IELTS
VOCABULARY

剑桥雅思阅读考点词真经

（机考笔试综合版）

刘洪波 编著

中国人民大学出版社
· 北京 ·

"阅读真经"三部曲，部部精心

"阅读真经"三部曲包括《雅思阅读真经5》《雅思阅读真经总纲》和《剑桥雅思阅读考点词真经》这三本书。

"真经"源于"武侠"。喜欢武侠的人，不只是喜欢"武"，更注重"侠"，激情四射，豪情万丈，仗义执言，用真诚和勤奋书写人生的辉煌。而要想撰写"真经"，需要四个条件：丰富的实践经验，深厚的文化底蕴，高超的概括能力和不断进取的热情和决心。

"真经"是刘洪波老师人生的分水岭，也是中国雅思培训行业对雅思考试卓越的贡献。

在2004年出版"阅读真经"之前，刘洪波老师只是一位优秀的老师。他在回国任教之前，在澳大利亚参加过11次雅思考试，拥有丰富的应试和培训经验。回国后，他在著名的英语培训学校成为最出色的雅思教师。他所培训的考生，涉及各个年龄段的0-N战"烤鸭"。他所接触的班型从1-N多种多样。凭着对澳大利亚教育的切身感悟，凭着对中国考生的深刻了解，凭着对英国剑桥雅思考试的深入理解与把握，他对雅思考试之敏感和熟悉程度无出其右者。他的经验和对教学的领悟浓缩成中国第一本雅思阅读针对性训练材料——《雅思阅读真经》，从而开创了真经流派。

"真经流派"用一句话概括，那就是"公平，公平，还是公平"。

"真经"的三个理念是：第一，消除文化差异、阅读习惯差异所造成的测试不公平，做好充分准备，使得考试尽量趋于合理。第二，通过备考养成正确的学习习惯，受益终生。第三，通过备考，做好留学准备，为未来的留学之路奠定基础。

所以，要选择"真经材料"，进行针对性训练。

"真经流派"在文化传播领域属于跨文化交流；从教学法上定义属于针对性训练；按照测试学理论属于考前有的放矢的科学准备；而从实践经验上说，蕴含丰富的经验和深厚的底蕴。

"真经流派"强调提前适应国外的阅读习惯和阅读内容，从而为应试和进一步深造做好准备。需知，雅思考试的内容是国外学习的模型和缩影，中国考生并不熟悉考题中的阅读内容。提前使用真正有针对性的准备材料，可以消除阅读偏好给考生带来的测试不公平，使得雅思考试对语言的评测更趋于科学和合理。这样的阅读材料选择需要深厚的功底，做这样的研究，是对跨文化交流和语言测试的卓越贡献。

让"真经"飞吧。

"真经流派"涉及听说读写四项，首先问世的是"阅读真经三部曲"及其衍生产品。

　　《雅思阅读真经 5》是最早的《阅读真经》各个层级的集大成者。该书精选典型文章、典型题目和考点词汇，任雅思阅读千变万化，总难逃真经的"天罗地网"。在编写过程中，研究了剑桥雅思考试 1—12 的文字表现形式，让考生充分熟悉试卷，在考场上产生"视觉亲切感"。

　　《雅思阅读真经 5》删除了被剑桥选重的文章，用最新题库文章加以替换。

　　《剑桥雅思阅读考点词真经》是"阅读提速"和"阅读提分"的秘密武器。因为提前熟悉了考点词和答案，在考场上定位、寻找关键词和答案会颇有灵感。该书内容活泼，容易携带，它将让所有的散碎时间变得生动而有效。

　　《剑桥雅思阅读考点词真经（机考笔试综合版）》增加了"剑 12"的典型词汇和考点词，完善了考点词理论，并对整个考点词的词库进行升级。这部分词汇是考生必须背诵的内容。附录中是完整的从"剑 4"到"剑 12"的词汇表，按照字母顺序排列，仅供自我评测使用。正文中的"剑 4、剑 5、剑 6"文本可以从本书附赠光盘中获得。

　　《雅思阅读真经总纲》是一本奇书。该书让考生充分浸入雅思阅读测试文化，完全理解各种出题手法和应试策略。简洁、明确，文辞华美，赏心悦目。如果不懂雅思，如果不爱教育，焉能至此！

　　让热情飞吧。

　　"阅读真经三部曲"的衍生品是丰富的网络课程和下载资料，是那个在澳大利亚奔波的 Ben 真诚的人生经历，是开创"真经流派"的 Harvey 的才华和自信，是涉足网络传播的 Bobo 的亲切和热情（详见《雅思阅读真经 5》推荐序）。

　　让才华飞吧。

　　一篇文章，散散乱乱，总为激情所扰。在出版之际，谨以此文为序。

真经 4：184284764

吕蕾微信公众号：lvlei1973

吕蕾微博：http://weibo.com/lvlei1973

吕蕾博客：http://blog.sina.com.cn/wonderfullei

一直播：76304044

如何使用本书

本书的动议基于下面几个理论：

一、记忆单词最有效的是根据文章的上下文，自然地有逻辑地记忆，而非背字典。如同我们从小是学习"人、口、手"，而非拿一本字典，先学提手旁，再记走之旁。我从来不提倡背任何的从 A 到 Z 的词汇书。这是贵学教育英语真经教学体系 GETS（Guixue English Teaching System）的区别性特征之一。本书以剑桥雅思 4–12 的文章为背景对词汇予以注释，通过阅读上下文记忆单词，使考生回归自然语言习得的逻辑习惯。

为了方便考生携带和体验，附录部分包含剑桥雅思 4–12 完整重点词汇，正文部分包含了剑桥雅思 6–12 重点词汇注释，"剑桥雅思 4""剑桥雅思 5""剑桥雅思 6"重点词汇在我的个人微信和光盘中提供。

二、学好一门外语不需要多本词汇书，一本就够了，但是要反复多遍，自己在词汇旁边做一些笔记，比如同义词、反义词、相关的话题词汇等。把这本书当成自己的伙伴，经常在上面添加一些笔记，相当于自己在不断修订升级，主动参与印象会更深刻，最后你可能还会对它产生感情。所以，这本书的排版留白很多，是留给考生的心得笔记区。

三、剑桥雅思 4–12 是全球雅思考生必做的真题。这本书包含阅读文章的重点词汇注释。所以，这本书是雅思考生必备的。

四、天下间所有阅读题其实是题目与原文的同义替换改写。所有阅读题的考点都是原文与题目的同义互换。在每篇文章的词汇注释后面，我把题目对应于原文的考点词汇罗列出来。

本书是国内第一本（全球范围内我不能确认）直接让考生透视雅思阅读题目考点的词汇书。换句话说，扒光了雅思命题者的绚丽外衣，使之"裸奔"。

考生把这本词汇书中每篇最后的"真题考点词替换清单"部分看一遍，等于做了一遍剑桥雅思 4–12。多么高效啊，1 个小时做完剑桥雅思真题 9 本书！

考生还可以用"真题考点词替换清单"来对照做题的思路，所以这本词汇书还是剑桥雅思 4–12 阅读题的解析！

有的题目的考点词替换没有罗列，因为在原文是原形出现，或词性不同而已；还有答案为 NG 的题目的考点词没有罗列。

考生理解了上面的这些话，那么雅思阅读完全就是送分的。

致谢

首先感谢学为贵阅读教师郭佳荣老师。应我邀请他为"剑桥雅思 10、11"挑选了全部"真题考点词替换清单"和核心词，收录在本书中。郭佳荣老师的经历有点传奇。他是一名羽毛球教练，原来雅思阅读考试 5.0 分，使用阅读真经体系后阅读迅速考到了 8.5 分，然后他选择来学为贵上课提高其他三项。他在课余时间主动帮助同学讲解阅读，以身说法传授真经。后来累积经验一步步从贵学助教、辅导老师、教师，最后成为贵学一线名师。

本书"剑桥雅思 12"的核心词和考点词清单由学为贵集团李娅宁老师、郭佳荣老师、纪燕伟老师编写。

本书包含的"剑桥雅思 5""剑桥雅思 6"的"真题考点词替换清单"是由李悦老师应我邀请完成。

本书包含的"剑桥雅思 4""剑桥雅思 7""剑桥雅思 8""剑桥雅思 9"的"真题考点词替换清单"由我亲自解析完成。

在本书的编写过程中，赵小锐、刘畅、谭乐、刘娟、付晓楠、田杨、冯涛、成岩、程玲、李慧芳、刘素良、焦磊、柏立明、焦鸿增、曹爱丽、张靖娴、袁伟、张美荣、刘伟、杨志、贾玉梅、李悦、李娅宁、纪燕伟也参与了资料收集及部分编写工作，在此一并感谢。

刘洪波微信公众号：liuhongbo-guixue

刘洪波微博：@ 刘洪波 - 学为贵

刘洪波博客：http://blog.sina.com.cn/lhbgx

刘洪波

2017 年 6 月

剑桥雅思阅读考点词

前言

——写于 2015 年

2012 年，贵学教育成立。作为她诞生之礼，我以她之名出版了《剑桥雅思听力考点词真经》和《剑桥雅思阅读考点词真经》，并同步公开了"雅思听力阅读考点词理论"的部分研究论文。当时，新浪教育、网易教育、搜狐教育同步转载了相关论文，引发了热议。

热议的意思就是有褒有贬。批评者认为我蔑视了几十年传统英语考试培训累积的各种技巧，一味强调同义替换；赞扬者则认为我开创了一个崭新的领域，教学理念领先整个行业很多年。

当然，我的学生们都自称"贵粉儿""脑残粉""真经死忠粉"，他们第一时间投入无比的热情开始研究听力阅读中的同义替换，开始背诵我提出的"考点词库"。我被他们的"盲目崇拜"感动得更加努力工作。

无论外界纷扰，我心宁静依旧。因为历史为证，《剑桥雅思听力考点词真经》和《剑桥雅思阅读考点词真经》是中国英语培训史上讲解同义替换的第一批出版专著。

多年过去，行业中越来越多的老师开始讲解和重视同义替换和考点词，中国雅思考生的听力、阅读平均分逐年上涨，全球排名稳步上升。

我很高兴，那才是我真正的收获。

论 文 摘 要

——写于 2012 年

雅思考生在接受培训时听得最多、说得最多的是定位词，又叫核心词（keywords）。殊不知比 keywords 更核心更重要的是考点词。因此，我写下两本书：《剑桥雅思阅读考点词真经》和《剑桥雅思听力考点词真经》，希望能帮助广大的考生洞察考试本源，化繁为简。也算公开提出一个新的教学研究方向，希望"考点词理论"能迅速扩展到托福、四六级考试、考研等考试中去，出版市场上从此流行"考点词"系列的书籍，培训课堂上开始流行"考点词"的教学术语，也算对国内英语培训业的发展尽到自己的一点责任。

考点词定义

考点词是在听力理解和阅读理解考试的每一道题目中，命题者所设计的最重要的题目和原文的同义替换单词（或反义词驳斥设计）。

考点词特点

如果考生认识这个单词，这道题就能做对；反之，则做错。

有的题目考点词不止一个。

雅思考点词的研究历程

2004 年，我在雅思阅读教学中讲："天下间的阅读理解和听力理解都是理解题目和原文之间的同义替换。无论任何题型，它们的命题思路都是一致的。因为题目中每一个单词所表达的含义都有对应的原文单词出处。听力与阅读都是如此。"

如果考生理解了这句话的含义，我就比喻为领悟了"无招胜有招"的意境。这个理论我在《雅思阅读真经总纲》中进行了详细的阐述和解释。 我提及"无招胜有招"这个理论，是因为它是雅思阅读、听力考点词库理论的基础。

2009 年春，英国剑桥大学 ESOL 向全球发行《剑桥雅思真题 7》。当我做到第一套题第一篇阅读时，发现第 13 题的命题考点与 2005 年出版的《剑桥雅思真题 5》的第三套题第三篇第 31 题的考点设计一致，对比如下：

《剑桥雅思真题 7》第 21 页第 13 题

题型：从原文选词填空
题目：The word "echolocation" was **first used** by someone working as a _____.
原文：The American zoologist Donald Griffin, who was largely responsible for the discovery of sonar in bats, **coined** the term "echolocation" to…
答案：**zoologist**

《剑桥雅思真题 5》第 73 页第 31 题

题型：哪一自然段包含题目信息
题目：where the expression AI was **first used**
原文：The field was launched, and the term "artificial intelligence" **coined**, at a conference in 1956…
答案：**B**

coin 一词作动词意思是"创造"，同义表达是"first use"。如果考生背过这个词义，那么这两道题都会轻松答对。

当时，我也没多想，接着往下做。只是在 coin 一词旁做了一个标记，提醒自己：以前讲"剑 5"，只说 coin 一词的动词含义很重要。而从今以后讲课，要提醒学生这个词非常重要，因为"剑 5"和"剑 7"两篇文章都考。它们都是历年考过的真题，一篇是动物类的，一篇是科技类的； 一个是填空题，一个是匹配题。但是，这两道题的考点都是 coin。

我接着往下做，又有新发现。

《剑桥雅思真题 7》第 46 页第 17 题

> 题型：哪一自然段包含题目信息
>
> 题目：one effect of chemicals on water sources
>
> 原文：…while the growth of algae is increasing in lakes because of the **fertiliser** run-off.
>
> 答案：**B**

《剑桥雅思真题 7》第 68 页第 9 题

> 题型：选项填空
>
> 题目：…and also use unwanted materials as _____.
>
> 原文：…and spread waste to **fertilise** the crop.
>
> 答案：**F fertilisers**

当时心中就有个想法：雅思命题者很喜欢这个词么，同一本"剑桥雅思"里就考了两次。 先不管了，做完这本书再说吧。 于是我做到了这道题：

《剑桥雅思真题 7》第 91 页第 11 题

> 题型：从原文选词填空
>
> 题目：The discovery on one pyramid of an object which **resembled** a _____ suggests…
>
> 原文：A wooden artifact found on the step pyramid at Saqqara **looks** uncannily **like** a modern glider.
>
> 答案：**modern glider**

这让我想起：

《剑桥雅思真题 4》第 30 页第 39 题

> 题型：选项填空
>
> 题目：…it was found that they made _____ choices.
>
> 原文：…we found that their choices closely **resembled** those made by the sighted subjects.
>
> 答案：**similar**

第一遍做完"剑7"，我确认了雅思阅读中三个重要的考点词：coin，fertilise 和 resemble。学员做完剑桥雅思真题，练了好多题；我做完剑桥雅思真题，最大的收获是这三个词。掩卷思考，心情激荡。我想我可能发现了雅思阅读考试中最核心的秘密。

接下来的思考是：为什么剑桥雅思在不同的年份、不同的考卷、不同的文章题材、不同的题型中都反复设置同一考点词呢？

有两个合乎逻辑的答案：第一，命题者少，许多题目是一个人出的，所以有个人风格，看到文章中有 coin，就习惯性出题 first used；第二，命题者多，但雅思命题官方有一个"考点词库"，会对命题者公布，告诉他们这些词很重要，符合雅思的学术难度，要求设计题目考查。显然第二种推断既合逻辑又合情理。

紧跟着的第二个问题是：为什么 coin，fertilise，resemble 这三个单词会进入"考点词库"，换句话说，为什么这三个单词如此重要，出国留学的考生必须会，剑桥雅思命题者碰到必考？

我想，可能是这样的：

coin 作动词指"创造"，常用于 coin a word/term，"创造了一个术语，造了一个新词"。在科技发展的历史上，全新的事物、技术和理论的诞生都需要新词来定义称呼。所以 coin 一词在学术论文中很常见，是对新理论下定义的标志。而且考生熟悉该词作名词的词义为"硬币"，易在将来留学海外做学术研究、阅读参考文献时出现困惑。因此该词的动词词义进入"考点词库"。

fertilise 作动词指"施肥"，名词是 fertiliser "化肥"。化肥的使用破坏了环境，对人类的健康有重大的影响。生死攸关的重要词汇，进入"考点词库"。

resemble 作动词指"相似，像"。同义词有 look like，be similar to。当我们想要把一个复杂事物或理论描述清晰时，我们经常会采用类比的手法：用一个读者都知道的、日常的、简单的东西去类比。这在学术论文中尤其常见。而且该词"长相"是形容词，实为重要动词。如不掌握，容易导致读者从语法上产生困惑，理解不了整个句子的含义。因此，该词进入"考点词库"。

以上都是我的猜想，连同我 coin 的术语"考点词库"，可能永远得不到剑桥雅思官方的证实。2011 年秋我应邀去剑桥 ESOL 访问，和剑桥雅思命题者面对面交流时，也不敢旁敲侧击地探询。官方一直对此讳莫如深，因为如有"考点词库"，那绝对就是剑桥雅思的最高机密之一。于是从 2009 年起，我开始着手研究自己心中的"雅思听力阅读考点词库"。当时《剑桥雅思》已经出到 7，已经有足够的真题素材可以对比研究，找出这些考点词。还原这个神秘的词库，让考生背记最重要的单词，意义非凡。断断续续地反复做题研究，过了两年。

2011 年，《剑桥雅思真题 8》全球出版发行，我开始做"剑 8"。

《剑桥雅思真题 8》第 21 页第 9 题

题型：填图
题目：escapement (**resembling**) _____
原文：...which was a lever-based device shaped **like** a ship's anchor.
答案：**anchor**

又考到 resemble。"剑 8"对于我的考点词研究没有太大的新贡献，佐证的作用更明显。到了 2012 年，我创立贵学教育，纳拥有十五年培训经验的北京雅思名师团队于旗下。我希望雅思真经教学体系流传天下，造福全球雅思学子。作为贵学真经教学体系 GETS（Guixue English Teaching System）的一个重要元素，"雅思听力阅读考点词库"也随之公开。

雅思阅读考点词库

——升级于 2015 年

说明：原创内容，受著作权法保护，教学引用请说明出处。

我精选了 538 个雅思阅读考点词，分成了 3 类，进行了重要性排序。如果考生熟知，对应雅思阅读 7 分以上能力。

第 1 类考点词

共 20 + 34 = 54 个

定义：雅思阅读文章中只要出现该词，90% 会被命题考查！不同的真题中被反复考查多次，超高频考点词！

背记：考生请严格按下表中重要性排行顺序记忆 20 个考点词。是的，我的学生学雅思阅读，第一个背的单词不是 abandon，abdomen，abnormal，而是 resemble，它在《剑桥雅思 9》和《剑桥雅思 10》中多次考到。请同时记忆下表真题命题方式中相对应的 34 个同义替换考点词（彩色单词）。不熟的单词请一定查出标注，同时建议思考相关反义词表达。

要求：滚瓜烂熟。

重要性排行	考点词	常考中文词义	雅思阅读真题命题方式
1	resemble	v. 像，与……相似	like, look like, be similar to
2	recognize	v. 认出，识别；承认	perceive, acknowledge, realize, appreciate, admit, identify, comprehend, understand, know
3	adjust	v. 调整，使适合	change, modify, shift, alter
4	approach	n. 方法	method, way
5	fundamental	adj. 基本的，基础的	rudimentary, preliminary, basic
6	rely on	依靠，依赖	depend on
7	domestic	adj. 家庭的；国内的	home, local, national
8	measure	v. 测量	calculate, assess, evaluate
9	trait	n. 特性，特征	characteristic, feature, property
10	coin	v. 创造	first used, invent
11	artificial	adj. 人造的，仿造的	synthetic, man-made
12	prompt	v. 促进，激起	initiate, immediately
13	exchange	v. 交换	share, apply A to B
14	underlie	v. 成为……基础	based on, ground, root
15	ignore	v. 忽视，不顾	neglect, overlook, underestimate
16	fertiliser	n. 化肥，肥料	chemical, toxic, unnatural
17	that*	pron. 那；那个	this, it, they, those, these, such * 指代是雅思阅读的重要考点
18	and*	conj. 和，而且	or, as well as, both…and, not only…but also…, other than, in addition, besides, on the one hand…on the other hand…, neither… nor… * 并列结构是雅思阅读的重要考点
19	rather than*	而非，不是	but, yet, however, whereas, nonetheless, nevertheless, notwithstanding, although, though, instead * 转折结构是雅思阅读的重要考点

20	**thanks to***	由于，幸亏	stem from, derive, owing to, due to, according to, because of, on account of, as a result of, leading to, because, since, for, in that, as, therefore, hence * 因果关系是雅思阅读的重要考点

第 2 类考点词

共 100 + 71 = 171 个（注：这类词中考点词与近义词有重复，故实际为 171 个考点词。）

定义：雅思阅读文章中只要出现该词，60% 会被命题考查！不同的真题中被考查过 1 次以上，重要考点词！

背记：考生请按下表中重要性排行顺序记忆 100 个考点词；同时记忆真题命题方式中相对应的 71 个同义替换考点词（彩色单词）。不熟的单词请一定查出标注，同时建议思考相关反义词表达。

要求：熟记 10 遍以上。

重要性排行	考点词	常考中文词义	雅思阅读真题命题方式
21	**diversity**	n. 多样性，差异	variety, difference
22	**detect**	v. 查明，发现	find, look for, seek, search
23	**isolate**	v. 使隔离，使孤立	inaccessible
24	**avoid**	v. 避免	escape, evitable
25	**budget**	n. 预算	fund, financial
26	**adapt to**	使适应	fit, suit
27	**alternative**	adj. 供替代的，供选择的 n. 替代品	substitute
28	**compensate**	n. 补偿，赔偿	make up, offset
29	**component**	n. 成分，要素	proportion
30	**military**	adj. 军事的	weapon, army
31	**criteria**	n. 标准	standard
32	**curriculum**	n. 课程	syllabus, course of study

33	feasible	*adj.* 可行的	realistic, viable
34	constrain	*v.* 束缚，限制	stop, control
35	deficiency	*n.* 缺陷，缺点	shortage, defect, weakness
36	supplement	*v.* 补充	provision
37	distinguish	*v.* 区别，辨别	separate, differentiate
38	analyze	*v.* 分析，解释	examine, diagnose
39	emphasize	*v.* 强调，着重	focus on, stress
40	enormous	*adj.* 庞大的，巨大的	massive, large
41	imitate	*v.* 模仿	mimic, copy
42	impair	*v.* 削弱，减少	damage, diminish, decrease
43	hinder	*v.* 阻碍	impede, prevent, deter, obstacle
44	legitimate	*adj.* 合法的	legal
45	limitation	*n.* 限制	restriction
46	convention	*n.* 手法；习俗	method; tradition
47	demanding	*adj.* 苛求的	troublesome
48	determine	*v.* 决定	decide
49	accelerate	*v.* 加速，促进；强调	speed up
50	ancient	*adj.* 古代的；古老的	aged, old
51	beneficial	*adj.* 有益的	helpful, advantageous, wholesome
52	chronic	*adj.* 慢性的，长期性的	lasting
53	conscious	*adj.* 有意识的，神志清醒的	aware, knowing
54	minimize	*v.* 最小化，使……减到最小	reduce, lessen
55	immunity	*n.* 免疫力	resistance
56	imperative	*adj.* 必要的，紧急的	compelling, necessary, urgent
57	secrete	*v.* 分泌	discharge, exude
58	exaggerate	*v.* 夸大，夸张	overstate
59	transmit	*v.* 传达，传输	pass, send, transfer

60	extinct	v. 灭绝	die out, lost
61	exclusive	adj. 独有的；排外的；专一的	only
62	guarantee	v. 保证，担保	assure
63	inherit	v. 继承	receive
64	witness	n. 见证，证据；目击者	view, see
65	magnetic	adj. 有磁性的	attractive
66	loss	n. 减少；亏损；失败；遗失	waste, gone
67	option	n. 选择	choice
68	prefer to	更喜欢	rather
69	priority	n. 优先权	preference, preferential
70	primary	adj. 主要的	principal, main
71	principle	n. 原理	rule
72	potential	n. 潜能 adj. 潜在的	possibility
73	quantity	n. 量，数量	number
74	settle	v. 解决；定居，稳定	fix, figure out
75	sophisticate	v. 使复杂	complicate
76	specific	adj. 明确的；特殊的	detailed, particular
77	survive	v. 存活，幸存	remain
78	swift	adj. 迅速的，敏捷的，立刻的	quick, rapid
79	unexpectedly	adv. 出乎意料地	surprising
80	surrounding	n. 环境	setting, environment
81	attempt	n. 试图，尝试	try, test
82	expertise	n. 专门技术	knowledge, skill
83	faculty	n. 能力，才能；全体教员	ability

84	donate	v. 捐赠	contribute
85	dynamics	n. 动力学	energy, force, move
86	incentive	n. 刺激，鼓励；动机	motive, stimulus
87	mortality	n. 死亡率	death
88	peripheral	adj. 外围的，次要的	unimportant, minor
89	vicinity	n. 邻近，附近	neighbourhood, nearby
90	threaten	v. 威胁，危及	endanger, jeopardize, risk, hazard
91	practice	n. 实行；练习	method, exercise
92	bacteria	n. 细菌	virus, germ, microbe
93	be subject to	受……支配	face
94	be liable to	易于……	potential
95	innate	adj. 天生的；内在的，直觉的	built-in, inborn
96	pattern	n. 模式	formation
97	therapy	n. 治疗，理疗	treatment
98	original	adj. 原始的，最初的	initial, first
99	confidential	adj. 机密的，秘密的	undisclosed, secret, hidden
100	cognitive	adj. 认知的	mental
101	comply with	照做，遵守	obey
102	consult	v. 查阅，商量，请教，咨询	ask for advice
103	superior	adj. 上级的；优秀的	higher, upper
104	co-operation	n. 合作，协作	support, work together
105	co-ordinate	v. 使……协调	organize, harmonize
106	differ	v. 使……相异；使……不同	vary
107	cue	n. 线索	hint, clue
108	signal	n. 信号	symbol, mark, sign
109	abandon	v. 放弃，遗弃	quit, give up, forsake, derelict
110	halt	n. 停止	stop, quit

111	**fragile**	*adj.* 脆弱的	vulnerable
112	**retain**	*v.* 记住	maintain
113	**vanish**	*n./v.* 消失，绝迹	disappear
114	**delivery**	*n.* 递送	send
115	**erode**	*v.* 侵蚀	rust, damage
116	**induce**	*v.* 引起，引诱	cause, lead to
117	**stable**	*adj.* 稳定的	constant, unchanged
118	**integrate**	*v.* 使……成整体	combine, whole
119	**equal**	*adj.* 平等的；相等的；胜任的	fair, even
120	**grant**	*v.* 拨款；授予	offer

第 3 类考点词

共 256 + 57 = 313 个

定义：雅思阅读真题文章中被考查过的单词，它们都是雅思阅读考点词。

背记：这 256 个单词的重要性一致，因此没有按照重要性排序；同时记忆真题命题方式中相对应的 57 个同义替换考点词（彩色单词）。不熟的单词请一定查出标注，同时建议思考相关反义词表达。

要求：熟记 5 遍以上。

考点词	常考中文词义	雅思阅读真题命题方式
accumulate	*v.* 累积，积聚	gather
addictive	*adj.* 上瘾的	habit
adversity	*n.* 逆境，不幸	trouble
aggression	*n.* 侵犯，侵害	attack
agreeable	*adj.* 令人愉快的；适合的；和蔼可亲的	pleasant
aid	*n.* 援助，帮助	help
allergic	*adj.* 过敏的；对……极讨厌的	irritate

altitude	n. 高度；海拔	height
application	n. 应用	utilization
approve	v. 批准	agree
array	n. 排列；大批	order
assign	v. 分配；指派	allocate
association	n. 协会，联盟；联系	union
attitude	n. 看法，态度	opinion
authority	n. 当局，权威	government
be consistent with	与……一致	compatible
bear	v. 承担；忍受	tolerate
blight	v. 损害；枯萎	destroy
boundary	n. 边界；底线	barrier
bungle	v. 搞糟，拙劣地工作	mishandle
burden	n. 负担	load
calamity	n. 灾难	disaster
capacity	n. 容量	volume
catastrophic	adj. 灾难的	disastrous
cater	v. 迎合；满足需要	serve
certify	v. 证明，保证	verify
civic	adj. 市民的	municipal
comment	n. 评论；意见 v. 评论	remark
commitment	n. 承诺，许诺，义务；致力	engagement
communal	adj. 公共的，公社的	public
commute	v. 通勤；用……交换	travel
compare	v. 与……相比较	contrast
conceal	v. 隐藏；隐瞒	hide

concentrate	v. 专心于；集中	focus
concur	v. 同意	agree
confer	v. 授予，给予	grant
conflict	n. 冲突，矛盾	unharmonious
confuse	v. 使混乱，使迷惑	puzzle
conservative	adj. 保守的	traditional
considerable	adj. 相当大的，重要的	significant
contingent	adj. 因情况而异的	uncertain
controversial	adj. 有争论的	disputable
correlation	n. 相关，关联	link
courtship	n. 求爱（时期）	mate
crash	n. 碰撞	collapse
credibility	n. 可信性	reliance
criminal	n. 罪犯，犯人	conviction
crisis	n. 危机	risk
criticism	n. 批评	condemn
curb	v. 限制，抑制	restrict
damp	adj. 潮湿的	wet
dazzle	v. 使目眩；使……眼花	flash
deadline	n. 最后期限	limit
delay	n. 延期，耽搁	postpone
democratic	adj. 民主的	republic
demographic	adj. 人口统计学的；人口学的	population statistic
dental	adj. 牙科的，牙齿的	teeth
depression	n. 抑郁，沮丧	frustration
designate	v. 指定，指派，标出	appoint

17

detain	v. 留住	hold
devastate	v. 毁坏，毁灭	wreck
disclose	v. 公开；揭露	expose
disparate	adj. 不同的	different
display	n. 显示	show
disrupt	v. 破坏	destroy
distract	v. 转移，分心	divert
distribute	v. 分配，分发	spread
documentation	n. 文件；文献	record
domain	n. 领域	field
dominant	adj. 占优势的，占支配地位的	overbearing
dramatic	adj. 戏剧化的；激动人心的；引人注意的	striking
drought	n. 干旱	dry
durable	adj. 持久的	lasting
eco-friendly	adj. 生态友好的，环保的	environmentally-friendly
elaborate	v. 详细阐述，详细叙述	illustrate
elderly	adj. 高龄的	aged
eliminate	v. 消除，排除	dispose
elusive	adj. 难懂的，难捉摸的；行踪隐秘的	hard
encyclopaedia	n. 百科全书	entire range of knowledge
entrepreneur	n. 企业家	boss
equator	n. 赤道	geography
erratically	adv. 不定地，无规律地	unpredictably

established	*adj.* 确定的；已制定的，已建立的	built
estate	*n.* 房地产	property
ethical	*adj.* 道德的	moral
eventually	*adv.* 最后，终于	finally
evidence	*n.* 迹象；证据	proof
evolve	*v.* 进化，发展；逐渐形成	develop
exceptional	*adj.* 异常的，特别出色的	extreme, utmost
exhausted	*adj.* 疲惫的，耗尽的	fatigue
experiment	*n.* 实验，试验	test
explicit	*adj.* 明确的	clear
exploit	*v.* 开发，利用	use
extend	*v.* 扩展，延伸，推广	expand
extract	*n.* 摘录 *v.* 提取	quotation
famine	*n.* 饥荒	hunger
finite	*adj.* 有限的	limited
fitness	*n.* 健康	health
foe	*n.* 敌人，危害物	enemy
format	*n.* 格式	structure
fragment	*n.* 碎片	piece
freeze	*n.* 冰冻，冻结	chill
fulfill	*v.* 满足，实现	execute
gene	*n.* 基因	factor
gifted	*adj.* 有天赋的，有才华的	talented
graphic	*adj.* 形象的；图解的	picture
habitat	*n.* 栖息地，住处	residence

harbour	*v.* 怀有 *n.* 海港	hold
hardship	*n.* 困苦；苦难	difficult
harsh	*adj.* 艰难的；严酷的	rough
hypothesis	*n.* 假设	assumption
impact	*n.* 影响	influence
impressive	*adj.* 感人的；给人深刻印象的	touching
in accordance with	依照；与……一致	conform
inaccurate	*adj.* 错误的	incorrect
inactive	*adj.* 不活跃的，不活动的	passive
inappropriate	*adj.* 不适当的	hard
indulge	*v.* 沉溺（于）	spoil
infest	*v.* 侵害；寄生于	plague
installment	*n.* 安装；分期付款	payment on its completion
intelligence	*n.* 智力	mind
intense	*adj.* 强烈的；紧张的；热情的	strong
interaction	*n.* 相互作用，交流互动	social activities
interference	*n.* 干涉	interdependence
interior	*n.* 内部 *adj.* 内部的	inner
interrupt	*v.* 中断	stop
introverted	*adj.* 内向的，含蓄的	shyness
involve	*v.* 包含，牵涉	associate
keen	*adj.* 热切的；急迫的，强烈的	strong

label	v. 打上标签	display
lack	v. 缺乏；不足	shortage
landscape	n. 风景	scene
likelihood	n. 可能性	chance
limb	n. 四肢	arm or leg
linguistic	adj. 语言（学）的	language
log	v. 记录 n. 原木	record
look-in	n. 成功的机会	opportunity, chance
lopsided	adj. 不平衡的	uneven
mainly	adv. 主要地，大体上	primarily
malfunction	v. 发生故障；不起作用	breakdown
mammal	n. 哺乳动物	creature
manage to do	设法完成某事	success
manifest	v. 出现，表现	obvious
manufacture	n. 生产	produce
marine	adj. 海产的；航海的，海运的	sea
mate	n. 配偶	spouse
mechanism	n. 机制，原理	method
mental	adj. 精神的，心理的	intelligent
mercury	n. 汞，水银	liquid metal
meteorological	adj. 气象学的	weather
migrate	v. 转移，迁移	move
moisture	n. 水分，湿度	humidity
monitor	v. 监控	surveillance
motif	n. 主题；图形	theme

mould	v. 模压，塑造；塑造成	form
native	adj. 本国的；土著的；天然的；天赋的	original
nocturnal	adj. 夜间的，夜间发生的	night
norm	n. 规范	regulation
notoriety	n. 名声	famous
objective	n. 目标，目的 adj. 客观的	goal
obligation	n. 义务	responsibility
obscure	v. 掩盖，使模糊不清	hide
obtain	v. 获得	get
odd	adj. 古怪的	strange
odour	n. 气味	smell
offensive	adj. 冒犯的，无礼的	hostile
official	n. 官员 adj. 官方的	authority
optimum	n. 最佳效果 adj. 最适宜的	best
ordinary	adj. 普通的；平凡的；平常的	common
organ	n. 器官；机构	a part of a body
out of the question	不可能	impossible
overcome	v. 克服	defeat
overtake	v. 赶上	surpass
paralyse	v. 使……麻痹；使……瘫痪	cannot move

paramount	*adj.* 最重要的，主要的	principal
participate	*v.* 参加	join
patient	*adj.* 有耐性的，能容忍的 *n.* 病人；患者	repetitive
peak	*n.* 最高峰，顶点 *v.* 使……达到顶峰	top
permit	*n.* 许可证，执照 *v.* 许可	allow
persuade	*v.* 说服，劝说	influence
pessimistic	*adj.* 悲观的	negative
phase	*n.* 阶段	process
physical	*adj.* 身体上的；物质的	body
plagiarise	*v.* 抄袭	copy
plenty of	大量的	many
plot	*v.* 密谋	plan
pose	*v.* 提出，造成，形成	cause
portable	*adj.* 便携的	conveyable
poverty	*n.* 贫穷	poor
praise	*n.* 赞扬	commend
predict	*v.* 预测，预知	expect
pressing	*adj.* 迫切的	urgent
private	*adj.* 私人的；私有的；私下的	personal
prohibit	*v.* 禁止	not allowed
prolong	*v.* 拉长，延长	extend
promote	*v.* 促进，推销	improve
prosper	*v.* 使成功，使繁荣	success

purify	v. 净化	clean
qualify	v. 取得资格	fulfill
radical	adj. 彻底的，根本的	utmost
range	n. 范围；幅度	scope
rare	adj. 稀有的	unusual
rate	n. 等级 v. 评估	rank; measure
react	v. 反应	respond
recreation	n. 娱乐，消遣	entertainment
reduction	n. 下降，减少	decrease
refer to	指（的是），涉及，提及	talk about
rehearsal	n. 排演；预演；练习	preparation
reject	v. 拒绝，排斥，丢弃	exclude
relevant	adj. 相关的	relative
religious	adj. 宗教的；虔诚的	sacred
reluctant	adj. 不情愿的	unwilling
reproduce	v. 繁殖	breed
responsible	adj. 负责的，可靠的；有责任的	liable
revision	n. 修正	editing
revive	v. 使复苏，恢复	renaissance
ruin	v. 毁灭	destroy
scenic	adj. 风景优美的	beautiful
shade	n. 遮阳；阴影	shelter
skepticism	n. 怀疑	doubt
soar	v. 激增	increase
solely	adv. 唯一地	alone
solicitor	n. 律师	lawyer

steer	v. 控制，引导	manage
stimulate	v. 刺激，激励	motivate
stride	n. 进展	progress
succumb	vi. 屈服	yield
subdivide	v. 把……细分	break down
subtle	adj. 微妙的	delicate
substance	n. 物质；实质	matter
sufficiency	n. 足量，充足	enough
supersede	v. 取代，代替	replace
suppress	v. 抑制；隐瞒	hold
supremacy	n. 至高无上，很高的地位	priority
suspicious	adj. 可疑的	odd
sustainable	adj. 可持续的	long-term
symptom	n. 症状，征兆	sign
tension	n. 紧张，不安	upset
term	n. 术语	word
throughout	adv. 自始至终，到处；全部 prep. 贯穿，遍及	anywhere
toll	n. 通行费 v. 征收	charge
trace	n. 追溯；痕迹	track
transcend	v. 胜过，超越	excel
transit	n. 运输；经过 v. 运送	send
tremendous	adj. 巨大的，惊人的	vast
trigger	n. 触发，引发，引起	begin
tropical	adj. 热带的	hot

unbiased	*adj.* 公正的，无偏见的	fair
uniform	*adj.* 始终如一的	consistent
valuable	*adj.* 宝贵的，有价值的	benefit
versatile	*adj.* 多功能的	all-around
view	*v.* 看	overlook
violent	*adj.* 暴力的；猛烈的	fierce
visible	*adj.* 明显的，看得见的	see
visual	*adj.* 视觉的	image
well-being	*n.* 健康，康乐	health

538 个雅思阅读考点词词库总表

这个词库总表是以上 3 类考点词的汇总，没有标注中文，是希望考生可以"望文生义"，用来测试自己的考点词掌握程度。同时，请扫描本书封底的二维码，下载"学为贵"App，输入本书封面的正版序列号，即可免费使用 538 个考点词的背记功能、全面测试、个人词汇量分析报告和考点词小游戏，帮助你轻松快速掌握它们。

abandon	accelerate	accumulate	acknowledge
adapt to	addictive	adjust	admit
adversity	aggression	agreeable	aid
allergic	allocate	alter	alternative
altitude	analyze	ancient	and
application	apply to	appreciate	approach
approve	array	artificial	assess
assign	association	assumption	assure
attempt	attitude	authority	avoid
aware	bacteria	barrier	based on
be consistent with	be liable to	be subject to	bear

beneficial	blight	boundary	budget
bungle	burden	calamity	calculate
capacity	catastrophic	cater	certify
change	characteristic	chronic	civic
clue	cognitive	coin	collapse
comment	commitment	communal	commute
compare	compatible	compensate	complicate
comply with	component	comprehend	conceal
concentrate	concur	condemn	confer
confidential	conflict	conform	confuse
conscious	conservative	considerable	constrain
consult	contingent	contrast	contribute
controversial	convention	conviction	co-operation
co-ordinate	correlation	courtship	crash
credibility	criminal	crisis	criteria
criticism	cue	curb	curriculum
damp	dazzle	deadline	defeat
defect	deficiency	delay	delicate
delivery	demanding	democratic	demographic
dental	depend on	depression	derive
designate	detailed	detain	detect
deter	determine	devastate	diagnose
differ	differentiate	diminish	disaster
discharge	disclose	disparate	display
disrupt	distinguish	distract	distribute
diversity	divert	documentation	domain
domestic	dominant	donate	dramatic
drought	durable	dynamics	eco-friendly

elaborate	elderly	eliminate	elusive
emphasize	encyclopaedia	endanger	engagement
enormous	entertainment	entrepreneur	environment
equal	equator	erode	erratically
escape	established	estate	ethical
evaluate	even	eventually	evidence
evitable	evolve	exaggerate	excel
exceptional	exchange	exclude	exclusive
execute	exhausted	expect	experiment
expertise	explicit	exploit	expose
extend	extinct	extract	extreme
exude	faculty	fair	famine
fatigue	feasible	feature	fertiliser
financial	finite	fit	fitness
focus on	foe	format	formation
fragile	fragment	freeze	frustration
fulfill	fund	fundamental	gene
germ	gifted	grant	graphic
guarantee	habitat	halt	harbour
hardship	harmonize	harsh	hazard
hinder	hint	hostile	hypothesis
identify	ignore	illustrate	imitate
immediately	immunity	impact	impair
impede	imperative	impressive	in accordance with
inaccessible	inaccurate	inactive	inappropriate
incentive	induce	indulge	infest
influence	inherit	initial	initiate
innate	installment	integrate	intelligence

intense	interaction	interference	interior
interrupt	introverted	invent	involve
isolate	jeopardize	keen	label
lack	landscape	legal	legitimate
likelihood	limb	limitation	linguistic
link	log	look-in	lopsided
loss	magnetic	main	mainly
make up	malfunction	mammal	manage to do
manifest	manufacture	marine	massive
mate	measure	mechanism	mental
mercury	meteorological	method	microbe
migrate	military	mimic	minimize
modify	moisture	monitor	moral
mortality	motif	motivate	motive
mould	municipal	native	necessary
neglect	nocturnal	norm	notoriety
obey	objective	obligation	obscure
obstacle	obtain	odd	odour
offensive	official	offset	only
opportunity	optimum	option	ordinary
organ	organize	original	out of the question
overcome	overlook	overtake	paralyse
paramount	participate	particular	patient
pattern	peak	perceive	peripheral
permit	persuade	pessimistic	phase
physical	plagiarise	plague	plenty of
plot	portable	pose	postpone
potential	poverty	practice	praise

predict	prefer to	preference	preliminary
pressing	prevent	primary	principal
principle	priority	private	prohibit
prolong	promote	prompt	proof
property	proportion	prosper	provision
purify	puzzle	qualify	quantity
quotation	radical	range	rare
rate	rather	rather than	react
realistic	realize	recognize	record
recreation	reduction	refer to	regulation
rehearsal	reject	relative	relevant
reliance	religious	reluctant	rely on
replace	reproduce	resemble	resistance
respond	responsible	restriction	retain
revision	revive	risk	rudimentary
ruin	scenic	scope	secrete
seek	setting	settle	shade
shelter	shift	signal	similar
skepticism	soar	solely	solicitor
sophisticate	specific	spoil	spouse
stable	standard	steer	stem from
stimulate	stimulus	stress	stride
subdivide	substance	substitute	subtle
succumb	sufficiency	suit	superior
supersede	supplement	suppress	supremacy
surpass	surrounding	surveillance	survive
suspicious	sustainable	swift	syllabus
symbol	symptom	synthetic	talented

tension	term	thanks to	that
theme	therapy	threaten	throughout
tolerate	toll	toxic	trace
track	trait	transcend	transit
transmit	tremendous	trigger	tropical
unbiased	underestimate	underlie	unexpectedly
uniform	utilization	valuable	vanish
variety	vary	vast	versatile
viable	vicinity	view	violent
virus	visible	visual	volume
vulnerable	well-being	wholesome	witness
wreck	yield		

最后重申

本部分的单词都是必须背的，因为它们每一个都对应真题、对应你的阅读考试分数。

要完全领悟考点词和真题的命题思路需要认真学习本书后面每篇真题考点词替换清单。

目录

Cambridge
IELTS
4

Test 1

↑ *Reading Passage 1*

真题考点词替换清单

题号	题目——原文
1	ignore—frequent 【反】
3	hold—harbour
	mistaken view—misconception
	study at school—curriculum
4	change—modification
7	follow on—be consistent with
10	where to live—habitats
11	loss—destruction
12	depend on—need continuing existence—survive
13	unexpectedly—surprising
	given—considering
	amount of—high level
	newspapers and television—media coverage
	world—global

↑ *Reading Passage 2: What Do Whales Feel?*

真题考点词替换清单

题号	题目——原文
15	underdeveloped—generated, rudimentary
19	exceptional—extremely keen
22	mating—courtship
24	follow—track
25	best developed—more than compensated for, well- developed

↑ *Reading Passage 3: Visual Symbols and the Blind*

真题考点词替换清单

题号	题目——原文
31	rapid—quickly

34	abstract—not directly
37	assigned—linked
39	similar—resembled
40	comprehend—appreciate, understand
	metaphors—symbol

Test 2

🔺 *Reading Passage 1: Lost for Words*

真题考点词替换清单

题号	题目——原文
1	variety—diversity
	as a result of—breeds
3	increasing appreciation—growing interest
4	teach—learn 【反】
5	more than one language—bilingualism
6	extinction—lost
7	determined—affect
8	reject—not to be induced
	established—old
13	loss—disappear
	inevitable—despite

🔺 *Reading Passage 2: Alternative Medicine in Australia*

真题考点词替换清单

题号	题目——原文
14	differ—unusual
	reluctant—conservative
15	consulted—visit
16	increasing—climb
19	higher—eroded 【反】
20	retraining—taking courses
23	long-term—chronic

♠ *Reading Passage 3: Play Is a Serious Business*

真题考点词替换清单

题号	题目——原文
27	unusual—not normally
	connections—communicate with each other
	beneficial—enhance creativity
28	recording—plot
29	physical hazards—deaths
30	mental activities—cognitive processes
31	reduction—less
	opportunities—look-in
33	rehearsal—get in shape, mould
34	strength—muscle
35	organ—brain
36	input—learning
	surroundings—environmental
37	wide range—variable, different
40	specific substance—particular chemical

Test 3

♠ *Reading Passage 1: Micro-enterprise Credit for Street Youth*

真题考点词替换清单

题号	题目——原文
2	loans—credit
3	poverty—demand for income
4	own business—entrepreneurship
6	provision—supplied with
9	any—not for everyone 【反】
11	only fixed—increasing 【反】
12	more money—charged interest
13	part of—in association with

📤 *Reading Passage 2: Volcanoes—Earth-shattering News*

真题考点词替换清单

题号	题目——原文
14	features of our planet—shaped the world, topography
17	unpredictability—not predictable
21	inactive—quiet
22	land—continents
	produced—provided
23	quickly—faster
25	quickly—swiftly
	violently—tremendous force

📤 *Reading Passage 3: Obtaining Linguistic Data*

真题考点词替换清单

题号	题目——原文
29	influenced—relevant
	situation—setting
30	self-conscious—being aware of
31	various—several
33	necessary—unavoidable
36	miss—limitations
37	comment—statements
	objectively—unbiased
38	focus on—deals only with
39	affect—depends on
40	additional—supplemented
	gained—derived

Test 4

↑ *Reading Passage 1: How Much Higher? How Much Faster?*

真题考点词替换清单

题号	题目——原文
1	date from—began
3	greatly—dramatic
6	gifted—genes
	recognised—identified, realised
9	inadequate—deficiencies
12	explain—understanding
13	understanding—knowledge
	basic—fundamental

↑ *Reading Passage 2: The Nature and Aims of Archaeology*

真题考点词替换清单

题号	题目——原文
20	subdivided—broken down
22	reasons—why
	shape—round, square
	domestic buildings—dwellings
24	valuable—importance, useful
27	compares—rather like

↑ *Reading Passage 3: The Problem of Scarce Resources*

真题考点词替换清单

题号	题目——原文
30	role—obligation
31	impact—stem from
32	limited—finite
33	sharp—dramatic
35	guaranteeing—ensure
36	independence—self-determining
38	population—demographic

General Training: Reading and Writing
Test A

↑ Section 1

真题考点词替换清单

题号	题目——原文
2	country surroundings—scenic woodland
4	fee—charge
5	stay the night—accommodation
6	greeting—welcome
7	relevant skills—previous experience
8	cheer up—lift spirits
9	a variety of ages—all the family
10	individual—each
11	take part—participation
12	overcome shyness—developing the confidence
13	rapid—in no time

↑ Section 2

真题考点词替换清单

题号	题目——原文
23	architecture—construction industry
24	company management—business practice
25	the disabled—people with special needs
26	secretarial tasks—office work
27	beauty therapy—facial massage and skin care

↑ Section 3: The History of Early Cinema

真题考点词替换清单

题号	题目——原文
28	plenty of—a great deal of
30	excellent—more impressive
33	profitable—commercial success
35	biggest—largest

7

38	make money—commercial success
39	own culture—traditional
40	size—proportion

General Training: Reading and Writing
Test B

↑ *Section 1*

真题考点词替换清单

题号	题目——原文
3	paid—settled
6	included—in addition to 【反】
8	replaced—restorations
9	provide the food—caterers, function, menu
10	lawyer—solicitors, legal services
12	somewhere to live—estate and property

↑ *Section 2*

真题考点词替换清单

题号	题目——原文
15	banana—tropical fruit
16	cattle farming—beef
17	recreation—fitness
18	elderly care—the aged support
19	infant—early childhood
20	beach protection—environmental issues
21	fish farming—marine industry

↑ *Section 3: Understanding Bee Behaviour*

真题考点词替换清单

题号	题目——原文
29	discovers—realised
30	discovers—found
32	distance—metres away
38	changing the position—moving further

Cambridge
IELTS
5

Test 1

↑ *Reading Passage 1: Johnson's Dictionary*

真题考点词替换清单

题号	题目——原文
1	contemporary texts—living language
2	limit for its completion—deadline
3	subtleties of—shades of
6	bring—confer
7	grant—offer
12	receive payment on its completion—installment
13	not all of the assistants survived—two of whom died

↑ *Reading Passage 2: Nature or Nurture?*

真题考点词替换清单

题号	题目——原文
14	a biological explanation—built up animal aggression
16	the identity—actor
17	expected—predict
20	help—positive effect
22	comply with—obey
24	positive survival mechanism—advantageous trait

↑ *Reading Passage 3: The Truth about the Environment*

真题考点词替换清单

题号	题目——原文
27	pessimistic view—getting worse
29	increase—fewer【反】
31	link to—associated with
32	slow down—accelerate【反】
33	selection of areas—lopsidedness
34	exaggerate—overstate
35	criticism—skepticism
36	meet their readers' expectation—provide what the public wants

题号	题目——原文
38	long-term—extend into our future
39	catastrophic impact—devastating problem
40	urgent—pressing

Test 2

⬆ *Reading Passage 1: Bakelite*

真题考点词替换清单

题号	题目——原文
1	like—similar
2	totally—entirely
3	in the field of—in the domain of alternative—substitutes
4	called—known as
5	e.g.—for example
8	intense—extreme
11	principle—feature
12	versatile material—thousand uses
13	limited range of colours—dazzling array of shades

⬆ *Reading Passage 2: What's So Funny?*

真题考点词替换清单

题号	题目——原文
15	above-average intelligence—superiority over others
16	nervous—tension
17	ignore—settle on【反】
18	artificial intelligence—language understanding and reasoning in machine
21	linked to—be critical for
23	involved with—associated with
24	most difficult tasks—extremely demanding job
25	react to—response to
26	individual—person
27	operation of the brain—how it works

Reading Passage 3: The Birth of Scientific English

真题考点词替换清单

题号	题目——原文
28	at first—original
29	protect ideas—keep discovery secrets
30	neither...nor—lack
32	scientist associated with royal society—many members of the royal society
33	overtaken—leading
35	strong competition—intellectual property

Test 3

Reading Passage 1: Early Childhood Education

真题考点词替换清单

题号	题目——原文
1	details of the range of family types—single-parent and two-parent families
3	failed—disappointing
4	positive outcomes—phenomenal
5	a variety of poor and wealthy families—a cross-section of socio-economic status
11	score highly—make a great stride

Reading Passage 2: Disappearing Delta

真题考点词替换清单

题号	题目——原文
14	interrupting a natural process—dams were built
16	threat—mercury
18	coastal erosion—land scoured away from the coastline
20	increase the fertility—protect the huge population
24	pollutant—waste
25	in the short term—in the immediate future

♠ Reading Passage 3: *The Return of Artificial Intelligence*

真题考点词替换清单

题号	题目——原文
27	military impact—battlefield
28	separate research areas—disparate fields
29	common topic—public consciousness
31	first used—coin
33	lowest point—peak【反】
37	potential—widespread

Test 4

♠ Reading Passage 1: *The Impact of Wilderness Tourism*

真题考点词替换清单

题号	题目——原文
4	the low financial cost—little or no initial investment
6	throughout the year—part of the year
8	evenly over the year—a relatively short season
10	revive—renaissance
12	produce and sell—business

♠ Reading Passage 2: *Flawed Beauty: The Problem with Toughened Glass*

真题考点词替换清单

题号	题目——原文
14	unusual—rare
15	suppress—what you hear is only the tip of the iceberg
17	examine—analyse
18	ordinary—standard
19	unexpectedly—without warning
22	warm—sunlight

Reading Passage 3: The Effects of Light on Plant and Animal Species

真题考点词替换清单

题号	题目——原文
27	plenty of—considerable
28	encourage—induce
32	cue—trigger
33	fast-growing plant—lower growth rate【反】
35	refer to as—known as
37	depend on—require
39	such as—like

General Training: Reading and Writing
Test A

Section 1

真题考点词替换清单

题号	题目——原文
3	a variety of colours—a variety of animal motifs
8	driest parts of Australia—desert
9	nesting sites—native birds
10	hiker, journey on foot—bushwalking
11	biking—two wheels
12	the A–Z of Australian native animals—encyclopaedia
13	graphic—pictorial
13	prehistoric animals—dinosaur
14	outdoor safety—survival techniques

Section 2

真题考点词替换清单

题号	题目——原文
19	no restrictions on the type of job—choose any job
21	transcript of results—assessment and results
22	interaction—social activities
23	A or B result—credit courses

Section 3: Lack of Sleep

真题考点词替换清单

题号	题目——原文
31	overcome sleep-related problems—get rid of pre-sleep worries and anxieties
33	man-made—synthetic
35	process—phase
37	stages—phase
39	move around—paralyse【反】

General Training: Reading and Writing
Test B

Section 2

真题考点词替换清单

题号	题目——原文
16	excluding—exclusive
20	obtain—not available【反】
22	best for surfing the web—broadband internet connection
24	new option—recent initiative
26	not belong to the College—privately owned
27	not have your own bathroom—communal bathroom

Section 3: Glow-worms

真题考点词替换清单

题号	题目——原文
28	threats—endanger
31	distribution—very part of the globe
32	attraction—open the cave to tourists
37	heat—temperature
40	damp—wet

Note

Cambridge
IELTS
6

Test 1

↑ Reading Passage 1: Australia's Sporting Success

真题考点词替换清单

题号	题目——原文
1	a number of—different
	exchange—applying to
	expertise—skills
2	visual imaging—images from digital camera
3	narrowing—focus on
4	reproduced—copying
5	optimum—much better
6	funded—finances
7	calculated—this much, this fast, these time
12	produced—developing
	plan—prepare
13	improve—sliced off

↑ Reading Passage 2: Delivering the Goods

真题考点词替换清单

题号	题目——原文
15	electronic delivery—over telephone lines
16	similar cost—no bigger
	local—domestic
17	weakening relationship—unrelated
	value—worth
18	greater—twice
19	guarantees—if【反】
20	prefer to—disproportionately
	nearby—geographic neighbours
24	components—disk drives
25	introduction—invention
	safely—damaged or stolen【反】
	efficiently—a great many stages【反】
26	international shipping—ocean shipping
	reduce—firmer hand【反】
	domestic—to and from the dock, truck and railroad

♠ Reading Passage 3: *Climate Change and the Inuit*

真题考点词替换清单

题号	题目——原文
28	difficult—hardship
	landscape—treeless, desert
29	supplies—provisions
30	well-being—health, crisis of identity, depression
31	respect—draw on, more credibility and weight
32	remains limited—still huge gaps
33	impossible—out of the question
34	catching—exploiting
	sustenance—surviving
36	harsh—hardships
	surroundings—environment
	successful—well adapted to
37	a few—a handful of
38	give up—abandoned
	ways—lifestyle
39	depend on—rely on
	mainly—heavily
40	produce—meat

Test 2

♠ Reading Passage 1: *Advantages of Public Transport*

真题考点词替换清单

题号	题目——原文
1	people power—democratic
2	travelling—commuting
3	higher incomes—wealthier
5	benefits—valuable, creativity
10	averagely—not special
11	limited—minimal
12	inappropriate—hard

Reading Passage 2: Greying Population Stays in the Pink

真题考点词替换清单

题号	题目——原文
14	falling—declining
15	speed—rate
	increasing—accelerate
17	due to—in the face of
	developments—advances
20	link—correlation
21	reduction—drop
22	cost—saved, financial burden
	predicted—expected
26	loneliness—emotionally isolated
	rises—higher

Reading Passage 3: Numeration

真题考点词替换清单

题号	题目——原文
27	necessary—paramount
28	hand signal—gestures
	restricted—limited
29	fulfill—qualify
	civic role—witness
30	separate from—independent of
31	characteristic—traces
32	sufficiency—enough
	quantity—how many
34	misunderstanding—confusion
39	newer—later

Test 3

⬆ *Reading Passage 1*

真题考点词替换清单

题号	题目——原文
2	focus on—settled upon
4	teaches—educate
5	actors—cinema star
6	important—worth trying
9	early—originally
11	passing—flow
12	uncertain—by no means obvious

⬆ *Reading Passage 2: Motivating Employees under Adverse Conditions*

真题考点词替换清单

题号	题目——原文
15	realistic—achievable, confident, valid
16	individuals—personalize
17	link—contingent on
18	fair—equal
21	team work—independence 【反】
22	feel—perceive
24	disclosed—openly communicating, visible
27	promotion—advancement

♠ Reading Passage 3: The Search for the Anti-aging Pill

真题考点词替换清单

题号	题目——原文
28	delay—slow
29	fewer—restriction
30	not many—few
	people—mortals
	attractive—harsh【反】
32	ate—fed
33	less likely—reduced risk
34	more—less【反】
36	reduced—decreased
	chance—likelihood
37	greater—lower【反】
38	less—minimizes
39	fewer—limit
40	focus on—emphasises

Test 4

♠ Reading Passage 1: Doctoring Sales

真题考点词替换清单

题号	题目——原文
2	financial incentives—honoraria
3	responsible—blame, responsibility
4	positive side—advantage
5	persuaded—influenced
6	studies—research
	shows—conclusion
	affected—works
8	limited—freedom【反】
9	moral—ethical
10	little use—primary sources【反】
11	visible—watch, see
13	legitimate—right
	make money—make a profit

↑ *Reading Passage 2: Do Literate Women Make Better Mothers?*

真题考点词替换清单

题号	题目——原文
14	teach—learnt【反】
	men and women—adults
17	attitudes—values
20	same—significantly lower【反】
21	stayed—remained unchanged
22	greatest change—impressive 21 points lower
26	money—budgets

↑ *Reading Passage 3*

真题考点词替换清单

题号	题目——原文
27	research—survey
33	lack of knowledge—not much was known
34	50%—halved
35	produce—develop
36	detailed—explicit
38	potential—be liable to
39	recognise the difference—distinguish

General Training: Reading and Writing
Test A

↑ Section 1

Caution Health Center Patient Information Leaflet

真题考点词替换清单

题号	题目——原文
1	outside—in addition to
2	first—initial
4	cancel—cannot keep
8	ask—request
	problem—symptoms, illness
9	move house—relocate

Bentley Hospital Catering Service

真题考点词替换清单

题号	题目——原文
10	not—nil
14	tell—report

Section 2

Bramley College International Scholarships

真题考点词替换清单

题号	题目——原文
19	twice—two
20	100%—full
21	50%—half

Using the Internet and CD-ROM Databases in the Library

真题考点词替换清单

题号	题目——原文
23	fee—charge
25	all times—any time
26	reserve—book

Section 3: The Water Crisis

真题考点词替换清单

题号	题目——原文
29	sectors—agriculture, industry
32	waste—leaks, losses
33	interdependence—interference
34	future—will, prospect
35	people—citizens
35	increasingly—more
37	application—use

General Training: Reading and Writing Test B

⬆ *Section 1*

The Employment Pages *Saturday Edition*

真题考点词替换清单

题号	题目——原文
1	teachers—academic staff, education
2	nurses—medical staff, hospital
3	university lecturer—academic staff
4	own business—self-employment
5	hotel—hospitality
6	public administration—government
7	agricultural—rural, farm
8	temporary—casual

Stanfield Theatre

真题考点词替换清单

题号	题目——原文
9	Internet—on-line
11	wheelchair—disabilities
14	get money back—refund

⬆ *Section 2*

Self-study Tips

真题考点词替换清单

题号	题目——原文
18	catalogue—log
19	important material—relevant pages
21	talk about—discuss

Study Centre Courses

真题考点词替换清单

题号	题目——原文
23	libraries—source material, cataloguing systems
25	acknowledging your sources—not to plagiarise
26	reading skills—skim, scan
27	grammar—tenses, language

Section 3: Pterosaurs

真题考点词替换清单

题号	题目——原文
30	confliction—disagreement
31	widespread destruction—calamity
32	all over the world—all continents
33	clear—definitely
34	hunted—catching
35	evolved—changed over time
36	failed—unable
38	take advantage of—use
40	across—wide

Cambridge

IELTS

7

Test 1

Reading Passage 1: Let's Go Bats

Paragraph A

prey [preɪ] n. 被捕食的动物

obstacle ['ɒbstəkl] n. 障碍

of one's own making 自作自受

economy [ɪ'kɒnəmɪ] n. 充分利用

exploit [ɪk'splɔɪt] v. 开发

living ['lɪvɪŋ] n. 生计

alternative [ɔ:l'tɜ:nətɪv] adj. 可选择的

thoroughly ['θʌrəlɪ] adv. 彻底地

occupy ['ɒkjʊpaɪ] v. 占有

favour ['feɪvə(r)] v. 有助于

make a go 成功

night-hunting [naɪt'hʌntɪŋ] adj. 夜间狩猎的

nocturnal [nɒk'tɜ:nl] adj. 夜间的，夜间发生的

ancestry ['ænsestrɪ] n. 祖先

mammal ['mæml] n. 哺乳动物

dinosaur ['daɪnəsɔ:(r)] n. 恐龙

dominate ['dɒmɪneɪt] v. 控制，支配

mammalian [mæ'meɪlɪən] adj. 哺乳动物的

scrap a living 艰难谋生

mass extinction 大量消亡，大灭绝

emerge [ɪ'mɜ:dʒ] v. 出现

substantial [səb'stænʃl] adj. 大量的

Paragraph B

engineering [ˌendʒɪ'nɪərɪŋ] n. 工程，工程学

in the absence of 在没有……的情况下

night-flighting [naɪt'flaɪtɪŋ] adj. 夜间飞行的

deep-sea [di:psi:] adj. 深海的

whale [weɪl] n. 鲸

dolphin ['dɒlfɪn] n. 海豚

muddy ['mʌdɪ] adj. 泥泞的

obstruct [əb'strʌkt] v. 阻塞

scatter ['skætə(r)] v. 分散

Paragraph C

manoeuvre [mə'nu:və(r)] v. 用策略

solution [sə'lu:ʃn] n. 解决方法

manufacture [ˌmænjʊ'fæktʃə(r)] v. 制造

lantern ['læntən] n. 灯笼，提灯

searchlight ['sɜːtʃlaɪt] n. 探照灯

firefly ['faɪəflaɪ] n. 萤火虫

bacteria [bæk'tɪərɪə] n. 细菌

consume [kən'sjuːm] v. 消耗

prohibitive [prə'hɪbətɪv] adj. 过高的

pinprick ['pɪnprɪk] n. 针刺，针孔

expose [ɪk'spəʊz] v. 暴露

detect [dɪ'tekt] v. 察觉，发现

fraction ['frækʃn] n. 部分

bounce [baʊns] v. 弹回，反射回

immensely [ɪ'menslɪ] adv. 极大地，无限地

headlight ['hedlaɪt] n. 汽车等的前灯

illuminate [ɪ'luːmɪneɪt] v. 照亮

signal ['sɪgnəl] n. 信号

expense [ɪk'spens] n. 损失，代价

weird [wɪəd] adj. 怪异的，不可思议的

Paragraph D

uncanny [ʌn'kænɪ] adj. 神秘的，离奇的

tell of 讲述

tricycle ['traɪsɪkl] n. 三轮车

block [blɒk] n. 街区

sensation [sen'seɪʃn] n. 感觉

phantom ['fæntəm] adj. 有名无实的；幽灵的，幻觉的

limb [lɪm] n. 四肢

echo ['ekəʊ] n. 回声，回音

presence ['prezns] n. 存在

discover [dɪ'skʌvə(r)] v. 发现

instrument ['ɪnstrəmənt] n. 器具，仪器

designer [dɪ'zaɪnə(r)] n. 设计者

adapt for 调整，使适应于

submarine [ˌsʌbmə'riːn] n. 潜艇

rely on 依赖

codename [kəʊdneɪm] n. 代码

sonar ['səʊnɑː(r)] n. 声呐

radar ['reɪdɑː(r)] n. 雷达

RDF 无线电测向机

Paragraph E

feat [fiːt] n. 成功，壮举

navigation [ˌnævɪ'geɪʃn] n. 航海，导航

strike a dumb 哑口无言

admiration [ˌædmə'reɪʃn] n. 钦佩，赞赏

technically ['teknɪklɪ] *adv.* 技术上地

underlying [ˌʌndə'laɪɪŋ] *adj.* 潜在的，根本的

mathematical [ˌmæθə'mætɪkl] *adj.* 数学的

zoologist [zəʊ'ɒlədʒɪst] *n.* 动物学家　　coin [kɔɪn] *v.* 创造

echolocation [ˌekəʊləʊ'keɪʃn] *n.* 回声测距，回声定位法

cover ['kʌvə(r)] *v.* 包括

Questions

perceive [pə'siːv] *v.* 察觉，感觉　　seabed ['siːbed] *n.* 海底，海床

sophisticated [sə'fɪstɪkeɪtɪd] *adj.* 复杂的

真题考点词替换清单

题号	题目——原文
1	other than—not the only
2	avoid dying out—manage to survive
5	military use—weapon, submarine
6	limb—arm or leg
8	calculate—measure
9	finding—detection
11	inaccurate—incorrect
11	refer to—talk about
11	because—since
12	based on—underlying
13	word—term
13	first used—coined

⬆ *Reading Passage 2: Making Every Drop Count*

Paragraph A

civilisation [sɪvɪlaɪ'zeɪʃən] *n.* 文明　　entwine [ɪn'twaɪn] *v.* 缠住，交织

manipulate [mə'nɪpjʊleɪt] *v.* 操作　　remote [rɪ'məʊt] *adj.* 遥远的

sophisticated [sə'fɪstɪkeɪtɪd] *adj.* 复杂的　　dam [dæm] *n.* 大坝

aqueduct ['ækwɪdʌkt] *n.* 沟渠   Roman ['rəʊmən] *n.* 罗马

height [haɪt] *n.* 高度

innovative ['ɪnəveɪtɪv] *adj.* 革新的，创新的

layout ['leɪaʊt] *n.* 布局，安排   pipe [paɪp] *n.* 管道

sewer ['suːə(r)] *n.* 下水道   occupant ['ɒkjəpənt] *n.* 居住者，居民

industrial [ɪn'dʌstrɪəl] *adj.* 工业的

Paragraph B

industrial revolution 工业革命   population explosion 人口爆炸

dramatically [drə'mætɪklɪ] *adv.* 剧烈地

unprecedented [ʌn'presɪdentɪd] *adj.* 空前的

monumental [ˌmɒnjʊ'mentl] *adj.* 不朽的   irrigation [ˌɪrɪ'geɪʃn] *n.* 灌溉

hydropower ['haɪdrəʊˌpaʊə] *n.* 水力发电   keep pace with 跟上，与……齐步前进

soaring ['sɔːrɪŋ] *adj.* 激增的，猛增的   artificial [ˌɑːtɪ'fɪʃl] *adj.* 人造的

electricity [ɪˌlek'trɪsətɪ] *n.* 电力   generate ['dʒenəreɪt] *v.* 生产，生成

turbine ['tɜːbaɪn] *n.* 涡轮机   spin [spɪn] *v.* 旋转

Paragraph C

dark side 负面   inferior to 比……差，不如

reiterate [rɪ'ɪtəreɪt] *v.* 重申，反复地做   drinking water 饮用水

adequate ['ædɪkwət] *adj.* 足够的

sanitation [ˌsænɪ'teɪʃn] *n.* 环境卫生，卫生设施

preventable [prɪ'ventəbl] *adj.* 可预防的

water-related ['wɔːtə(r)rɪ'leɪtɪd] *adj.* 与水相关的

estimate ['estɪmət] *v.* 估计

Paragraph D

jeopardize ['dʒepədaɪz] *v.* 危害，使陷危地

compensation [ˌkɒmpen'seɪʃn] n. 补偿

make way for 让步

reservoir ['rezəvwɑː(r)] n. 水库

species ['spiːʃiːz] n. 物种

endangered [ɪn'deɪndʒəd] adj. 濒临灭绝的

withdrawal [wɪð'drɔːəl] n. 取回，取得

free-flowing [friː'fləʊɪŋ] adj. 自由流淌的

ecosystem ['iːkəʊsɪstəm] n. 生态系统

thrive [θraɪv] v. 繁荣，兴旺

degrade [dɪ'greɪd] v. 降级

productivity [ˌprɒdʌk'tɪvəti] n. 生产力

aquifer ['ækwɪfə(r)] n. 蓄水层

pump down 排空

replenish [rɪ'plenɪʃ] v. 补充

dispute [dɪ'spjuːt] n. 争论

tension ['tenʃn] n. 紧张，不安

Paragraph E

outset ['aʊtset] n. 开始，开端

millennium [mɪ'leniəm] n. 千禧年

provision [prə'vɪʒn] n. 供应

shift [ʃɪft] v. 改变

priority [praɪ'ɒrəti] n. 优先权

infrastructure ['ɪnfrəstrʌktʃə(r)] n. 基础设施

option ['ɒpʃn] n. 选择

resort [rɪ'zɔːt] n. 凭借，手段

philosophy [fə'lɒsəfi] n. 哲学；指导思想

Paragraph F

unexpectedly [ˌʌnɪk'spektɪdli] adj. 没有预料到的，没想到的

predict [prɪ'dɪkt] v. 预测

diminish [dɪ'mɪnɪʃ] v. 减少

output ['aʊtpʊt] n. 产量

soar [sɔː(r)] v. 激增

Paragraph G

remarkable [rɪ'mɑːkəbl] adj. 卓越的

figure out 想出

efficiency [ɪ'fɪʃnsi] n. 效率

rethink [ˌriː'θɪŋk] v. 反思

tenfold ['tenfəʊld] adv. 十倍

quadruple [kwɒ'druːpl] v. 翻两番，使成四倍

conserve [kən's3ːv] v. 保存，保藏

approximately [ə'prɒksɪmətlɪ] *adv.* 大约，近似地

commercial [kə'mɜːʃl] *adj.* 商业的　　inflation [ɪn'fleɪʃn] *n.* 通货膨胀

Paragraph H

specification [ˌspesɪfɪ'keɪʃn] *n.* 规格　　accountability [əˌkaʊntə'bɪlətɪ] *n.* 责任

warranted ['wɒrəntɪd] *adj.* 担保的　　criteria [kraɪ'tɪərɪə] *n.* 标准

budget ['bʌdʒɪt] *n.* 预算

Questions

call for 要求　　revision [rɪ'vɪʒn] *n.* 修正

address [ə'dres] *v.* 对付　　standard ['stændəd] *n.* 标准

imitate ['ɪmɪteɪt] *v.* 模仿　　domestic [də'mestɪk] *adj.* 家庭的

ownership ['əʊnəʃɪp] *n.* 所有权

真题考点词替换清单

题号	题目——原文
14	ancient—history, roman empire
15	relevance to health—clean drinking water, sanitation, disease
16	environmental—people, fish, ecosystems, soil, agricultural
17	scientist—expert
	call for—demanding
	revision—change, shift
18	surprising—unexpected
	reduce, downward—diminish, slow, fall
20	need—must
	raise—higher
	standard—specification, criteria
22	increasing—soaring
	due to—because of
	primarily—mainly
25	lead to—thanks to
	domestic—in homes

Reading Passage 3: Educating Psyche

Paragraph 1

psyche ['saɪkɪ] *n.* 灵魂

radical ['rædɪkl] *adj.* 彻底的，根本的，激进的

imagination [ɪˌmædʒɪ'neɪʃn] *n.* 想象   unconscious [ʌn'kɒnʃəs] *adj.* 无意识的

propose [prə'pəʊz] *v.* 提出   suggestion [sə'dʒestʃən] *n.* 暗示

Paragraph 2

instructional [ɪn'strʌkʃənl] *adj.* 指导的，教育的

connection [kə'nekʃn] *n.* 联系   mental ['mentl] *adj.* 精神的

reactivity [ˌriːæk'tɪvɪtɪ] *n.* 反应   durable ['djʊərəbl] *adj.* 持久的

perceive [pə'siːv] *v.* 察觉

peripheral [pə'rɪfərəl] *adj.* 外围的，次要的

binding ['baɪndɪŋ] *n.* 装订   typeface ['taɪpfeɪs] *n.* 字形，字体

concentrate ['kɒnsntreɪt] *v.* 集中，专注   mannerism ['mænərɪzəm] *n.* 特殊习惯

auditorium [ˌɔːdɪ'tɔːrɪəm] *n.* 观众席   air-conditioning ['eərkən'dɪʃnɪŋ] *n.* 空调

elusive [ɪ'luːsɪv] *adj.* 难懂的，难捉摸的   readily ['redɪlɪ] *adv.* 容易地，乐意地

hypnosis [hɪp'nəʊsɪs] *n.* 催眠   relive [ˌriː'lɪv] *v.* 再生

imaginatively [ɪ'mædʒɪnətɪvlɪ] *adv.* 想象地

psychodrama ['saɪkəʊdrɑːmə] *n.* 心理剧疗法

Paragraph 3

phenomenon [fə'nɒmɪnən] *n.* 现象   attribute to 导致

counterproductive [ˌkaʊntəprə'dʌktɪv] *adj.* 效率低下的

memorise ['meməraɪz] *v.* 记忆，储存   fatigue [fə'tiːg] *n.* 疲劳，疲乏

reflect [rɪ'flekt] *v.* 反映

suggestopedia [sə.dʒestə'piːdɪə] *n.* 暗示感应教学法

curriculum [kə'rɪkjələm] *n.* 课程　　　　capacity [kə'pæsətɪ] *n.* 容量

Paragraph 4

illustration [.ɪlə'streɪʃn] *n.* 解释　　　　variant ['veərɪənt] *n.* 变化

session ['seʃn] *n.* 讲习会　　　　　　classical ['klæsɪkl] *adj.* 古典的，经典的

solemnly ['sɒləmlɪ] *adv.* 严肃地　　　dynamic [daɪ'næmɪk] *n.* 动感

baroque [bə'rɒk] *adj.* 巴洛克式的，复杂的

normal ['nɔːml] *adj.* 正常的　　　　attempt [ə'tempt] *n.* 试图，尝试

Paragraph 5

beforehand [bɪ'fɔːhænd] *adv.* 事先，预先　　expectation [.ekspek'teɪʃn] *n.* 预期，期待

preliminary [prɪ'lɪmɪnərɪ] *adj.* 开始的　　likewise ['laɪkwaɪz] *adv.* 同样地，也

devote assist 投入协助　　　　　　instruct [ɪn'strʌkt] *v.* 指示，通知

Paragraph 6

stimulate ['stɪmjʊleɪt] *v.* 激励　　　recall [rɪ'kɔːl] *v.* 回想

communicate [kə'mjuːnɪkeɪt] *v.* 沟通，交流

improvised [ɪmprə'vaɪzd] *adj.* 即兴的

dramatization [.dræmətə'zeɪʃn] *n.* 编剧，改编成戏剧

distinctive [dɪ'stɪŋktɪv] *adj.* 有特色的，与众不同的

assume [ə'sjuːm] *v.* 认为

automatic [.ɔːtə'mætɪk] *adj.* 自动的，无意识的

effortless ['efətləs] *adj.* 不费力气的　　accomplish [ə'kʌmplɪʃ] *v.* 完成

paraconsciously ['pærə'kɒnʃəslɪ] *adv.* 超意识地

accessible [ək'sesəbl] *adv.* 易接近的

conventional [kən'venʃənl] *adj.* 惯例的，传统的

grammar ['græmə(r)] n. 语法

idiom ['ɪdɪəm] n. 成语，习语

Paragraph 7

trance [trɑːns] n. 恍惚

yoga ['jəʊɡə] n. 瑜伽

ceremony ['serəmənɪ] n. 仪式

faith healing （靠祈祷等治病的）信仰疗法

essential [ɪ'senʃl] adj. 基本的，本质的

placebo [plə'siːbəʊ] n. 安慰剂

tap [tæp] v. 激活

authority [ɔː'θɒrətɪ] n. 权威

precisely [prɪ'saɪslɪ] adv. 精确地，恰恰

categorical [ˌkætə'ɡɒrɪkl] adj. 绝对的

accredited [ə'kredɪtɪd] adj. 公认的，可信任的

procedure [prə'siːdʒə(r)] n. 过程

Silva mind-control 西瓦心灵术，控制法

ritual ['rɪtʃʊəl] n. 仪式

acknowledge [ək'nɒlɪdʒ] v. 承认

dispense [dɪ'spens] v. 执行

autocratic [ˌɔːtə'krætɪk] adj. 专制的

capsule ['kæpsjuːl] n. 胶囊

designate ['dezɪɡneɪt] v. 指定，指派

Paragraph 8

notoriety [ˌnəʊtə'raɪətɪ] n. 名声

spectacular [spek'tækjələ(r)] adj. 壮观的，惊人的

associate [ə'səʊʃɪeɪt] n. 同事，伙伴

mediocre [ˌmiːdɪ'əʊkə(r)] adj. 普通的，平凡的

mind set 思维定式

emulate ['emjʊleɪt] v. 模仿

motivate ['məʊtɪveɪt] v. 激发；激励

Questions

valid ['vælɪd] adj. 有根据的

variable ['veərɪəbl] n. 变量

be similar to 相似

prefer to 更喜欢

overload [ˌəʊvə'ləʊd] v. 超载

demanding [dɪ'mɑːndɪŋ] adj. 苛求的

conventional [kən'venʃənl] adj. 传统的

retain [rɪ'teɪn] v. 记住

真题考点词替换清单

题号	题目——原文
27	way—approach
	not traditional—radical new
28	unimportant—peripheral
33	conventional—not unusual
36	retain—learn
	vocabulary—words
37	admit—acknowledge
39	well known—gain some notoriety

Test 2

🔼 *Reading Passage 1: Why Pagodas don't Fall Down*

Paragraph 1

sweep [swiːp] *v.* 席卷

flimsy ['flɪmzɪ] *adj.* 脆弱的，易损坏的

pagoda [pə'gəʊdə] *n.* 宝塔

lightning ['laɪtnɪŋ] *n.* 闪电

disastrous [dɪ'zɑːstrəs] *adj.* 灾难性的

elevated ['elɪveɪtɪd] *adj.* 高尚的

devastate ['devəsteɪt] *v.* 毁坏，毁灭

magnificent [mæg'nɪfɪsnt] *adj.* 壮丽的，华丽的

storey ['stɔːrɪ] *n.* 楼层

unscathed [ʌn'skeɪðd] *adj.* 未受伤的

typhoon [taɪ'fuːn] *n.* 台风

wooden ['wʊdn] *adj.* 木质的

collapse [kə'læps] *v.* 倒塌

civil war 内战

topple ['tɒpl] *v.* 推翻

flatten ['flætn] *v.* 摧毁，夷平

level ['levl] *v.* 夷为平地

Paragraph 2

mystify ['mɪstɪfaɪ] *v.* 使神秘化，使迷惑

stable ['steɪbl] *adj.* 稳定的

slender ['slendə(r)] *adj.* 细长的

confident ['kɒnfɪdənt] *adj.* 自信的

erect [ɪ'rekt] v. 建造

steel [stiːl] n. 钢铁

reinforced [riːɪn'fɔːst] adj. 加强的，加固的

concrete ['kɒŋkriːt] n. 混凝土

dozen ['dʌzn] n. 一打，十二个

shock absorber 减震器

dampen ['dæmpən] v. 抑制

sideways ['saɪdweɪz] adj. 向侧面的

skyscraper ['skaɪskreɪpə(r)] n. 摩天大楼

masterpiece ['mɑːstəpiːs] n. 杰作

Paragraph 3

peg [peg] n. 钉，桩

wedge [wedʒ] n. 楔子

hesitation [ˌhezɪ'teɪʃn] n. 犹豫

majestic [mə'dʒestɪk] adj. 庄严的，宏伟的

soar [sɔː(r)] v. 升高到

carpenter ['kɑːpəntə(r)] n. 木匠

trick [trɪk] n. 诀窍，花招

sway [sweɪ] v. 摇动，摇摆

settle ['setl] v. 稳定

Paragraph 4

Buddhism ['bʊdɪzəm] n. 佛教

attach [ə'tætʃ] v. 依附，贴上

staircase ['steəkeɪs] n. 楼梯

watchtower ['wɒtʃtaʊə(r)] n. 瞭望楼

be dispensed with 被免除

batter ['bætə(r)] v. 猛击

eaves [iːvz] n. 屋檐

gush [gʌʃ] v. 冲刷

overhang ['əʊvəhæŋ] n. （房屋楼层的）悬挑部分，飞檐

Paragraph 5

width [wɪdθ] n. 宽度

porcelain ['pɔːsəlɪn] n. 瓷，瓷器

tile [taɪl] n. 瓷砖，瓦片

earthenware ['ɜːθnweə(r)] n. 陶器，土器

Paragraph 6

resilience [rɪ'zɪliəns] n. 恢复力，顺应力

trunk-like [trʌŋklaɪk] adj. 像树干的

pillar ['pɪlə(r)] *n.* 柱子

flex [fleks] *v.* 折曲，柔软地摆动

startling ['stɑːtlɪŋ] *adj.* 令人吃惊的

Paragraph 7

structural ['strʌktʃərəl] *adj.* 建筑的，结构的

stationary ['steɪʃənrɪ] *adj.* 固定的

pendulum ['pendjələm] *n.* 钟摆

craftsman ['krɑːftsmən] *n.* 工匠

grasp [grɑːsp] *v.* 抓住

principle ['prɪnsəpl] *n.* 原则

stack [stæk] *n.* 堆

slither ['slɪðə(r)] *n.* 滑动

fro [frəʊ] *adv.* 向后地

consecutive [kən'sekjətɪv] *adj.* 连贯的，连续不断的

constrain [kən'streɪn] *v.* 限制

Paragraph 8

taper ['teɪpə(r)] *v.* 逐渐变细

successive [sək'sesɪv] *adj.* 连续的

vertical ['vɜːtɪkl] *adj.* 垂直的

corresponding [ˌkɒrə'spɒndɪŋ] *adj.* 相应的

counterpart ['kaʊntəpɑːt] *n.* 对应物

stack [stæk] *v.* 堆积，堆叠

regulation [ˌregjʊ'leɪʃn] *n.* 校准，规则

Paragraph 9

extra-wide ['ekstrəwaɪd] *adj.* 额外宽的

tightrope walker 走钢丝者

balancing ['bælənsɪŋ] *n.* 平衡

jolt [dʒəʊlt] *n.* 摇晃

graceful ['greɪsfl] *adj.* 优雅的

abrupt [ə'brʌpt] *adj.* 突然的

anticipate [æn'tɪsɪpeɪt] *v.* 预期，预料到

Questions

interior [ɪn'tɪərɪə(r)] *adj.* 内部的

post [pəʊst] *n.* 站，哨所

dynamics [daɪ'næmɪks] *n.* 动力学

真题考点词替换清单

题号	题目——原文
2	destroyed—unscathed【反】
4	absorb—sway and settle, rather than fight
	severe weather conditions—nature's forces
5	interior—inner
	access to top—staircases
7	observation post—watchtowers
8	up to half—fifty per cent or more
9	original—first
	religious—buddhism, temples
10	loosely over each other—independent of one another
11	stop—constrain
12	dynamics—shake, snake dance
13	fitted loosely—simply stacked
	on top of each other—one on top of another

🔺 *Reading Passage 2: The True Cost of Food*

Paragraph A

challenge ['tʃælɪndʒ] *n.* 挑战

relative ['relətɪv] *adj.* 相对的

enervation [ˌenə'veɪʃn] *n.* 贫瘠

wildlife ['waɪldlaɪf] *n.* 野生动物

agriculture ['ægrɪkʌltʃə(r)] *n.* 农业

immediate [ɪ'miːdɪət] *adj.* 直接的

collateral [kə'lætərəl] *adj.* 附属的

destruction [dɪ'strʌkʃn] *n.* 破坏

welfare ['welfeə(r)] *n.* 安宁

Paragraph B

mechanisation [ˌmekənaɪ'zeɪʃən] *n.* 机械化

fertiliser ['fɜːtɪlaɪzə] *n.* 肥料，化肥

pesticide ['pestɪsaɪd] *n.* 杀虫剂

monoculture ['mɒnəkʌltʃə(r)] *n.* 单一品种种植

battery ['bætrɪ] *n.* 电池

rearing ['rɪərɪŋ] *n.* 饲养

livestock ['laɪvstɒk] *n.* 牲畜，家畜

genetic [dʒə'netɪk] *adj.* 遗传的，基因的

engineering [ˌendʒɪ'nɪərɪŋ] *n.* 工程

onward ['ɒnwəd] *adj.* 向前的

unstoppable [ʌn'stɒpəbl] *adj.* 无法阻碍的，无法停止的

yield [jiːld] *n.* 产量，收益

soar [sɔː(r)] *v.* 激增

colossal [kə'lɒsl] *adj.* 巨大的

farmland ['fɑːmlænd] *n.* 农田

skylark ['skaɪlɑːk] *n.* 云雀

partridge ['pɑːtrɪdʒ] *n.* 鹧鸪

lapwing ['læpwɪŋ] *n.* 田凫

bunting ['bʌntɪŋ] *n.* 鹀

vanish ['vænɪʃ] *v.* 消失

stretch [stretʃ] *n.* 一片

hedgerow ['hedʒrəʊ] *n.* 灌木树篱

landscape ['lændskeɪp] *n.* 风景

faecal ['fiːkl] *adj.* 粪的

filth [fɪlθ] *n.* 污秽

salmon ['sæmən] *n.* 鲑鱼

loch [lɒk] *n.* 湖，海湾

fertility [fə'tɪlətɪ] *n.* 肥沃，富饶

continuous [kən'tɪnjʊəs] *adj.* 连续的

industrial [ɪn'dʌstrɪəl] *adj.* 工业的

algae ['ældʒiː] *n.* 藻类，海藻

run-off 溢流

Paragraph C

battlefield ['bætlfiːld] *n.* 战场

consumer [kən'sjuːmə] *n.* 消费者

economist [ɪ'kɒnəmɪst] *n.* 经济学家

externality [ˌekstɜː'nælətɪ] *n.* 外部效应

transaction [træn'zækʃn] *n.* 交易

borne [bɔːn] *v.* 承担；运输

financial [faɪ'nænʃl] *adj.* 金融的

aesthetic [iːs'θetɪk] *adj.* 美学的，审美的

Paragraph D

quantify ['kwɒntɪfaɪ] *v.* 量化，确定数量

amount to 合计，达到

staggering ['stægərɪŋ] *adj.* 令人惊愕的

remarkable [rɪ'mɑːkəbl] *adj.* 卓越的

leading ['liːdɪŋ] *adj.* 主要的

thinker ['θɪŋkə(r)] *n.* 思想家

University of Essex 埃塞克斯大学

calculate ['kælkjʊleɪt] v. 计算

repairing [rɪ'peərɪŋ] n. 修复

equivalent [ɪ'kwɪvələnt] adj. 等价的

hectare ['hekteə(r)] n. 公顷

arable ['ærəbl] adj. 可开垦的

pasture ['pɑːstʃə(r)] n. 草地，牧场

conservative [kən'sɜːvətɪv] adj. 保守的

estimate ['estɪmət] n. 估计

Paragraph E

nitrate ['naɪtreɪt] n. 硝酸盐

phosphate ['fɒsfeɪt] n. 磷酸盐

bug [bʌg] n. 臭虫，小虫

cryptosporidium [ˌkrɪptəʊspə'rɪdɪəm] n. 隐孢子虫

habitat ['hæbɪtæt] n. 栖息地

emission [ɪ'mɪʃn] n. 排放

erosion [ɪ'rəʊʒn] n. 侵蚀

organic [ɔː'gænɪk] adj. 有机的

carbon ['kɑːbən] n. 碳

poisoning ['pɔɪzənɪŋ] n. 中毒

memorable ['memərəbl] adj. 显著的

conclusion [kən'kluːʒn] n. 结论

threefold ['θriːfəʊld] adj. 三倍的

supposedly [sə'pəʊzɪdli] adv. 可能

over the counter 直接交易

enormous [ɪ'nɔːməs] adj. 巨大的

subsidy ['sʌbsədɪ] n. 补贴，津贴

prop [prɒp] v. 支持

intensive [ɪn'tensɪv] adj. 集中的

mess [mes] n. 混乱

Paragraph F

urgent ['ɜːdʒənt] adj. 紧急的

feasible ['fiːzəbl] adj. 可行的

sustainable [sə'steɪnəbl] adj. 可持续的

diverse [daɪ'vɜːs] adj. 不同的，多样的

sector ['sektə(r)] n. 部门

thriving [θraɪvɪŋ] adj. 繁荣的

rural ['rʊərəl] adj. 农村的

Paragraph G

replace [rɪ'pleɪs] v. 代替

viable ['vaɪəbl] adj. 可行的

alternative [ɔːl'tɜːnətɪv] n. 替换物

premium ['priːmɪəm] n. 额外费用

recommend [ˌrekə'mend] *v.* 推荐

require [rɪ'kwaɪə(r)] *v.* 需要

comprise [kəm'praɪz] *v.* 包含

agrochemical [ˌægrəʊ'kemɪkl] *adj.* 农用化学品的

norm [nɔːm] *n.* 规范

commitment [kə'mɪtmənt] *n.* 承诺

Questions

purify ['pjʊərɪfaɪ] *v.* 净化

recognise ['rekəgnaɪz] *v.* 认识到

attitude ['ætɪtjuːd] *n.* 态度

deteriorate [dɪ'tɪərɪəreɪt] *v.* 恶化

initiate [ɪ'nɪʃɪeɪt] *v.* 开始实施

真题考点词替换清单

题号	题目——原文
14	purify—removal of the bug
	domestic water—drinking water
15	stages—first, then, then, and now
16	term—what economists refer to as externalities
	hidden—not appear
17	chemicals—fertilizer
	water sources—lakes
18	decline—vanish
21	illness caused by food—food poisoning
22	conclude—draw a conclusion
	higher than—threefold
23	realistic—feasible
	reduce reliance on—break away from
24	too big a jump—unable to adapt to
25	initiate—introduction
	change—more...than the current norm
26	change—shift
	both... and—as well as

Reading Passage 3: Makete Integrated Rural Transport Project

Section A

disappointing [ˌdɪsəˈpɔɪntɪŋ] *adj.* 令人失望的

conventional [kənˈvenʃənl] *adj.* 惯例的，传统的

rethink [ˌriːˈθɪŋk] *v.* 反思

rural [ˈrʊərəl] *adj.* 农村的，乡下的

tackle [ˈtækl] *v.* 处理

request [rɪˈkwest] *n.* 请求，需要

availability [əˌveɪləˈbɪlətɪ] *n.* 可用性，有效性

Tanzania [ˌtænzəˈniːə] *n.* 坦桑尼亚

integrated [ˈɪntɪɡreɪtɪd] *adj.* 综合的

adopt [əˈdɒpt] *v.* 采用

household [ˈhaʊshəʊld] *n.* 家庭，一家人

obtain [əbˈteɪn] *v.* 获得

essential [ɪˈsenʃl] *adj.* 基本的，必要的

underlying [ˌʌndəˈlaɪɪŋ] *adj.* 潜在的，根本的

assumption [əˈsʌmpʃn] *n.* 设想

co-ordinate [kəʊˈɔːdɪneɪt] *v.* 使……协调

Section B

virtually [ˈvɜːtʃʊəlɪ] *adv.* 事实上，几乎

isolate [ˈaɪsəleɪt] *v.* 使隔离，使孤立

regional [ˈriːdʒənl] *adj.* 区域的

rare [reə(r)] *adj.* 稀有的

alternative [ɔːlˈtɜːnətɪv] *adj.* 选择性的

donkey [ˈdɒŋkɪ] *n.* 驴子

primarily [praɪˈmerəlɪ] *adv.* 主要地

slippery [ˈslɪpərɪ] *adj.* 滑的

propose [prəˈpəʊz] *v.* 提出

socio-economic [ˈsəʊsiːəʊˌiːkəˈnɒmɪk] *adj.* 社会经济的

survey [ˈsɜːveɪ] *n.* 调查

indicate [ˈɪndɪkeɪt] *v.* 表明

regard [rɪˈɡɑːd] *v.* 与……有关

locality [ləʊˈkælətɪ] *n.* 地点

firewood [ˈfaɪəwʊd] *n.* 柴火，木柴

grinding mill 磨坊

Section C

determine [dɪˈtɜːmɪn] *v.* 决定

identify [aɪˈdentɪfaɪ] *v.* 确定

burden [ˈbɜːdn] *n.* 负担

approach [əˈprəʊtʃ] *n.* 方法

implement ['ɪmplɪmənt] *v.* 补充

mobility [məʊ'bɪlətɪ] *n.* 移动性

district ['dɪstrɪkt] *n.* 区域

truck [trʌk] *n.* 卡车

mechanical [mə'kænɪkl] *adj.* 机械的

consideration [kən.sɪdə'reɪʃn] *n.* 考虑

short-cut ['ʃɔːtkʌt] *n.* 捷径

hillside ['hɪlsaɪd] *n.* 山坡

arduous ['ɑːdjʊəs] *adj.* 费力的

handrail ['hændreɪl] *n.* 扶手

footbridge ['fʊtbrɪdʒ] *n.* 人行桥

uncommon [ʌn'kɒmən] *adj.* 不寻常的

technologically [.teknə'lɒdʒɪklɪ] *adv.* 技术上地

motor vehicle 机动车

constrain [kən'streɪn] *v.* 限制

appropriate [ə'prəʊprɪeɪt] *adj.* 适当的

promotion [prə'məʊʃn] *n.* 推广

manufacturable [mænjʊ'fæktʃərəbl] *adj.* 可制造的

wheelbarrow ['wiːlbærəʊ] *n.* 独轮手推车

Section D

selected [sɪ'lektɪd] *adj.* 挑选出来的

refinement [rɪ'faɪnmənt] *n.* 改良

institutionalisation [.ɪnstɪ'tjuːʃənəlaɪzeɪʃn] *n.* 制度化，体制化

accompanying [ə'kʌmpəniɪŋ] *adj.* 附随的

maintenance ['meɪntənəns] *n.* 维护，维修

readily ['redɪlɪ] *adv.* 容易地，无困难地

fluctuate ['flʌktʃʊeɪt] *v.* 使波动

request [rɪ'kwest] *n.* 需要

participate [pɑː'tɪsɪpeɪt] *v.* 参加

efficiency [ɪ'fɪʃnsɪ] *n.* 效率

motorised ['məʊtəraɪzd] *adj.* 机动化的

poverty ['pɒvətɪ] *n.* 贫穷

modification [.mɒdɪfɪ'keɪʃn] *n.* 修改，修正

carpenter ['kɑːpəntə(r)] *n.* 木匠

shilling ['ʃɪlɪŋ] *n.* 先令

transportation [.trænspɔː'teɪʃn] *n.* 运输

breeding ['briːdɪŋ] *n.* 繁殖，饲养

affordable [ə'fɔːdəbl] *adj.* 负担得起的

initiative [ɪ'nɪʃətɪv] *n.* 首创精神

renting ['rentɪŋ] *n.* 出租

investment [ɪn'vestmənt] *n.* 投资

illustrate ['ɪləstreɪt] *v.* 说明

supplementary [.sʌplɪ'mentrɪ] *adj.* 补充的

Section E

criticize ['krɪtɪsaɪz] v. 批评

authority [ɔː'θɒrəti] n. 当局

hand down 宣布，把……传下去

villager ['vɪlɪdʒə(r)] n. 村民

Section F

improved [ɪm'pruːvd] adj. 改良的

inexpensive [ˌɪnɪk'spensɪv] adj. 便宜的

dedicated ['dedɪkeɪtɪd] adj. 专注的，有奉献精神的

awareness [ə'weənəs] n. 意识

reference ['refrəns] n. 参考

Questions

preference ['prefrəns] n. 偏爱

prior to 在……之前

inaccessible [ˌɪnæk'sesəbl] adj. 无法进入的

affordable [ə'fɔːdəbl] adj. 负担得起的

hinder ['hɪndə(r)] v. 阻碍

真题考点词替换清单

题号	题目——原文
27	identify—understand, know, research, survey
	transport problems—isolated, bad shape, access impossible, extremely rare, restricted, slippery, dangerous
29	co-operation—support and understanding
	officials—authorities
32	inaccessible—isolated
34	20% outside—80% within
36	construction—building
37	buses and trucks—motorized vehicles
	hinder—not successful
38	local people—communities
	lend a hand—participate in
39	isolation for part of the year—accessible throughout the year

Test 3

Reading Passage 1: Ant Intelligence

Paragraph 1

intelligent [ɪn'telɪdʒənt] *adj.* 智能的，聪明的

spring to mind 使人突然想起

ape [eɪp] *n.* 猿猴

sufficiently [sə'fɪʃntlɪ] *adv.* 足够地

hint [hɪnt] *n.* 一点，微量

ant [ænt] *n.* 蚂蚁

considerable [kən'sɪdərəbl] *adj.* 相当大的，重要的

scrutiny ['skruːtənɪ] *n.* 详细审查，监视

demonstrate ['demənstreɪt] *v.* 表明

spark [spɑːk] *n.* 火花，痕迹

cognition [kɒg'nɪʃn] *n.* 认识，知识

reject ['riːdʒekt] *v.* 抵制，拒绝

investigation [ɪnˌvestɪ'geɪʃn] *n.* 调查

Paragraph 2

repel [rɪ'pel] *v.* 击退

attack [ə'tæk] *n.* 袭击

contact ['kɒntækt] *v.* 联系，接触

auditory ['ɔːdətrɪ] *adj.* 听觉的

channel ['tʃænl] *n.* 通道

chant [tʃɑːnt] *n.* 圣歌

jingle ['dʒɪŋgl] *n.* 叮当声

slogan ['sləʊgən] *n.* 标语

martial ['mɑːʃl] *adj.* 军事的，战争的

arouse [ə'raʊz] *v.* 引起，唤醒

propagate ['prɒpəgeɪt] *v.* 传播，传送

mood [muːd] *n.* 心情

biologist [baɪ'ɒlədʒɪst] *n.* 生物学家

embarrassment [ɪm'bærəsmənt] *n.* 难堪

fungi ['fʌndʒaɪ] *n.* 真菌，菌类

aphid ['eɪfɪd] *n.* 蚜虫

livestock ['laɪvstɒk] *n.* 家畜

launch [lɔːntʃ] *v.* 发动，投入

spray [spreɪ] *n.* 喷雾

confuse [kən'fjuːz] *v.* 使混乱，使迷惑

slave [sleɪv] *n.* 奴隶

engage in 从事

ceaselessly ['siːsləslɪ] *adv.* 不停地

Paragraph 3

transmission [træns'mɪʃn] n. 传送，传递

encode [ɪn'kəʊd] v. 编码，译码

gene [dʒiːn] n. 基因

instinct ['ɪnstɪŋkt] n. 本能，直觉

master ['mɑːstə(r)] v. 控制，征服

progress ['prəʊgres] v. 进步

fungus ['fʌŋgəs] n. 真菌

herding ['hɜːdɪŋ] n. 畜群

sophisticated [sə'fɪstɪkeɪtɪd] adj. 富有经验的，久经世事的

overtake [ˌəʊvə'teɪk] v. 赶上

agribusiness ['æɡrɪbɪznəs] n. 农业综合企业

Paragraph 4

sustainable [sə'steɪnəbl] adj. 可持续的

crop [krɒp] n. 农作物

adaptable [ə'dæptəbl] adj. 能适应的

Paragraph 5

digest [daɪ'dʒest] v. 消化，吸收

cellulose ['seljʊləʊs] n. 纤维素

cultivate ['kʌltɪveɪt] v. 培养，耕作

antibiotics [ˌæntɪbaɪ'ɒtɪks] n. 抗生素

weed [wiːd] n. 杂草

fertilise ['fɜːtəlaɪz] v. 使肥沃，施肥

Paragraph 6

unchanged [ʌn'tʃeɪndʒd] adj. 不变的

distant ['dɪstənt] adj. 遥远的

colleague ['kɒliːg] n. 同事

screen [skriːn] v. 拍摄

diverse [daɪ'vɜːs] adj. 不同的，多样的

domesticate [də'mestɪkeɪt] v. 驯养，教化

species ['spiːʃiːz] n. 物种

impressively [ɪm'presɪvlɪ] adv. 令人难忘地

modify ['mɒdɪfaɪ] v. 修改

swap [swɒp] v. 交换，交易

strain [streɪn] n. 血缘，品种

colony ['kɒlənɪ] n. 聚居地，（动植物的）群体

Paragraph 7

prehistoric [ˌpriːhɪ'stɒrɪk] adj. 史前的

exposure [ɪk'spəʊʒə(r)] n. 暴露

urban ['ɜːbən] *adj.* 城市的

chamber ['tʃeɪmbə(r)] *n.* 房间，室

setting ['setɪŋ] *n.* 布置，环境

tunnel ['tʌnl] *n.* 隧道

Paragraph 8

amazed [ə'meɪzd] *adj.* 吃惊的，惊奇的

magnificent [mæg'nɪfɪsnt] *adj.* 宏伟的

supercolony ['suːpə(r)'kɒlənɪ] *n.* 巨大巢穴

megalopolis [ˌmegə'lɒpəlɪs] *n.* 特大城市

interconnected [ˌɪntəkə'nektɪd] *adj.* 相互连接的

territory ['terətrɪ] *n.* 范围，领域

accomplish [ə'kʌmplɪʃ] *v.* 完成，实现

Paragraph 9

enduring [ɪn'djʊərɪŋ] *adj.* 持久的

meshed [meʃt] *adj.* 网状的

ancestor ['ænsestə(r)] *n.* 祖先

masterpiece ['mɑːstəpiːs] *n.* 杰作

primitive ['prɪmətɪv] *adj.* 原始的，简单的

intricately ['ɪntrɪkətlɪ] *adv.* 错综复杂地

outstrip [ˌaʊt'strɪp] *v.* 超过，胜过

hail [heɪl] *v.* 致敬，向……欢呼

cave painting 洞穴壁画，洞窟画

albeit [ˌɔːl'biːɪt] *conj.* 虽然；即使

Paragraph 10

conduct [kən'dʌkt] *v.* 实施，进行

navigate ['nævɪgeɪt] *v.* 导航，定位

combine [kəm'baɪn] *v.* 使联合，使结合

framework ['freɪmwɜːk] *n.* 框架，结构

foraging ['fɒrɪdʒɪŋ] *adj.* 觅食的

bearing ['beərɪŋ] *n.* 方位

landmark ['lændmɑːk] *n.* 地标

consult [kən'sʌlt] *v.* 查阅，商量

Paragraph 11

transmit [træns'mɪt] *v.* 传达，传输

mobilise ['məʊbɪlaɪz] *v.* 调动，使流通

scout [skaʊt] *v.* 侦查员

maze [meɪz] *n.* 迷宫

session ['seʃn] *n.* 时间

forager ['fɒrɪdʒə] *n.* 强征队员

proceed [prə'siːd] v. 开始，发生

precaution [prɪ'kɔːʃn] n. 预防，警惕

odour ['əʊdə(r)] n. 气味

clue [kluː] n. 线索，情节

sequence ['siːkwəns] n. 顺序

compass ['kʌmpəs] n. 罗盘

Paragraph 12

exhaustive [ɪg'zɔːstɪv] adj. 详尽的，彻底的

attach to 使依恋

laboratory [lə'bɒrətrɪ] n. 实验室

spot [spɒt] n. 斑点

Questions

edible ['edəbl] adj. 可食用的

genetic [dʒə'netɪk] adj. 基因的

interbreed [ˌɪntə'briːd] v. 品种杂交

secretion [sɪ'kriːʃn] n. 分泌物

真题考点词替换清单

题号	题目——原文
1	same—compared to【反】
2	encourage—forcing house
4	making calculations—integrating
	position—bearing
5	were able to—prevent【反】
	smell—odour
8	natural secretion—secrete antibiotics
9	weed-killers—control weeds
	unwanted materials—waste
10	genetic—DNA
	constantly—regularly
	upgrade—improve or modify
	exchanging—swapping and sharing
	species—strains
12	affect—ruin
13	waste energy—use enormous amounts of energy

▲ Reading Passage 2: Population Movements and Genetics

Paragraph A

distribution [ˌdɪstrɪ'bjuːʃn] *n.* 分布，分配

archaeological [ˌɑːkɪə'lɒdʒɪkl] *adj.* 考古学的

fossil ['fɒsl] *adj.* 化石的　　　　　sound [saʊnd] *adj.* 可靠的，合理的

footing ['fʊtɪŋ] *n.* 基础，立足处　　obtain [əb'teɪn] *v.* 获得

genetic [dʒə'netɪk] *adj.* 基因的，遗传的

Paragraph B

Siberia [saɪ'bɪərɪə] *n.* 西伯利亚　　launching ['lɒntʃɪŋ] *n.* 发射，开始

colonizer ['kɒlənaɪzə(r)] *n.* 移民　　migration [maɪ'greɪʃn] *n.* 迁移，移民

Bering Strait 白令海峡

Paragraph C

anthropologist [ˌænθrə'pɒlədʒɪst] *n.* 人类学家

variant ['veərɪənt] *n.* 变体　　　　protein ['prəʊtiːn] *n.* 蛋白质

immunoglobin [ɪmjʊ'nəgləʊbɪn] *n.* 免疫球蛋白

fluid ['fluːɪd] *adj.* 流动的　　　　portion ['pɔːʃn] *n.* 部分

interbreed [ˌɪntə'briːd] *v.* 异种交配

allotype ['ələtaɪp] *n.* （同种）异型抗免疫球蛋白

calibrate ['kælɪbreɪt] *v.* 矫正，调整　　indication [ˌɪndɪ'keɪʃn] *n.* 表明

Paragraph D

sample ['sɑːmpl] *v.* 取样　　　　correspond [ˌkɒrə'spɒnd] *v.* 符合，一致

Inuit ['ɪnjɔɪt] *n.* 因纽特人　　　　Aleut ['ælɪʊt] *n.* 阿留申人

deduce [dɪ'djuːs] *v.* 推论，推断

ancestral [æn'sestrəl] *adj.* 祖先的，祖传的

hunter ['hʌntə(r)] *n.* 猎人

Paragraph E

conclusion [kən'kluːʒn] *n.* 结论　　geneticist [dʒə'netɪsɪst] *n.* 遗传学者

mitochondrial [ˌmaɪtəʊˈkɒndrɪəl] *adj.* 线粒体的

separated [ˈsepəreɪtɪd] *adj.* 分开的　　peninsula [pəˈnɪnsjələ] *n.* 半岛

descend [dɪˈsend] *v.* 遗传

Paragraph F

throw some light 提供一些线索，给……照亮

biological [ˌbaɪəˈlɒdʒɪkl] *adj.* 生物的

characteristics [ˌkærɪktəˈrɪstɪks] *n.* 特征，特性

minimally [ˈmɪnɪməli] *adv.* 最低限度地

specimen [ˈspesɪmən] *n.* 样品，样本　　majority [məˈdʒɒrəti] *n.* 大多数

prehistoric [ˌpriːhɪˈstɒrɪk] *adj.* 史前的　　link to 与……有联系，相关

trait [treɪt] *n.* 特性，特征　　incisor [ɪnˈsaɪzə(r)] *n.* 切牙，门牙

shovel [ˈʃʌvl] *v.* 用铲子铲，用勺子舀　　scoop [skuːp] *v.* 挖

premolar [ˈpriːˈməʊlə] *n.* 前磨牙，前臼齿

triple-rooted 三层次的　　molar [ˈməʊlə(r)] *n.* 臼齿，磨牙

Paragraph G

linguist [ˈlɪŋgwɪst] *n.* 语言学家　　belong to 属于

credence [ˈkriːdns] *n.* 证据，凭证　　favour [ˈfeɪvə] *v.* 赞成，喜欢

notion [ˈnəʊʃn] *n.* 概念，见解　　account for 占，对……作出解释

backing [ˈbækɪŋ] *n.* 支持

真题考点词替换清单

题号	题目——原文
16	closeness—distance 【反】
17	results—found, showed, deduced
18	further evidence—other research support
	genetic—geneticist, DNA
19	dental—teeth, tooth
	examination—studies
26	prehistoric and modern—ancient and modern
	Americans and Asians—New and Old World

⬆ *Reading Passage 3*

Paragraph 1

heritage ['herɪtɪdʒ] *n.* 遗产，传统

increasing [ɪn'kriːsɪŋ] *adj.* 渐增的

threaten ['θretn] *v.* 威胁

threat [θret] *n.* 威胁，恐吓

geography [dʒɪ'ɒgrəfɪ] *n.* 地理，地形

deterioration [dɪˌtɪərɪə'reɪʃn] *n.* 恶化，退化

mismanagement [ˌmɪs'mænɪdʒmənt] *n.* 管理不当，处理失当

woodland ['wʊdlənd] *n.* 林地，森林

conference ['kɒnfərəns] *n.* 会议

combat ['kɒmbæt] *v.* 反对，与……战斗

ecosystem ['iːkəʊsɪstəm] *n.* 生态系统

initial [ɪ'nɪʃl] *adj.* 最初的

confine [kən'faɪn] *v.* 限制

Mediterranean [ˌmedɪtə'reɪnɪən] *adj.* 地中海的

Nordic ['nɔːdɪk] *adj.* 北欧的，日耳曼民族的

discard [dɪs'kɑːd] *v.* 抛弃，放弃

decline [dɪ'klaɪn] *n.* 下降；衰退

imbalance [ɪm'bæləns] *n.* 不平衡，不安定

increasingly [ɪn'kriːsɪŋlɪ] *adv.* 越来越多地

frontier ['frʌntɪə(r)] *n.* 前沿，边界

climate ['klaɪmət] *n.* 气候

Ministerial Conference 部长大会

destruction [dɪ'strʌkʃn] *n.* 毁坏

extension [ɪk'stenʃn] *n.* 延期，伸展

preparatory [prɪ'pærətrɪ] *adj.* 预备的

joint action 联合行动

border ['bɔːdə] *v.* 与……接壤

Paragraph 2

biological [ˌbaɪə'lɒdʒɪkl] *adj.* 生物的

recreational [ˌrekrɪ'eɪʃənl] *adj.* 娱乐的，消遣的

lung [lʌŋ] *n.* 肺

photosynthesis [ˌfəʊtəʊ'sɪnθəsɪs] *n.* 光合作用

oxygen ['ɒksɪdʒən] *n.* 氧气，氧

transformation [ˌtrænsfə'meɪʃn] *n.* 转化，转换

solar energy 太阳能

fulfill [fʊl'fɪl] *v.* 满足，实现

planet ['plænɪt] *n.* 行星

non-polluting ['nɒnpə'luːtɪŋ] *adj.* 无污染的

power plant 发电厂

renew [rɪ'njuː] v. 更新

condemn [kən'dem] v. 使……处于（不利的境况）

unrivaled [ʌn'raɪvəld] adj. 无敌的，无可比拟的

unwind [ˌʌn'waɪnd] v. 放松，解开

leisure ['leʒə(r)] adj. 空闲的，有余的

hiking ['haɪkɪŋ] n. 徒步旅行

dawn [dɔːn] n. 黎明，破晓

recognise ['rekəgnaɪz] v. 承认，认可

Paragraph 3

myth [mɪθ] n. 神话

effectively [ɪ'fektɪvlɪ] adv. 有效地

exploit [ɪk'splɔɪt] v. 开发，利用

transcend [træn'send] v. 胜过，超越

inevitable [ɪn'evɪtəbl] adj. 不可避免的

declaration [ˌdeklə'reɪʃn] n. 宣布，宣告

coherent [kəʊ'hɪərənt] adj. 连贯的，一致的

continuity [ˌkɒntɪ'njuːətɪ] n. 连续性

unforeseen [ˌʌnfɔː'siːn] adj. 无法预料的

potential [pə'tenʃl] n. 潜能，可能性

maintain [meɪn'teɪn] v. 维持

Paragraph 4

accompany [ə'kʌmpənɪ] v. 陪伴，伴随

policy-making ['pɒləsi'meɪkɪŋ] n. 决策

extension [ɪk'stenʃn] n. 延长，延期

systematization [ˌsɪstəmətaɪ'zeɪʃn] n. 系统化

surveillance [sɜː'veɪləns] n. 监视，监督

monitor ['mɒnɪtə(r)] v. 监控

proportion [prə'pɔːʃn] n. 部分

needle ['niːdl] n. 针叶

continent ['kɒntɪnənt] n. 大陆，陆地

species ['spiːʃiːz] n. 物种

cumulative ['kjuːmjələtɪv] adj. 累积的

atmospheric [ˌætməs'ferɪk] adj. 大气的，大气层的

pollutant [pə'luːtənt] n. 污染物

culprit ['kʌlprɪt] n. 引起问题的事物

nitrogen ['naɪtrədʒən] n. 氮

sulphur dioxide 二氧化硫

accentuate [ək'sentʃʊeɪt] v. 强调

drought [draʊt] n. 干旱

hard winter 严冬，寒冬

soil imbalance 土壤失衡

acidification [əˌsɪdɪfɪ'keɪʃən] *n.* 酸化，土地酸化

preserve [prɪ'zɜːv] *v.* 保存，保护

diversity [daɪ'vɜːsəti] *n.* 多样性，差异

databank ['deɪtəbæŋk] *n.* 数据库

preventative [prɪ'ventətɪv] *adj.* 预防性的

minister ['mɪnɪstə(r)] *n.* 部长

rapidly ['ræpɪdlɪ] *adv.* 迅速地

thinly ['θɪnlɪ] *adv.* 稀疏地

scattered ['skætəd] *adj.* 分散的

permanent ['pɜːmənənt] *adj.* 永久的

skiing ['skiːɪŋ] *n.* 滑雪运动

preferential [ˌprefə'renʃl] *adj.* 优先的，特惠的

relaunch [ˌriː'lɔːntʃ] *v.* 重新启动

physiology [ˌfɪzɪ'ɒlədʒɪ] *n.* 生理学

scholarship ['skɒləʃɪp] *n.* 奖学金

framework ['freɪmwɜːk] *n.* 框架，结构

harmonize ['hɑːmənaɪz] *v.* 使和谐

identify [aɪ'dentɪfaɪ] *v.* 确定，识别

motivation [ˌməʊtɪ'veɪʃn] *n.* 动机

participant [pɑː'tɪsɪpənt] *n.* 参与

discussion [dɪ'skʌʃn] *n.* 讨论

representative [ˌreprɪ'zentətɪv] *n.* 代表

Questions

boundary ['baʊndrɪ] *n.* 边界

co-ordinate [kəʊ'ɔːdənɪt] *v.* 配合

allocate ['æləkeɪt] *v.* 分配

真题考点词替换清单

题号	题目——原文
28	excluded—discarded
31	natural—artificial【反】
32	limited—transcend【反】
	boundaries—frontiers
33	possibility—inevitable
34	information is to be gathered—surveillance, monitor
35	all kinds of species—genetic diversity
36	information be collected and shared—databank
37	fragile—most at risk
	priority—preferential
38	resources—scholarships, financial support
39	better co-ordinated—framework, network, harmonizing
40	plans—resolutions, proposes

Test 4

⬆ Reading Passage 1: Pulling Strings to Build Pyramids

pyramid ['pɪrəmɪd] n. 金字塔

reckon ['rekən] v. 估计，猜想

hanging in the air 未完成的

Paragraph 1

conventional [kən'venʃənl] adj. 传统的

slave [sleɪv] n. 奴隶

drag [dræg] v. 拖，拉

sledge [sledʒ] n. 雪橇

consultant [kən'sʌltənt] n. 顾问

kite [kaɪt] n. 风筝

peruse [pə'ruːz] v. 详细考察

monument ['mɒnjʊmənt] n. 纪念碑

hieroglyph ['haɪərəɡlɪf] n. 象形文字，图画文字

odd [ɒd] adj. 古怪的

posture ['pɒstʃə(r)] n. 姿势

rope [rəʊp] n. 绳索

mechanical [mə'kænɪkl] adj. 机械的

giant ['dʒaɪənt] adj. 巨大的

Paragraph 2

intrigue [ɪn'triːɡ] v. 激起……兴趣

aeronautics [ˌeərə'nɔːtɪks] n. 航空学

fascinate ['fæsɪneɪt] v. 使着迷

keen [kiːn] adj. 强烈的

puzzle ['pʌzl] v. 使迷惑

spark [spɑːk] v. 鼓舞，激起

apparently [ə'pærəntlɪ] adv. 显然地

possibility [ˌpɒsə'bɪlətɪ] n. 可能性

investigate [ɪn'vestɪɡeɪt] v. 调查，研究

lifter ['lɪftə] n. 升降机

Paragraph 3

stone column 石柱

horizontal [ˌhɒrɪ'zɒntl] adj. 水平的

vertical ['vɜːtɪkl] adj. 垂直的

calculation [ˌkælkjʊ'leɪʃn] n. 计算，估算

scale-model [skeɪl'mɒdl] n. 比例模块

wind-tunnel ['waɪnd'tʌnl] n. 风洞

convince [kən'vɪns] v. 说服，使确信

modest ['mɒdɪst] adj. 适度的

sustain [sə'steɪn] v. 维持

pulley ['pʊlɪ] n. 滑轮

magnify ['mægnɪfaɪ] v. 放大，夸大

applied [ə'plaɪd] adj. 应用的

rig [rɪg] v. 操纵，装配

tent-shaped [tentʃeɪpt] adj. 帐篷形状的

scaffold ['skæfəʊld] n. 脚手架

suspend [sə'spend] v. 吊，悬挂

apex ['eɪpeks] n. 顶

roll [rəʊl] v. 滚动

trolley ['trɒlɪ] n. 手推车

Paragraph 4

unlikely [ʌn'laɪklɪ] adj. 不太可能的

rectangular [rek'tæŋgjələ(r)] adj. 矩形的

nylon ['naɪlɒn] n. 尼龙

sail [seɪl] n. 帆，篷

stunned [stʌnd] adj. 受惊的

Paragraph 5

blow [bləʊ] v. 吹，风吹

jerk [dʒɜːk] n. 猛拉，猛推

massive ['mæsɪv] adj. 大量的，巨大的

construction [kən'strʌkʃn] n. 建设

brute [bruːt] adj. 粗野的

Paragraph 6

specialist ['speʃəlɪst] n. 专家

unconvince [ʌnkən'vɪns] v. 使不信服，使不确信

kite-lifting [kaɪtlɪftɪŋ] adj. 风筝升降的

associate professor 副教授

Egyptology [ˌiːdʒɪp'tɒlədʒɪ] n. 埃及古物学

Paragraph 7

harness ['hɑːnɪs] v. 使用，驾驭

accomplished [ə'kʌmplɪʃt] adj. 熟练的

sailor ['seɪlə(r)] n. 水手

wooden ['wʊdn] adj. 木制的

flight [flaɪt] n. 飞行，飞翔

artifact ['ɑːtəˌfækt] n. 人工制品

uncannily [ʌn'kænɪlɪ] adv. 神秘地，不寻常地

glider ['glaɪdə(r)] n. 滑翔机

sophistication [sə,fɪstɪ'keɪʃn] *n.* 复杂；老于世故

civilization [,sɪvəlaɪ'zeɪʃn] *n.* 文明   dump [dʌmp] *v.* 倾倒

flaming ['fleɪmɪŋ] *adj.* 燃烧的   debris ['debriː] *n.* 碎片，残骸

foe [fəʊ] *n.* 敌人，危害物

Paragraph 8

machinery [mə'ʃiːnəri] *n.* 机械   adobe [ə'dəʊbɪ] *n.* 土砖

arch [ɑːtʃ] *n.* 拱桥   hint [hɪnt] *n.* 提示

Questions

resemble [rɪ'zembl] *v.* 相似

真题考点词替换清单

题号	题目——原文
1	generally believed—conventional picture
	people—slaves
9	lift—bear the weight
	large—massive
10	use—harnessing
	discovery—found
11	object—artifact
	resemble—looks like
12	experimented with—developing
13	weapons—foes
	sending—deliver

Reading Passage 2: Endless Harvest

Paragraph 1

explorer [ɪk'splɔːrə(r)] *n.* 探险家   fur hunter 毛皮猎人

volcanic [vɒl'kænɪk] *adj.* 火山的   archipelago [,ɑːkɪ'peləgəʊ] *n.* 群岛，列岛

land mass 大陆块   inhabitant [ɪn'hæbɪtənt] *n.* 居民

Alaska [ə'læskə] *n.* 阿拉斯加

Paragraph 2

combined [kəm'baɪnd] *adj.* 组合的，联合的

coastline ['kəʊstlaɪn] *n.* 海岸线

nutrient-rich ['njuːtrɪəntrɪtʃ] *adj.* 营养丰富的

seabird ['siːbɜːd] *n.* 海鸟

shellfish ['ʃelfɪʃ] *n.* 甲壳类动物

mollusk ['mɒləsk] *n.* 软体动物

bounty ['baʊntɪ] *n.* 丰富，慷慨

commercial [kə'mɜːʃl] *adj.* 商业的

fishery ['fɪʃərɪ] *n.* 渔业，水产业

Paragraph 3

herring ['herɪŋ] *n.* 鲱，青鱼

groundfish ['graʊndfɪʃ] *n.* 低栖鱼，低层鱼

cod [kɒd] *n.* 鳕鱼

sole [səʊl] *n.* 鳎（可食用比目鱼）

perch [pɜːtʃ] *n.* 鲈鱼

pollock ['pɒlək] *n.* 鳕鱼类

cultural ['kʌltʃərəl] *adj.* 文化的

salmon ['sæmən] *n.* 鲑鱼

pump [pʌmp] *v.* 抽水

rhythmic ['rɪðmɪk] *adj.* 有节奏的，间隙的

circulating ['sɜːkjʊleɪtɪŋ] *adj.* 循环的

nourishment ['nʌrɪʃmənt] *n.* 食物，营养品

predictable [prɪ'dɪktəbl] *adj.* 可预言的

abundance [ə'bʌndəns] *n.* 充裕，丰富

flourish ['flʌrɪʃ] *v.* 茂盛，活跃

spawner [s'pɔːnə(r)] *n.* 已成熟的雌鱼

eagle ['iːgl] *n.* 鹰

ultimately ['ʌltɪmətlɪ] *adv.* 根本，基本上

Chinook [tʃɪ'nuːk] *n.* 切努克人

chum [tʃʌm] *n.* 狗鲑

coho ['kəʊhəʊ] *n.* 银大马哈鱼，银鲑

silver ['sɪlvə(r)] *n.* 银

sockeye ['sɒkaɪ] *n.* 红鲑

humpback ['hʌmpbæk] *n.* 座头鲸

spawn [spɔːn] *v.* 产卵

commercially [kə'mɜːʃəlɪ] *adv.* 商业上

producer [prə'djuːsə(r)] *n.* 生产者

ex-vessel [eks'vesl] *n.* 以前的船

Paragraph 4

catch [kætʃ] *n.* 捕捉；捕获物

overfish ['əʊvə'fɪʃ] *v.* 过度捕捞

crash [kræʃ] *n.* 碰撞

severe [sɪ'vɪə(r)] *adj.* 严峻的

declare [dɪ'kleə(r)] v. 宣布，断言

disaster area 灾区

statehood ['steɪthʊd] n. 国家层面

sustainable [sə'steɪnəbl] adj. 可持续的

harvest ['hɑːvɪst] n. 收获，产量

occasion [ə'keɪʒn] n. 时机，机会

federal ['fedərəl] adj. 联邦的

onset ['ɒnset] n. 开始

mandate ['mændeɪt] v. 授权，托管

statewide ['steɪtwaɪd] adj. 遍及全州的

in excess of 超过，多于

Paragraph 5

primary ['praɪmərɪ] adj. 主要的

biologist [baɪ'ɒlədʒɪst] n. 生物学家

adult fish 成鱼

counting ['kaʊntɪŋ] n. 计算

aeroplane ['eərəpleɪn] n. 飞机

pre-set [priː'set] adj. 预置的，提前设定的

stock [stɒk] n. 贮备，库存

abundance [ə'bʌndəns] n. 充足，充裕

monitor ['mɒnɪtə(r)] v. 监控

streamside ['striːmsaɪd] n. 河边地带

sonar ['səʊnɑː(r)] n. 声呐

fisherman ['fɪʃəmən] n. 渔人，渔夫

halt [hɔːlt] n. 停止

prosper ['prɒspə(r)] v. 使成功，使繁荣

Paragraph 6

commission [kə'mɪʃn] v. 委任

certify ['sɜːtɪfaɪ] v. 证明，保证

label ['leɪbl] n. 标签，商标

responsibility [rɪˌspɒnsə'bɪlətɪ] n. 责任

undergo [ˌʌndə'gəʊ] v. 经历，经受

official [ə'fɪʃl] n. 官员

organization [ˌɔːgənaɪ'zeɪʃn] n. 组织，机构

review [rɪ'vjuː] n. 回顾；评论

enable [ɪ'neɪbl] v. 使能够

recognise ['rekəgnaɪz] v. 认出

criteria [kraɪ'tɪərɪə] n. 标准

panel ['pænl] n. 小组

representative [ˌreprɪ'zentətɪv] n. 代表

Paragraph 7

observer [əb'zɜːvə(r)] n. 观察者

collapse [kə'læps] v. 倒塌，瓦解

certification [ˌsɜːtɪfɪ'keɪʃn] n. 证明，保证

subsistence [səb'sɪstəns] n. 生存，存在

priority [praɪˈɒrəti] *n.* 优先权

devastate [ˈdevəsteɪt] *v.* 毁灭

Paragraph 8

crisis [ˈkraɪsɪs] *n.* 危机

impact [ˈɪmpækt] *n.* 影响

contend [kənˈtend] *v.* 主张

climatic [klaɪˈmætɪk] *adj.* 气候的

shift [ʃɪft] *n.* 变化

prompt [prɒmpt] *v.* 促进，激起

cumulative [ˈkjuːmjələtɪv] *adj.* 累积的

El Nino/La Nina 厄尔尼诺／拉尼娜现象

culminate [ˈkʌlmɪneɪt] *v.* 使结束

Paragraph 9

announce [əˈnaʊns] *v.* 宣布

qualify [ˈkwɒlɪfaɪ] *v.* 限制，使……有资格

grant [grɑːnt] *v.* 授予

permission [pəˈmɪʃn] *n.* 允许，许可

required [rɪˈkwaɪəd] *adj.* 必需的

Questions

authority [ɔːˈθɒrəti] *n.* 权威

sufficient [səˈfɪʃnt] *adj.* 足够的

permit [pəˈmɪt] *v.* 许可

deny [dɪˈnaɪ] *v.* 否认

authority [ɔːˈθɒrəti] *n.* 权威，权力

sufficient [səˈfɪʃnt] *adj.* 充足的

真题考点词替换清单

题号	题目——原文
16	life—animals, people
	dependent on—heart, soul, blood, nourishment
19	sharp decrease—crashes
21	keep a check—monitoring
22	authority—can
	stop—halt
23	successful—prosper
24	recognise—certifies
26	label—display

🔺 Reading Passage 3: Effects of Noise

Paragraph 1

plausible ['plɔːzəbl] *adj.* 貌似有理的

prefer [prɪ'fɜː(r)] *v.* 宁愿，更喜欢

initially [ɪ'nɪʃəlɪ] *adv.* 最初

a wide range of 各式各样的

burst [bɜːst] *n.* 突发

physiological [ˌfɪzɪə'lɒdʒɪkl] *adj.* 生理学的

disruptive [dɪs'rʌptɪv] *adj.* 令人困扰的

arousal [ə'raʊzl] *n.* 反应，感受

suppose [sə'pəʊz] *v.* 假设，认为

adjust to 调整，使适应

capable ['keɪpəbl] *adj.* 能够，能胜任

expose [ɪk'spəʊz] *v.* 曝光，暴露

measure ['meʒə(r)] *v.* 测量，估量

reaction [rɪ'ækʃn] *n.* 反应

subject ['sʌbdʒɪkt] *n.* 实验对象

decline [dɪ'klaɪn] *v.* 下降

Paragraph 2

adaptation [ˌædæp'teɪʃn] *n.* 适应

troublesome ['trʌblsəm] *adj.* 讨厌的，使人苦恼的

require [rɪ'kwaɪə(r)] *v.* 要求，需要

interfere [ˌɪntə'fɪə(r)] *v.* 妨碍，干涉

dial ['daɪəl] *n.* 仪表盘

air-traffic [eər'træfɪk] *adj.* 空中交通的

track [træk] *v.* 追踪

wheel [wiːl] *n.* 方向盘

concentrate ['kɒnsntreɪt] *v.* 集中

monitor ['mɒnɪtə(r)] *v.* 监控

aeroplane pilot 飞行员

similarly ['sɪmələlɪ] *adv.* 同样地

steering ['stɪərɪŋ] *n.* 操纵，掌舵

Paragraph 3

significant [sɪg'nɪfɪkənt] *adj.* 重大的，有意义的

finding ['faɪndɪŋ] *n.* 结果

tune out 关掉

background ['bækgraʊnd] *n.* 背景

circumstance ['sɜːkəmstəns] *n.* 环境，局面

predictability [prɪˌdɪktə'bɪlətɪ] *n.* 可预测性

chronic ['krɒnɪk] *adj.* 漫长的，长期的

unexpected [ˌʌnɪk'spektɪd] *adj.* 意外的，想不到的

intrusion [ɪn'truːʒn] *n.* 侵入

space [speɪs] *v.* 隔开

amount [ə'maʊnt] *n.* 数量，总额

overall [ˌəʊvə'rɔːl] *adj.* 全部的

occur [ə'kɜː(r)] *v.* 发生

random ['rændəm] *adj.* 随机的，任意的

interval ['ɪntəvl] *n.* 间隔，间距

annoying [ə'nɔɪɪŋ] *adj.* 讨厌的，恼人的

portion ['pɔːʃn] *n.* 部分

proofread ['pruːfriːd] *v.* 校对

after-effect ['ɑːftə(r)ɪ'fekt] *n.* 后果

error ['erə(r)] *n.* 错误

Paragraph 4

apparently [ə'pærəntlɪ] *adv.* 显然地

fatigue [fə'tiːg] *n.* 疲劳，疲乏

take its toll 造成损伤，损害

Paragraph 5

variable ['veərɪəbl] *n.* 变数，可变因素

eliminate [ɪ'lɪmɪneɪt] *v.* 消除

individual [ˌɪndɪ'vɪdʒʊəl] *n.* 个人

option ['ɒpʃn] *n.* 选项

sufficient [sə'fɪʃnt] *adj.* 足够的，充分的

Paragraph 6

transient ['trænzɪənt] *adj.* 短暂的

lasting ['lɑːstɪŋ] *adj.* 持久的

realistic [ˌriːə'lɪstɪk] *adj.* 现实的

compare [kəm'peə(r)] *v.* 与……相比较

distract [dɪ'strækt] *v.* 转移，分心

distractible [dɪ'stræktəbl] *adj.* 易分心的

follow-up ['fɒləʊʌp] *adj.* 后续的

distractibility [dɪstræktə'bɪlɪtɪ] *n.* 注意力分散

match [mætʃ] *v.* 匹配

investigator [ɪn'vestɪgeɪtə(r)] *n.* 研究者，调查员

comparable ['kɒmpərəbl] *adj.* 可比较的，比得上的

ethnicity [eθ'nɪsətɪ] *n.* 种族地位

Questions

disrupt [dɪs'rʌpt] v. 破坏

problem-solving ['prɒbləm'sɒlvɪŋ] n. 决策

occurrence [ə'kʌrəns] n. 发生

manifest ['mænɪfest] v. 出现，表现

pitch [pɪtʃ] n. 调子

真题考点词替换清单

题号	题目——原文
27	difficulty—having to adjust
28	problem-solving—work out problems
30	situations—background
	intense—quit loud
33	made—produced
34	manifests—take its toll
	later—takes a while
35	difficult to concentrate—disruptive
37	not arise—eliminate
	stop—control, turn off
40	capacity—ability

General Training: Reading and Writing
Test A

⬆ Section 1

Eastern Energy

advice [əd'vaɪs] n. 建议

matter ['mætə(r)] n. 事件；原因

connect with 与……有关

bill [bɪl] n. 账单

query ['kwɪəri] n. 疑问

regarding [rɪ'gɑːdɪŋ] prep. 关于

electricity supply 电力供应

notice ['nəʊtɪs] n. 注意

require [rɪ'kwaɪə(r)] v. 需要，要求

arrangement [ə'reɪndʒmənt] n. 安排

move [muːv] n. 移居

meter reading 仪表读数

occupant ['ɒkjəpənt] *n.* 居住者

interrupt [ˌɪntə'rʌpt] *v.* 中断

hold responsibility for 对……负责

various ['veərɪəs] *adj.* 各种各样的

digital display meter 数字显示仪表

efficient [ɪ'fɪʃnt] *adj.* 足够的

password ['pɑːswɜːd] *n.* 密码

complain [kəm'pleɪn] *v.* 抱怨

heating ['hiːtɪŋ] *n.* 供暖

household ['haʊshəʊld] *n.* 家庭

contact ['kɒntækt] *v.* 联系

payment ['peɪmənt] *n.* 付款，支付

dial meter 刻度盘仪表

assistance [ə'sɪstəns] *n.* 帮助

enquiry [ɪn'kwaɪərɪ] *n.* 询问

helpline ['helplaɪn] *n.* 热线服务电话

complaints handling team 投诉处理团队

真题考点词替换清单

题号	题目——原文
4	throughout—anywhere
7	not charged—free

Using Your New Microwave Oven

microwave ['maɪkrəweɪv] *n.* 微波

recommend [ˌrekə'mend] *v.* 推荐，建议

check [tʃek] *v.* 检查

dry out 变干

frequently ['friːkwəntlɪ] *adv.* 频繁地

pastry ['peɪstrɪ] *n.* 油酥点心，糕点

sausage ['sɒsɪdʒ] *n.* 香肠，腊肠

casing ['keɪsɪŋ] *n.* 香肠的（肠衣）

fork [fɔːk] *n.* 叉子

soup [suːp] *n.* 汤

essential [ɪ'senʃl] *adj.* 基本的，主要的

exceed [ɪk'siːd] *v.* 超过

heat [hiːt] *v.* 加热

catch fire 着火

bread item 面包类食物

processed meat 加工肉

non-porous ['nɒn'pɔːrəs] *adj.* 无孔的

pierce [pɪəs] *v.* 刺破

burst [bɜːst] *v.* 爆炸

sauce [sɔːs] *n.* 酱油

beverage ['bevərɪdʒ] n. 饮料

boiling point 沸点

bubble ['bʌbl] v. 使冒泡，沸腾

warm up 变热

steam [stiːm] n. 蒸汽

stir [stɜː(r)] v. 搅拌

wipe out 擦净

squeeze [skwiːz] v. 挤

interior [ɪnˈtɪərɪə(r)] n. 内部

microwave oven 微波炉

evidence ['evɪdəns] n. 迹象

overheat [ˌəʊvəˈhiːt] v. 使过热

piping hot 滚热的

emit [ɪˈmɪt] v. 发出

operation [ˌɒpəˈreɪʃn] n. 操作

soapy [ˈsəʊpɪ] adj. 涂有肥皂的

grease [griːs] n. 油脂

unplug [ˌʌnˈplʌg] v. 拔掉电源

Questions

moisture [ˈmɔɪstʃə(r)] n. 水分

liquid [ˈlɪkwɪd] n. 液体

真题考点词替换清单

题号	题目——原文
8	rapid—times are much shorter
9	quantities—amounts
10	low in moisture—dry
11	skins—casings
12	liquids—soup, boiling point
13	re-heating—a second time
14	clean—wiped out, cloth

 Section 2

Choosing Premises for a New Business

dominate [ˈdɒmɪneɪt] v. 支配，控制

premise [ˈpremɪs] n. 店面，办公地

overwhelming [ˌəʊvəˈwelmɪŋ] adj. 压倒性的，势不可当的

temptation [tempˈteɪʃn] n. 引诱

rectify [ˈrektɪfaɪ] v. 改正

priority [praɪˈɒrətɪ] n. 优先权

properly [ˈprɒpəlɪ] adv. 适当地

threaten [ˈθretn] v. 威胁

promising ['prɒmɪsɪŋ] *adj.* 有前途的

swing [swɪŋ] *v.* 摆动

initial [ɪ'nɪʃl] *adj.* 最初的

vary ['veərɪ] *v.* 变化

rent [rent] *n.* 租金

particularly [pə'tɪkjələlɪ] *adv.* 特别地

manufacturing [ˌmænjʊ'fæktʃərɪŋ] *n.* 制造业

storage ['stɔːrɪdʒ] *n.* 存储，仓库

van [væn] *n.* 厢式货车

deliver [dɪ'lɪvə(r)] *v.* 递送

parking ['pɑːkɪŋ] *n.* 停车

restriction [rɪ'strɪkʃn] *n.* 限制

crucial ['kruːʃl] *adj.* 重要的，决定性的

prospect ['prɒspekt] *n.* 前途

flexibility [ˌfleksə'bɪlətɪ] *n.* 灵活性，弹性

internally [ɪn'tɜːnəlɪ] *adv.* 内部地

extend [ɪk'stend] *v.* 延伸，推广

landlord ['lændlɔːd] *n.* 房东

rebuilding ['riːˌbɪldɪŋ] *n.* 重建

consider [kən'sɪdə(r)] *v.* 考虑到

rigid ['rɪdʒɪd] *adj.* 严格的

conservation [ˌkɒnsə'veɪʃn] *n.* 保存，保护

principal ['prɪnsəpl] *adj.* 首要的，最重要的

ironically [aɪ'rɒnɪklɪ] *adv.* 讽刺地

commit [kə'mɪt] *v.* 使……承担任务

outlay ['aʊtleɪ] *n.* 费用，支出

enormously [ɪ'nɔːməslɪ] *adv.* 巨大地

centrally ['sentrəlɪ] *adv.* 在中心

via ['vaɪə] *prep.* 通过

rely on 依靠

lorry ['lɒrɪ] *n.* 卡车，货车

nearby [ˌnɪə'baɪ] *adj.* 附近的

staff [stɑːf] *n.* 员工，职员

tighten ['taɪtn] *v.* 变紧

guidance ['gaɪdns] *n.* 指导

obstruct [əb'strʌkt] *v.* 妨碍

alter ['ɔːltə(r)] *v.* 变化

knock down 拆除

spare land 空地

contract ['kɒntrækt] *n.* 合同

alteration [ˌɔːltə'reɪʃn] *n.* 修改

authority [ɔː'θɒrətɪ] *n.* 当局

density ['densətɪ] *n.* 密度

housing ['haʊzɪŋ] *n.* 房屋

Questions

impressive [ɪm'presɪv] *adj.* 印象深刻的

principal ['prɪnsəpl] *adj.* 主要的

真题考点词替换清单

题号	题目——原文
15	impressive—importance
16	depend on—rely on
	principal—main
17	produce goods—manufacturing
18	removed—knocking down
19	permitted—allowed
20	close to—near

California State College

employee [ɪm'plɔɪiː] *n.* 雇员

pick up 获得

department [dɪ'pɑːtmənt] *n.* 部门

workweek ['wɜːkwiːk] *n.* 一星期工作时间

overtime ['əʊvətaɪm] *adj.* 加班的，超时的

supervisor ['suːpəvaɪzə(r)] *n.* 监督人

in excess of 超过

additional [ə'dɪʃənl] *adj.* 额外的

staff [stɑːf] *n.* 职员

obtain [əb'teɪn] *v.* 获得

pre-tax ['prɪ'tæks] *adj.* 税前的

deduction [dɪ'dʌkʃn] *n.* 扣除

pay cash 付现金

Safety Department 安全部门

fine [faɪn] *n.* 罚款

automatic [ˌɔːtə'mætɪk] *adj.* 自动的

prior to 在……之前

payday ['peɪdeɪ] *n.* 发薪日

paycheck ['peɪtʃek] *n.* 付薪水的支票

non-exempt employee 非免税员工

approve [ə'pruːv] *v.* 批准

receive [rɪ'siːv] *v.* 获得

compensation [ˌkɒmpen'seɪʃn] *n.* 补偿

parking zone 停车区

permit [pə'mɪt] *n.* 许可

payroll ['peɪrəʊl] *n.* 工资单

Human Resources 人力资源部

license number 执照号码

ticket ['tɪkɪt] *v.* 对……开交通违规罚单

apply [ə'plaɪ] *v.* 申请

duplicate ['djuːplɪkət] *n.* 副本

release [rɪ'liːs] *v.* 释放

temporary ['tempərɪ] *adj.* 临时的

full-time [fu:ltaɪm] *adj.* 全职的

approximately [ə'prɒksɪmətlɪ] *adv.* 大约

course [kɔ:s] *n.* 进程

calendar year 历年

prorated [prəʊ'reɪtɪd] *adj.* 按比例分配的

schedule ['ʃedju:l] *n.* 计划表

initiate [ɪ'nɪʃɪeɪt] *v.* 开始

grant [grɑ:nt] *v.* 授予

request [rɪ'kwest] *v.* 请求

authorize ['ɔ:θəraɪz] *v.* 批准

entitle [ɪn'taɪtl] *v.* 使……有权利

span [spæn] *n.* 跨度，范围

grace [greɪs] *n.* 优惠

Questions

authorize ['ɔ:θəraɪz] *v.* 批准

真题考点词替换清单

题号	题目——原文
21	collect—pick up
22	authorize—approve
23	paid extra—additional compensation
24	taken off—deduction
25	calculate—worked out
	method—system
26	fill in—complete

↑ Section 3: A Very Special Dog

Paragraph 1

flight [flaɪt] *n.* 班机

Tullamarine International Airport 图拉马莱恩国际机场

baggage ['bægɪdʒ] *n.* 行李

conveyor belt 传送带

reclaim [rɪ'kleɪm] *v.* 回收利用

annexe ['æneks] *n.* 附加物

roaring ['rɔ:rɪŋ] *adj.* 轰鸣的

vent [vent] *n.* 出口

grinding ['graɪndɪŋ] *adj.* 刺耳的

generator ['dʒenəreɪtə(r)] *n.* 发电机

bark [bɑ:k] *v.* 犬吠

sleek [sli:k] *adj.* 圆滑的

labrador ['læbrədɔ:(r)] *n.* 一种纽芬兰猎犬

wag [wæg] *v.* 摇摆   tail [teɪl] *n.* 尾巴

Paragraph 2

cavalcade [ˌkævl'keɪd] *n.* 骑兵队伍   luggage ['lʌɡɪdʒ] *n.* 行李

beneath [bɪ'ni:θ] *prep.* 在……下面   all-smelling [ɔ:lsmelɪŋ] *adj.* 嗅的

nondescript ['nɒndɪskrɪpt] *adj.* 难以区分的

hardback ['hɑ:dbæk] *n.* 精装版   suitcase ['su:tkeɪs] *n.* 手提箱

styrofoam ['staɪrəfəʊm] *n.* 泡沫聚苯乙烯

pepper ['pepə(r)] *n.* 胡椒   wrap [ræp] *v.* 包裹

freezer ['fri:zə(r)] *n.* 冰箱   heat-sealed [hi:tsi:ld] *adj.* 热封的

plastic ['plæstɪk] *adj.* 塑料的   hashish ['hæʃi:ʃ] *n.* 印度大麻制剂

Paragraph 3

concealed [kən'si:ld] *adj.* 隐蔽的

super-sniffer ['su:pə(r)s'nɪfə(r)] *n.* 超级嗅探

persistent [pə'sɪstənt] *adj.* 坚持的   scratch [skrætʃ] *v.* 抓

alert [ə'lɜ:t] *v.* 使警觉   handler ['hændlə(r)] *n.* 训练者

breed [bri:d] *n.* 品种，种类   dedicate ['dedɪkeɪt] *v.* 致力，贡献

solely ['səʊllɪ] *adv.* 唯一地   detect [dɪ'tekt] *v.* 察觉，发觉

drug [drʌɡ] *n.* 毒品   grade [greɪd] *n.* 级别

Paragraph 4

wholly ['həʊllɪ] *adv.* 完全地   illegal [ɪ'li:ɡl] *adj.* 非法的

entirely [ɪn'taɪəlɪ] *adv.* 完全地   sphere [sfɪə(r)] *n.* 范围

comparatively [kəm'pærətɪvlɪ] *adv.* 比较地   esoteric [ˌesə'terɪk] *adj.* 难懂的

neurobiology [njʊərəʊbaɪ'ɒlədʒɪ] *n.* 神经生物学

turn out 结果是   unswerving [ʌn'swɜ:vɪŋ] *adj.* 坚定的

concentration [ˌkɒnsen'treɪʃən] *n.* 集中　　trait [treɪt] *n.* 特性

neurobiologist [njʊərəʊbaɪ'ɒlədʒɪst] *n.* 神经生物学家

mechanism ['mekənɪzəm] *n.* 机制，原理　　determine [dɪ't3:mɪn] *v.* 决定

flip [flɪp] *v.* 蹦跳　　deficit ['defɪsɪt] *n.* 缺乏

incidence ['ɪnsɪdəns] *n.* 发生率，影响　　diagnosis [ˌdaɪəg'nəʊsɪs] *n.* 诊断

controversial [ˌkɒntrə'v3:ʃl] *adj.* 有争论的

Paragraph 5

traditionally [trə'dɪʃənəlɪ] *adv.* 习惯上，传统地

pound [paʊnd] *n.* 兽栏　　breeder ['bri:də(r)] *n.* 饲养员

senior ['si:nɪə(r)] *adj.* 年长的　　instructor [ɪn'strʌktə(r)] *n.* 指导员

doctoral student 博士生

Paragraph 6

define [dɪ'faɪn] *v.* 定义，明确　　detector dog 缉毒犬

praise [preɪz] *n.* 赞扬　　disposal [dɪ'spəʊzl] *n.* 处理

hunting ['hʌntɪŋ] *n.* 打猎　　instinct ['ɪnstɪŋkt] *n.* 本能

stamina ['stæmɪnə] *n.* 精力，活力　　sniff [snɪf] *v.* 嗅，闻

taxing ['tæksɪŋ] *adj.* 费力的　　jam-packed [dʒæmpækt] *adj.* 拥挤不堪的

crowd [kraʊd] *n.* 群众，一群　　cargo ship 货船

Paragraph 7

remaining [rɪ'meɪnɪŋ] *adj.* 剩余的　　cognitive ['kɒgnətɪv] *adj.* 认知的

capable ['keɪpəbl] *adj.* 能够的　　despite [dɪs'paɪt] *prep.* 尽管

distraction [dɪ'strækʃn] *n.* 注意力分散　　dockside ['dɒksaɪd] *n.* 坞边

selective attention 选择性注意力　　potentially [pə'tenʃəlɪ] *adv.* 潜在地

persevere [ˌp3:sɪ'vɪə(r)] *v.* 坚持　　sustained attention 持久性注意力

Paragraph 8

assess [əˈses] *v.* 评定

scale [skeɪl] *n.* 范围

patch [pætʃ] *n.* 小块土地

feeble [ˈfiːbl] *adj.* 虚弱的，弱的

paddock [ˈpædək] *n.* 小围场

obsessive [əbˈsesɪv] *adj.* 着迷的，急迫的

mark [mɑːk] *v.* 打分数

toss [tɒs] *v.* 投掷

score [skɔː(r)] *v.* 评价

distracted [dɪˈstræktɪd] *adj.* 思想不集中的

phenomenal [fəˈnɒmɪnl] *adj.* 异常的

Paragraph 9

overlapping [əʊvəˈlæpɪŋ] *adj.* 重叠的

ignore [ɪgˈnɔː(r)] *v.* 忽视

cue [kjuː] *n.* 提示

military [ˈmɪlətri] *adj.* 军事的

operator [ˈɒpəreɪtə(r)] *n.* 操作员

cluttered [ˈklʌtə(r)d] *adj.* 混乱的

interval [ˈɪntəvl] *n.* 间隔，间距

spot [spɒt] *v.* 认出

visual [ˈvɪʒʊəl] *adj.* 视觉的

vigilance [ˈvɪdʒɪləns] *n.* 警戒

radar [ˈreɪdɑː(r)] *n.* 雷达

blip [blɪp] *n.* 物体光点

infrequently [ɪnˈfriːkwəntli] *adv.* 稀少地

Paragraph 10

signal [ˈsɪgnəl] *n.* 信号

unpredictable [ˌʌnprɪˈdɪktəbl] *adj.* 不可预测的

odour [ˈəʊdə(r)] *n.* 气味

routine [ruːˈtiːn] *adj.* 日常的

postcard [ˈpəʊstkɑːd] *n.* 明信片

bulging [ˈbʌldʒɪŋ] *adj.* 膨胀的

molecule [ˈmɒlɪkjuːl] *n.* 分子

focused [ˈfəʊkəst] *adj.* 专心的

heroin [ˈherəʊɪn] *n.* 海洛因

sack [sæk] *n.* 麻布袋

Paragraph 11

attentional [əˈtenʃənəl] *adj.* 注意的

cure [kjʊə(r)] *v.* 治疗处理

component [kəmˈpəʊnənt] *n.* 成分

Questions

reflex [ˈriːfleks] *v.* 反射

真题考点词替换清单

题号	题目——原文
29	genetic qualities—new breeding
30	not easily distracted—concentration
33	noisy—roaring
34	maintain concentration—focusing on
35	constant—for long periods
36	approval—praise
37	widely accepted—controversial【反】
38	notice—spot
40	concealed—hidden
	miss—escapes

General Training: Reading and Writing
Test B

♠ *Section 1*

Call Anywhere in the State for One Low Short-distance Rate

access ['ækses] *adj.* 向公众开放的   leisure time 闲暇时间

executive [ɪɡ'zekjətɪv] *adj.* 行政的，经营的

highflier ['haɪflaɪə(r)] *n.* 繁忙用户，有抱负心的人

design [dɪ'zaɪn] *v.* 设计   moderate ['mɒdərət] *adj.* 适度的

high-volume ['haɪv'ɒlju:m] *adj.* 大容量的   charge [tʃɑːdʒ] *v.* 收费

rate [reɪt] *n.* 等级   saving ['seɪvɪŋ] *n.* 节约

off-peak [ɒfpiːk] *adj.* 非高峰时间的   strain [streɪn] *v.* 使紧张

budget ['bʌdʒɪt] *n.* 预算   competitive [kəm'petətɪv] *adj.* 竞争的

minimum ['mɪnɪməm] *n.* 最小化   apply [ə'plaɪ] *n.* 应用

client ['klaɪənt] *n.* 客户   arise [ə'raɪz] *v.* 上升

value ['vælju:] *v.* 重视   convenience [kən'viːnjəns] *n.* 便利

overhead [ˌəʊvə'hed] *n.* 经常费用

slightly ['slaɪtlɪ] *adv.* 稍微地

communication [kəˌmjuːnɪ'keɪʃn] *n.* 通讯

billing ['bɪlɪŋ] *n.* 开具账单

round up 使成整数

be subject to 受……支配

frequent ['friːkwənt] *adj.* 频繁的

discounted ['dɪskaʊntɪd] *adj.* 已折扣的

critical ['krɪtɪkl] *adj.* 重要的

increment ['ɪnkrəmənt] *n.* 盈余，增额

cent [sent] *n.* 分

smartcard ['smɑːtkɑːd] *n.* 智能卡

Questions

cost-effective [kɒstɪ'fektɪv] *adj.* 性价比高的

Westwinds Farm Campsite

booking ['bʊkɪŋ] *n.* 预订

campsite ['kæmpsaɪt] *n.* 营地

consideration [kənˌsɪdə'reɪʃn] *n.* 考虑

observe [əb'zɜːv] *v.* 遵守

litter ['lɪtə(r)] *n.* 垃圾

shower ['ʃaʊə(r)] *n.* 淋浴

washing area 洗漱区

disturb [dɪ'stɜːb] *v.* 打扰

tolerate ['tɒləreɪt] *v.* 忍受

plenty ['plentɪ] *n.* 足够

reserve [rɪ'zɜːv] *v.* 保留

guarantee [ˌgærən'tiː] *v.* 保证

camper ['kæmpə(r)] *n.* 露营者

whilst [waɪlst] *conj.* 同时

dispose [dɪ'spəʊz] *v.* 处理

bin [bɪn] *n.* 箱子

toilet ['tɔɪlət] *n.* 厕所

obstruct [əb'strʌkt] *v.* 妨碍，阻碍

disorderly [dɪs'ɔːdəlɪ] *adv.* 无秩序地

prohibit [prə'hɪbɪt] *v.* 禁止

portable ['pɔːtəbl] *adj.* 便携的

admittance [əd'mɪtns] *n.* 进入，进入权

真题考点词替换清单

题号	题目——原文
13	not allowed—prohibited
14	not allowed—refuse

⬆ *Section 2*

The Law on Minimum Pay

entitle [ɪn'taɪtl] *v.* 使……有权利

minimum pay 最低工资

national minimum wage 国家最低工资标准

amongst [ə'mʌŋst] *prep.* 在……之中

unpaid [ˌʌn'peɪd] *adj.* 未付的

specify ['spesɪfaɪ] *v.* 指定

rate [reɪt] *n.* 价格

applicable [ə'plɪkəbl] *adj.* 可适用的

training ['treɪnɪŋ] *n.* 训练

provision [prə'vɪʒn] *n.* 规定

accommodation [əˌkɒmə'deɪʃn] *n.* 住宿

gross pay 工资总额

item ['aɪtəm] *n.* 条款，项目

payroll ['peɪrəʊl] *n.* 工资单

bonus ['bəʊnəs] *n.* 奖金，红利

commission [kə'mɪʃn] *n.* 佣金

tip [tɪp] *n.* 小费

gratuity [grə'tjuːəti] *n.* 小费；退职金

complain [kəm'pleɪn] *v.* 投诉

employer [ɪm'plɔɪə(r)] *n.* 雇主

fine [faɪn] *v.* 罚款

trade union 工会

Revenue and Customs 税务及海关总署

helpline ['helplaɪn] *n.* 服务热线电话

inspect [ɪn'spekt] *v.* 检查

ground [graʊnd] *n.* 范围

available [ə'veɪləbl] *adj.* 可得的

tribunal [traɪ'bjuːnl] *n.* 裁决

complaint [kəm'pleɪnt] *n.* 投诉

真题考点词替换清单

题号	题目——原文
16	receiving—getting
18	via—through
19	speak to—talk with
20	look at—inspect
	boss—employer

Dealing with Your Office Emails

benefit ['benɪfɪt] *n.* 好处

improve [ɪm'pruːv] *v.* 提高

efficiency [ɪ'fɪʃnsɪ] *n.* 效率

statistics [stə'tɪstɪks] *n.* 统计

wade [weɪd] *v.* 费力行走

spam [spæm] *n.* 垃圾邮件

inbox ['ɪnbɒks] *n.* 收件箱

virus ['vaɪrəs] *n.* 病毒

prioritize [praɪ'ɒrətaɪz] *v.* 按重要性排列

identify [aɪ'dentɪfaɪ] *v.* 确定，识别

sender ['sendə(r)] *n.* 发送人

urgent ['ɜːdʒənt] *adj.* 紧急的

responsibility [rɪ,spɒnsə'bɪlətɪ] *n.* 责任

require [rɪ'kwaɪə(r)] *v.* 需要

acknowledgement [ək'nɒlɪdʒmənt] *n.* 感谢

follow-up ['fɒləʊʌp] *n.* 后续工作

advisable [əd'vaɪzəbl] *adj.* 可取的，适当的

complicated ['kɒmplɪkeɪtɪd] *adj.* 复杂的

rushed [rʌʃt] *adj.* 匆忙的

definite ['defɪnət] *adj.* 确切的

one line 一行

valuable ['væljuəbl] *adj.* 宝贵的

indicate ['ɪndɪkeɪt] *v.* 显示

unsolicited [,ʌnsə'lɪsɪtɪd] *adj.* 未经请求的

clutter up 胡乱地填满

infect [ɪn'fekt] *v.* 传染

guidance ['gaɪdns] *n.* 指导

a large volume of 大量的

hear from 收到……信

expect [ɪk'spekt] *v.* 期望

sphere [sfɪə(r)] *n.* 范围

forward ['fɔːwəd] *v.* 转寄

prompt [prɒmpt] *adj.* 及时的

recipient [rɪ'sɪpɪənt] *adj.* 容易接受的

brief [briːf] *adj.* 简要的

真题考点词替换清单

题号	题目——原文
24	need—require
25	easy—uncomplicated
27	sender—recipient 【反】

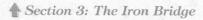 ## Section 3: The Iron Bridge

the iron bridge 铁桥

universally [,juːnɪ'vɜːsəlɪ] *adv.* 普遍地

recognise ['rekəgnaɪz] *v.* 认为是　　Industrial Revolution 工业革命

Paragraph A

cross [krɒs] *v.* 横过　　River Severn 塞文河

cast-iron [kɑːst'aɪən] *adj.* 铸铁的　　erect [ɪ'rekt] *v.* 建造

structure ['strʌktʃə(r)] *n.* 结构　　iron-caster ['aɪən'kɑːstə(r)] *n.* 铸工

Paragraph B

equivalent [ɪ'kwɪvələnt] *n.* 对应物，等价物

motorway ['məʊtəweɪ] *n.* 高速公路　　extensively [ɪk'stensɪvlɪ] *adv.* 广阔地

navigable ['nævɪgəbl] *adj.* 可航行的　　purpose ['pɜːpəs] *n.* 目的

navigate ['nævɪgeɪt] *v.* 航行　　goods [gʊdz] *n.* 货物

coal [kəʊl] *n.* 煤　　iron product 铁产品

wool [wʊl] *n.* 羊毛制品　　grain [greɪn] *n.* 粮食

cider ['saɪdə(r)] *n.* 苹果酒　　upstream [ˌʌp'striːm] *adv.* 向上游的

luxury ['lʌkʃərɪ] *n.* 奢侈品　　riverbank ['rɪvəbæŋk] *n.* 河岸

wharf [wɔːf] *n.* 码头　　load [ləʊd] *v.* 装载

unload [ˌʌn'ləʊd] *v.* 卸载

Paragraph C

patent ['pætnt] *v.* 取得……专利权　　steel-making ['stiːlmeɪkɪŋ] *n.* 炼钢

furnace ['fɜːnɪs] *n.* 火炉，熔炉　　property ['prɒpətɪ] *n.* 财产

apprenticeship [ə'prentɪʃɪp] *n.* 学徒　　coke [kəʊk] *n.* 焦炭

derive [dɪ'raɪv] *v.* 源于

economical [ˌiːkə'nɒmɪkl] *adj.* 经济的，节约的

alternative [ɔːl'tɜːnətɪv] *n.* 替代品　　charcoal ['tʃɑːkəʊl] *n.* 木炭

fuel ['fjuːəl] *n.* 燃料　　abundant [ə'bʌndənt] *adj.* 丰富的

limestone ['laɪmstəʊn] *n.* 石灰岩

Paragraph D

pioneer [ˌpaɪə'nɪə(r)] v. 开辟，做先驱

store [stɔ:(r)] n. 贮藏

surrounding [sə'raʊndɪŋ] adj. 周围的

delay [dɪ'leɪ] n. 延期，耽搁

construct [kən'strʌkt] v. 建造

ferry ['ferɪ] v. 用渡船运送

particularly [pə'tɪkjələlɪ] adv. 特别地

ironworks ['aɪənwɜ:ks] n. 钢铁厂

architect ['ɑ:kɪtekt] n. 建筑师

Paragraph E

section ['sekʃn] n. 截面

remarkably [rɪ'mɑ:kəblɪ] adv. 显著地，非常地

feat [fi:t] n. 功绩，壮举

civil engineering project 土木工程

fund [fʌnd] v. 投资，资助

painting ['peɪntɪŋ] n. 绘画

estimate ['estɪmət] n. 估计

district ['dɪstrɪkt] n. 区域

pedestrian [pə'destrɪən] n. 行人

span [spæn] n. 跨度

unheard of 前所未闻的

open to traffic 通车

commission [kə'mɪʃn] v. 委托制作

engraving [ɪn'greɪvɪŋ] n. 雕刻作品

debt [det] n. 债务

flourish ['flʌrɪʃ] v. 繁荣

Ironbridge Gorge World Heritage Site 铁桥峡谷世界文化遗产

Paragraph F

pioneering [ˌpaɪə'nɪərɪŋ] adj. 首创的

account [ə'kaʊnt] n. 记录

experiment [ɪk'sperɪmənt] n. 实验

assumption [ə'sʌmpʃn] n. 假定，设想

sketch [sketʃ] n. 素描，略图

under construction 在建设中

eye-witness ['aɪwɪtnəs] n. 目击者

discovery [dɪ'skʌvərɪ] n. 发现

shed new light on 为……提供更多线索

watercolor ['wɔ:təkʌlə] n. 水彩画

numerous ['nju:mərəs] adj. 许多的

Paragraph G

assume [ə'sjuːm] *v.* 假定，认为

unimpeded [ˌʌnɪm'piːdɪd] *adj.* 畅通无阻的

contradict [ˌkɒntrə'dɪkt] *v.* 与……抵触

fake [feɪk] *n.* 假货

depict [dɪ'pɪkt] *v.* 描述

archaeological [ˌɑːkɪə'lɒdʒɪkl] *adj.* 考古学的

photographic [ˌfəʊtə'græfɪk] *adj.* 摄影的

title ['taɪtl] *v.* 把……称为，加标题于

barge [bɑːdʒ] *n.* 游艇

historian [hɪ'stɔːrɪən] *n.* 历史学家

half-scale [hɑːfskeɪl] *adj.* 一半比例的

survey ['sɜːveɪ] *n.* 调查

Paragraph H

casting ['kɑːstɪŋ] *n.* 铸造

slightly ['slaɪtlɪ] *adv.* 稍微地

bolt [bəʊlt] *v.* 拴住

fit together 组合

probability [ˌprɒbə'bɪlətɪ] *n.* 可能性

individually [ˌɪndɪ'vɪdʒʊəlɪ] *adv.* 单独地

weld [weld] *v.* 焊接

metal ['metl] *n.* 金属

joint [dʒɔɪnt] *n.* 结合处

Paragraph I

Swedish ['swiːdɪʃ] *adj.* 瑞典的

apparently [ə'pærəntlɪ] *adv.* 显然地，明显地

drawing ['drɔːɪŋ] *n.* 图画

valuable ['væljʊəbl] *adj.* 有价值的

真题考点词替换清单

题号	题目——原文
29	leading to—approach
30	closed to traffic—open only to pedestrians
38	raise money—funded
39	attractive—cheaper, more efficient
40	connected to each other—fitted together, joints

Note

Cambridge
IELTS
8

Test 1

🔺 *Reading Passage 1: A Chronicle of Timekeeping*

Paragraph A

archaeological [ˌɑːkɪə'lɒdʒɪkl] *adj.* 考古学的

advent ['ædvent] *n.* 到来，出现   Roman Empire 罗马帝国

Babylonian [ˌbæbɪ'ləʊnjən] *n.* 巴比伦人   calendar ['kælɪndə] *n.* 日历

co-ordinate [kəʊ'ɔːdɪnət] *v.* 协调；调整   communal [kə'mjuːnl] *adj.* 公共的

shipment ['ʃɪpmənt] *n.* 运输   planting ['plɑːntɪŋ] *n.* 栽培，种植

harvesting ['hɑːvɪstɪŋ] *n.* 收获   solar day 太阳日

successive [sək'sesɪv] *adj.* 连续的   rotate [rəʊ'teɪt] *v.* 使转动

axis ['æksɪs] *n.* 轴，轴线   lunar month 太阴月，农历月

orbit ['ɔːbɪt] *n.* 轨道   solar year 太阳年

accompany [ə'kʌmpəni] *v.* 伴随   revolution [ˌrevə'luːʃn] *n.* 旋转

Paragraph B

artificial light 人造光   equator [ɪ'kweɪtə] *n.* 赤道

wax and wane 月圆月缺，盈亏；兴衰成败

conspicuous [kən'spɪkjʊəs] *adj.* 显而易见的

hence [hens] *adv.* 因此   latitude ['lætɪtjuːd] *n.* 纬度

lunar cycle 农历周期   clime [klaɪm] *n.* 地方

chart [tʃɑːt] *n.* 图表

Paragraph C

formulate ['fɔːmjʊleɪt] *v.* 制定，用公式表达

municipal [mjuː'nɪsɪpl] *adj.* 城市的   approximate [ə'prɒksɪmət] *v.* 接近于

decan ['dekən] *n.* 黄道十度分度   Sirius ['sɪrɪəs] *n.* 天狼星

annual ['ænjʊəl] *adj.* 每年的   flooding ['flʌdɪŋ] *n.* 洪汛，泛滥

Nile [naɪl] *n.* 尼罗河

cosmic ['kɒzmɪk] *adj.* 宇宙的

dozen ['dʌzn] *n.* 十二个

duration [djʊ'reɪʃn] *n.* 期间，持续时间

length [leŋθ] *n.* 长度

disseminate [dɪ'semɪneɪt] *v.* 传播

span [spæn] *v.* 跨越

interval ['ɪnt3vəl] *n.* 时间间隔，间距

temporal ['tempərəl] *adj.* 时间的

vary ['veərɪ] *v.* 变化

equinox ['iːkwɪnɒks] *n.* 春分，秋分

Paragraph D

track [træk] *v.* 追踪

sundial ['sʌndaɪəl] *n.* 日晷

counterpart ['kaʊntəpɑːt] *n.* 极相似的事物

basin ['beɪsn] *n.* 盆

denote [dɪ'nəʊt] *v.* 指示

device [dɪ'vaɪs] *n.* 装置

satisfactorily [ˌsætɪs'fæktərɪlɪ] *adv.* 令人满意地

Mediterranean [ˌmedɪtə'reɪnɪən] *n.* 地中海

inventor [ɪn'ventə] *n.* 发明家

shadow ['ʃædəʊ] *n.* 阴影

water clock 滴漏，水钟

drip [drɪp] *v.* 滴下，溢出

dip [dɪp] *v.* 浸入

freezing ['friːzɪŋ] *adj.* 冰冻的，严寒的

Paragraph E

advent ['ædv3nt] *n.* 到来，出现

suit [suːt] *v.* 适合

scheme [skiːm] *n.* 方案，计划

astronomical [ˌæstrə'nɒmɪkl] *adj.* 天文学的

sunset ['sʌnset] *n.* 日落，傍晚

split [splɪt] *v.* 使分开

mechanical [mə'kænɪkl] *adj.* 机械的

arise [ə'raɪz] *v.* 出现

supersede [ˌsuːpə'siːd] *v.* 取代

commence [kə'mens] *v.* 开始

Paragraph F

weight-driven [weɪt'drɪvn] *adj.* 重量驱动的

Bedfordshire ['bedfədʃɪə] *n.* 贝德福德郡

timekeeper ['taɪmkiːpə] *n.* 钟表

descend [dɪ'send] v. 下降

motive force 动力

gear wheel 齿轮

escapement [ɪ'skeɪpmənt] n. 擒纵装置

coil [kɔɪl] v. 盘绕，把……卷成圈

fusee [fjuː'ziː] n. 引信

mainspring ['meɪnsprɪŋ] n. 主要动机

pendulum ['pendjələm] n. 钟摆

devise [dɪ'vaɪz] v. 设计，发明

swing [swɪŋ] v. 摆动

arc [ɑːk] n. 弧（度）

efficient [ɪ'fɪʃnt] adj. 有效率的

Paragraph G

address [ə'dres] v. 解决，处理

variation [ˌveərɪ'eɪʃn] n. 变化

anchor ['æŋkə(r)] n. 锚

lever-based ['liːvə(r)beɪst] adj. 基于杠杆原理的

release [rɪ'liːs] v. 释放

precise [prɪ'saɪs] adj. 精确的

beat [biːt] v. 有节奏地敲打

floor-standing [flɔː(r)'stændɪŋ] adj. 落地的

case design 案例设计

Paragraph H

instrument ['ɪnstrəmənt] n. 仪器

quartz-crystal [kwɔːts'krɪstl] adj. 石英水晶的

beam [biːm] v. 发送

Global Positioning System 全球定位系统

calibrate ['kælɪbreɪt] v. 校正

navigation [ˌnævɪ'geɪʃn] n. 航海

stock-trading [stɒk'treɪdɪŋ] adj. 股票交易的

power-distribution ['paʊə(r)ˌdɪstrɪ'bjuːʃn] n. 配电

grid [grɪd] n. 输电网

integral ['ɪntɪgrəl] adj. 完整的

time-based [taɪmbeɪst] adj. 基于时间的，以时间为基准的

Questions

simultaneous [ˌsɪml'teɪnɪəs] adj. 同时的

cabinet ['kæbɪnət] n. 橱柜

aviation [ˌeɪvɪ'eɪʃn] *n.* 航空　　　　prompt [prɒmpt] *n.* 提示

coincidental [kəʊˌɪnsɪ'dentl] *adj.* 一致的，巧合的

oversimplified [ˌəʊvər'sɪmplɪfaɪd] *adj.* 过于简单化的

真题考点词替换清单

题号	题目——原文
1	cold—freezing
2	geography—equator, latitudes, northern, northward
2	farming—agriculture
4	uniform—eventually, superseded
7	cabinet shape—floor-standing case
8	organize—co-ordinate, regulate
8	public—communal
9	resembling—like
13	each—once

🔺 *Reading passage 2: Air Traffic Control in the USA*

Paragraph A

occur [ə'kɜː(r)] *v.* 发生　　　　Grand Canyon 大峡谷（美）

establishment [ɪ'stæblɪʃmənt] *n.* 确立

Federal Aviation Administration 联邦航空管理局

oversee [ˌəʊvə'siː] *v.* 监视，监督　　　congested [kən'dʒestɪd] *adj.* 拥挤的

procedure [prə'siːdʒə(r)] *n.* 程序

Paragraph B

rudimentary [ˌruːdɪ'mentrɪ] *adj.* 初步的　　air traffic control 空中交通管制

controller [kən'trəʊlə(r)] *n.* 控制员　　　manual ['mænjʊəl] *adj.* 手动的

vicinity [və'sɪnətɪ] *n.* 邻近，附近　　　beacon ['biːkən] *n.* 灯塔

flashing light 闪光灯　　　approximate [ə'prɒksɪmət] *v.* 接近于

metropolitan [ˌmetrə'pɒlɪtən] *n.* 大都市的人

Paragraph C

radar ['reɪdɑː(r)] *n.* 雷达

radio communication 无线电通信

full-scale [fʊlskeɪl] *adj.* 全面的

regulation [ˌreɡjʊ'leɪʃn] *n.* 管理

fortuitous [fɔː'tjuːɪtəs] *adj.* 偶然的

advent ['ædvent] *n.* 出现

jet engine 喷射发动机

pilot ['paɪlət] *n.* 飞行员

margin ['mɑːdʒɪn] *n.* 边缘

Paragraph D

depart [dɪ'pɑːt] *v.* 出发，起程，起飞

variety [və'raɪəti] *n.* 多样

accommodate [ə'kɒmədeɪt] *v.* 适应

Paragraph E

put into effect 实施，使生效

virtual ['vɜːtʃʊəl] *adj.* 事实上的

blanket ['blæŋkɪt] *v.* 覆盖

bind [baɪnd] *v.* 约束

recreational [ˌrekrɪ'eɪʃənl] *adj.* 娱乐的，消遣的

impose [ɪm'pəʊz] *v.* 限制，强加

afford [ə'fɔːd] *v.* 给予，提供

Paragraph F

meteorological [ˌmiːtɪərə'lɒdʒɪkl] *adj.* 气象的

reliance [rɪ'laɪəns] *n.* 信赖，依靠

visual ['vɪʒʊəl] *adj.* 视觉的

cue [kjuː] *n.* 线索

necessitate [nə'sesɪteɪt] *v.* 迫使，使成必要

altitude ['æltɪtjuːd] *n.* 海拔

navigational [ˌnævɪ'ɡeɪʃənl] *adj.* 航海的

panel ['pænl] *n.* 仪表板

devise [dɪ'vaɪz] *v.* 设计

airspace ['eəspeɪs] *n.* 领空，空间

possess [pə'zes] *v.* 拥有

rating ['reɪtɪŋ] *n.* 等级

Paragraph G

designate ['dezɪɡneɪt] *v.* 指定，标出

stem from 起源于

aviation [ˌeɪvɪ'eɪʃn] *n.* 航空

turboprop ['tɜːbəʊprɒp] *n.* 涡轮螺旋桨飞机

realm [relm] *n.* 领域   efficient [ɪ'fɪʃnt] *adj.* 有效率的

instrument-rated ['ɪnstrəmənt'reɪtɪd] *adj.* 用设备测评的

instrumentation [ˌɪnstrəmen'teɪʃn] *n.* 使用仪器

govern ['gʌvn] *v.* 支配，控制   correspond [ˌkɒrəs'pɒnd] *v.* 符合，一致

municipal [mju:'nɪsɪpl] *adj.* 地方自治的

medium-sized ['miːdɪəm'saɪzd] *adj.* 中型的

encompass [ɪn'kʌmpəs] *v.* 包含   rigorous ['rɪgərəs] *adj.* 严密的

explicit [ɪk'splɪsɪt] *adj.* 明确的   obey [ə'beɪ] *v.* 遵守

approach [ə'prəʊtʃ] *n.* 方法，途径   clearance ['klɪərəns] *n.* 空隙

cruise [kruːz] *v.* 巡航；漫游

真题考点词替换清单

题号	题目——原文
14	disaster—accident
	prompt—resulted in
16	oversimplified—incomplete
17	altitude—356m above, higher
18	weather—meteorological
19	defining—designated
20	created—establishment
26	average—medium

🔺 *Reading Passage 3: Telepathy*

Introduction

communicate [kə'mjuːnɪkeɪt] *v.* 交流   telepathy [tə'lepəθɪ] *n.* 心灵感应；传心术

community [kə'mjuːnəti] *n.* 社区，团体   spark [spɑːk] *v.* 激起，引起

bitter ['bɪtə(r)] *adj.* 激烈的   controversy ['kɒntrəvɜːsɪ] *n.* 争论

Paragraph 1

parapsychologist [ˌpærəsaɪˈkɒlədʒɪst] *n.* 通灵者

derision [dɪˈrɪʒn] *n.* 嘲笑

sceptical [ˈskeptɪkl] *adj.* 怀疑的

claim [kleɪm] *n.* 声称

rigorous [ˈrɪgərəs] *adj.* 严密的

implication [ˌɪmplɪˈkeɪʃn] *n.* 含义

uncover [ʌnˈkʌvə] *v.* 发现，揭开

Paragraph 2

constitute [ˈkɒnstɪtjuːt] *v.* 组成，构成

compelling [kəmˈpelɪŋ] *adj.* 引人注意的

genuine [ˈdʒenjʊɪn] *adj.* 真实的

brink [brɪŋk] *n.* 边缘

collapse [kəˈlæps] *n.* 倒塌，失败

definitive [dɪˈfɪnətɪv] *adj.* 明确的

proof [pruːf] *n.* 证据

sceptic [ˈskeptɪk] *n.* 怀疑论者

advocate [ˈædvəkeɪt] *n.* 支持者

alike [əˈlaɪk] *adv.* 相似地

concur [kənˈkɜː(r)] *v.* 同意

impressive [ɪmˈpresɪv] *adj.* 给人深刻印象的

ganzfeld [ˈgɑːntsfelt] *adj.* 超感官知觉全域试验的

telepathic [ˌtelɪˈpæθɪk] *adj.* 心灵感应术的

meditation [ˌmedɪˈteɪʃn] *n.* 冥想，沉思

involve [ɪnˈvɒlv] *v.* 包含

faint [feɪnt] *adj.* 微弱的

swamp [swɒmp] *v.* 使沉没，淹没

detect [dɪˈtekt] *v.* 探测，察觉

tranquility [træŋˈkwɪlɪtɪ] *n.* 心神稳定

Paragraph 3

participant [pɑːˈtɪsɪpənt] *n.* 参与者

reclining [rɪˈklaɪnɪŋ] *adj.* 倾斜的

sealed [siːld] *adj.* 密封的

filter [ˈfɪltə] *n.* 滤波器，滤色镜

identification [aɪˌdentɪfɪˈkeɪʃn] *n.* 鉴定，识别

image bank 图片库

sender [ˈsendə] *n.* 发出者

beam [biːm] *v.* 发出

receiver [rɪˈsiːvə] *n.* 接收者

session [ˈseʃn] *n.* 会议

hit-rate [hɪtreɪt] *n.* 命中率

pioneer [ˌpaɪəˈnɪə] *n.* 先锋

statistical [stəˈtɪstɪkl] *adj.* 统计的

Paragraph 4

implication [ˌɪmplɪˈkeɪʃn] *n.* 暗示，表明   reveal [rɪˈviːl] *v.* 反映，揭示

crucial [ˈkruːʃl] *adj.* 重要的   flaw [flɔː] *n.* 瑕疵，缺点

routinely [ruːˈtiːnlɪ] *adv.* 例行地，惯常地

overlook [ˌəʊvəˈlʊk] *v.* 忽略

conventional [kənˈvenʃənl] *adj.* 传统的；惯例的

sensory [ˈsensərɪ] *adj.* 感觉的   leakage [ˈliːkɪdʒ] *n.* 泄漏

outright [ˈaʊtraɪt] *adj.* 完全的   fraud [frɔːd] *n.* 欺骗

Paragraph 5

switch [swɪtʃ] *v.* 转变   automated [ˈɔːtəʊmeɪtɪd] *adj.* 自动化的

variant [ˈveərɪənt] *n.* 变化   minimise [ˈmɪnɪmaɪz] *v.* 最小化

flawed [flɔːd] *adj.* 有缺陷的

meta-analysis [ˈmetəˈnæləsɪs] *n.* 荟萃分析，元分析

Paragraph 6

consistency [kənˈsɪstənsɪ] *n.* 一致性   defender [dɪˈfendə] *n.* 拥护者

marginally [ˈmɑːdʒɪnəlɪ] *adv.* 少量地

apparent [əˈpærənt] *adj.* 明显的，表面上的

Paragraph 7

mainstream [ˈmeɪnstriːm] *n.* 主流   reject [ˈriːdʒekt] *v.* 排斥

plausible [ˈplɔːzəbl] *adj.* 貌似真实的，似乎合理的

mechanism [ˈmekənɪzəm] *n.* 原理

Paragraph 8

esoteric [ˌesəˈterɪk] *adj.* 难懂的   theoretical [ˌθɪəˈretɪkl] *adj.* 理论上的

quantum [ˈkwɒntəm] *n.* 量子论   entanglement [ɪnˈtæŋglmənt] *n.* 纠缠

demonstrate [ˈdemənstreɪt] *v.* 证明

parapsychology [ˌpærəsaɪˈkɒlədʒɪ] *n.* 通灵学

prompt [prɒmpt] v. 提示

probing ['prəʊbɪŋ] n. 探索，探查

eventually [ɪ'ventʃʊəlɪ] adv. 最终地

existence [ɪg'zɪstəns] n. 存在

Questions

trial ['traɪəl] n. 试验

suitable ['suːtəbl] adj. 适当的

alter ['ɔːltə(r)] v. 变更

真题考点词替换清单

题号	题目——原文
27	agree—concur
	impressive—significance
28	suitable—relaxing
29	alter—change
31	pick out—choose
37	limit—minimizing

Test 2

⬆ *Reading Passage 1: Sheet Glass Manufacture: The Float Process*

Paragraph 1

Mesopotamian [ˌmesəʊpə'teɪmjən] n. 美索不达米亚人

mixture ['mɪkstʃə(r)] n. 混合，混合物

soda ash 碳酸钠

lime [laɪm] n. 石灰

Celsius ['selsɪəs] n. 摄氏度

molten ['məʊltən] adj. 熔化

harden ['hɑːdn] v. 使变硬

cool [kuːl] v. 使冷却

spin [spɪn] v. 旋转

surface ['sɜːfɪs] n. 表面

unblemished [ʌn'blemɪʃt] adj. 无瑕的

intensive [ɪn'tensɪv] adj. 集中的

Paragraph 2

flat [flæt] adj. 平坦的，扁平的

glassmaker ['glɑːsˌmeɪkə] n. 玻璃工人

ribbon ['rɪbən] n. 带状

squeeze [skwiːz] v. 挤压

molten ['məʊltən] *adj.* 炽热的，融化的

roller ['rəʊlə(r)] *n.* 滚子

mangle ['mæŋgl] *n.* 轧布机

virtually ['vɜːtʃʊəlɪ] *adv.* 几乎；实质上

thickness ['θɪknəs] *n.* 厚度

grind [graɪnd] *v.* 磨掉

polish ['pɒlɪʃ] *v.* 磨光，擦亮

rub [rʌb] *v.* 摩擦

Paragraph 3

float process 浮法玻璃生产法

manufacture [ˌmænjʊ'fæktʃə] *n.* 生产

tinted ['tɪntɪd] *adj.* 着色的，带色彩的

coated ['kəʊtɪd] *adj.* 上涂料的

a bed of 一层

eliminate [ɪ'lɪmɪneɪt] *v.* 消除

tin [tɪn] *n.* 锡

Paragraph 4

concept ['kɒnsept] *n.* 理念

gravity ['grævətɪ] *n.* 引力，重力

guarantee [ˌgærən'tiː] *v.* 保证

horizontal [ˌhɒrɪ'zɒntl] *adj.* 水平的

pour [pɔː(r)] *v.* 倒入

underside ['ʌndəˌsaɪd] *n.* 底面

parallel to 与……平衡

transport ['trænspɔːt] *v.* 运输

tension ['tenʃn] *n.* 拉力

interaction [ˌɪntər'ækʃn] *n.* 相互作用

coincidence [kəʊ'ɪnsɪdəns] *n.* 巧合，一致

Paragraph 5

pilot plant 试验工厂

convince [kən'vɪns] *v.* 使确信

full-scale [fʊlskeɪl] *adj.* 全面的

marketable ['mɑːkɪtəbl] *adj.* 可销售的，市场的

continuous [kən'tɪnjʊəs] *adj.* 连续的

Paragraph 6

optical ['ɒptɪkl] *adj.* 光学的

refining [rɪ'faɪnɪŋ] *n.* 精炼

homogenise [hə'mɒdʒɪnaɪz] *v.* 使均匀

simultaneously [ˌsɪml'teɪnɪəslɪ] *adv.* 同时地

furnace ['fɜːnɪs] *n.* 火炉，熔炉   coating zone 涂层区

relief [rɪ'liːf] *n.* 减轻

Paragraph 7

principle ['prɪnsəpl] *n.* 原理

sub-millimetre [sʌb'mɪlɪmiːtə(r)] *n.* 亚毫米

mar [mɑː(r)] *v.* 损毁，损坏   inclusion [ɪn'kluːʒn] *n.* 内含物

bubble ['bʌbl] *n.* 气泡   inspection [ɪn'spekʃn] *n.* 检查

sand grain 沙粒   tremor ['tremə(r)] *n.* 颤动

ripple ['rɪpl] *n.* 波纹   upstream ['ʌpˌstriːm] *adj.* 向上游的

unaided eye （不借助设备的）肉眼   downstream [ˌdaʊn'striːm] *adj.* 顺流的

steer [stɪə(r)] *v.* 控制，引导   cutter ['kʌtə(r)] *n.* 切割机

flaw [flɔː] *n.* 瑕疵，缺点

Paragraph 8

requirement [rɪ'kwaɪəmənt] *n.* 要求；必要条件

pattern ['pætn] *n.* 模式；图案

minimize ['mɪnɪmaɪz] *v.* 最小化，使……减到最小

真题考点词替换清单

题号	题目——原文
2	remained—stayed
3	slow—long time
4	varying—any
11	instant—for years 【反】
12	improved—highest quality
13	humans—unaided eye

↑ *Reading Passage 2: The Little Ice Age*

Paragraph A

detailed ['diːteɪld] *adj.* 详细的，详尽的   climatic [klaɪ'mætɪk] *adj.* 气候上的

shift [ʃɪft] *n.* 变化

embark on 从事，着手

context ['kɒntekst] *n.* 背景，上下文

oppose [ə'pəʊz] *v.* 反对

humanity [hju:'mænəti] *n.* 人类，人性

at the mercy of 受……支配

entire [ɪn'taɪə] *adj.* 整个的，全部的

glacial ['gleɪʃl] *adj.* 冰冷的，冰河时代的

episode ['epɪsəʊd] *n.* 片段，插曲；一段情节

adapt [ə'dæpt] *v.* 适应

irregular [ɪ'regjələ(r)] *adj.* 无规律的

dazzling ['dæzlɪŋ] *adj.* 耀眼的，眼花缭乱的

opportunism [ˌɒpə'tju:nɪzəm] *n.* 机会主义，投机主义

strategy ['strætədʒɪ] *n.* 策略

harsh [hɑ:ʃ] *adj.* 严酷的

drought [draʊt] *n.* 干旱

unaccustomed [ˌʌnə'kʌstəmd] *adj.* 不习惯的

adopt [ə'dɒpt] *v.* 采取

stock-raising [stɒk'reɪzɪŋ] *n.* 家畜饲养

revolutionise [ˌrevə'lu:ʃənaɪz] *v.* 变革

pre-industrial ['pri:ɪn'dʌstrɪəl] *adj.* 工业化以前的

civilization [ˌsɪvəlaɪ'zeɪʃn] *n.* 文明

price [praɪs] *n.* 代价

famine ['fæmɪn] *n.* 饥荒

Paragraph B

roughly ['rʌflɪ] *adv.* 大约

bitterly ['bɪtəlɪ] *adv.* 极其，非常

glacier ['glæsɪə(r)] *n.* 冰川

pack ice 积冰

unprecedented [ʌn'presɪdentɪd] *adj.* 空前的

freeze [fri:z] *n.* 冻结

seesaw ['si:sɔ:] *n.* 上下动；跷跷板

quarter-century ['kwɔ:tə(r)'sentʃərɪ] *n.* 二十五年

intensely [ɪn'tenslɪ] *adv.* 极度地

easterly wind 东风

abrupt [ə'brʌpt] *adj.* 突然的

mild [maɪld] *adj.* 温和的

heat wave 热浪，热波

Paragraph C

reconstruct [ˌriːkən'strʌkt] v. 重建，修复

systematic [ˌsɪstə'mætɪk] adj. 系统的

observation [ˌɒbzə'veɪʃn] n. 观察，观察报告

tropical ['trɒpɪkl] adj. 热带的 　　　　proxy record 代用记录

tree ring 树木的年轮 　　　　ice core 冰核

supplement ['sʌplɪmənt] v. 补充 　　　incomplete [ˌɪnkəm'pliːt] adj. 不完整的

account [ə'kaʊnt] n. 记录 　　　　northern hemisphere 北半球

equator [ɪ'kweɪtə(r)] n. 赤道 　　　amplify ['æmplɪfaɪ] v. 扩大

drill [drɪl] v. 钻孔 　　　　Antarctica [æn'tɑːktɪk] n. 南极洲

Greenland [griːnlænd] n. 格陵兰岛 　　Peruvian Andes 秘鲁的安第斯山脉

variation [ˌveərɪ'eɪʃn] n. 变化

Paragraph D

narrative ['nærətɪv] adj. 叙事的 　　Medieval Warm Period 中世纪暖期

Norse [nɔːs] n. 挪威人 　　　　voyager ['vɒɪdʒə] n. 航海者

uniform ['juːnɪfɔːm] adj. 始终如一的

Paragraph E

ice pack 流冰群，大片浮冰 　　　voyage ['vɒɪdʒ] v. 航行，航海

reroute [riː'ruːt] v. 重新定航线 　　descended on 降临

perish ['perɪʃ] v. 死亡

continent-wide ['kɒntɪnəntwaɪd] adj. 全大陆的

decidedly [dɪ'saɪdɪdlɪ] adv. 明显，毫无疑问地

stormy ['stɔːmɪ] adj. 多风暴的 　　culminate ['kʌlmɪneɪt] v. 达到极值

commodity [kə'mɒdətɪ] n. 商品 　　cod [kɒd] n. 鳕鱼

herring ['herɪŋ] n. 鲱鱼，青鱼 　　fishing fleet 渔船队

Basque [bɑːsk] n. 巴斯克人 　　　Dutch [dʌtʃ] n. 荷兰人

stem from 起源于

fodder ['fɒdə] *n.* 饲料

crop [krɒp] *n.* 农作物

productivity [ˌprɒdʌk'tɪvəti] *n.* 产量

self-sufficient [selfsə'fɪʃnt] *adj.* 自给自足的

livestock ['laɪvstɒk] *n.* 家畜

Paragraph F

migration [maɪ'greɪʃn] *n.* 迁移，移民

land-hungry [lænd'hʌŋgri] *adj.* 渴望占有土地的

famine ['fæmɪn] *n.* 饥荒

blight [blaɪt] *n.* 荒芜

hectare ['hekteə] *n.* 公顷

woodland ['wʊdlənd] *n.* 林地

axe [æks] *n.* 斧

intensive [ɪn'tensɪv] *adj.* 集中的，加强的

clearance ['klɪərəns] *n.* 清除，空隙

release [rɪ'liːs] *v.* 释放

trigger ['trɪgə] *v.* 引发，引起

fossil fuel 矿物燃料

proliferate [prə'lɪfəreɪt] *v.* 使激增

soar [sɔː(r)] *v.* 高涨

steep [stiːp] *adj.* 急剧上升的

regime [reɪ'ʒiːm] *n.* 体制，模式

prolonged [prə'lɒŋd] *adj.* 持续很久的

hurricane ['hʌrɪkən] *n.* 飓风，暴风

真题考点词替换清单

题号	题目——原文
14	today—modern, current
15	thousand years—ten centuries
16	enough food—against famine
17	impact on—caused
18	documentation—records, written accounts
	limited—only
	mainly—largely
20	rather than—far from
22	no rain—drought
23	abroad—migration
24	cutting down—fell
25	discovered—explored, visited

Reading Passage 3: The Meaning and Power of Smell

Introduction

olfaction [ɒl'fækʃn] *n.* 嗅觉

psychological [ˌsaɪkə'lɒdʒɪkl] *adj.* 心理上的

aroma [ə'rəʊmə] *n.* 芳香

consciously ['kɒnʃəsli] *adv.* 自觉地，有意识地

faculty ['fæklti] *n.* 能力

impair [ɪm'peə(r)] *v.* 削弱，减少

well-being [wel'biːɪŋ] *n.* 健康，康乐

Paragraph A

survey ['sɜːveɪ] *n.* 调查

conduct [kən'dʌkt] *v.* 进行，实施

Concordia University 康卡迪亚大学

participant [pɑː'tɪsɪpənt] *n.* 参与者

comment on 对……评论

evoke [ɪ'vəʊk] *v.* 引起

scent [sent] *n.* 气味

a rush of joy 一阵欢乐

foul [faʊl] *adj.* 污秽的

odour ['əʊdə] *n.* 气味

grimace [grɪ'meɪs] *v.* 做苦相

disgust [dɪs'gʌst] *n.* 厌恶，嫌恶

respondent [rɪ'spɒndənt] *n.* 应答者

olfactory [ɒl'fæktərɪ] *adj.* 嗅觉的

label ['leɪbl] *v.* 打上标签，分类

fragrant ['freɪgrənt] *adj.* 芳香的，愉快的

perception [pə'sepʃn] *n.* 感觉，知觉

sensation [sen'seɪʃn] *n.* 感觉

Paragraph B

cue [kjuː] *n.* 线索

bonding ['bɒndɪŋ] *n.* 结合，紧密

survey ['sɜːveɪ] *n.* 调查

infant ['ɪnfənt] *n.* 婴儿

spouse [spaʊs] *n.* 配偶

well-known [welnəʊn] *adj.* 著名的

distinguish [dɪ'stɪŋgwɪʃ] *v.* 区别，辨别

reveal [rɪ'viːl] *v.* 显示，揭露

register ['redʒɪstə(r)] *v.* 记录；注册

Paragraph C

sensory ['sensəri] *adj.* 感觉的，知觉的

undervalue [ˌʌndə'væljuː] *v.* 低估，看轻

feeble ['fiːbl] *adj.* 微弱的　　　　　　olfactory [ɒl'fæktərɪ] *adj.* 嗅觉的，味道的

possess [pə'zes] *v.* 持有

remarkable [rɪ'mɑːkəbl] *adj.* 卓越的，非凡的

acute [ə'kjuːt] *adj.* 敏锐的

Paragraph D

elusive [ɪ'luːsɪv] *adj.* 难捉摸的　　　　realm [relm] *n.* 领域

capture ['kæptʃə(r)] *v.* 捕获，抓住　　　make do with 设法应付

realm [relm] *n.* 领域，范围

recollection [ˌrekə'lekʃn] *n.* 回忆，回忆起的事物

implication [ˌɪmplɪ'keɪʃn] *n.* 含义，暗示

Paragraph E

fundamental [ˌfʌndə'mentl] *adj.* 基本的　　to be answered 有待解决，有待回答

odourless ['əʊdələs] *adj.* 无气味的

unanswered [ʌn'ɑːnsəd] *adj.* 未回答的，未解决的

objectively [əb'dʒektɪvlɪ] *adv.* 客观地

non-physical ['nɒn'fɪzɪkl] *adj.* 非物质的，无形的

component [kəm'pəʊnənt] *n.* 成分，组件　　inevitable [ɪn'evɪtəbl] *adj.* 不可避免的

Paragraph F

invest [ɪn'vest] *v.* 赋予　　　　　　offensive [ə'fensɪv] *adj.* 冒犯的，无礼的

interact [ˌɪntər'ækt] *v.* 互相影响　　　intimate ['ɪntɪmət] *adj.* 亲密的

charged [tʃɑːdʒd] *adj.* 充满感情的　　　attach to 依附

interiorise [ɪn'tɪərɪəˌraɪz] *v.* 内化，使看法深入内心

essence ['esns] *n.* 本质

Questions

demonstrate ['demənstreɪt] *v.* 证明　　　male [meɪl] *n.* 男性

female ['fiːmeɪl] *n.* 女性　　　　　　reject ['riːdʒekt] *v.* 抵制

limitation [ˌlɪmɪ'teɪʃn] *n.* 限制　　　measurement ['meʒəmənt] *n.* 测量

真题考点词替换清单

题号	题目——原文
27	relationship—association
	smell—scent, odour
	feelings—emotion, joy, disgust, agreeable
29	not appreciated—undervalued
30	talking about—languages, vocabulary
33	ability—faculty
	damaged—impaired
34	realizing—considered
37	recognise—distinguish
	husbands and wives—marriage partners
38	linguistic—languages
	lack—doesn't exist
39	do not smell—odourless
40	unpleasant—offensive

Test 3

 Reading Passage 1: Striking Back at Lightning with Lasers

Paragraph 1

seldom ['seldəm] *adv.* 很少，不常

dramatic [drə'mætɪk] *adj.* 引人注意的，惊人的

thunderstorm ['θʌndəstɔːm] *n.* 雷暴雨　　strike [straɪk] *v.* 打击，冲击

fury ['fjʊərɪ] *n.* 狂怒　　　　　　　　inflict [ɪn'flɪkt] *v.* 造成，遭受

roll in 滚滚而来　　　　　　　　　　　leisurely ['leʒəlɪ] *adv.* 悠闲地

golf [gɒlf] *n.* 高尔夫

terrifying ['terɪfaɪɪŋ] *adj.* 令人恐惧的，骇人的

dice [daɪs] *n.* 骰子；概率

lightning ['laɪtnɪŋ] *n.* 闪电

inviting [ɪn'vaɪtɪŋ] *adj.* 诱人的

golfer ['gɒlfə] *n.* 打高尔夫的人

bolt [bəʊlt] *n.* 闪电

property ['prɒpəti] *n.* 财产

Paragraph 2

hit [hɪt] *v.* 打击，袭击

strategy ['strætədʒɪ] *n.* 战略

brave [breɪv] *v.* 勇敢地面对

laser ['leɪzə] *n.* 激光

thundercloud ['θʌndəklaʊd] *n.* 雷雨云

trial ['traɪəl] *n.* 试验

neutralise ['njuːtrəlaɪz] *v.* 中和

armoury ['ɑːmərɪ] *n.* 兵工厂

discharge [dɪs'tʃɑːdʒ] *v.* 放出

Paragraph 3

command [kə'mɑːnd] *n.* 命令，指令

trail [treɪl] *v.* 追踪

generate ['dʒenəreɪt] *v.* 产生

fund [fʌnd] *v.* 投资，资助

precise [prɪ'saɪs] *adj.* 精确的

voltage ['vəʊltɪdʒ] *n.* 电压

rocket ['rɒkɪt] *n.* 火箭

wire ['waɪə] *n.* 电线

survive [sə'vaɪv] *v.* 幸存

power grid 电力网

measurement ['meʒəmənt] *n.* 测量

bear up 支持

Paragraph 4

trigger ['trɪgə(r)] *v.* 引发

branch [brɑːntʃ] *n.* 分支

occasionally [ə'keɪʒnəlɪ] *adv.* 偶尔

Paragraph 5

stream [striːm] *n.* 一连串

project ['prɒdʒekt] *n.* 项目

invest [ɪn'vest] *v.* 投资

promising ['prɒmɪsɪŋ] *adj.* 有希望的，有前途的

emerge [ɪ'mɜːdʒ] *v.* 出现

populated ['pɒpjʊleɪtɪd] *adj.* 人口集中的

back [bæk] *v.* 支持

laboratory [lə'bɒrətrɪ] *n.* 实验室

Paragraph 6

high-powered [haɪ'paʊəd] *adj.* 高性能的；强有力的

reveal [rɪ'viːl] *v.* 反映

extract ['ekstrækt] *v.* 提取

electron [ɪ'lektrɒn] *n.* 电子

atom ['ætəm] *n.* 原子

ion ['aɪən] *n.* 离子

generate ['dʒenəreɪt] *v.* 使形成

ionisation [ˌaɪənaɪ'zeɪʃən] *n.* 电离作用

conduct [kən'dʌkt] *v.* 导电

uncontrollable [ˌʌnkən'trəʊləbl] *adj.* 无法控制的

surge [sɜːdʒ] *n.* 涌动的气流

conductor [kən'dʌktə(r)] *n.* 导体

close by 在附近

cloud-zapper 击云器

install [ɪn'stɔːl] *v.* 安装

key [kiː] *adj.* 关键的，主要的

portable ['pɔːtəbl] *adj.* 轻便的

international sporting event 国际体育赛事

beam [biːm] *v.* 发送

brew [bruː] *v.* 酿造，酝酿

Paragraph 7

stumbling ['stʌmblɪŋ] *adj.* 障碍的

block [blɒk] *n.* 障碍物

nifty ['nɪftɪ] *adj.* 精巧的

offing ['ɒfɪŋ] *n.* 在视野内的远处海面（即将到来）

manageable ['mænɪdʒəbl] *adj.* 易管理的，易操作的

Paragraph 8

commercial [kə'mɜːʃl] *adj.* 商业的

reckon ['rekən] *v.* 认为，猜想

forthcoming [ˌfɔːθ'kʌmɪŋ] *adj.* 即将来临的

field test 现场试验

turning point 转折点

an avalanche of 突然一阵的，蜂拥而来的，如雪片飞来的

eventually [ɪ'ventʃʊəlɪ] *adv.* 最后，总共

Paragraph 9

benefit ['benɪfɪt] *v.* 使……得益

fingertip ['fɪŋɡətɪp] *n.* 指尖

mighty ['maɪtɪ] *adj.* 强有力的

current ['kʌrənt] *n.* （水，气，电）流

meteorology [ˌmiːtɪə'rɒlədʒɪ] *n.* 气象学

forecast ['fɔːkɑːst] *v.* 预报，预测

Paragraph 10

confront [kən'frʌnt] *v.* 面临，遭遇

meteorological [ˌmiːtɪərə'lɒdʒɪkl] *adj.* 气象学的

menace ['menəs] *n.* 威胁，恐吓

hail [heɪl] *n.* 冰雹

induce [ɪn'djuːs] *v.* 引起，引诱

lightning flash 电闪，闪光

torrential rain 暴雨，倾盆大雨

moisture ['mɔɪstʃə(r)] *n.* 水分，湿度

formation [fɔː'meɪʃn] *n.* 形成

hailstone ['heɪlstəʊn] *n.* 冰雹

crop [krɒp] *n.* 庄稼

laser-toting ['leɪzə(r)təʊtɪŋ] *adj.* 携带激光的

Questions

golf course 高尔夫球场

weather forecaster 气象预报员

intensely [ɪn'tenslɪ] *adv.* 强烈地

真题考点词替换清单

题号	题目——原文
2	building—property
4	financial support—funded
6	difficulty—block
7	removing—extract
	from—out of
8	control—guide
12	depend on—turning point
	tests in real—field tests

↟ *Reading Passage 2: The Nature of Genius*

Paragraph 1

genius ['dʒiːnɪəs] *n.* 天才

prodigy ['prɒdədʒɪ] *n.* 奇才

gens [dʒenz] *n.* 来源，氏族

term [tɜːm] *n.* 术语

begetter [bɪˈgetə(r)] *n.* 父；生产者

cult [kʌlt] *n.* 祭仪

divinity [dɪˈvɪnəti] *n.* 神学，神

paterfamilias [ˌpeɪtəfəˈmɪliæs] *n.* 家长，一家之长

perpetuate [pəˈpetʃueɪt] *v.* 保持，使……不朽

represent [ˌreprɪˈzent] *v.* 代表

characteristics [ˌkærɪktəˈrɪstɪks] *n.* 特点

thence [ðens] *adv.* 因此

attribute [ˈætrɪbjuːt] *n.* 特质

derive [dɪˈraɪv] *v.* 起源于

guiding [ˈgaɪdɪŋ] *adj.* 给予引导的，有影响的，领导性的

astrology [əˈstrɒlədʒɪ] *n.* 占星术

genetics [dʒəˈnetɪks] *n.* 遗传学

exceptional [ɪkˈsepʃənl] *adj.* 异常的，特别出色的

Paragraph 2

gift [gɪft] *n.* 天赋

ambivalent [æmˈbɪvələnt] *adj.* 矛盾的

envy [ˈenvɪ] *v.* 嫉妒

mistrust [ˌmɪsˈtrʌst] *v.* 不信任，怀疑

mythology [mɪˈθɒlədʒɪ] *n.* 神话

giftedness [gɪfˈtɪdnəs] *n.* 天才

talented [ˈtæləntɪd] *adj.* 有才能的

defective [dɪˈfektɪv] *adj.* 有缺陷的

impractical [ɪmˈpræktɪkl] *adj.* 不切实际的，不现实的

eccentric [ɪkˈsentrɪk] *adj.* 古怪的，反常的

weakling [ˈwiːklɪŋ] *n.* 怯懦的人

madness [ˈmædnəs] *n.* 疯狂，疯子

unrecognised [ʌnˈrekəgnaɪzd] *adj.* 未被承认的，未被认可的

unrewarded [ˌʌnrɪˈwɔːdɪd] *adj.* 未获得报偿的

adversity [ədˈvɜːsəti] *n.* 逆境，不幸

enrich [ɪnˈrɪtʃ] *v.* 使丰富，使富足

highbrow [ˈhaɪbraʊ] *n.* 卖弄知识的人，知识分子

egghead [ˈeghed] *n.* 受过高等教育的人，书呆子

blue-stocking [bluːˈstɒkɪŋ] *n.* 女才子

wiseacre [ˈwaɪzeɪkə] *n.* 自以为聪明者

know-all [ˈnəʊɔːl] *n.* 万事通

boffin [ˈbɒfɪn] *n.* 研究员，科学工作者

denigration [ˌdenɪˈgreɪʃn] *n.* 贬义词

Paragraph 3

considerable [kən'sıdərəbl] *adj.* 相当大的，重要的

significant [sıg'nıfıkənt] *adj.* 重大的，有意义的

aspect ['æspekt] *n.* 部分　　　　　frequency ['fri:kwənsı] *n.* 频率

tutor ['tju:tə] *n.* 家庭教师，导师　　beneficial [ˌbenı'fıʃl] *adj.* 有益的

adjustment [ə'dʒʌstmənt] *n.* 调整，调节　frequency ['fri:kwənsı] *n.* 频率

fascinating ['fæsıneıtıŋ] *adj.* 迷人的，吸引人的

anecdote ['ænıkdəʊt] *n.* 轶事，奇闻　　similarity [ˌsımə'lærətı] *n.* 类似，相似点

exception [ık'sepʃn] *n.* 例外

norm-referenced [nɔ:m'refrənst] *adj.* 参照标准的

collate [kə'leıt] *v.* 核对，校对　　　upbringing ['ʌpbrıŋıŋ] *n.* 养育

school [sku:l] *v.* 教育

exceptional [ık'sepʃənl] *adj.* 异常的，例外的

infant mortality 婴儿死亡率　　　　life expectancy 平均寿命

home tutoring 家庭教育　　　　　　nobility [nəʊ'bılətı] *n.* 贵族

bullying ['bʊlıŋ] *n.* 恃强欺弱的行为　corporal ['kɔ:pərəl] *adj.* 肉体的

privileged ['prıvəlıdʒd] *adj.* 享有特权的　paediatrics [ˌpi:dı'ætrıks] *n.* 儿科学

objective [əb'dʒektıv] *adj.* 客观的

Paragraph 4

peak [pi:k] *n.* 最高峰，顶点　　　　visible ['vızəbl] *adj.* 明显的，看得见的

observer [əb'zɜ:və(r)] *n.* 观察者　　mist [mıst] *n.* 模糊不清之物

vantage point 优势　　　　　　　　apply to 应用于

outstanding [aʊt'stændıŋ] *adj.* 杰出的　continuum [kən'tınjʊəm] *n.* 连续

mundane [mʌn'deın] *adj.* 世俗的，世界的

mediocre [ˌmi:dı'əʊkə] *adj.* 普通的，平凡的

observation [ˌɒbzə'veıʃn] *n.* 观察，检测　incapable [ın'keıpəbl] *adj.* 无能力的

musician [mju'zıʃn] *n.* 音乐家　　　　vice verse 反之亦然

nurture ['nɜ:tʃə(r)] v. 养育

trigger ['trɪɡə(r)] v. 引起

channel ['tʃænl] n. 通道

gifted ['ɡɪftɪd] adj. 有天赋的，有才华的

Paragraph 5

marvel ['mɑ:vl] v. 对……感到惊异

achievement [ə'tʃi:vmənt] n. 成就

manifestation [ˌmænɪfe'steɪʃn] n. 表现，显示

demonstrate ['demənstreɪt] v. 证明

hard-won [hɑ:dwʌn] adj. 来之不易的，难得的

Kepler ['keplə] n. 开普勒（人名）

Einstein ['aɪnˌstaɪn] n. 爱因斯坦

commonplace ['kɒmənpleɪs] adj. 平凡的

schoolchildren ['sku:ltʃɪldrən] n. 小学生

outrageous [aʊt'reɪdʒəs] adj. 令人吃惊的

fabric ['fæbrɪk] n. 织物，布

supremacy [su:'preməsɪ] n. 至高无上，很高的地位

outstrip [ˌaʊt'strɪp] v. 超过，胜过

miler ['maɪlə] n. 一英里赛跑的运动员

jogging ['dʒɒɡɪŋ] n. 慢跑

Paragraph 6

uniquely [jʊ'ni:klɪ] adv. 独特地

instruction [ɪn'strʌkʃn] n. 指示

emulate ['emjʊleɪt] v. 模仿

unpalatable [ʌn'pælətəbl] adj. 讨人厌的，使人不悦的

fame [feɪm] n. 名声

perseverance [ˌpɜ:sɪ'vɪərəns] n. 坚持不懈，不屈不挠

single-mindedness ['sɪŋɡl'maɪndɪdnəs] n. 专心；忠贞

dedication [ˌdedɪ'keɪʃn] n. 奉献

restriction [rɪ'strɪkʃn] n. 限制

integrity [ɪn'teɡrətɪ] n. 正直，诚实

Paragraph 7

descriptive [dɪ'skrɪptɪv] adj. 叙述的，描写性的

precision [prɪ'sɪʒn] n. 精确

delude [dɪ'lu:d] v. 迷惑，使失望

humanity [hju:'mænətɪ] n. 人类，人道

Questions

exhausted [ɪgˈzɔːstɪd] *adj.* 疲惫的，耗尽的

inherit [ɪnˈherɪt] *v.* 继承

in essence 实质上

lessen [ˈlesn] *v.* 减轻，减少

contradict [ˌkɒntrəˈdɪkt] *v.* 与……相矛盾

taken for granted 理所当然，想当然

retain [rɪˈteɪn] *v.* 保持

真题考点词替换清单

题号	题目——原文
14	exhausted—burn out
16	inherited—in families
17	never appreciate—unrecognised
18	difficulties—adversity
21	any—particular
23	lessen—minimise
	significance—supremacy

⬆ *Reading Passage 3: How does the Biological Clock Tick?*

Paragraph A

tick [tɪk] *v.* 滴答地记录；标以记号

life span 寿命

biologically [ˌbaɪəˈlɒdʒɪklɪ] *adv.* 生物学上地

statement [ˈsteɪtmənt] *n.* 叙述

subject [ˈsʌbdʒɪkt] *v.* 受……影响

unusable [ˌʌnˈjuːzəbl] *adj.* 不能用的

comparable [ˈkɒmpərəbl] *adj.* 比得上的

restricted [rɪˈstrɪktɪd] *adj.* 有限的

artificially [ˌɑːtɪˈfɪʃəlɪ] *adv.* 人造地

wear and tear 磨损，消耗

organism [ˈɔːgənɪzəm] *n.* 有机体，生物体

Paragraph B

static [ˈstætɪk] *adj.* 静态的

wear down 使疲劳，损耗

occur [əˈkɜː] *v.* 发生

constitute [ˈkɒnstɪtjuːt] *v.* 组成

aging [ˈeɪdʒɪŋ] *n.* 衰老

law [lɔː] *n.* 规律

thermodynamics [ˌθɜːməʊdaɪ'næmɪks] *n.* 热力学

inexorable [ɪn'eksərəbl] *adj.* 无法改变的

biological [ˌbaɪə'lɒdʒɪkl] *adj.* 生物的

dynamic [daɪ'næmɪk] *adj.* 有活力的

permanent ['pɜːmənənt] *adj.* 永久的

exchange [ɪks'tʃeɪndʒ] *v.* 交换

molecule ['mɒlɪkjuːl] *n.* 分子

renew [rɪ'njuː] *v.* 使更新

destruction [dɪ'strʌkʃn] *n.* 毁灭

equilibrium [ˌiːkwɪ'lɪbrɪəm] *n.* 平衡，均衡

spring [sprɪŋ] *n.* 泉水

Paragraph C

inevitable [ɪn'evɪtəbl] *adj.* 必然的，不可避免的

possess [pə'zes] *v.* 持有

nevertheless [ˌnevəðə'les] *conj.* 然而，不过

characteristics [ˌkærɪktə'rɪstɪks] *n.* 特征

genetic [dʒə'netɪk] *adj.* 遗传的，基因的

optimal ['ɒptɪməl] *adj.* 最佳的

immortality [ˌɪmɔː'tæləti] *n.* 不朽，长生不老

disturb [dɪ'stɜːb] *v.* 弄乱，妨碍

mechanism ['mekənɪzəm] *n.* 原理

existent [ɪg'zɪstənt] *adj.* 存在的，生存的

mutation [mjuː'teɪʃn] *n.* 突变

adaptation [ˌædæp'teɪʃn] *n.* 适应

evolution [ˌiːvə'luːʃn] *n.* 进化

Paragraph D

striking ['straɪkɪŋ] *adj.* 惊人的

parameter [pə'ræmɪtə] *n.* 参数，系数

attain [ə'teɪn] *v.* 实现；获得

upper limit 上限

mammoth ['mæməθ] *adj.* 巨大的

species ['spiːʃiːz] *n.* 物种

duration [djʊ'reɪʃn] *n.* 持续时间

nutrition [njʊ'trɪʃn] *n.* 营养

unicellular [ˌjuːnɪ'seljələ] *adj.* 单细胞的

Paragraph E

determine [dɪ'tɜːmɪn] *v.* 确定

propose [prə'pəʊz] *v.* 提出

internal clock 生物钟

fixed [fikst] *adj.* 固定的

metabolic [ˌmetə'bɒlik] *adj.* 新陈代谢的

mathematical [ˌmæθə'mætɪkl] *adj.* 数学上的

body mass 体重

in comparison to 与……相比

inverted [ɪn'vɜːtɪd] *adj.* 倒转的，颠倒的

valid ['vælɪd] *adj.* 有根据的

systematic [ˌsɪstə'mætɪk] *adj.* 系统的

Paragraph F

frugally [frʊ'gəlɪ] *adv.* 节约地

crocodile ['krɒkədaɪl] *n.* 鳄鱼

tortoise ['tɔːtəs] *n.* 乌龟

prey [preɪ] *n.* 捕获

captivity [kæp'tɪvətɪ] *n.* 囚禁

hibernation [ˌhaɪbə'neɪʃn] *n.* 冬眠，过冬

lethargy ['leθədʒɪ] *n.* 昏睡

bat [bæt] *n.* 蝙蝠

hedgehog ['hedʒhɒg] *n.* 刺猬

consumption [kən'sʌmpʃn] *n.* 消耗

comrade ['kɒmreɪd] *n.* 伙伴

account for 对……作出解释，说明……的原因

energetically [ˌenə'dʒetɪklɪ] *adv.* 精力充沛地

intensively [ɪn'tensɪvlɪ] *adv.* 强烈地，集中地

Paragraph G

sparing ['speərɪŋ] *adj.* 节约的

cardiovascular [ˌkɑːdɪəʊ'væskjələ] *adj.* 心血管的

prolong [prə'lɒŋ] *v.* 延长

relaxation [ˌriːlæk'seɪʃn] *n.* 放松，休息

adequate ['ædɪkwət] *adj.* 足够的

equable ['ekwəbl] *adj.* 平静的

balanced ['bælənst] *adj.* 平衡的

personality [ˌpɜːsə'nælətɪ] *n.* 个性

self-observation [selfˌɒbzə'veɪʃn] *n.* 自我观察，自我审查

critical ['krɪtɪkl] *adj.* 决定性的

consistency [kən'sɪstənsɪ] *n.* 一致性

真题考点词替换清单

题号	题目——原文
27	differences—not the same
28	why—reason, because
	dying—immortality【反】
29	stable—constant
32	prolonging—extend, increase
33	in accordance with—according to
	principles—laws
36	pose a problem—disturb
40	conserving—sparing

Test 4

🔺 *Reading Passage 1: Land of the Rising Sum*

Paragraph A

significantly [sɪɡ'nɪfɪkəntlɪ] *adv.* 值得注目地

mathematical [ˌmæθə'mætɪkl] *adj.* 数学上的

attainment [ə'teɪnmənt] *n.* 成绩，成就

sample ['sɑːmpl] *adj.* 作为代表或范例的

comparison [kəm'pærɪsn] *n.* 比较，对照

establish [ɪ'stæblɪʃ] *v.* 建立，确定

score [skɔː(r)] *n.* 分数

proportion [prə'pɔːʃn] *n.* 部分，比例

attainer [ə'teɪnə] *n.* 取得成就者

incidentally [ˌɪnsɪ'dentlɪ] *adv.* 偶然地

variation [ˌveərɪ'eɪʃn] *n.* 变化

reasonably ['riːznəblɪ] *adv.* 合理地

consistent [kən'sɪstənt] *adj.* 始终如一的，一致的

achieve [ə'tʃiːv] *v.* 达到目的，完成

Paragraph B

virtually ['vɜːtʃʊəlɪ] *adv.* 事实上，几乎

sector ['sektə(r)] *n.* 部门，部分

spacious ['speɪʃəs] *adj.* 宽敞的

standardise ['stændədaɪz] *v.* 使……标准化

let off 排放；放过

formal ['fɔ:ml] *adj.* 正式的

mutual ['mju:tʃʊəl] *adj.* 共同的，相互的

unstream [ʌn'stri:m] *v.* 不再把······按智力分班

considerable [kən'sɪdərəbl] *adj.* 相当大的

identity [aɪ'dentətɪ] *n.* 一致，认同感

rank [ræŋk] *v.* 排名

competition [ˌkɒmpə'tɪʃn] *n.* 竞争

steam [sti:m] *n.* 精力

address [ə'dres] *n.* 致辞

bowing ['bəʊɪŋ] *n.* 鞠躬

loyalty ['lɔɪəltɪ] *n.* 忠诚，忠实

concentration [ˌkɒnsen'treɪʃən] *n.* 集中

Paragraph C

basis ['beɪsɪs] *n.* 基础

remarkably [rɪ'mɑ:kəblɪ] *adv.* 非常地；显著地

demonstrate ['demənstreɪt] *v.* 展示

free compulsory education 免费义务教育

presumably [prɪ'zju:məblɪ] *adv.* 大概，推测起来

inexpensive [ˌɪnɪk'spensɪv] *adj.* 便宜的

set out 开始

accessible [ək'sesəbl] *adj.* 可理解的

centralized ['sentrəˌlaɪzd] *adj.* 集中的，中央集权的

curriculum [kə'rɪkjələm] *n.* 课程

keen [ki:n] *adj.* 热心的；敏锐的

cartoon [kɑ:'tu:n] *n.* 卡通片；连环漫画

deliver [dɪ'lɪvə] *v.* 实现，履行

Paragraph D

pattern ['pætn] *n.* 模式

comment on 发表评论，发表意见

elaborate [ɪ'læbəreɪt] *v.* 详细阐述，详细叙述

principle ['prɪnsəpl] *n.* 原则

ignorance ['ɪgnərəns] *n.* 不知，不懂

solution [sə'lu:ʃn] *n.* 解决方案，答案

avoid [ə'vɔɪd] *v.* 避免

repetition [ˌrepə'tɪʃn] *n.* 重复

elaboration [ɪˌlæbəˈreɪʃn] *n.* 详细阐述　　set [set] *v.* 设置（问题）

individually [ˌɪndɪˈvɪdʒuəlɪ] *adv.* 单独地　　rarely [ˈreəlɪ] *adv.* 很少地

supplementary [ˌsʌplɪˈmentrɪ] *adj.* 补充的，追加的

worksheet [ˈwɜːkʃiːt] *n.* 工作表，工作单，作业

distribute [dɪˈstrɪbjuːt] *v.* 分配，分发　　impression [ɪmˈpreʃn] *n.* 效果

comprehensive [ˌkɒmprɪˈhensɪv] *adj.* 广泛的；综合的

coverage [ˈkʌvərɪdʒ] *n.* 覆盖范围　　combine with 联合，结合

homogeneity [ˌhɒmədʒəˈniːətɪ] *n.* 同质，同种

render [ˈrendə] *v.* 放弃　　circulate [ˈsɜːkjəleɪt] *v.* 循环；巡视

cope [kəʊp] *v.* 处理

Paragraph E

mixed-ability [mɪkstəˈbɪlətɪ] *adj.* 学生能力不一的

extra work 额外的任务　　observe [əbˈzɜːv] *v.* 观察，注意

struggler [ˈstrʌglə] *n.* 奋斗者，有困难的人

assist [əˈsɪst] *v.* 帮助　　seek [siːk] *v.* 寻求

foster [ˈfɒstə] *v.* 培养　　scarcely [ˈskeəslɪ] *adv.* 几乎不

adequate [ˈædɪkwət] *adj.* 足够的　　keep up 赶上

inform of 告知，通知　　evening tuition 夜校，晚班

Paragraph F

contributing [kənˈtrɪbjuːtɪŋ] *adj.* 作贡献的，起作用的

attitude [ˈætɪtjuːd] *n.* 态度　　emphasis [ˈemfəsɪs] *n.* 重点，强调

couple with 结合　　accuracy [ˈækjərəsɪ] *n.* 准确性

supportive [səˈpɔːtɪv] *adj.* 支持的　　repetitively [rɪˈpetətɪvlɪ] *adv.* 重复地

quote [kwəʊt] *v.* 引用　　unjustified [ʌnˈdʒʌstɪfaɪd] *adj.* 不正当的

observe [əbˈzɜːv] *v.* 注意到，说

inspirational [ˌɪnspəˈreɪʃənl] *adj.* 鼓舞人心的

真题考点词替换清单

题号	题目——原文
3	format—pattern
4	less successful students—strugglers, slow learners
5	key—major contributing factors
6	wider range—greater variation
10	well organized—logically developed
11	patiently—repetition
	carefully—elaboration
13	much effort—hard work
	correct—accuracy
	emphasised—focus on

Reading Passage 2: Biological Control of Pests

Paragraph 1

pest [pest] *n.* 害虫

continuous [kənˈtɪnjʊəs] *adj.* 持续的

reckless [ˈrekləs] *adj.* 鲁莽的，不顾后果的

synthetic [sɪnˈθetɪk] *adj.* 合成的，人造的

pose [pəʊz] *v.* 造成

crop [krɒp] *n.* 农作物，庄稼

counter-productive [ˌkaʊntəprəˈdʌktɪv] *adj.* 产生相反效果的

engender [ɪnˈdʒendə] *v.* 产生，造成

disorder [dɪsˈɔːdə(r)] *n.* 失调

pesticide [ˈpestɪsaɪd] *n.* 杀虫剂

contribute to 导致

breed [briːd] *n.* 品种，种类

chemical-resistant [ˈkemɪklrɪˈzɪstənt] *adj.* 抗化学药品的

lethal [ˈliːθl] *adj.* 致命的，致死的

superbug [ˈsuːpəbʌg] *n.* 超级病菌

Paragraph 2

species [ˈspiːʃiːz] *n.* 物种

resistance [rɪˈzɪstəns] *n.* 抵抗力

potent [ˈpəʊtnt] *adj.* 有效的

disease-spreading [dɪˈziːzˈspredɪŋ] *adj.* 传播病菌的

immune [ɪˈmjuːn] *adj.* 免疫的　　insecticide [ɪnˈsektɪsaɪd] *n.* 杀虫剂，农药

Paragraph 3

glaring [ˈɡleərɪŋ] *adj.* 明显的　　harmful [ˈhɑːmfl] *adj.* 有害的

application [ˌæplɪˈkeɪʃn] *n.* 应用　　wipe out 消灭

non-targeted [nɒnˈtɑːɡɪtɪd] *adj.* 非针对性的

organism [ˈɔːɡənɪzəm] *n.* 有机体，生物体

population [ˌpɒpjʊˈleɪʃn] *n.* 种群

agroecologist [æɡrəʊiːˈkɒlədʒɪst] *n.* 农业生态学家

treadmill [ˈtredmɪl] *n.* 跑步机

syndrome [ˈsɪndrəʊm] *n.* 综合症状，并发症状

tremendous [trəˈmendəs] *adj.* 巨大的　　potential [pəˈtenʃl] *n.* 潜能

diversity [daɪˈvɜːsəti] *n.* 多样性　　withstand [wɪðˈstænd] *v.* 抵挡，反抗

bear [beə(r)] *v.* 生子　　offspring [ˈɒfsprɪŋ] *n.* 后代，子孙

built-in [ˌbɪltˈɪn] *adj.* 内在的，天生的

Paragraph 4

havoc [ˈhævək] *n.* 大破坏，浩劫　　illustrate [ˈɪləstreɪt] *v.* 说明

bask [bɑːsk] *v.* 沉浸于

chemical-based [ˈkemɪklbeɪst] *adj.* 依靠化学药品的

intensive [ɪnˈtensɪv] *adj.* 广泛的　　avidly [ˈævɪdli] *adv.* 贪心地，热心地

boost [buːst] *v.* 促进，增加　　yield [jiːld] *n.* 产品，收益

proliferation [prəˌlɪfəˈreɪʃn] *n.* 增殖　　variety [vəˈraɪəti] *n.* 种类；多样

Paragraph 5

alarming [əˈlɑːmɪŋ] *adj.* 令人担忧的　　outbreak [ˈaʊtbreɪk] *n.* 发作；爆发

necessitate [nəˈsesɪteɪt] *v.* 使成为必要　　spraying [ˈspreɪɪŋ] *n.* 喷雾，喷洒

outlay ['aʊtleɪ] *n.* 经费，支出

account for 占到

invasion [ɪn'veɪʒn] *n.* 入侵，侵犯

cotton ['kɒtn] *n.* 棉花

push to the wall 把……逼上绝路

Paragraph 6

inadequate [ɪn'ædɪkwət] *adj.* 不足的，不充分的

property ['prɒpətɪ] *n.* 性能

adverse effect 副作用

DDT 滴滴涕（一种杀虫剂）

mutation [mjuː'teɪʃn] *n.* 突变

agency ['eɪdʒənsɪ] *n.* 中介，机构

Paragraph 7

escalating ['eskəleɪtɪŋ] *adj.* 上升的

indiscriminate [ˌɪndɪ'skrɪmɪnət] *adj.* 任意的，不加选择的

application [ˌæplɪ'keɪʃn] *n.* 应用

sound [saʊnd] *adj.* 合理的，有效的

natural enemy 天敌

field [fiːld] *n.* 领域

potential [pə'tenʃl] *n.* 可能性，潜力

low-cost [ləʊkɒst] *adj.* 低成本的

perpetual [pə'petʃʊəl] *adj.* 永久的，不断的

minimum ['mɪnɪməm] *n.* 最小量

detrimental [ˌdetrɪ'mentl] *adj.* 有害的，不利的

side-effect [saɪd'iːfekt] *n.* 副作用

non-polluting ['nɒnpə'luːtɪŋ] *adj.* 无污染的

self-dispersing [selfdɪs'pɜːsɪŋ] *adj.* 自行驱散的

peril ['perəl] *n.* 危险

effective [ɪ'fektɪv] *adj.* 有效的

selective [sɪ'lektɪv] *adj.* 选择性的

popularity [ˌpɒpjʊ'lærətɪ] *n.* 普及

limited ['lɪmɪtɪd] *adj.* 有限的

in contrast to 与……比起来

bio-control [biːəʊkən'trəʊl] *n.* 生物控制

Paragraph 8

Commonwealth Institute of Biological Control 英联邦生物防治研究所

global ['gləʊbl] *adj.* 全球的

network ['netwɜːk] *n.* 网络

laboratory [lə'bɒrətrɪ] *n.* 实验室

field station 野外观测站，野外台

active ['æktɪv] *adj.* 活跃的

non-commercial [ˌnɒnkə'mɜːʃəl] *adj.* 非商业性的

engage [ɪn'geɪdʒ] *v.* 使参加

predator ['predətə(r)] *n.* 捕食者

parasite ['pærəsaɪt] *n.* 寄生虫

serve [sɜːv] *v.* 可作……用

clearing-house ['klɪrɪŋˌhaʊs] *n.* 信息交流中心

Paragraph 9

seed-feeding [siːd'fiːdɪŋ] *adj.* 以草种为食的

weevil ['wiːvl] *n.* 象鼻虫

native to 原产自……

obnoxious [əb'nɒkʃəs] *adj.* 讨厌的

exert [ɪg'zɜːt] *v.* 施以……影响

devious ['diːvɪəs] *adj.* 偏僻的，间接的

influence ['ɪnfluəns] *n.* 影响

Hyderabad-based ['haɪdərəbɑːdbeɪst] *adj.* 总部位于海德巴拉的

Argentina [ˌɑːdʒən'tiːnə] *n.* 阿根廷

eradication [ɪˌrædɪ'keɪʃn] *n.* 根除

hyacinth ['haɪəsɪnθ] *n.* 风信子

nuisance ['njuːsns] *n.* 讨厌的东西，麻烦事

perfect ['pɜːfɪkt] *v.* 使完美

prey [preɪ] *v.* 捕食

notorious [nəʊ'tɔːrɪəs] *adj.* 臭名昭著的

defoliant [ˌdiː'fəʊlɪənt] *n.* 落叶剂，脱叶剂

Paragraph 10

flourishing ['flʌrɪʃɪŋ] *adj.* 旺盛的，繁茂的

coconut ['kəʊkənʌt] *n.* 椰子，椰子肉

grove [grəʊv] *n.* 果园

plague [pleɪg] *v.* 使受灾祸

leaf-mining [liːf'maɪnɪŋ] *adj.* 破坏叶子的

larval ['lɑːvl] *adj.* 幼虫状态的，潜在的

indigenous [ɪn'dɪdʒənəs] *adj.* 本土的

grass-scale [grɑːsskeɪl] *adj.* 大规模的

devour [dɪ'vaʊə(r)] *v.* 吞噬

forage ['fɒrɪdʒ] *n.* 草料，饲料

beetle ['biːtl] *n.* 甲虫

canal [kə'næl] *n.* 管道

clutch [klʌtʃ] *n.* 控制

hectare ['hekteə] *n.* 公顷

infest [ɪn'fest] *v.* 侵扰，寄生于

Salvinia molesta 槐萍

rice field 稻田

真题考点词替换清单

题号	题目——原文
14	imbalance—disorders
15	no responding—resistance
17	spent—outlay
19	innate—built-in
	immunity—resistance
21	free from danger—safe
24	blighted—plagued
26	plague—infest

🔺 *Reading Passage 3: Collecting Ant Specimens*

Paragraph 1

ant [ænt] *n.* 蚂蚁

jar [dʒɑː(r)] *n.* 罐

exhaustive [ɪg'zɔːstɪv] *adj.* 详尽的，彻底的

survey ['sɜːveɪ] *n.* 调查

estimate ['estɪmət] *v.* 估计

collection [kə'lekʃn] *n.* 采集，收集

classification [ˌklæsɪfɪ'keɪʃn] *n.* 分类

desirable [dɪ'zaɪərəbl] *adj.* 合适的，需要的

determination [dɪˌtɜːmɪ'neɪʃn] *n.* 测定

ecological [ˌiːkə'lɒdʒɪkl] *adj.* 生态学的

compatible [kəm'pætəbl] *adj.* 可兼容的，能共存的

taxonomist [tæk'sɒnəmɪst] *n.* 分类学者

stray [streɪ] *adj.* 迷路的；离群的

complicated ['kɒmplɪkeɪtɪd] *adj.* 复杂的

species ['spiːʃiːz] *n.* 物种

abundance [ə'bʌndəns] *n.* 充裕，丰富

taxonomy [tæk'sɒnəmɪ] *n.* 分类法

cast [kɑːst] *n.* 阵容，成员

variation [ˌveərɪ'eɪʃn] *n.* 变种

identifiable [aɪˌdentɪ'faɪəbl] *adj.* 可辨认的

overlook [ˌəʊvə'lʊk] *v.* 忽略

limited ['lɪmɪtɪd] *adj.* 有限的

specimen ['spesɪmən] *n.* 样本，标本

taxonomic [ˌtæksə'nɒmɪk] *adj.* 分类学的

investigation [ɪnˌvestɪ'geɪʃn] *n.* 调查研究

Paragraph 2

hand collecting 徒手收集

bait [beɪt] *n.* 诱饵

litter ['lɪtə(r)] *n.* 垃圾，枯枝落叶

sampling ['sɑːmplɪŋ] *n.* 取样

pitfall ['pɪtfɔːl] *n.* 陷阱

trap [træp] *n.* 陷阱，圈套

occur [ə'kɜː(r)] *v.* 出现

log [lɒg] *n.* 原木

rotten ['rɒtən] *adj.* 腐烂的

vegetation [ˌvedʒə'teɪʃn] *n.* 植被，植物

trunk [trʌŋk] *n.* 树干

bark [bɑːk] *n.* 树皮

nest [nest] *n.* 巢穴

forage ['fɒrɪdʒ] *v.* 搜寻

foraging column 觅食队伍

nocturnal [nɒk'tɜːnl] *adj.* 夜间活动的

confine [kən'faɪn] *v.* 限制，局限

aspirator ['æspɪreɪtə] *n.* 抽吸器

pooter ['puːtə(r)] *n.* 吸虫管

forcep [fɔː'sep] *n.* 钳子

moistened ['mɔɪsnd] *adj.* 弄湿的

paint brush 漆刷

sting [stɪŋ] *v.* 刺痛，蜇

tube [tjuːb] *n.* 管子

capacity [kə'pæsəti] *n.* 容量

ethanol ['eθənɒl] *n.* 乙醇

mishandle [ˌmɪs'hændl] *v.* 处理不当

Paragraph 3

concentrate ['kɒnsəntreɪt] *v.* 聚集

forager ['fɒrɪdʒə] *n.* 觅食者

elusive [ɪ'luːsɪv] *adj.* 难捉摸的，行踪隐秘的

utilize ['juːtəlaɪz] *v.* 利用

shrub [ʃrʌb] *n.* 灌木

light-colored [laɪt'kʌlə(r)d] *adj.* 浅色的

test-tube ['testtjuːb] *n.* 试管

vial ['vaɪəl] *n.* 玻璃小瓶

capture ['kæptʃə(r)] *v.* 捕获，抓住

surrounding [sə'raʊndɪŋ] *adj.* 周围的

leaf litter 落叶层

Paragraph 4

layer ['leɪə] *n.* 层

debris ['debriː] *n.* 碎片，残骸

extract ['ekstrækt] *v.* 提取

marshy [mɑːʃiː] *adj.* 沼泽的

coarse [kɔːs] *adj.* 粗糙的

sample ['sɑːmpl] *v.* 取样，抽样调查

funnel ['fʌnl] *n.* 漏斗

sift [sɪft] *v.* 过滤，筛选

twig [twɪg] *n.* 小枝，嫩叶

Paragraph 5

container [kən'teɪnə(r)] *n.* 容器

diameter [daɪ'æmɪtə] *n.* 直径

personal preference 个人喜好

ethylene ['eθɪliːn] *n.* 乙烯

propylene ['prəʊpəliːn] *n.* 丙烯

maintenance ['meɪntənəns] *n.* 维护，维持

intervention [ˌɪntə'venʃn] *n.* 介入，干预

preservative [prɪ'zɜːvətɪv] *n.* 防腐剂

vary ['veərɪ] *v.* 变化

undertake [ˌʌndə'teɪk] *v.* 承担，从事

glycol ['glaɪkɒl] *n.* 乙二醇，甘醇

evaporate [ɪ'væpəreɪt] *v.* 蒸发

encounter [ɪn'kaʊntə(r)] *v.* 偶然碰见

真题考点词替换清单

题号	题目——原文
29	range—different
32	wet habitats—rain forests and marshy areas
33	hard to find—elusive
34	little—minimal
35	container—tubes

General Training: Reading and Writing Test A

Section 1

Holiday Plus

package ['pækɪdʒ] *n.* 整套事务

wilderness ['wɪldənəs] *n.* 原野，荒野

heritage-listed ['herɪtɪdʒ'lɪstɪd] *adj.* 被列为古迹的

lodge [lɒdʒ] *n.* 旅馆

retreat [rɪ'triːt] *n.* 休息寓所

buffet ['bʊfeɪ] *n.* 自助餐　　soft drink 软饮料，不含酒精的饮料

available [ə'veɪləbl] *adj.* 可得的，可用的

canoeing [kə'nuːɪŋ] *n.* 划独木舟　　open-air ['əʊpəneə(r)] *adj.* 户外的

tennis court 网球场　　horse-riding [hɔːs'raɪdɪŋ] *n.* 骑马

optional ['ɒpʃənl] *adj.* 可选择的

self-drive [self'draɪv] *adj.* 租车自己驾驶的

pelican ['pelɪkən] *n.* 鹈鹕，塘鹅（一种食鱼鸟）

resort [rɪ'zɔːt] *n.* 度假胜地　　coral ['kɒrəl] *adj.* 珊瑚的

Great Barrier Reef 大堡礁（澳洲）　　refurbishment [ˌriː'fɜːbɪʃmənt] *n.* 整修

flight [flaɪt] *n.* 航班　　cedar ['siːdə] *n.* 雪松，香柏

blend [blend] *n.* 混合　　sophistication [səˌfɪstɪ'keɪʃn] *n.* 复杂

ambience ['æmbɪəns] *n.* 周围环境，气氛

cater for 迎合，满足

真题考点词替换清单

题号	题目——原文
2	tour—trip
4	not open—close

Sydney Travel College

travel insurance 旅游保险　　compulsory [kəm'pʌlsəri] *adj.* 必需的

assume [ə'sjuːm] *v.* 假设，承担

overseas [ˌəʊvə'siːz] *adj.* 海外的，国外的

requirement [rɪ'kwaɪəmənt] *n.* 要求　　reciprocal [rɪ'sɪprəkl] *adj.* 互惠的

arrangement [ə'reɪndʒmənt] *n.* 安排

emergency [ɪ'mɜːdʒənsɪ] *n.* 紧急情况，突发事件

personnel [ˌpɜːsəˈnel] *n.* 全体人员

accompany [əˈkʌmpəni] *v.* 陪伴，伴随

pre-existing [ˈpriːɪɡˈzɪstɪŋ] *adj.* 先存在的

disability [ˌdɪsəˈbɪləti] *n.* 残疾

claim [kleɪm] *n.* 要求，声明

luggage [ˈlʌɡɪdʒ] *n.* 行李

theft [θeft] *n.* 偷盗

belongings [bɪˈlɒŋɪŋz] *n.* 财产，所有物；行李

receipt [rɪˈsiːt] *n.* 收据

payment [ˈpeɪmənt] *n.* 偿还

briefcase [ˈbriːfkeɪs] *n.* 公文包

backpack [ˈbækpæk] *n.* 双肩背包

portable [ˈpɔːtəbl] *adj.* 便携的

CD player **CD** 音碟机

non-refundable [nɒnrɪˈfʌndəbl] *adj.* 不可退款的

deposit [dɪˈpɒzɪt] *n.* 保证金

unforeseen [ˌʌnfɔːˈsiːn] *adj.* 无法预料的

unforeseeable [ˌʌnfɔːˈsiːəbl] *adj.* 不可预见的，无法预料的

circumstance [ˈsɜːkəmstəns] *n.* 情况

真题考点词替换清单

题号	题目——原文
8	minor—non-emergency
9	a parent—a family member
	bring—accompany
10	had before—pre-existing
13	laptop—portable computers
	stolen—theft

 Section 2

Kenichi Software: Security Guidelines for Staff

Paragraph 1

security [sɪˈkjʊərəti] *n.* 安全

on the premises 在……前提下

authorization [ˌɔːθəraɪˈzeɪʃn] *n.* 授权，批准

odd [ɒd] *adj.* 古怪的

Paragraph 2

detain [dɪ'teɪn] v. 留住

unauthorized [ʌn'ɔ:θəraɪzd] adj. 非法的

inspect [ɪn'spekt] v. 检查

property ['prɒpəti] n. 财产

request [rɪ'kwest] v. 需要

on the grounds 由于……原因

removal [rɪ'mu:vl] n. 挪用，移动

motor vehicle 机动车

submit [səb'mɪt] v. 服从

Paragraph 3

be subject to 遭受

disciplinary ['dɪsəplɪnəri] adj. 纪律的，训诫的

Paragraph 4

issue ['ɪʃu:] v. 发给

safeguard ['seɪfgɑ:d] v. 保护

Human Resources 人力资源，人力资源部

contractor [kən'træktə(r)] n. 立契约者

one-off [wʌnɒf] adj. 一次性的

badge [bædʒ] n. 徽章

oblige [ə'blaɪdʒ] v. 强制

Paragraph 5

access ['ækses] n. 使用权

trivial ['trɪviəl] adj. 不重要的，琐碎的

disclosure [dɪs'kləʊʒə(r)] n. 披露，揭发

supplier [sə'plaɪə(r)] n. 供应商

essential [ɪ'senʃl] adj. 必要的

outsider [ˌaʊt'saɪdə] n. 外人

Paragraph 6

confidential [ˌkɒnfi'denʃl] adj. 机密的，秘密的

specification [ˌspesɪfɪ'keɪʃn] n. 规格，说明书

drawings ['drɔ:ɪŋz] n. 图纸，图示

divulge [daɪ'vʌldʒ] v. 泄露

manager ['mænɪdʒə(r)] n. 经理

proceeding [prə'si:dɪŋ] n. 程序，诉讼

relate to 与……相关

hand over 上交

account [ə'kaʊnt] n. 账目，账单

initiate [ɪ'nɪʃieɪt] v. 发起

misuse [ˌmɪs'juːs] *n.* 滥用　　　　　afterwards ['ɑːftəwədz] *adv.* 后来

真题考点词替换清单

题号	题目——原文
15	suspicious—odd, unusual
	report—inform
16	stop—detain
17	face—be subject to
18	human resources—staff
19	confidential—disclosure
20	hand in—hand over

Is Everyone Entitled to Paid Holidays?

Paragraph 1

Working Time Regulations 工作时间条例　　come into force 生效，开始实施

amend [ə'mend] *v.* 修改，改善　　　　majority [mə'dʒɒrəti] *n.* 大多数

entitle [ɪn'taɪtl] *v.* 使……有权利　　junior ['dʒʊnjə] *adj.* 后进的；下级的

Paragraph 3

accrual [ə'kruːəl] *n.* 应计项目；自然增长　　approval [ə'pruːvl] *n.* 批准

Paragraph 4

counter ['kaʊntə(r)] *adj.* 相反的

Paragraph 5

shutdown ['ʃʌtdaʊn] *n.* 停工

Paragraph 6

carry over 延期　　　　　　　　　　contract ['kɒntrækt] *n.* 合同

lieu [luː] *n.* 代替　　　　　　　　　outstanding [aʊt'stændɪŋ] *adj.* 未偿付的

provided [prə'vaɪdɪd] *conj.* 假如，倘若

Paragraph 7

specify ['spesɪfaɪ] *v.* 指定　　　　　union representative 工会代表

真题考点词替换清单

题号	题目——原文
21	excluded—not covered
22	minimum—no fewer than
	annual—a year
25	possible—e.g.(for example)

🔺 Section 3: Snake Oil

Paragraph A

cowboy ['kaʊbɔɪ] *n.* 牧童

roam [rəʊm] *v.* 流浪，漫游

gunfight ['gʌnfaɪt] *n.* 枪战

phrase [freɪz] *n.* 词汇

dismissive [dɪs'mɪsɪv] *adj.* 表示轻视的

patent ['pætnt] *adj.* 新奇的，专利的

miraculous [mɪ'rækjələs] *adj.* 不可思议的，奇迹的

cure [kjʊə(r)] *n.* 治愈

baldness [bɔːldnəs] *n.* 秃头

snakebite ['sneɪkbaɪt] *n.* 蛇咬伤

cattle ['kætl] *n.* 牛，牲畜

stealing ['stiːlɪŋ] *n.* 偷盗

live up to 符合，达到预期标准

consequently ['kɒnsɪkwəntlɪ] *adv.* 因此，结果

evaluate [ɪ'væljʊeɪt] *v.* 评价

Paragraph B

remarkable [rɪ'mɑːkəbl] *adj.* 非凡的

dismiss [dɪs'mɪs] *v.* 解散

outrageous [aʊt'reɪdʒəs] *adj.* 令人吃惊的

positively ['pɒzətɪvlɪ] *adv.* 当然，肯定地

remedy ['remədɪ] *n.* 治疗

ingredient [ɪn'griːdɪənt] *n.* 原料

Echinacea [ˌekə'neɪʃɪə] *n.* 紫锥花属

potent ['pəʊtnt] *adj.* 有效的

promoter [prə'məʊtə(r)] *n.* 发起人

cure-all [k'juːrɪəl] *n.* 万灵药

lay [leɪ] *adj.* 外行的

qualification [ˌkwɒlɪfɪ'keɪʃn] *n.* 任职资格

eliminate [ɪ'lɪmɪneɪt] *v.* 消除

a host of 许多

ailment ['eɪlmənt] *n.* 小病

Paragraph C

native to 生长于

coneflower ['kəʊnˌflaʊə] *n.* 金菊花

poultice ['pəʊltɪs] *n.* 药膏状

wound [wuːnd] *n.* 伤口

sting [stɪŋ] *n.* 蜇伤

gum [gʌm] *n.* 牙龈

measles ['miːzlz] *n.* 麻疹

arthritis [ɑːˈθraɪtɪs] *n.* 关节炎

Paragraph D

pharmacist ['fɑːməsɪst] *n.* 药剂师

folk remedy 偏方

nonsense ['nɒnsns] *n.* 胡说

convert [kən'vɜːt] *v.* 改变

nasal ['neɪzl] *adj.* 鼻的

congestion [kən'dʒestʃən] *n.* 堵塞

tincture ['tɪŋktʃə(r)] *n.* 酊剂

incidentally [ˌɪnsɪ'dentlɪ] *adv.* 偶然地

Paragraph E

antibiotics [ˌæntɪbaɪ'ɒtɪks] *n.* 抗生素

herbalist ['hɜːbəlɪst] *n.* 草药医生

homeopath ['həʊmɪəpæθ] *n.* 同种疗法医师

extensive [ɪk'stensɪv] *adj.* 广泛的

plot [plɒt] *n.* 阴谋

conduct [kən'dʌkt] *v.* 实施

echinacin [ekɪ'neɪsɪn] *n.* 海胆碱

flowering top 开花顶部

ointment ['ɔɪntmənt] *n.* 药膏

liquid ['lɪkwɪd] *n.* 液体

internal [ɪn'tɜːnl] *adj.* 内部的

external [ɪk'stɜːnl] *adj.* 外部的

Paragraph F

genuinely ['dʒenjɔɪnlɪ] *adv.* 真诚地

amused [ə'mjuːzd] *adj.* 愉快的

confirm [kən'fɜːm] *v.* 确定，证实

treatment ['triːtmənt] *n.* 治疗，疗法

infection [ɪn'fekʃn] *n.* 感染

a range of 一系列

bacteria [bæk'tɪərɪə] *n.* 细菌

protozoa [ˌprəʊtə'zəʊə] *n.* 原生细菌

intriguing [ɪn'triːgɪŋ] *adj.* 有趣的

extract ['ekstrækt] *v.* 提取

enthusiastic [ɪnˌθjuːzɪ'æstɪk] *adj.* 狂热的

convert [kən'vɜːt] *n.* 皈依者

packaged ['pækɪdʒd] *adj.* 包装过的

remedy ['remədɪ] *n.* 补救，治疗

supplement ['sʌplɪmənt] *n.* 补充物

shelves [ʃelvz] *n.* 架子

pharmacy ['fɑːməsɪ] *n.* 药房

equivalent [ɪ'kwɪvələnt] *n.* 对应物

practical ['præktɪkl] *adj.* 实用的

Paragraph G

prairie ['preərɪ] *n.* 大草原

drought-resistant ['draʊtrɪ'zɪstənt] *adj.* 抗旱的

tolerant ['tɒlərənt] *adj.* 抗……的，可忍受的

distinctive [dɪ'stɪŋktɪv] *adj.* 与众不同的

perennial [pə'renɪəl] *adj.* 多年生的

erect [ɪ'rekt] *adj.* 竖立的

hairy ['heərɪ] *adj.* 多毛的

spotted ['spɒtɪd] *adj.* 有斑点的

stem [stem] *n.* 干，茎

daisy ['deɪzɪ] *n.* 雏菊

floret ['flɒrət] *n.* 小花

cone [kəʊn] *n.* 球果

oval ['əʊvl] *adj.* 椭圆状的

lance-shaped ['lɑːnsʃ'eɪpt] *adj.* 长矛状的

coarsely [kɔːslɪ] *adv.* 粗糙地

toothed [tuːθt] *adj.* 锯齿状的

Paragraph H

property ['prɒpətɪ] *n.* 特性

manufacturer [ˌmænjʊ'fæktʃərə] *n.* 制造商，生产商

first frost 初霜

真题考点词替换清单

题号	题目——原文
28	earlier—long before
	application—used
29	research—tested
34	believed—risky, failed【反】
38	kill—against
	microbes—bacteria

General Training: Reading and Writing Test B

Section 1

Consumer Advice on Buying Shoes

Step 1

purchase ['pɜːtʃəs] *n.* 购买

refund ['riːfʌnd] *n.* 退款，偿还

exchange [ɪks'tʃeɪndʒ] *v.* 交换

inspection [ɪn'spekʃn] *n.* 检查

claim [kleɪm] *n.* 声称

faulty ['fɔːltɪ] *adj.* 出毛病的，有问题的

credit note 信用票据

unwanted [ˌʌn'wɒntɪd] *adj.* 多余的

put off 推延，阻止

Step 2

get anywhere 有进展

consult [kən'sʌlt] *v.* 请教

available [ə'veɪləbl] *adj.* 可得到的

Step 3

cover ['kʌvə(r)] *v.* 包括；报道，采访

resulting [rɪ'zʌltɪŋ] *adj.* 作为结果的

Step 4

resort [rɪ'zɔːt] *n.* 手段

take legal action 提出诉讼，采取法律行动

leaflet ['liːflət] *n.* 传单

alternatively [ɔːl'tɜːnətɪvlɪ] *adv.* 可选择地

procedure [prə'siːdʒə] *n.* 程序

真题考点词替换清单

题号	题目——原文
1	unwanted—change your mind
	straightaway—at once, immediately
	receipt—proof of purchase
	probably—likely
3	factory—manufacturer
6	contributes—pay
8	bought—sell 【反】

Lost Cards

debit ['debɪt] *n.* 借方

theft [θeft] *n.* 盗窃

insurance [ɪn'ʃʊərəns] *n.* 保险

plastic money 信用卡

shield [ʃiːld] *n.* 盾

issue ['ɪʃuː] *v.* 发行

notify ['nəʊtɪfaɪ] *v.* 通知

forge [fɔːdʒ] *v.* 伪造

withdraw [wɪð'drɔː] *v.* 提款

memorise ['meməraɪz] *v.* 记忆

precaution [prɪ'kɔːʃn] *n.* 预防，警惕

suspect [sə'spekt] *v.* 怀疑，猜想

provided [prə'vaɪdɪd] *conj.* 假如，倘若

run up 积欠

scheme [skiːm] *n.* 计划

account card 记账卡

registry ['redʒɪstrɪ] *n.* 注册

blank [blæŋk] *adj.* 空白的

sum [sʌm] *n.* 金额

negligence ['neglɪdʒəns] *n.* 疏忽

disguise [dɪs'gaɪz] *v.* 假装，掩饰

真题考点词替换清单

题号	题目——原文
9	lose—missing
11	get in touch—notified
13	buys—withdraws

 Section 2

Recycling at Work—Handy Hints to Employers

handy ['hændɪ] *adj.* 便利的，手边的

estimate ['estɪmət] *v.* 估计

revenue ['revənjuː] *n.* 收益

top [tɒp] *v.* 超过……，达到……顶点

recycling [ˌriː'saɪklɪŋ] *n.* 回收利用

audit ['ɔːdɪt] *n.* 审计，查账

hint [hɪnt] *n.* 暗示

avoidable [ə'vɔɪdəbl] *adj.* 可避免的

efficient [ɪ'fɪʃnt] *adj.* 有效的

generate ['dʒenəreɪt] *v.* 产生

scheme [skiːm] *n.* 计划

switch [swɪtʃ] *v.* 转换

contractor [kən'træktə(r)] *n.* 承包人

consumption [kən'sʌmpʃn] *n.* 消耗

poster ['pəʊstə(r)] *n.* 海报，广告

query ['kwɪəri] *n.* 疑问，质问

newsletter ['njuːzletə(r)] *n.* 实时通讯

workplace ['wɜːkpleɪs] *n.* 工作场所，车间

discard [dɪs'kɑːd] *v.* 抛弃

disposable [dɪ'spəʊzəbl] *adj.* 用完即可丢弃的，一次性的

plastic ['plæstɪk] *adj.* 塑料的

mug [mʌg] *n.* 杯子

donate [dəʊ'neɪt] *v.* 捐赠

replace [rɪ'pleɪs] *v.* 代替，替换

recycling [ˌriː'saɪklɪŋ] *n.* 回收利用

duplex ['djuːpleks] *adj.* 双重的

allocate ['æləkeɪt] *v.* 分配

motivation [ˌməʊtɪ'veɪʃn] *n.* 动机；推动

inevitable [ɪn'evɪtəbl] *adj.* 不可避免的

variety [və'raɪəti] *n.* 多样

ceramic [sə'ræmɪk] *adj.* 陶瓷的

upgrade [ˌʌp'greɪd] *v.* 升级

charity ['tʃærəti] *n.* 慈善团体

真题考点词替换清单

题号	题目——原文
16	cut—reduced
	stationery—paper
17	displayed—putting up
19	unwanted—waste
	used for—serve...purposes
20	refreshments—tea
21	sent—donating

How to Answer Any Interview Question

to start 首先

consultant [kən'sʌltənt] *n.* 顾问

executive [ɪg'zekjətɪv] *n.* 执行者，经理

deliver [dɪ'lɪvə(r)] *v.* 传送

politician [ˌpɒlə'tɪʃn] *n.* 政治家

tip [tɪp] *n.* 建议

coach [kəʊtʃ] *v.* 指导

handle ['hændl] *v.* 处理

employer [ɪm'plɔɪə(r)] *n.* 雇主，老板

press [pres] *n.* 新闻

candidate [ˈcændɪdeɪt] n. 应试者

transition [trænˈzɪʃn] n. 转变

qualification [ˌkwɒlɪfɪˈkeɪʃn] n. 资格

deliver [dɪˈlɪvə(r)] v. 传送

effectively [ɪˈfektɪvlɪ] adv. 有效地

prior to 在……之前

viable [ˈvaɪəbl] adj. 可行的

tailor [ˈteɪlə(r)] v. 裁剪，使合适

recall [rɪˈkɔːl] v. 回忆，回想

blemish [ˈblemɪʃ] n. 瑕疵，缺点

steer clear of 绕开，避开

turnaround [ˈtɜːnəraʊnd] n. 好转，转机

query [ˈkwɪərɪ] n. 质问

convey [kənˈveɪ] v. 传达

formula [ˈfɔːmjələ] n. 公式

diligent [ˈdɪlɪdʒnt] adj. 勤勉的，用功的

beforehand [bɪˈfɔːhænd] adv. 事先，预先

insight [ˈɪnsaɪt] n. 洞察力

shareholder [ˈʃeəhəʊldə(r)] n. 股东

require [rɪˈkwaɪə(r)] v. 需要

cope with 处理

dodge [dɒdʒ] v. 托词，避开

at all costs 不惜一切代价地

真题考点词替换清单

题号	题目——原文
22	not to imitate—unlike
	ignore—take notice
23	recommended—advises
24	request—ask
25	studying—reading
26	avoid—steer clear

Section 3: Taking Point

Paragraph 1

fuel [ˈfjuːəl] v. 提高

prospect [ˈprɒspekt] n. 前途

minority [maɪˈnɒrɪtɪ] n. 少数

monolingual [ˌmɒnəˈlɪŋgwəl] adj. 仅用一种语言的

claim [kleɪm] v. 声称

intelligence [ɪnˈtelɪdʒəns] n. 智力

bright [braɪt] adj. 光明的

Paragraph 2

root [ruːt] *n.* 根源

marker ['mɑːkə(r)] *n.* 标识

embarrassed [ɪm'bærəst] *adj.* 尴尬的

comment on 评价

Maori ['maʊəriː] *n.* 毛利语

point out 指出

bilingual [ˌbaɪ'lɪŋgwəl] *adj.* 双语的

Paragraph 3

agreement [ə'griːmənt] *n.* 协议，同意

expert ['eksp3ːt] *n.* 专家

bilingual [ˌbaɪ'lɪŋgwəl] *adj.* 双语的

schoolmate ['skuːlmeɪt] *n.* 同学

Paragraph 4

professor [prə'fesə(r)] *n.* 教授

view [vjuː] *n.* 观点

Paragraph 5

linguistics [lɪŋ'gwɪstɪks] *n.* 语言学

Freiburg University 弗赖堡大学

tend to 倾向

display [dɪ'spleɪ] *n.* 表现

problem-solving ['prɒbləm'sɒlvɪŋ] *adj.* 解决问题的

further ['f3ːðə(r)] *adj.* 更远的，更深的

Paragraph 6

enthusiasm [ɪn'θjuːzɪæzəm] *n.* 热忱，热心

attitude ['ætɪtjuːd] *n.* 看法，意见

blame [bleɪm] *v.* 责备

Paragraph 7

immigrant ['ɪmɪgrənt] *n.* 移民

possibility [ˌpɒsə'bɪlətɪ] *n.* 可能性

Turkish ['t3ːkɪʃ] *adj.* 土耳其的

Paragraph 8

nursery school 幼儿园

take up 开始从事

concern [kən's3ːn] *v.* 关系到

Paragraph 9

seldom ['seldəm] *adv.* 很少，不常

New Zealander 新西兰人

Paragraph 10

socialize ['səʊʃəlaɪz] v. 使社会化   kindergarten ['kɪndəgɑːtn] n. 幼儿园

bilingualism [baɪ'lɪŋwəlɪzəm] n. 双语，双语现象

battlefield ['bætlfiːld] n. 战场   identity [aɪ'dentətɪ] n. 身份；同一性

Paragraph 11

approach [ə'prəʊtʃ] n. 方法，途径   pressure ['preʃə(r)] v. 迫使

Paragraph 12

outsider [ˌaʊt'saɪdə(r)] n. 外人

Paragraph 13

scenario [sə'nɑːrɪəʊ] n. 方案；剧本   aware [ə'weə(r)] adj. 意识到的，知道的

Paragraph 15

marketing specialist 营销专家   trade fair 商品交易会，贸易展销会

真题考点词替换清单

题号	题目——原文
32	faster—more easily
37	provides opportunities—open the door
38	work—job

Cambridge
IELTS
9

Test 1

Reading Passage 1: William Henry Perkin

Paragraph 1

prompt [prɒmpt] v. 促进，激励；激起，唤起

solidify [sə'lɪdɪfaɪ] v. 加强，使固化　　stumble upon 偶然发现

Paragraph 2

immerse [ɪ'mɜːs] v. 沉迷……中，陷入　　devotion [dɪ'vəʊʃn] n. 忠诚；热爱；奉献

perceive [pə'siːv] v. 意识到；发觉，察觉

eminent ['emɪnənt] adj. 著名的，知名的，杰出的

Paragraph 3

enrolment [ɪn'rəʊlmənt] n. 入学；注册，登记

fortune ['fɔːtʃuːn] n. 财富

Paragraph 4

derive from 由……起源，取自　　surpass [sə'pɑːs] v. 超越，超过

desirability [dɪˌzaɪərə'bɪləti] n. 愿望，渴求

synthetic [sɪn'θetɪk] adj. 合成的，人造的

substitute ['sʌbstɪtjuːt] n. 代替者，替补

Paragraph 5

mysterious [mɪ'stɪərɪəs] adj. 神秘的；不可思议的

sludge [slʌdʒ] n. 沉淀物　　substance ['sʌbstəns] n. 物质，材料

incorporate [ɪn'kɔːpəreɪt] v. 使混合

unexpected [ˌʌnɪk'spektɪd] adj. 意外的，想不到的

Paragraph 6

textile ['tekstaɪl] n. 纺织品，织物　　dye [daɪ] n. 染料，颜色

excretion [ɪk'skriːʃn] n. 排泄，排泄物　　muddy ['mʌdi] adj. 模糊的，浑浊的

hue [hjuː] n. 色彩，色调　　backdrop ['bækdrɒp] n. 背景

Paragraph 7

fabric ['fæbrɪk] *n.* 织物，布；质地

fascinating ['fæsɪneɪtɪŋ] *adj.* 有巨大吸引力的，迷人的

commercial [kə'mɜːʃl] *adj.* 商业的，贸易的

Paragraph 8

fierce [fɪəs] *adj.* 激烈的，猛烈的，凶猛的

boost [buːst] *n.* 繁荣，提高，增加

flatter ['flætə(r)] *v.* 使高兴，使荣幸；奉承，恭维

gown [gaʊn] *n.* 长袍，长外衣   clamour ['klæmə(r)] *v.* 大声地要求

Paragraph 9

stain [steɪn] *v.* 给……染色，着色

invisible [ɪn'vɪzəbl] *adj.* 看不见的，无形的

bacteria [bæk'tɪəriə] *n.* 细菌（单数形式为 bacterium）

artificial [ˌɑːtɪ'fɪʃl] *adj.* 人造的，人工的，虚假的

真题考点词替换清单

题号	题目——原文
1	recognise—perceive
	ability—talent
2	enroll—attend
3	employ—become 【反】
4	still—not long after that
	discovery—breakthrough
	make—bring
	rich—fortune
	famous—fame
6	hope—attempt
	drug—medical treatment
8	group in society—the rich
	be associated—so...that...

题号	题目——原文
9	potential—possibilities
	immediately—instant
	understand—recognition
10	name—known as
	finally—later...commonly
11	consult—ask advice
	set up—give birth to
12	invent—produce...first
13	disease—vaccine【反】
	now—current
	targeted—against
	synthetic—artificial

Reading Passage 2: Is There Anybody Out There?

haunt [hɔːnt] v. 困扰，时时萦绕心头

humanity [hjuːˈmænəti] n. 人类；人性；人道

poise [pɔɪz] n. 泰然自若，自信；体态

civilisation [ˌsɪvəlaɪˈzeɪʃn] n. 文明，文化；文明社会

attempt [əˈtempt] n. & v. 试图，尝试

Paragraph A

curiosity [ˌkjʊəriˈɒsəti] n. 好奇心；奇人，奇物

foster [ˈfɒstə(r)] v. 养育；培养；促进

sufficient [səˈfɪʃnt] adj. 足够的，充足的；有能力胜任的

cog [kɒɡ] n. 齿轮

horizon [həˈraɪzn] n. 视野，眼界；地平线

wipe out 彻底摧毁，灭绝，了结

galaxy [ˈɡæləksi] n. 银河，银河系；星系

threat [θret] n. 威胁，恐吓；凶兆

nuclear [ˈnjuːkliə(r)] adj. 原子能的，原子核的

Paragraph B

ignore [ɪg'nɔ:(r)] *v.* 忽视，不顾 evidence ['evɪdəns] *n.* 证据；迹象；明显

emerge [ɪ'mɜːdʒ] *v.* 出现，浮现，暴露

conservative [kən'sɜːvətɪv] *adj.* 保守的，传统的

assumption [ə'sʌmpʃn] *n.* 假设，假定

radically ['rædɪklɪ] *adv.* 彻底地，完全地，根本地

recognise ['rekəgnaɪz] *v.* 认出，识别，辨别

resemble [rɪ'zembl] *v.* 与……相像，类似于

restrictively [rɪ'strɪktɪvlɪ] *adv.* 限制（性）地，约束（性）地

carbon ['kɑːbən] *n.* 碳

Paragraph C

severely [sɪ'vɪə(r)lɪ] *adv.* 严重地；严格地

estimate ['estɪmət] *v.* 估计，评价；预测

Paragraph D

alien ['eɪlɪən] *adj.* 国外的；相异的 attenuate [ə'tenjʊeɪt] *v.* 减弱，衰弱，变小

frequency ['friːkwənsɪ] *n.* 频率；频繁性 telescope ['telɪskəʊp] *n.* 望远镜

dramatically [drə'mætɪklɪ] *adv.* 巨大地，引人注目地，戏剧性地

hardware ['hɑːdweə(r)] *n.* 硬件；武器装备

sensitivity [ˌsensə'tɪvətɪ] *n.* 敏感；敏感性，感受性

Paragraph E

ethical ['eθɪkl] *adj.* 民族的；伦理的，道德的

address [ə'dres] *v.* 处理，解决；演讲 urgency ['ɜːdʒənsɪ] *n.* 紧迫，急迫；急事

debate [dɪ'beɪt] *n.&v.* 讨论，争论，辩论 draft [drɑːft] *v.* 起草，制定

真题考点词替换清单

题号	题目——原文
14	underlying—ground
15	likelihood—guess, estimate, perhaps, might
16	seeking—looking for
16	transmission—sending
18	life expectancy—lifetime
18	Earth—a planet like ours
19	searching for—looking for
19	signal—radio waves
20	most powerful—the world's largest
21	help—pass on the benefits
21	overcome—dealing with
21	serious problems—threats
22	trying to find—looking for
22	resemble in many ways—pretty well like
22	humans—us
24	picked up—detection
26	promptly—immediately
26	respond—react, reply

Reading Passage 3: The History of the Tortoise

Paragraph 1

tortoise ['tɔːtəs] *n.* 乌龟，陆龟

enterprising ['entəpraɪzɪŋ] *adj.* 大胆的，有魄力的

parched [pɑːtʃt] *adj.* 炎热的，干旱的　　desert ['dezət] *n.* 沙漠，荒地

cellular ['seljələ(r)] *adj.* 细胞的；由细胞组成的

fluid ['fluːɪd] *n.* 液体，流体　　　　　　mammal ['mæml] *n.* 哺乳动物

snail [sneɪl] *n.* 蜗牛

worm [wɜːm] *n.* 虫，蠕虫

invasion [ɪn'veɪʒn] *n.* 入侵，闯入

migration [maɪ'greɪʃn] *n.* 迁移

Paragraph 2

reproduction [ˌriːprə'dʌkʃn] *n.* 繁殖，生殖

abandon [ə'bændən] *v.* 放弃，抛弃

intermediate [ˌɪntə'miːdɪət] *n.* 中间体，中间物；调解人

cousin ['kʌzn] *n.* 远亲

revert [rɪ'vɜːt] *v.* 恢复；回到……上

marine [mə'riːn] *adj.* 海的，海中的

ancestor ['ænsestə(r)] *n.* 祖先

equivalent [ɪ'kwɪvələnt] *adj.* 相等的

gill [gɪl] *n.* 鳃

vertebrate ['vɜːtɪbrət] *adj.* 有脊椎的

Paragraph 3

descend [dɪ'send] *v.* 遗传下来；来自；下来

terrestrial [tə'restrɪəl] *adj.* 陆地的，陆生的

dinosaur ['daɪnəsɔː(r)] *n.* 恐龙

fossil ['fɒsl] *n.* 化石

fragment ['frægmənt] *n.* 碎片；片段

streamlined ['striːmlaɪnd] *adj.* 流线型的

Paragraph 4

species ['spiːʃiːz] *n.* 物种，种类

triangular [traɪ'æŋgjələ(r)] *adj.* 三角形的；三方面的

graph [græf] *n.* 图表，曲线图

plot [plɒt] *v.* 标绘

overlap [ˌəʊvə'læp] *n.* 重叠部分；重叠，重合

cluster ['klʌstə(r)] *n.* 簇，组

Paragraph 5

apparently [ə'pærəntlɪ] *adv.* 显然地，显而易见地

branch [brɑːntʃ] *n.* 分支

aquatic [ə'kwætɪk] *adj.* 水生的

constitute ['kɒnstɪtjuːt] *v.* 构成，组成

Paragraph 6

remarkable [rɪˈmɑːkəbl] *adj.* 值得注意的，引人注目的

remote [rɪˈməʊt] *adj.* （亲属关系）远的

真题考点词替换清单

题号	题目——原文
27	had to—must, without...none...could...
	before—prior
	transfer from sea to land—invasion of land
28	changes—redesign
29	lack—never
	ancestors—earlier marine
30	resembled—look like
32	determine—tell
	incomplete—only fragments
33	appearance—look like
	determined—surely
	habitat—lived...in the water
34	taken from—obtained
35	data, information—three measurements
	recorded—plot
	comparing—against
36	dense—tight
	top—upper part
38	positioned—show up
	about—approximately
39	position—right
	indicated—no doubt
	ancient creatures—fossils
40	most significant—remarkable
	transition from sea to land—return
	more than once—double

Test 2

Reading Passage 1

Paragraph A

impairment [ɪm'peəmənt] *n.* 缺陷，损伤

auditory ['ɔːdətrɪ] *adj.* 听觉的，听觉器官的

detrimental [ˌdetrɪ'mentl] *adj.* 有害的，不利的

Paragraph B

preliminary [prɪ'lɪmɪnərɪ] *adj.* 初步的，初级的

collaborative [kə'læbərətɪv] *adj.* 合作的，协作的

interaction [ˌɪntər'ækʃn] *n.* 互动，互相影响

comprehend [ˌkɒmprɪ'hend] *v.* 理解，领会

Paragraph C

deficit ['defɪsɪt] *n.* 缺隙

maximum ['mæksɪməm] *adj.* 最大的，最大极限的

generate ['dʒenəreɪt] *v.* 造成，引起

Paragraph D

reverberation [rɪˌvɜːbə'reɪʃn] *n.* 回声，回响

disability [ˌdɪsə'bɪlətɪ] *n.* 残疾，无能　　verbal ['vɜːbl] *adj.* 言语的，口头的

vulnerable ['vʌlnərəbl] *adj.* 易受伤的，脆弱的

autistic [ɔː'tɪstɪk] *n.* 自闭症患者，孤僻症患者

disorder [dɪs'ɔːdə(r)] *n.* 失调，混乱

Paragraph E

discrepancy [dɪs'krepənsɪ] *n.* 矛盾，不符合（之处）

sensory ['sensərɪ] *adj.* 感觉的，感官的

distressing [dɪ'stresɪŋ] *adj.* 使人痛苦的，令人苦恼的

quantify ['kwɒntɪfaɪ] *v.* 量化，确定……的数量

stimulus ['stɪmjələs] *n.* 刺激，刺激物，促进因素（复数形式为 stimuli）

intrusive [ɪn'truːsɪv] *adj.* 打扰的，侵入的

adversely ['ædvɜːslɪ] *adv.* 不利地，有害地

Paragraph F

sustaining [sə'steɪnɪŋ] *adj.* 持续的   persistence [pə'sɪstəns] *n.* 坚持

screen out 筛选出

Paragraph G

penetrate ['penɪtreɪt] *v.* 透（渗）入；刺入，刺穿

exacerbate [ɪg'zæsəbeɪt] *v.* 使恶化，使加重

optimum ['ɒptɪməm] *adj.* 最佳的，最适宜的，最有利的

undiagnosed [ʌn'daɪəgnəʊzd] *adj.* 未确诊的，尚未找到原因的

Paragraph H

embark [ɪm'bɑːk] *v.* 开始或从事（尤指新的或难的事），乘船

consultation [ˌkɒnsl'teɪʃn] *n.* 请教，咨询，磋商

barrier ['bærɪə(r)] *n.* 障碍，妨碍   vitally ['vaɪtəlɪ] *adv.* 极其，致命地

Paragraph I

formulate ['fɔːmjuleɪt] *v.* 制定，规划

imperative [ɪm'perətɪv] *adj.* 必要的，势在必行的

promulgate ['prɒmlgeɪt] *v.* 颁布，公布

真题考点词替换清单

题号	题目——原文
	national policy—New Zealand Disability Strategy
1	initiative—embark
2	global—international
	team effort—working party
3	hypothesis—suggested
	reason—amounts to
	growth—heightened

题号	题目——原文
4	demand—imperative
	suitable—appropriate
	worldwide—international
	regulations—standards
5	medical conditions—impairment, disorders
	more at risk—extremely vulnerable
6	proportion—%
	auditory—hearing
7	period—decades
8	upset—painful and distressing
9	not been diagnosed—undiagnosed
10	aims to—is to
	give—provide
11	current teaching methods—modern teaching practices
12	cooling systems—air-conditioning units
13	to increase awareness—only limited attention【反】

Reading Passage 2: Venus in Transit

Paragraph A

transit ['trænzɪt] *n.* 凌日

astronomical [ˌæstrə'nɒmɪkl] *adj.* 天文学的

astronomer [ə'strɒnəmə(r)] *n.* 天文学家，天文学者

allege [ə'ledʒ] *v.* 宣称，断言，辩称

outperform [ˌaʊtpə'fɔːm] *v.* 胜过，做得比……更好

accuracy ['ækjərəsɪ] *n.* 精确（性），准确（性）

Paragraph B

extraordinary [ɪk'strɔːdnrɪ] *adj.* 非凡的，不寻常的

innermost ['ɪnəməʊst] *adj.* 最深处的，最里面的

desolate ['desələt] *adj.* 荒凉的，无人的

calculate ['kælkjʊleɪt] *v.* 计算，估计　　parallax ['pærəlæks] *n.* 视差

Paragraph C

fundamental [ˌfʌndə'mentl] *adj.* 基础的；重要的

orbital ['ɔːbɪtl] *adj.* 轨道的

Paragraph D

inspire [ɪn'spaɪə(r)] *v.* 鼓舞，激励，启迪　　pin down 使明确说明，确定

scale [skeɪl] *n.* 规模，比例　　solar ['səʊlə(r)] *adj.* 太阳的，日光的

deserve [dɪ'zɜːv] *v.* 值得，应得　　sympathy ['sɪmpəθɪ] *n.* 同情（心），慰问

thwart [θwɔːt] *v.* 阻挠，挫败　　besiege [bɪ'siːdʒ] *v.* 包围

flee [fliː] *v.* 逃跑，逃掉　　equator [ɪ'kweɪtə(r)] *n.* 赤道

Paragraph E

precise [prɪ'saɪs] *adj.* 精确的；重要的　　smear [smɪə(r)] *v.* 将……弄模糊，弄脏

circular ['sɜːkjələ(r)] *adj.* 圆的　　diffraction [dɪ'frækʃn] *n.* 衍射，反射

exhibit [ɪg'zɪbɪt] *v.* 表现，呈现　　refract [rɪ'frækt] *v.* 使（光线）折射

Paragraph F

radar ['reɪdɑː(r)] *n.* 雷达　　cosmic ['kɒzmɪk] *adj.* 宇宙的

extend [ɪk'stend] *v.* 扩展，延伸

Paragraph G

spectacle ['spektəkl] *n.* 奇观，壮观，景象

pave [peɪv] *v.* 为……铺平道路，铺设　　vital ['vaɪtl] *adj.* 至关重要的，生死攸关的

breakthrough ['breɪkθruː] *n.* 突破，重要的新发现

detect [dɪ'tekt] *v.* 探测

真题考点词替换清单

题号	题目——原文
14	different ways—extended to
15	event—the fact that
	prevented—not helped, thwarted
16	potential, future—might prove to be
	discoveries—breakthroughs
	leading on from—paved the way
17	physical states—"black drop" effect
	failed—difficult, problem, impossible, dogged
18	calculated—determined
	the distance of the Sun from the Earth—AU
	fair degree of accuracy—reasonably accurate
19	understood—realise
	worked out—measure
	comparing—calculating
20	realised—had shown
	time—speeds
	go round—orbital
	depends on—governed
21	witnessed—saw
	unable—ruled out
22	see—observe
23	second—next
	ironically, clouded out, dispiriting—managed to observe【反】
24	appears—looks
	shape, distorted—not circular
26	work out—measure, calculate

Reading Passage 3: A Neuroscientist Reveals How to Think Differently

Paragraph 1

neuroscientist ['njʊərəsaɪəntɪst] *n.* 神经科学家

innovation [ˌɪnə'veɪʃn] *n.* 创新，改革

Paragraph 2

iconoclastic [aɪˌkɒnəˈklæstɪk] *adj.* 打破旧习的

distinct [dɪˈstɪŋkt] *adj.* 不同的，有区别的

perception [pəˈsepʃn] *n.* 认知能力，感悟能力

utilize [ˈjuːtəlaɪz] *v.* 利用，使用　　　constraint [kənˈstreɪnt] *n.* 限制，约束

drumbeat [ˈdrʌmbiːt] *n.* 鼓声

Paragraph 3

budget [ˈbʌdʒɪt] *n.* 预算　　　bulb [bʌlb] *n.* 灯泡

evolve [ɪˈvɒlv] *v.* （使）进化，（使）演变，（使）逐步形成

impede [ɪmˈpiːd] *v.* 阻碍，阻止　　　confront [kənˈfrʌnt] *v.* 面对，碰到

interpret [ɪnˈtɜːprɪt] *v.* 解释　　　shortcut [ˈʃɔːtkʌt] *n.* 捷径，近路

photon [ˈfəʊtɒn] *n.* 光子，光量子

Paragraph 4

pitfall [ˈpɪtfɔːl] *n.* 陷阱，圈套　　　curse [kɜːs] *n.* 诅咒，咒骂

statistical [stəˈtɪstɪkl] *adj.* 统计的，统计学的

likelihood [ˈlaɪklɪhʊd] *n.* 可能性

Paragraph 5

bombard [bɒmˈbɑːd] *v.* 轰炸，炮轰　　　novelty [ˈnɒvltɪ] *n.* 新奇事物

expose [ɪkˈspəʊz] *v.* 暴露

embrace [ɪmˈbreɪs] *v.* 欣然接受或采取；包括，包含

Paragraph 6

tend to 趋向，朝某方向　　　trigger [ˈtrɪɡə(r)] *v.* 触发，引发，激发

variant [ˈveərɪənt] *n.* 变体　　　inhibit [ɪnˈhɪbɪt] *v.* 妨碍，抑制

trivial [ˈtrɪvɪəl] *adj.* 不重要的，琐碎的

Paragraph 7

empathy [ˈempəθɪ] *n.* 共鸣，同感　　　cognition [kɒɡˈnɪʃn] *n.* 认知，认知力

intertwine [ˌɪntəˈtwaɪn] *v.* 缠结在一起，缠绕

enthusiasm [ɪnˈθjuːzɪæzəm] *n.* 热情，热忱

Paragraph 8

artistic [ɑːˈtɪstɪk] *adj.* 艺术的

alienation [ˌeɪlɪəˈneɪʃn] *n.* 疏远，疏远感，脱离

asset [ˈæset] *n.* 有价值的或有用的人；财富

真题考点词替换清单

题号	题目——原文
27	link—secrets
	achievement—success
28	distinctive—different
29	because—thus
	rely on—draw on
	previous events—past experience
30	result—product
31	avoids—do not
	traps—pitfall
32	exposure—encountered
	different events—things...never...before
	forces—bombard
	think—see
33	unusually—extraordinary
	receptive—willingness
	new—fresh, different
37	psychological—mental
	illness—disorder
38	and—too
40	many fields—every area
	and—from...to...
	scientific—technology

Test 3

Reading Passage 1: Attitudes to Language

Paragraph 1

systematic [ˌsɪstə'mætɪk] *adj.* 有系统的，有条理的

objective [əb'dʒektɪv] *adj.* 客观的

linguistic [lɪŋ'gwɪstɪk] *adj.* 语言的；语言学的

deteriorate [dɪ'tɪərɪəreɪt] *v.* （使）恶化，（使）变坏

invective [ɪn'vektɪv] *n.* 痛骂，猛烈抨击　　polemic [pə'lemɪk] *n.* 论战，争论，辩论

Paragraph 2

criticise ['krɪtɪsaɪz] *v.* 批评，挑剔，评论

exempt [ɪg'zempt] *adj.* 被免除的，被豁免的

aptitude ['æptɪtjuːd] *n.* 才能，资质，天资　　survival [sə'vaɪvl] *n.* 生存

Paragraph 3

prescriptivism [prɪ'skrɪptəˌvɪzəm] *n.* 规定主义（指传统语法）

ought to 应当，应该，理应

encounter [ɪn'kaʊntə(r)] *v.* 相遇，不期而遇

adherent [əd'hɪərənt] *n.* 支持者，拥护者

deviation [ˌdiːvɪ'eɪʃn] *n.* 背离，偏离

Paragraph 4

approach [ə'prəʊtʃ] *n.* 途径，方法

grammarian [grə'meərɪən] *n.* 语法家，文法家

threefold ['θriːfəʊld] *adj.* 三倍的；三重的　　dispute [dɪ'spjuːt] *n.* 争端，争论

reliance [rɪ'laɪəns] *n.* 依赖，依靠，信赖　　chaos ['keɪɒs] *n.* 混乱，紊乱，一团糟

authoritarian [ɔːˌθɒrɪ'teərɪən] *adj.* 权力主义的，独裁主义的

alternative [ɔːl'tɜːnətɪv] *n.* 取舍，二中选一　　*adj.* 另外的，二选一的

motivate ['məʊtɪveɪt] *v.* 激发，促动

widespread ['waɪdspred] *adj.* 普遍的，分布广的

maintain [meɪn'teɪn] *v.* 维护，维持，保护

Paragraph 5

diversity [daɪ'vɜːsəti] *n.* 多样化，多样性   evaluate [ɪ'væljʊeɪt] *v.* 评价，评估

halt [hɔːlt] *n. & v.* 停止，中止，暂停

advocate ['ædvəkeɪt] *n.* 提倡（者），拥护（者）

custom ['kʌstəm] *n.* 习惯，惯例   legislation [ˌledʒɪs'leɪʃn] *n.* 立法，法律

tenet ['tenɪt] *n.* 原则，信条   analysis [ə'næləsɪs] *n.* 分析

Paragraph 6

opposition [ˌɒpə'zɪʃn] *n.* 反对，敌对，对抗

valid ['vælɪd] *adj.* 有效的；正当的   liberalism ['lɪbərəlɪzəm] *n.* 自由主义

elitist [ɪ'liːtɪst] *n.* 精英，优秀人才

真题考点词替换清单

题号	题目——原文
1	arguments—debate
	reason why—so
2	small—minor
	more strongly than—as easily as 【反】
3	assessment—judge
	affected—influence
6	pointless—not to, impossible tasks
	attempt to—try to
	stop—halting
7	only…after—already 【反】
8	misrepresented—extreme, painting unreal pictures
10	great importance—best, reliance on
12	based on—original, only just standard
13	historical—18th century

Reading Passage 2: Tidal Power

Paragraph A

tidal ['taɪdl] *adj.* 潮汐的，潮水的

turbine ['tɜ:baɪn] *n.* 涡轮机

electricity [ɪˌlek'trɪsəti] *n.* 电力，电流

operate ['ɒpəreɪt] *v.* 运转

principle ['prɪnsəpl] *n.* 原则，原理

current ['kʌrənt] *n.* 水流

constant ['kɒnstənt] *adj.* 恒定的，不变的

prospect ['prɒspekt] *n.* 前景；景象

renewable [rɪ'nju:əbl] *adj.* 可再生的，可更新的

emission [ɪ'mɪʃn] *n.* 排放，排放量

Paragraph B

competitive [kəm'petətɪv] *adj.* 有竞争力的，竞争的

Paragraph C

blade [bleɪd] *n.* 叶片，刀片

sustainable [sə'steɪnəbl] *adj.* 可持续的

predictable [prɪ'dɪktəbl] *adj.* 可预测的，可预见的

hostile ['hɒstaɪl] *adj.* 不利的；敌对的，有敌意的

propeller [prə'pelə(r)] *n.* 螺旋桨

self-sufficient [selfsə'fɪʃnt] *adj.* 自给自足的

drastically ['drɑ:stɪklɪ] *adv.* 大大地，彻底地

abandon [ə'bændən] *v.* 放弃，丢弃

identify [aɪ'dentɪfaɪ] *v.* 确定，识别

commercial [kə'mɜ:ʃl] *adj.* 商业的

marine [mə'ri:n] *adj.* 海的，海洋的

subsidiary [səb'sɪdɪəri] *n.* 子公司，附属公司　*adj.* 辅助的

potential [pə'tenʃl] *adj.* 潜在的，可能的

Paragraph D

generator ['dʒenəreɪtə(r)] *n.* 发电机

diameter [daɪ'æmɪtə(r)] *n.* 直径

grid [grɪd] *n.* 电网

maintenance ['meɪntənəns] *n.* 维修，保养

seaweed ['si:wi:d] *n.* 海藻，海草

Paragraph E

cable ['keɪbl] *n.* 电缆

Paragraph F

bubble ['bʌbl] *n.* 气泡，水泡

submerge [səb'mɜːdʒ] *v.* 淹没

robust [rəʊ'bʌst] *adj.* 坚固的，牢固的

vibration [vaɪ'breɪʃn] *n.* 振动

debris ['debriː] *n.* 碎片，残渣

extraction [ɪk'strækʃn] *n.* 取出，抽出

真题考点词替换清单

题号	题目——原文
14	site—station
15	a way—via the cable
	bring back—re-imported
16	previous—originally
17	possibility—prospects
18	more…than—unlike
	reliable—predictable, constant
19	cut down—reducing
	air pollution—carbon dioxide emissions
20	contribute to—if…, Britain would be able to
21	income—earner
22	vicinity—around
	particular features—heavily indented, strong tidal currents
23	raised—lifted
	extraction—clean
24	comparatively—relatively
	in danger—at risk
	due to—from
25	result from—causes

Reading Passage 3: Information Theory—the Big Idea

Paragraph A

code [kəʊd] *n.* 编码，代码

impact ['ɪmpækt] *n.* 影响

voyager ['vɒɪɪdʒə(r)] *n.* 旅行者，航行者

physics ['fɪzɪks] *n.* 物理学

probe [prəʊb] *n.* 探测器，探测仪；探针

launch [lɔːntʃ] *v.* 发射

spectacular [spek'tækjələ(r)] *adj.* 壮观的，精彩的

soar [sɔ:(r)] *v.* 高飞，飞腾　　　exposure [ɪk'spəʊʒə(r)] *n.* 暴露

freezing ['fri:zɪŋ] *adj.* 结冰的，严寒的

circuit ['sɜ:kɪt] *n.* 电路，线路　　spare [speə(r)] *n.* 备用零件；备用品

target ['tɑ:gɪt] *n.* 目标，对象

Paragraph B

triumph ['traɪʌmf] *n.* 成功，胜利　　highlight ['haɪlaɪt] *v.* 强调，突出

astonishing [ə'stɒnɪʃɪŋ] *adj.* 惊人的　　gadget ['gædʒɪt] *n.* 小装置，小器械

shun [ʃʌn] *v.* 避开，回避

acclaim [ə'kleɪm] *n.&v.* 喝彩，欢呼；赞扬　　satellite ['sætəlaɪt] *n.* 卫星；人造卫星

convey [kən'veɪ] *v.* 传输，运送；传递，传达

Paragraph C

prestigious [pre'stɪdʒəs] *adj.* 著名的，有声望的

capture ['kæptʃə(r)] *v.* 捕获，捕捉，获得

vague [veɪg] *adj.* 模糊的，不清楚的　　guarantee [ˌgærən'ti:] *v.* 保证，担保

interfere [ˌɪntə'fɪə(r)] *v.* 干扰，干涉

Paragraph D

capacity [kə'pæsəti] *n.* 容量，性能　　absolute ['æbsəlu:t] *adj.* 绝对的，完全的

Paragraph E

devise [dɪ'vaɪz] *v.* 想出，设计　　feat [fi:t] *n.* 成就，功绩

spacecraft ['speɪskrɑ:ft] *n.* 宇宙飞船，航天器

crumple ['krʌmpl] *v.* 弄皱，变皱　　crisps [krɪsps] *n.* 薯片

ultimate ['ʌltɪmət] *adj.* 最后的，最终的；最大的，极限的

Paragraph F

redundant [rɪ'dʌndənt] *adj.* 多余的，累赘的

ambiguous [æm'bɪgjʊəs] *adj.* 含糊的，不清楚的

compression [kəm'preʃn] *n.* 压缩；浓缩　　cram [kræm] *v.* 塞进，填满

真题考点词替换清单

题号	题目——原文
29	fame—acclaim
30	machine—check-out lasers
	interpreting—read
	information—price
	incomplete—even, crumpled
31	incident—event
32	initially—originally
	intended to—set out
	achieve—aim
	research—work
33	transmitted—sent
	pictures—images
	both…and…—and
34	left—out of
35	scientists—experts
	stop working—failing
36	hope—solution
	tell—message, instruct
	replace...with...—use...to change...
	distance—kilometers from Earth
	difficult—not easy
37	was used—by means of
38	starting point—basic, fundamental
	attempt—set about
	send—transmit
	messages—information
	from place to place—over distances
39	amount—units of bits
	sent—pass, communication
	given time—rate, per second
	determined—depends on, limit, maximum
	reference—given
40	products—mobile videophone
	more than—close to Shannon's ultimate limit 【反】

Test 4

Reading Passage 1: The Life and Work of Marie Curie

Paragraph 1

radioactivity [ˌreɪdɪəʊækˈtɪvəti] *n.* 放射性，辐射能

sole [səʊl] *adj.* 单独的，唯一的

Paragraph 2

prodigious [prəˈdɪdʒəs] *adj.* 巨大的；异常的，惊人的

medal [ˈmedl] *n.* 奖章，奖牌，勋章   investment [ɪnˈvestmənt] *n.* 投资，投入

earning [ˈɜːnɪŋ] *n.* 收入，获利

Paragraph 4

significance [sɪɡˈnɪfɪkəns] *n.* 意义，重要性

phenomenon [fəˈnɒmɪnən] *n.* 现象，事迹

Paragraph 5

mineral [ˈmɪnərəl] *n.* 矿物，矿石，矿物质

superior [suːˈpɪərɪə(r)] *adj.* 较高的，较好的，优先的

element [ˈelɪmənt] *n.* 元素，要素   radium [ˈreɪdɪəm] *n.* 镭

radiation [ˌreɪdɪˈeɪʃn] *n.* 辐射，放射物   struggle [ˈstrʌɡl] *v.* 奋斗，努力，争取

Paragraph 6

interrupt [ˌɪntəˈrʌpt] *v.* 打断，截断，阻止   appoint [əˈpɔɪnt] *v.* 任命，约定

demonstration [ˌdemənˈstreɪʃn] *n.* 证明，论证

Paragraph 7

henceforth [ˌhensˈfɔːθ] *adv.* 从今以后，今后

devote [dɪˈvəʊt] *v.* 奉献，把……奉献（给）；把……专用（于）

professorship [prəˈfesəʃɪp] *n.* 教授职位   vacant [ˈveɪkənt] *adj.* 空缺的，空闲的

isolation [ˌaɪsəˈleɪʃn] *n.* 孤立；隔离，分开；离析

Paragraph 8

wounded ['wuːndɪd] *adj.* 负伤的，受伤的

in earnest 认真地，正式地　　　　substance ['sʌbstəns] *n.* 物质，材料

application [ˌæplɪ'keɪʃn] *n.* 应用，运用

Paragraph 9

triumphant [traɪ'ʌmfənt] *adj.* 成功的　　campaign [kæm'peɪn] *n.* 运动

Paragraph 10

accumulate [ə'kjuːmjəleɪt] *v.* 积累，堆积

abundant [ə'bʌndənt] *adj.* 大量的，丰富的，充足的

decisive [dɪ'saɪsɪv] *adj.* 决定性的　　exposure [ɪk'spəʊʒə(r)] *n.* 暴露

tube [tjuːb] *n.* 管，管状物

Paragraph 11

contribution [ˌkɒntrɪ'bjuːʃn] *n.* 贡献　　immense [ɪ'mens] *adj.* 极大的，巨大的

subsequent ['sʌbsɪkwənt] *adj.* 随后的，后来的

真题考点词替换清单

题号	题目——原文
1	joint—with; both—sole【反】
4	stop—interrupt
5	took over—left vacant
	position—professorship
9	received recognition—was awarded the Noble Prize
10	medical technique—treatment
11	saw—understood
	importance—need
	collecting—accumulate
	both…and…—not only…(but) also
13	suffered from—died

Reading Passage 2: Young Children's Sense of Identity

Paragraph A

emergence [ɪ'mɜːdʒəns] *n.* 出现，发生   feature ['fiːtʃə(r)] *n.* 特征，特点

Paragraph B

distinction [dɪ'stɪŋkʃn] *n.* 区别，特质   caregiver ['keəgɪvə(r)] *n.* 照料者，护理者

propose [prə'pəʊz] *v.* 提议，建议，计划   limb [lɪm] *n.* 肢

mimic ['mɪmɪk] *v.* 模仿，模拟，学样

vocalization [ˌvəʊkəlaɪ'zeɪʃn] *n.* 发声，发声法

contingent [kən'tɪndʒənt] *adj.* 因情况而异的，视情况而定的

reflection [rɪ'flekʃn] *n.* 反映，反射

Paragraph D

interaction [ˌɪntər'ækʃn] *n.* 互相影响，互动

empirical [ɪm'pɪrɪkl] *adj.* 凭经验的，经验主义的

scarce [skeəs] *adj.* 缺乏的

Paragraph E

category ['kætəgərɪ] *n.* 种类，类别；范畴   element ['elɪmənt] *n.* 元素，要素

colleague ['kɒliːg] *n.* 同事，同僚，同行   derive [dɪ'raɪv] *v.* 源于，来自，得到

Paragraph F

inextricably [ˌɪnɪk'strɪkəblɪ] *adv.* 无法摆脱地，解不开地

bound [baʊnd] *v.* 束缚，捆绑   conceive [kən'siːv] *v.* 构思，设想，想象

essentially [ɪ'senʃəlɪ] *adv.* 本质上，根本上

Paragraph G

milestone ['maɪlstəʊn] *n.* 里程碑，划时代事件

dab [dæb] *v.* 轻拍；很快地涂抹   cue [kjuː] *n.* 暗示，提示，线索

Paragraph H

graphic ['græfɪk] *adj.* 图的，用图表示的

display [dɪ'spleɪ] *n.* 显示   rage [reɪdʒ] *n.* 愤怒

longitudinal [ˌlɒŋɡɪ'tjuːdɪnl] *adj.* 经度的，纵向的

intensity [ɪn'tensəti] *n.* 强烈，强度

frustration [frʌ'streɪʃn] *n.* 挫折，挫败，失意

struggle ['strʌɡl] *n.&v.* 奋斗，努力，争取   ownership ['əʊnəʃɪp] *n.* 所有权，所有

notable ['nəʊtəbl] *adj.* 值得注意的，显著的

真题考点词替换清单

题号	题目——原文
14	researchers—Lewis and Brooks-Gunn
	study—experiment
	method—dabbed some red powder on the noses of children
15	imitation—mimic, copying
	role—source of information
16	age—second birthday
	identify—recognize
	static—without…movement
	image—visually, seeding
17	reason—because of
	limitation—difficulties, cannot
	link—feature
	possible—may
18	culture—Western societies
19	examples—such as
	features—characteristics
	contribute to—is made up of
20	never…without…—impossible…outside
	relationships with other people—social experience

题号	题目——原文
21	is related to—was concerned with
	mastery—control, affect
	things—objects
	and—This is followed by…
22	aggressive—anger, struggle, war, disputing
	leads to—the link
23	observing—see
	contributes to—leads to
	self—distinct from other
24	image, face—looking, mirror, see
	handling objects—control physical objects
25	problems—difficulties

Reading Passage 3: The Development of Museums

Paragraph A

conviction [kən'vɪkʃn] *n.* 信念

historical [hɪ'stɒrɪkl] *adj.* 历史的，有历史根据的

relics ['relɪks] *n.* 遗产，遗物　　　　testimony ['testɪmənɪ] *n.* 证据，证明

artefact ['ɑːtɪfækt] *n.* 手工艺品，人工制品

chronicle ['krɒnɪkl] *n.* 编年史，年代记

veracity [və'ræsətɪ] *n.* 真实　　　　endure [ɪn'djʊə(r)] *v.* 持续，持久

showcase ['ʃəʊkeɪs] *n.* 玻璃柜台，玻璃陈列柜

subtle ['sʌtl] *adj.* 微妙的，难以察觉或描述的

ordinary ['ɔːdnrɪ] *adj.* 普通的，平凡的，平常的

exclusive [ɪk'skluːsɪv] *adj.* 专用的，独有的

domain [də'meɪn] *n.* 范围，领域，领土

Paragraph B

alter ['ɔːltə(r)] *v.* 改变，更改　　　　heritage ['herɪtɪdʒ] *n.* 遗产，继承物

imperial [ɪm'pɪərɪəl] *adj.* 帝国的，皇家的

prototype ['prəʊtətaɪp] *n.* 原型；典范

virtual ['vɜːtʃʊəl] *adj.* 实质上的，事实上的

intolerable [ɪn'tɒlərəbl] *adj.* 不能忍受的，无法容忍的

Paragraph C

distinction [dɪ'stɪŋkʃn] *n.* 区别   evaporate [ɪ'væpəreɪt] *v.* 消失，蒸发

adopt [ə'dɒpt] *v.* 采用，采取，采纳

authenticity [ˌɔːθen'tɪsətɪ] *n.* 可靠性，真实性

presentation [ˌprezn'teɪʃn] *n.* 显示，介绍

enormous [ɪ'nɔːməs] *adj.* 巨大的，庞大的

jungle ['dʒʌŋgl] *n.* 丛林

Paragraph D

undergo [ˌʌndə'gəʊ] *v.* 经历，承受

competitive [kəm'petətɪv] *adj.* 竞争的，有竞争力的

Paragraph E

accuracy ['ækjərəsɪ] *n.* 精确（性），准确（性）

depict [dɪ'pɪkt] *v.* 描绘，描画，描述   correspond [ˌkɒrə'spɒnd] *v.* 符合，相应

dominant ['dɒmɪnənt] *adj.* 支配的，统治的，占优势的

gesture ['dʒestʃə(r)] *n.* 手势，姿势

contemporary [kən'temprərɪ] *adj.* 现代的，当代的

prejudice ['predʒʊdɪs] *n.* 成见，偏见

Paragraph F

bias ['baɪəs] *n.* 偏见

inevitable [ɪn'evɪtəbl] *adj.* 不可避免的，必然发生的

notion ['nəʊʃn] *n.* 观念，见解

真题考点词替换清单

题号	题目——原文
27	views—attitudes
	current—recently
	change—altered, now
	mixed—does not share this opinion
28	fewer differences—distinction...is evaporating
	public attractions—museums, heritage sites and theme parks
29	commercial-income—generating
	pressures—difficult, increasing need
	people—those who...
	in charge—engaged in
30	meet visitor expectations—corresponds to public perceptions
	interpreting the facts—historical accuracy must be increasingly altered
31	today—recently
	past—used to
	the public—ordinary visitor
32	current—recently, now
	trends—attitudes
	emphasise—key word
	personal involvement—experience
33	less easy—is gradually evaporating
35	reveal—tell
	present—contemporary
	beliefs—perceptions of the world
	past—ancestors
36	only—not everything
	durable—transitory 【反】, survives
	objects—materials, castles, palaces
	remain—survives
	because—has to do with

题号	题目——原文
37	consumer—market forces
	avoid—move away from
38	people—visitors
39	boundaries—walled area
	changed little—more than five times【反】
40	false—only, bias
	used to—in the past

General Training: Reading and Writing

Test A

Section 1

Questions 1-6

Paragraph A

snack [snæk] *n.* 小吃，零食   essential [ɪ'senʃl] *adj.* 必要的，必需的

enthusiasm [ɪn'θjuːzɪæzəm] *n.* 热情，热忱

absolute ['æbsəluːt] *adj.* 绝对的，无条件的

drop in 拜访，来访

Paragraph B

apply [ə'plaɪ] *v.* 申请   applicant ['æplɪkənt] *n.* 应聘者，申请者

reference ['refrəns] *n.* 推荐信   wage [weɪdʒ] *n.* 薪酬（多指周薪）

nanny ['nænɪ] *n.* 保姆   carer ['keərə(r)] *n.* 看护者

Paragraph C

formal ['fɔːml] *adj.* 正式的；正规的   qualification [ˌkwɒlɪfɪ'keɪʃn] *n.* 资格

sensible ['sensəbl] *adj.* 明智的，通情达理的

imaginative [ɪ'mædʒɪnətɪv] *adj.* 富有想象力的

detail ['diːteɪl] *n.* 细节，详情，详细内容

paragraph D

cleaner ['kliːnə(r)] *n.* 保洁员，清洁工　　block [blɒk] *n.* 大楼，大厦

paragraph E

mature [mə'tʃʊə(r)] *adj.* 成熟的，稳重的

experienced [ɪk'spɪərɪənst] *adj.* 富有经验的

administrator [əd'mɪnɪstreɪtə(r)] *n.* 管理者，管理人员

secretary ['sekrətrɪ] *n.* 秘书，文秘　　soft furnishing 室内家装，室内装潢

paragraph F

cafe ['kæfeɪ] *n.* 小餐厅，小餐馆　　venture ['ventʃə(r)] *n.* 冒险，探险

negotiate [nɪ'gəʊʃɪeɪt] *v.* 谈判，协商

Paragraph G

let [let] *v.* 出租　　　　　　　　start up 开始，发动

catering ['keɪtərɪŋ] *n.* 餐饮供应，酒席承办

well-paid [welpeɪd] *adj.* 薪酬优厚的

真题考点词替换清单

题号	题目——原文
1	few hours a week—2 hours per day
	early morning—finish work before the offices open
2	no experience—formal qualifications not as important as sensible
	full-time—Mon-Fri, 8.30-5.00
	short-term—Jan-July
3	no experience—experience not essential
	cannot work on weekdays—Sat & Sun only

题号	题目——原文
4	more than 20 years' experience—experienced
	run a business—start up on their own
5	full-time—full-time cook
6	well-paid—excellent wages

Questions 7-14

intercity [ˌɪntəˈsɪtɪ] *adj.* 城市之间的

sleeper [ˈsliːpə(r)] *n.* 卧铺

subject to 取决于，依赖于

reservation [ˌrezəˈveɪʃn] *n.* 保留，预订

berth [bɜːθ] *n.* （轮船、火车的）卧铺

cabin [ˈkæbɪn] *n.* 客舱

fare [feə(r)] *n.* 票价

biscuit [ˈbɪskɪt] *n.* 饼干

continental breakfast 欧式早餐，英式早餐

Paragraph A

book [bʊk] *v.* 预订，预约

unbeatable [ʌnˈbiːtəbl] *adj.* 无敌的，无与伦比的

non-refundable [nɒnrɪˈfʌndəbl:] *adj.* 不能退款的

Paragraph B

apex [ˈeɪpeks] *n.* 顶端，顶点，顶峰

bargain [ˈbɑːgən] *n.* 物美价廉的商品

outward [ˈaʊtwəd] *adj.* 向外的，外出的

payment [ˈpeɪmənt] *n.* 所付款额

administrative charge 管理附加费，手续费

Paragraph C

valid [ˈvælɪd] *adj.* 有效的

peak [piːk] *n.* 巅峰，顶点，最高点

departure [dɪˈpɑːtʃə(r)] *n.* 离开，启程，出发

count [kaʊnt] *v.* 计算，清点，算做

previous [ˈpriːvɪəs] *adj.* 之前的，先前的

Paragraph D

flexible [ˈfleksəbl] *adj.* 机动的，灵活的

standard class 标准舱

Paragraph E

exclusive [ɪk'sklu:sɪv] *adj.* 专用的，专属的

inclusive [ɪn'klu:sɪv] *adj.* 包含的

Paragraph F

package ['pækɪdʒ] *n.* 包价（旅游），套餐

Paragraph G

option ['ɒpʃn] *n.* 选项   turn up 到达，出现

真题考点词替换清单

题号	题目——原文
7	advantages—special
	with a friend—for two people
8	cannot use, Friday—except all these peak days: all Fridays
9	without restriction—valid, all
10	booked up to 7 days before departure—by booking at least a week before outward travel
	cheapest—unbeatable price
11	restriction on departure time—only available for travel after 9 a.m.
12	cannot get your money back—non-refundable
13	out on Monday and back the next day—must include a Saturday night away
14	cannot use, between midnight and 10 a.m.—allows...between 10 a.m. and midnight 【反】

Section 2

Questions 15-21

Paragraph 1

project ['prɒdʒekt] *v.* 展现，展示   professional image 职业形象，专业形象

in keeping with 与……保持一致   client ['klaɪənt] *n.* 客户

input ['ɪnpʊt] *n.* 投入

site [saɪt] *n.* 地点，场所

on a daily basis 每天

Paragraph 2

alternatively [ɔːl'tɜːnətɪvlɪ] *adv.* 作为选择地，或者

appropriate [ə'prəʊprɪət] *adj.* 合适的，适当的

accessory [ək'sesərɪ] *n.* 配件，配饰

torn [tɔː'n] *adj.* 破损的（tear 的过去分词转化成的形容词）

frayed [freɪd] *adj.* 磨破的，磨损的（fray 的过去分词转化成的形容词）

pressed [prest] *adj.* 熨平的，平展的

wrinkled ['rɪŋkld] *adj.* 起皱褶的（wrinkle 的过去分词转化成的形容词）

contingency [kən'tɪndʒənsɪ] *n.* 偶然性，可能性

exert [ɪg'zɜːt] *v.* 运用，使用

judgement ['dʒʌdʒmənt] *n.* 评断，判断

supervisor ['suːpəvaɪzə(r)] *n.* 监督者，监管者

Paragraph 3

footwear ['fʊtweə(r)] *n.* 鞋类

conservative [kən'sɜːvətɪv] *adj.* 保守的，传统的

walking shoes 轻便鞋

dress shoes 正装皮鞋

loafer ['ləʊfə(r)] *n.* 平底便鞋

flat [flæt] *n.* 平底鞋

dress heels 正装跟鞋

backless shoes 露脚背的鞋

open toe shoes 露脚背的鞋，鱼嘴鞋

Paragraph 4

tasteful ['teɪstfl] *adj.* 雅致的

item ['aɪtəm] *n.* 物品

flashy ['flæʃɪ] *adj.* 闪光的，晃眼的

Paragraph 5

makeup ['meɪk,ʌp] *n.* 化妆，化妆品

cologne [kə'ləʊn] *n.* 古龙水

excessive [ɪkˈsesɪv] *adj.* 过多的，过度的　　allergic reaction 过敏反应

substance [ˈsʌbstəns] *n.* 物质　　moderation [ˌmɒdəˈreɪʃn] *n.* 适度，适量

Paragraph 6

head cover 头盖，头罩

Paragraph 7

casual [ˈkæʒʊəl] *adj.* 随便的，非正式的　　logo [ˈləʊɡəʊ] *n.* 标志，徽标

in case 以防，万一　　violation [ˌvaɪəˈleɪʃn] *n.* 违反，违背

meet [miːt] *v.* 满足　　persist [pəˈsɪst] *v.* 依旧存在，继续存在

verbal [ˈvɜːbl] *adj.* 口头的　　in line with 符合，与……一致

真题考点词替换清单

题号	题目——原文
15	aim—objective
	to present...to clients—to project...
16	state of clothes, must be—should be pressed and never wrinkled
17	brightly colored—flashy
18	avoid too much—in moderation
19	allowed—permitted
20	recommend—strongly encouraged
21	breaking—fails
	repeatedly ignored—problem persists

Questions 22-27

Paragraph 1

review [rɪˈvjuː] *v.* 复查，复审　　in the light of 基于，按照

array [əˈreɪ] *n.* 一大组，一大批　　entitlement [ɪnˈtaɪtlmənt] *n.* 应得权益

graduate trainee [ˈɡrædʒʊətˌtreɪˈniː] *n.* 毕业实习生，毕业培训生

promotion [prə'məʊʃn] *n.* 晋升　　　　outset ['aʊtset] *n.* 起初，开始

Paragraph 2

non-contributory [nɒnkən'trɪbjətərɪ] *adj.* 无须供款的，不必缴费的

salary pension scheme 薪酬抚恤金计划

payable ['peɪəbl] *adj.* 应支付的，可支付的

qualify ['kwɒlɪfaɪ] *v.* 达到标准，证明合格

eligible ['elɪdʒəbl] *adj.* 合格的，有资格的

Paragraph 3

assurance [ə'ʃʊərəns] *n.* 保险

equivalent [ɪ'kwɪvələnt] *adj.* 相当的，相等的

nominated beneficiary 被指定的受益人

Paragraph 5

subsidise ['sʌbsɪdaɪz] *v.* 补助

Paragraph 6

residential [ˌrezɪ'denʃl] *adj.* 住宅的，与居住有关的

Paragraph 7

extensive [ɪk'stensɪv] *adj.* 广泛的　　　netball ['netbɔːl] *n.* 无网篮球

squash [skwɒʃ] *n.* 壁球　　　　　　　gliding ['glaɪdɪŋ] *n.* 滑翔

Paragraph 8

body ['bɒdɪ] *n.* 机构，组织

Paragraph 10

sabbatical [sə'bætɪkl] *n.* 休假

Paragraph 11

occupational [ˌɒkjʊ'peɪʃənl] *adj.* 与职业有关的

staff [stɑːf] *v.* 担任，提供

Paragraph 12

along with（除……之外）还，以及　　one-off [wʌnɒf] *adj.* 一次性的

amusement park 游乐场

真题考点词替换清单

题号	题目——原文
23	pension—pension scheme
	work a minimum of—to most staff who have completed
24	take a holiday, provided by the company—offer subsidised holiday accommodation for staff
25	pay half the seat price—ticket subsidies of 50%
26	financial assistance for—financial support
27	in difficult circumstance—particular hardship

Section 3: Out of the Ashes

Paragraph A

break out 突然发生，爆发

fire brigade 消防队

first floor【英】第二层

sweep up 清扫，清理

blaze [bleɪz] *n.* 烈火

porcelain ['pɔːsəlɪn] *n.* 瓷器

conservator [kən's3ːvətə(r)] *n.* 保护者，救护者

mobilise ['məʊbəlaɪz] *v.* 调动，组织

bulk supplies of 大量的

desperately ['despərətlɪ] *adv.* 非常，特别，极其

salvage ['sælvɪdʒ] *n.* 抢救，营救

stoke [stəʊk] *v.* 烧火

survive [sə'vaɪv] *v.* 幸存，幸免于难

apart from 除……之外，除去

retreat [rɪ'triːt] *v.* 撤退，撤走

steward ['stjuːəd] *n.* 管家

rage [reɪdʒ] *v.* 肆虐

stationer ['steɪʃənə(r)] *n.* 文具店

blotting paper 吸墨纸

paragraph B

sludge [slʌdʒ] *n.* 泥浆，烂泥

char [tʃɑː(r)] *v.* 烧黑，熏黑

timber ['tɪmbə(r)] *n.* 木材，木料

devastation [ˌdevə'steɪʃn] *v.* 毁坏，摧毁

charcoal ['tʃɑːkəʊl] *n.* 木炭

ground floor 【英】第一层

utter ['ʌtə(r)] *adj.* 彻底的，完全的

Paragraph C

swing into action 立刻行动起来

grid [grɪd] *n.* 格子

sift [sɪft] *v.* 筛选，甄别

mark...out 划分，区分

debris ['debriː] *n.* 碎片，残片

categorise ['kætəgəraɪz] *v.* 分类，归类

Paragraph D

remnant ['remnənt] *n.* 残骸，残存

wrap [ræp] *v.* 包；隐藏

dismantle [dɪs'mæntl] *v.* 拆开，拆卸

lantern ['læntən] *n.* 灯笼

reprieve [rɪ'priːv] *v.* 缓解，舒缓

Paragraph E

scale [skeɪl] *n.* 规模

restoration [ˌrestə'reɪʃnː] *n.* 修复，复原

commentator ['kɒmənteɪtə(r)] *n.* （电台或广播的）时事评论员

vandalism ['vændəlɪzəm] *n.* 蓄意破坏

call upon 要求

unsound [ˌʌn'saʊnd] *adj.* 不稳固的

undertake [ˌʌndə'teɪk] *v.* 从事，承担

property ['prɒpəti] *n.* 财产

setting ['setɪŋ] *n.* 状况，环境

Paragraph F

intricate ['ɪntrɪkət] *adj.* 复杂的，繁冗的

tender ['tendə(r)] *v.* 提供；投标

woodcarver ['wʊdkɑːvə] *n.* 木匠，雕刻匠

plasterer ['plɑːstərə(r)] *n.* 泥水匠，石膏匠

arise [ə'raɪz] *v.* 出现，产生

ascertain [ˌæsə'teɪn] *v.* 确定，确立

fore [fɔː(r)] *n.* 前沿，一线

Paragraph H

visibly ['vɪzəbli] *adv.* 明显地，显而易见地

haunt [hɔːnt] *n.* 故居

testament ['testəmənt] *n.* 证据，证明

真题考点词替换清单

题号	题目——原文
28	sorting—categories
30	improvement—upgrading,updating
31	carry out the repair work—doing the intricate restoration work
32	rebuild Uppark—restoration programme
33	reacted to—debate
34	completed—finish
35	rescued immediately—the courage and swift action
36	large quantities—the bulk
39	reasons—three main reasons

General Training: Reading and Writing Test B

Section 1

Questions 1–7

Paragraph 1

discount ['dɪskaʊnt] *v.* 打折

Paragraph 2

apply [ə'plaɪ] *v.* 申请

proof [pruːf] *n.* 证明，证据

birth certificate 出生证明

driving licence 驾驶证

passport ['pɑːspɔːt] *n.* 护照

medical card 医疗卡

acceptable [ək'septəbl] *adj.* 可以接受的，认可的

mature [mə'tʃʊə(r)] *adj.* 成熟的，成年的   eligibility [ˌelɪdʒə'bɪlətɪ] *n.* 资格

headteacher [hed'tiːtʃər] *n.* 校长   tutor ['tjuːtə(r)] *n.* 导师

sign [saɪn] *v.* 签字，签署   application form 申请表

latter ['lætə(r)] *n.* 后者   officially [ə'fɪʃəlɪ] *adv.* 官方地，正式地

stamp [stæmp] *v.* 盖章，盖戳   be defined as 被定义为

Paragraph 3

rail-appointed travel agent 铁路运营方指定的旅行社

authorised student travel office 被授权的学生旅游办公室

leaflet ['liːflət] *n.* 传单，单页

passport-sized ['pɑːspɔːtsaɪzd] *adj.* 护照尺寸的

Paragraph 4

Bank Holiday 银行假日（在英国指法定节假日）

minimum fare 最低票价

Paragraph 5

bear [beə(r)] *v.* 具有   signature ['sɪgnətʃə(r)] *n.* 签名，签署

invalid [ɪn'vælɪd] *adj.* 无效的   purchase facility 购买设备

full fare 全额   inspection [ɪn'spekʃn] *n.* 检查，检验

Paragraph 6

Belgium ['beldʒəm] *n.* 比利时   charge [tʃɑːdʒ] *v.* 收取，征收（费用等）

submit [səb'mɪt] *v.* 提交   holder ['həʊldə(r)] *n.* 持有者

transferable [træns'fɜːrəbl] *adj.* 可转让的

board [bɔːd] *v.* 登（车、船、飞机等）   eligible ['elɪdʒəbl] *adj.* 合格的，有资格的

真题考点词替换清单

题号	题目——原文
1	over 25—a mature student over this age
2	photographs—photos
3	certain time—before 10 a.m. Monday to Friday (except during July and August)
4	impossible—invalid
5	not transferable to...—be used by anybody else
7	must pay—will be charged

Questions 8-14

distinct [dɪ'stɪŋkt] *adj.* 不同的

discount ['dɪskaʊnt] *n.* 折扣

alter ['ɔːltə(r)] *v.* 改变

senior citizen 老年人，年长者

global-trotter ['gləʊbl'trɒtə(r)] *n.* 环球旅行者

railpass [reɪlpɑːs] *n.* 铁路通行卡

econopass [ɪ'kɔːnəpɑːs] *n.* 经济通行卡

departure [dɪ'pɑːtʃə(r)] *n.* 出发，启程

be up to 是……的职责

suitcase ['suːtkeɪs] *n.* 旅行箱

charter ['tʃɑːtə(r)] *v.* 租，包租

delay [dɪ'leɪ] *v.* 推迟、延误

concession [kən'seʃn] *n.* (对某类人) 减价

in the case of 在……的情况下

maximum ['mæksɪməm] *n.* 最大值

option ['ɒpʃn] *n.* 选择，选项

outward trip 旅程

refund ['riːfʌnd] *v.* 退款

applicable [ə'plɪkəbl] *adj.* 适用的

access to 接近，进入

luggage ['lʌgɪdʒ] *n.* 行李

destination [ˌdestɪ'neɪʃn] *n.* 目的地

elderly ['eldəli] *adj.* 年长的，年老的

get in touch with 与……取得联系

spare [speə(r)] *v.* 给，留出

真题考点词替换清单

题号	题目——原文
8	concession—discount
9	large groups—over 25 passengers
	reserve—reservations
10	cancel—refund
11	paying—a charge of
13	responsibility to make sure—it is up to you to check

Section 2

Questions 15-20

Paragraph 1

immigrant ['ɪmɪgrənt] *n.* 移民

credential [krə'denʃl] *n.* 凭证，资质

degree [dɪ'griː] *n.* 学位

partially ['pɑːʃəlɪ] *adv.* 部分地

properly ['prɒpəlɪ] *adv.* 完全地，充分地

certificate [sə'tɪfɪkət] *n.* 证书

diploma [dɪ'pləʊmə] *n.* 文凭

Paragraph 2

hire ['haɪə(r)] *v.* 聘用，雇用

evaluate [ɪ'væljʊeɪt] *v.* 评估，评价

attain [ə'teɪn] *v.* 获得

personnel [ˌpɜːsə'nel] *n.* 员工

human resources 人力资源

Paragraph 3

apply for 申请，应聘

apprenticeship [ə'prentɪʃɪp] *n.* 学徒身份

on-the-job 在工作中的

potential [pə'tenʃl] *n.* 潜力，潜能

employment [ɪm'plɔɪmənt] *n.* 职业

hands on 动手实践的

credit ['kredɪt] *n.* 学分

security [sɪ'kjʊərətɪ] *n.* 稳定

Paragraph 4

assess [ə'ses] *v.* 评定，评估

accredit [ə'kredɪt] *v.* 委托，授权

posting ['pəʊstɪŋ] *n.* 岗位，职位   process ['prəʊses] *n.* 过程

secure [sɪ'kjʊə(r)] *v.* 获得，获取   screen [skriːn] *v.* 筛

Paragraph 5

establish [ɪ'stæblɪʃ] *v.* 安顿   integrate ['ɪntɪgreɪt] *v.* 融合，整合

workplace ['wɜːkpleɪs] *n.* 单位，公司，车间

mosaic [məʊ'zeɪɪk] *n.* 马赛克，镶嵌，拼接

diversity [daɪ'vɜːsətɪ] *n.* 多样性

Paragraph 6

arrival [ə'raɪvl] *n.* 到达者，抵达者   academic [ˌækə'demɪk] *adj.* 学术的

qualification [ˌkwɒlɪfɪ'keɪʃn] *n.* 资格，资质

initially [ɪ'nɪʃəlɪ] *adv.* 开始，最初   stability [stə'bɪlətɪ] *n.* 稳定性

workforce ['wɜːkfɔːs] *n.* 劳动力

真题考点词替换清单

题号	题目——原文
	make sure—ensure
15	academic qualifications—educational qualifications
18	provide stability—job security
20	enter the workforce—into the workforce
	increase—improving

Questions 21–27

Paragraph 1

presentation [ˌprezn'teɪʃn] *n.* 展示   department [dɪ'pɑːtmənt] *n.* 部门

client ['klaɪənt] *n.* 客户   reaction [ri'ækʃn] *n.* 反应

panic ['pænɪk] *v.* 惊慌，恐慌

compliment ['kɒmplɪmənt] *n.* 赞美，称赞，恭维

Paragraph 2

condense [kən'dens] v. 浓缩，精简   allot [ə'lɒt] v. 分配

a short attention span 不能长久集中注意力；分心

Paragraph 3

point [pɔɪnt] n. 要点   overall [ˌəʊvər'ɔːl] adj. 全部的

demonstrate ['demənstreɪt] v. 展示，说明   concept ['kɒnsept] n. 观点，想法

Paragraph 4

prop [prɒp] n. 道具   alive [ə'laɪv] adj. 活泼的，有生气的

hold up 举起   receiver [rɪ'siːvə(r)] n. 接收器

signal ['sɪgnəl] v. 标志，表示

Paragraph 5

dynamic [daɪ'næmɪk] adj. 有活力的   anecdote ['ænɪkdəʊt] n. 轶事

start off 开始

enthusiastically [ɪnˌθjuːzɪ'æstɪklɪ] adv. 充满激情地

curiosity [ˌkjʊərɪ'ɒsətɪ] n. 好奇   energetic [ˌenə'dʒetɪk] adj. 充满活力的

identify [aɪ'dentɪfaɪ] v. 识别   briefly ['briːflɪ] adv. 简短地

Paragraph 6

ending ['endɪŋ] n. 结尾   memorable ['memərəbl] adj. 难忘的

participate [pɑː'tɪsɪpeɪt] v. 参与   humorous ['hjuːmərəs] adj. 幽默

Paragraph 7

memorise ['meməraɪz] v. 记住   word-for-word 逐字地

stilted ['stɪltɪd] adj. 生硬的，死板的   deliver [dɪ'lɪvə(r)] v. 传递，表达

effortlessly ['efətləslɪ] adv. 不费力地   burst [bɜːst] n. 迸发，爆发

confidence ['kɒnfɪdəns] n. 信心   sail through 顺利完成

Paragraph 8

regard [rɪ'ɡɑːd] v. 认为

appreciation [əˌpriːʃɪ'eɪʃn] n. 感激，感谢

interact [ˌɪntər'ækt] v. 互动

真题考点词替换清单

题号	题目——原文
21	invitation—being asked to
25	listeners—audience
27	prepare well—a burst of confidence

Section 3: The Birdmen

Paragraph 1

mechanise ['mekənaɪz] v. 使机械化

put an end to 终止，结束

enthusiast [ɪn'θjuːzɪæst] n. 狂热者，发烧友

ultimate ['ʌltɪmət] adj. 终极的

fantasy ['fæntəsɪ] n. 梦幻，幻想

jet [dʒet] n. 喷气

pack [pæk] n. 包裹，背包

vertically [vɜːtɪklɪ] adv. 垂直地

forwards ['fɔːwədz] adv. 向前

backwards ['bækwədz] adv. 向后

stuntman ['stʌntmæn] n. 特技表演者

strap [stræp] v. 捆绑，捆扎

propel [prə'pel] v. 推进，推动

Paragraph 2

paramotoring [ˌpærə'məʊtərɪŋ] n. 动力滑翔伞运动

parachute ['pærəʃuːt] v. 用降落伞降落　n. 降落伞

paragliding ['pærəɡlaɪdɪŋ] n. 滑翔伞运动

get about 移动

comparable ['kɒmpərəbl] adj. 相似的，类似的

in term of 就……而言

ill-suited [ɪl'suːtɪd] adj. 不适合的

commute [kə'mjuːt] v. 往返于两地之间

take off 起飞

Paragraph 3

close call 险象环生，死里逃生

inspection [ɪn'spekʃn] n. 检查

exhaust pipe 排烟管，排气管

harness ['hɑːnɪs] *n.* 固定装置

melt [melt] *v.* 熔化

put sb.off 阻止，使……失去兴趣，使……失去勇气

enthusiastic [ɪnˌθjuːzɪ'æstɪk] *adj.* 热情的

take up 开始从事，关注，对……产生兴趣

regret [rɪ'gret] *v.* 悔恨，后悔

pick up 购买

land [lænd] *v.* 着陆

scare [skeə(r)] *v.* 使惊恐，害怕

Paragraph 4

not in the same league as 不像……一样好

acrobatics [ˌækrə'bætɪks] *n.* 特技飞行

daredevil ['deədevl] *n.* 蛮勇的人，冒失鬼

skim [skɪm] *v.* 掠过

fountain ['faʊntən] *n.* 喷泉

grab [græb] *v.* 攥，握

Paragraph 5

cockpit ['kɒkpɪt] *n.* 驾驶舱

submarine [ˌsʌbmə'riːn] *n.* 潜水艇

Paragraph 6

soar [sɔː(r)] *v.* 急速上升

dive [daɪv] *v.* 俯冲

skydiver ['skaɪdaɪvə(r)] *n.* 跳伞运动员

monitor ['mɒnɪtə(r)] *v.* 检测

turbine ['tɜːbaɪn] *n.* 涡轮机

release [rɪ'liːs] *v.* 释放

float [fləʊt] *v.* 漂浮

unfold [ʌn'fəʊld] *v.* 展开，打开

composite ['kɒmpəzɪt] *n.* 混合物，合成物，复合材料

approach [ə'prəʊtʃ] *v.* 接触，接洽

specialise in 主营，专营

miniature ['mɪnətʃə(r)] *adj.* 微型的，小型的

rigid ['rɪdʒɪd] *adj.* 坚硬的，坚固的

aerodynamic ['eərəʊdaɪ'næmɪk] *adj.* 空气动力的

carbon ['kɑːbən] *n.* 炭

foldable [fəʊld'eɪbl] *adj.* 可折叠的

Paragraph 7

ambition [æm'bɪʃn] *n.* 抱负，夙愿

tension ['tenʃn] *n.* 紧张

narrowly ['nærəʊlɪ] *adv.* 一点，稍微

in short supply 供不应求

thoroughly ['θʌrəlɪ] *adv.* 完全地，彻底地

thrust [θrʌst] *n.* 推力

swing [swɪŋ] *v.* 摇摆，摇晃

fortunate ['fɔːtʃənət] *adj.* 幸运的

pastime ['pɑːstaɪm] *n.* 休闲，娱乐

exceed [ɪk'siːd] *v.* 超过，超越

真题考点词替换清单

题号	题目——原文
29	dangerous—scared, death
30	likes—enjoyed
31	military—the air force
32	first—initially
	firm—company
34	top speed—soaring
36	equipment—special wings
	enabling—managed to do
37	promote—advertise
39	mistake—regret
40	prevent—trouble, impossibility
	leaving the ground—taking off

Cambridge
IELTS
10

Test 1

Reading Passage 1: Stepwells

millennium [mɪˈleniəm] *n.* 一千年

fundamental [ˌfʌndəˈmentl] *adj.* 基本的，根本的

document [ˈdɒkjʊmənt] *v.* 用文件证明

spectacular [spekˈtækjələ(r)] *adj.* 壮观的，惊人的

monuments [ˈmɒnjʊmənts] *n.* 遗迹   era [ˈɪərə] *n.* 时代

bygone [ˈbaɪɡɒn] *adj.* 过去的

Paragraph 1

inhabitant [ɪnˈhæbɪtənt] *n.* 居民；居住者   access [ˈækses] *n.* 进入；使用权；通路

bathing [ˈbeɪðɪŋ] *n.* 沐浴；游泳   irrigation [ˌɪrɪˈɡeɪʃn] *n.* 灌溉

utilitarian [ˌjuːtɪlɪˈteəriən] *adj.* 功利的；实利的

application [ˌæplɪˈkeɪʃn] *n.* 应用；申请

Paragraph 2

architecturally [ˌɑːkɪˈtektʃərəlɪ] *adv.* 建筑上地；关于建筑地

complex [ˈkɒmpleks] *n.* 复合体；综合设施

dotted [ˈdɒtɪd] *adj.* 星罗棋布的；有点的

Paragraph 3

comprise [kəmˈpraɪz] *v.* 包含；由……组成

descending [dɪˈsendɪŋ] *v.* 下降

recede [rɪˈsiːd] *v.* 后退；减弱   negotiate [nɪˈɡəʊʃieɪt] *v.* 谈判，协商

Paragraph 4

sloping side 斜边

elaborate [ɪˈlæbərət] *v.* 精心制作；从简单成分合成

via [ˈvaɪə] *prep.* 渠道，通过；经由   pillar [ˈpɪlə(r)] *n.* 柱子；柱状物

pavilion [pə'vɪlɪən] *n.* 楼阁；大帐篷

sheltered ['ʃeltəd] *adj.* 受保护的；掩蔽的

relentless [rɪ'lentləs] *adj.* 残酷的；不间断的

intricate ['ɪntrɪkət] *adj.* 复杂的；错综的

decorative ['dekərətɪv] *adj.* 装饰性的；装潢用的

sculpture ['skʌlptʃə(r)] *n.* 雕塑   embellish [ɪm'belɪʃ] *v.* 修饰；装饰

churn [tʃɜːn] *v.* 搅拌

Paragraph 5

derelict ['derəlɪkt] *adj.* 玩忽职守的；无主的

Paragraph 6

undergo [ˌʌndə'gəʊ] *v.* 经历   restoration [ˌrestə'reɪʃn] *n.* 恢复；复位

Paragraph 7

silt [sɪlt] *v.* 使淤塞；充塞

pristine ['prɪstiːn] *adj.* 原始的，古时的；纯朴的

carve [kɑːv] *v.* 雕刻   niche [niːʃ] *n.* 壁龛

monument ['mɒnjʊmənt] *n.* 纪念碑；历史遗迹

Paragraph 8

reservoir ['rezəvwɑː(r)] *n.* 水库；蓄水池   hallmark ['hɔːlmɑːk] *n.* 印记

geometrical [ˌdʒiːə'metrɪkl] *adj.* 几何的   terrace ['terəs] *n.* 阶地；露台

intricately ['ɪntrɪkətlɪ] *adv.* 杂乱地   shrine [ʃraɪn] *n.* 圣祠

Paragraph 9

intricately ['ɪntrɪkətlɪ] *adv.* 杂乱地   commission [kə'mɪʃn] *v.* 委任

Paragraph 10

aesthetically [es'θetɪklɪ] *adv.* 审美地；美学观点上地

zigzag ['zɪgzæg] v. 成之字形   descend [dɪ'send] v. 下降

striking ['straɪkɪŋ] adj. 显著的，突出的   veranda [və'rændə] n. 游廊；走廊

ornate [ɔː'neɪt] adj. 华丽的；装饰的

Paragraph 11

colonnaded [ˌkɒlə'neɪdɪd] adj. 有柱廊的；有列柱的

Paragraph 12

medieval [ˌmedɪ'iːvl] adj. 原始的；仿中世纪的

preserving [prɪ'zɜːvɪŋ] n. 保留，保存   flock [flɒk] n. 群

far-flung [fɑː(r)flʌŋ] adj. 遥远的；广泛的；广布的

Gaza [gɑːzə] n. 加沙（地中海岸港市）

ingenuity [ˌɪndʒə'njuːətɪ] n. 独创性；精巧；精巧的装置

Question

storey ['stɔːrɪ] n. 楼层；叠架的一层

真题考点词替换清单

题号	题目——原文
1	all over the world—unique to this region 【反】
2	collection—gathering
2	a range of function—leisure, relaxation, worship
5	alter—high/low
6	part of—include
6	sheltered—shade
6	visitors—people
7	serious climate event—drought
8	nowadays—today
10	pattern—formation
11	looks like—resemble
12	provide—supported
12	view—overlook

🔺 *Reading Passage 2: EUROPEAN TRANSPORT SYSTEMS 1990—2010*

Paragraph A

conceive [kən'si:v] *v.* 构思；以为；持有

vigorous ['vɪgərəs] *adj.* 有力的；精力充沛的

facilitate [fə'sɪlɪteɪt] *v.* 促进；使便利；使更容易

teleworking ['telɪwɜ:kɪŋ] *n.* 电子办公；在家中上班

teleservice [tel's3:vɪs] *n.* 远程服务

substantial [səb'stænʃl] *adj.* 大量的；实质的

fleet [fli:t] *n.* 舰队

Paragraph B

internal frontiers 内部边界

abolish [ə'bɒlɪʃ] *v.* 彻底废除；摧毁

flow [fləʊ] *n.* 流动

emphasise ['emfəsaɪz] *v.* 强调；加强……的语气

labour intensive 劳动集约

assembly [ə'semblɪ] *n.* 装配；集会，集合

Paragraph C

haulage ['hɔ:lɪdʒ] *n.* 拖运；拖曳

inherit [ɪn'herɪt] *v.* 继承

tip [tɪp] *v.* 翻倒；倾覆

enlarged [ɪn'lɑ:dʒd] *adj.* 放大的；增大的；扩展的

Paragraph D

imperative [ɪm'perətɪv] *n.* 命令；需要；规则

sustainable development 可持续发展

Paragraph E

consumption [kən'sʌmpʃn] *n.* 消费；消耗

emission [ɪ'mɪʃn] *n.* 排放

reverse [rɪ'vɜːs] *v.* 扭转

sector ['sektə(r)] *n.* 部门

estimate ['estɪmət] *n.* 估计；预算

culprit ['kʌlprɪt] *n.* 罪魁祸首

Paragraph F

deterioration [dɪˌtɪərɪə'reɪʃn] *n.* 恶化；退化；堕落

Paragraph G

solely ['səʊllɪ] *adv.* 单独地，唯一地

complementary [ˌkɒmplɪ'mentrɪ] *adj.* 补足的，补充的

curb [kɜːb] *v.* 控制；勒住

revitalise [ˌriː'vaɪtəlaɪz] *v.* 使有新的活力

ratio ['reɪʃɪəʊ] *n.* 比率，比例

occupancy rate 租用率

baton ['bætɒn] *n.* 指挥棒；接力棒

Paragraph H

efficiency [ɪ'fɪʃnsɪ] *n.* 效率；效能

regional cohesion 区域凝聚力

saturated arteries 饱和动脉

logistics [lə'dʒɪstɪks] *n.* 后勤；物流

uncoupling [ˌʌn'kʌplɪŋ] *n.* 解偶联

Paragraph I

comprise [kəm'praɪz] *v.* 包含；由……组成

integrated ['ɪntɪɡreɪtɪd] *adj.* 综合的；完整的；互相协调的

Questions

escalate ['eskəleɪt] *v.* 逐步上升

restricting [rɪs'trɪktɪŋ] *n.* 整形，限制

rebalance [rɪ'bæləns] *n.* 再平衡；调整

prohibitively [prə'hɪbətɪvlɪ] *adv.* 过高地

真题考点词替换清单

题号	题目——原文
14	rapid—spectacular
	passenger—private
15	distances—hundreds or even thousands of kilometers away from
16	awaiting—candidate for entry
17	fresh and important—new imperatives
	long-term—sustainable
19	charging—pricing
	alone—solely
	policies—approach
	restricting—curb
20	improving—increase
21	all the step—a series of
	change—alternative
	patterns—modes
22	need—requirement
	growing—increase
	despite—although
23	closer to—hundreds or even thousands of kilometers away from 【反】
26	predicted—expected

🔺 *Reading Passage 3: The psychology of innovation*

Paragraph 1

innovation [ˌɪnə'veɪʃn] *n.* 创新，革新；新方法

stimulate ['stɪmjʊleɪt] *v.* 鼓舞，激励

Paragraph 2

recruitment [rɪ'kruːtmənt] *n.* 招聘

Paragraph 3

jam [dʒæm] *v.* 拥挤

quintet [kwɪn'tet] *n.* 五重奏

fuse [fjuːz] *v.* 混合

instinctively [ɪn'stɪŋktɪvlɪ] *adv.* 本能地

Paragraph 4

hard-wired [hɑːd'waɪəd] *adj.* 硬连线的，硬接线的

counter-intuitive ['kaʊntə(r)ɪn'tjuːɪtɪv] *adj.* 反直觉的；违反语感的

seize [siːz] *v.* 抓住；夺取

invariably [ɪn'veərɪəblɪ] *adv.* 总是；不变地；一定地

Paragraph 5

delicate ['delɪkət] *adj.* 微妙的；精美的

collaborative [kə'læbərətɪv] *adj.* 合作的，协作的

Paragraph 6

syndrome ['sɪndrəʊm] *n.* 综合征；综合症状

array [ə'reɪ] *n.* 数组；大批

rival ['raɪvl] *n.* 对手；竞争者

stun [stʌn] *v.* 使震惊；给以深刻的印象

pursuing [pə'sjuːɪŋ] *n.* 追逐；追赶

sought [sɔːt] *v.* 寻找

Paragraph 7

tap into 挖掘；接进

resisted [rɪ'zɪstɪd] *adj.* 受到抵抗的

veteran ['vetərən] *n.* 老手；富有经验的人

advocate ['ædvəkeɪt] *v.* 提倡，主张，拥护

Paragraph 8

visualizing ['vɪʒʊəlaɪzɪŋ] *n.* 肉眼观察

prototyping [prəʊtə'taɪpɪŋ] *n.* 样机研究；原型设计

deepen ['diːpən] *v.* 使加深；使强烈

Paragraph 9

inhibit [ɪn'hɪbɪt] *v.* 抑制；禁止

regrettable [rɪ'gretəbl] *adj.* 令人遗憾的；可惜的

opt out 决定退出；插播

passivity [pæ'sɪvətɪ] *n.* 被动性；被动结构；无抵抗

overbearing [ˌəʊvə'beərɪŋ] *adj.* 傲慢的；压倒一切的

Paragraph 10

scale [skeɪl] *n.* 规模；比例

interchange ['ɪntətʃeɪndʒ] *n.* 互换；交换

revolutionized [ˌrevə'luːʃənaɪzd] *adj.* 革命化的；被彻底改革的

Paragraph 11

simultaneously [ˌsɪml'teɪnɪəslɪ] *adv.* 同时地

Questions

concise [kən'saɪs] *adj.* 简明的，简洁的

loyalty ['lɔɪəltɪ] *n.* 忠诚；忠心

dominant boss 占主导地位的老板

真题考点词替换清单

题号	题目——原文
27	share—understand, believe in
28	conscious—aware
29	strengthen—deepen
	commitment—engagement
30	valued—be given full attention
31	remain—still at the company

题号	题目——原文
32	avoid risk—play it safe
33	chance—gambles
34	dominant—overbearing
	ignore—deadly passivity
35	share—interchange
37	most people—every individual
40	manager—boss
	approval—speech
	persuasive—powerful
	colleague—peer

Test 2

🔺 *Reading Passage 1: Tea and the Industrial Revolution*

Paragraph A

anthropological [ˌænθrəpə'lɒdʒɪkl] *adj.* 人类学的；人类学上的

wrestling ['reslɪŋ] *n.* 摔跤；扭斗　　　enigma [ɪ'nɪgmə] *n.* 谜

Paragraph B

affluent ['æflʊənt] *adj.* 富裕的；丰富的

mass-produced [mæsprə'djuːst] *adj.* 大量生产的，大批生产的

market-driven economy 市场经济　　　criteria [kraɪ'tɪərɪə] *n.* 标准，条件

industrialising [ɪn'dʌstrɪəlaɪzɪŋ] *n.* 工业化　　　sufficient [sə'fɪʃnt] *adj.* 足够的；充分的

Paragraph C

cupboard ['kʌbəd] *n.* 碗柜；食橱

antiseptic [ˌæntɪ'septɪk] *adj.* 防腐的，抗菌的；非常整洁的

tannin ['tænɪn] *n.* 丹宁酸；鞣酸

ingredient [ɪnˈɡriːdɪənt] *n.* 原料；要素；组成部分

flourish [ˈflʌrɪʃ] *v.* 繁荣，兴旺；茂盛；活跃

dysentery [ˈdɪsəntrɪ] *n.* 痢疾

deduction [dɪˈdʌkʃn] *n.* 扣除，减除；推论；减除额

scepticism [ˈskeptɪsɪzəm] *n.* 怀疑；怀疑论；怀疑主义

wary [ˈweərɪ] *adj.* 谨慎的；机警的；唯恐的；考虑周到的

favourable [ˈfeɪvərəbl] *adj.* 有利的；赞成的；令人满意的

appraisal [əˈpreɪzl] *n.* 评价；估价（尤指估价财产，以便征税）；估计

Paragraph D

alight [əˈlaɪt] *v.* 下来；飞落

burst [bɜːst] *n.* 爆发，突发；爆炸

infant [ˈɪnfənt] *n.* 婴儿；幼儿；未成年人

halve [hɑːv] *v.* 对半分开；均分；把……减半

reduction [rɪˈdʌkʃn] *n.* 减少；下降；缩小

Paragraph E

reveal [rɪˈviːl] *v.* 透露；显露；揭秘

water-borne disease 水传疾病

deduce [dɪˈdjuːs] *v.* 推理

malt [mɔːlt] *n.* 麦芽

Paragraph F

sanitation [ˌsænɪˈteɪʃn] *n.* 环境卫生；卫生设备；下水道设施

grip [ɡrɪp] *n.* 紧握；柄；支配；握拍方式；拍柄绷带

prevalence [ˈprevələns] *n.* 流行；普遍；广泛

coincidence [kəʊˈɪnsɪdəns] *n.* 巧合；一致；同时发生

relatively ['relətɪvlɪ] *adv.* 相当地；相对地，比较地

clipper ['klɪpə(r)] *n.* 快速帆船；大剪刀；剪削者；理发剪

dip [dɪp] *v.* 蘸

purifying ['pjʊərɪfaɪŋ] *n.* 净化；精制

Paragraph G

combination lock 暗码锁；号码锁

forge [fɔːdʒ] *v.* 锻造

tea-soaked [tiːsəʊkt] *adj.* 用茶浸泡后的

literacy ['lɪtərəsɪ] *n.* 读写能力；精通文学

essence ['esns] *n.* 本质，实质；精华；香精

abandoned [ə'bændənd] *adj.* 被抛弃的；无约束的

Question

comparison [kəm'pærɪsn] *n.* 比较；类似

真题考点词替换清单

题号	题目——原文
1	time—18th century
	place—in Britain
2	conditions—factors
	required—need
	industrialisation—the revolution
3	two keys—tea and beer
4	increase—burst/ growth
6	comparisons with Japan—looked to Japan
7	unemployment—give up/ out of work
9	without succumbing—prevent
10	disagree—strengthened by support 【反】
11	after—then
	reduction—burst/ growth 【反】
13	mortality—death

⬆ *Reading Passage 2: Gifted children and learning*

Paragraph A

provision [prə'vɪʒn] *n.* 规定；条款；准备

interaction [ɪn'tɜ:(r)'ækʃn] *n.* 相互作用；互动

decidedly [dɪ'saɪdɪdlɪ] *adv.* 果断地；断然地；明显；毫无疑问

age-norm [eɪdʒnɔ:m] *n.* 年龄常模

manipulate [mə'nɪpjʊleɪt] *v.* 操纵；操作；巧妙地处理；篡改

predict creativity 预测创造力

Paragraph B

emerge [ɪ'mɜ:dʒ] *v.* 浮现；摆脱；暴露

qualitative ['kwɒlɪtətɪv] *adj.* 定性的；质的，性质上的

compensate ['kɒmpenseɪt] *v.* 补偿；付报酬

self-regulation [self,regjʊ'leɪʃn] *n.* 自动调节

metacognition [me'tækɔ:gnɪʃən] *n.* 元认知；后设认知

monitoring ['mɒnɪtə(r)ɪŋ] *n.* 监视，监控；检验，检查

evaluation [ɪ,væljʊ'eɪʃn] *n.* 评价；[审计]评估；估价；求值

Paragraph C

demonstrate ['demənstreɪt] *v.* 证明；示威

succinctly [sək'sɪŋktlɪ] *adv.* 简洁地；简便地

merely ['mɪəlɪ] *adv.* 仅仅，只不过；只是

Paragraph D

diminish [dɪ'mɪnɪʃ] *v.* 使减少；使变小　　　autonomy [ɔ:'tɒnəmɪ] *n.* 自治，自治权

spoon-feeding [spuːn'fiːdɪŋ] v. 用匙喂；溺爱；填鸭式教育

initiate [ɪ'nɪʃɪeɪt] v. 开始，发起

deprived [dɪ'praɪvd] adj. 缺少食物的；缺乏足够教育的

Paragraph E

vital ['vaɪtl] adj. 至关重要的；生死攸关的；有活力的

domain [də'meɪn] n. 领域；域名；产业；地产

expertise [ˌekspɜː'tiːz] n. 专门知识；专门技术；专家的意见

Paragraph F

facilitate [fə'sɪlɪteɪt] v. 促进；帮助；使容易

harness ['hɑːnɪs] v. 利用

Questions

accurate ['ækjərət] adj. 精确的

self-reliance [selfrɪ'laɪəns] n. 自力更生，依靠自己；自恃

真题考点词替换清单

题号	题目——原文
14	domestic——home
15	too much guidance——overdirect
16	anxiety——negative emotions
17	favour——useful
	social-disadvantaged children——children from deprived areas
18	accurate——fewer errors
	produce——make
	less time——shorten
	exercises——the practice

题号	题目——原文
19	self-reliance—independent
	goal—highest levels of expertise
20	channel their feelings—emotional forces
	assist—improve…efficiently
21	close relatives—close relationship
	benefits—positive
	support—provision
22	really successful—outstanding performance
	individuals—students
	learnt—know
	a considerable amount—a great deal
	their subject—specific domain
23	strong—close
	connection—relationship
	availability—backup
24	do not have—lack of
25	involves—include
26	rely on—have a tendency to

Reading Passage 3: Museums of fine art and their public

Paragraph 1

reproductions [ˌriːprə'dʌkʃns] *n.* 复制品

Paragraph 2

manuscript ['mænjʊskrɪpt] *n.* 手稿；原稿

precisely [prɪ'saɪslɪ] *adv.* 精确地；恰恰   interpreting [ɪn'tɜːprɪtɪŋ] *n.* 解释；口译

medium ['miːdɪəm] *n.* 方法；媒体；媒介；中间物

signify ['sɪɡnɪfaɪ] *v.* 表示；意味

Paragraph 3

facsimile [fæk'sɪmɪlɪ] *n.* 复印本

workshop apprentices 车间学徒

incomparably [ɪnˈkɒmprəblɪ] *adv.* 无比地；无敌地

scale [skeɪl] *n.* 规模；比例　　　　duplication [ˌdjuːplɪˈkeɪʃn] *n.* 复制；副本

Paragraph 4

implicit [ɪmˈplɪsɪt] *adj.* 含蓄的；暗示的；盲从的

recognition [ˌrekəɡˈnɪʃn] *n.* 识别；承认，认出；重视；赞誉；公认

Paragraph 5

severe limitation 严重缺陷

Paragraph 6

repository [rɪˈpɒzətrɪ] *n.* 贮藏室，仓库；知识库；智囊团

reinforce [ˌriːɪnˈfɔːs] *n.* 加固；加强

numerous [ˈnjuːmərəs] *adj.* 许多的，很多的

possess [pəˈzes] *v.* 控制；使掌握；持有；迷住；拥有，具备

status [ˈsteɪtəs] *n.* 地位；状态；情形；重要身份

Paragraph 7

monetary [ˈmʌnɪtrɪ] *adj.* 货币的；财政的

evidently [ˈevɪdəntlɪ] *adv.* 显然，明显地；清楚地

deter [dɪˈtɜː(r)] *v.* 制止，阻止；使打消念头

spontaneous [spɒnˈteɪnɪəs] *adj.* 自发的；自然的；无意识的

immediate [ɪˈmiːdɪət] *adj.* 立即的；直接的；最接近的

self-reliant [selfrɪˈlaɪənt] *adj.* 自力更生的；自恃的

Paragraph 8

be struck by ……所感动，被……所触动，被……打动

sheer [ʃɪə(r)] *n.* 偏航；透明薄织物

realistically [ˌriːə'lɪstɪklɪ] *adv.* 现实地；实际地；逼真地

Paragraph 9

distressing [dɪ'stresɪŋ] *adj.* 使痛苦的；悲伤的；使烦恼的

prescribed [prɪ'skraɪbd] *adj.* 规定的　　encounter [ɪn'kaʊntə(r)] *v.* 邂逅

superficially [ˌsjuːpə'fɪʃəlɪ] *adv.* 表面地；浅薄地

Paragraph 10

critical ['krɪtɪkl] *adj.* 鉴定的；批评的，爱挑剔的；危险的；决定性的；评论的

authentic [ɔː'θentɪk] *adj.* 真正的，真实的；可信的

participatory [paːˌtɪsɪ'peɪtərɪ] *adj.* 供人分享的；吸引参与的

abundance [ə'bʌndəns] *n.* 充裕，丰富

Paragraph 11

render ['rendə(r)] *v.* 提出；描绘；放弃；报答；归还；宣布

permanently ['pɜːmənəntlɪ] *adv.* 永久地，长期不变地

high-fidelity [haɪfɪ'delətɪ] *n.* 高保真；高保真度

awe [ɔː] *n.* 敬畏

establishment [ɪ'stæblɪʃmənt] *n.* 确立，制定；公司；设施

Questions

instruct [ɪn'strʌkt] *v.* 指导；通知；命令；教授

replication [ˌreplɪ'keɪʃn] *n.* 复制；回答；反响

regrettable [rɪ'gretəbl] *adj.* 令人遗憾的；可惜的；可悲的；抱歉的

superiority [suːˌpɪərɪ'ɒrətɪ] *n.* 优越，优势；优越性

underlying ideas 基本的想法

large-scale [lɑːdʒskeɪl] *adj.* 大规模的，大范围的；大比例尺的

真题考点词替换清单

题号	题目——原文
27&28	not—rather than
29&30	however—yet
	in historical times—in the 16th century
	instruct—assign
31	this may not be—unfortunately/ this seem to
33	be willing to—be deterred from 【反】
35	unlike—difference; specific—prescribed time
37	conflict—perfect harmony 【反】
38	encourage—give the confidence; opinions openly—express their views
39	high quality—high-fidelity
40	are likely to—may be

Test 3

🔺 *Reading Passage 1: The Context, Meaning and Scope of Tourism*

Paragraph A

primitive ['prɪmətɪv] *adj.* 原始的，远古的；简单的，粗糙的

aristocrat ['ærɪstəkræt] *n.* 贵族   resort [rɪ'zɔːt] *n.* 度假村；度假胜地

Paragraph B

advent ['ædvənt] *n.* 到来；出现；基督降临；基督降临节

subsequent ['sʌbsɪkwənt] *adj.* 后来的，随后的

Paragraph C

segment ['segmənt] *n.* 片段；段数   gross national product 国民生产总值

profound [prə'faʊnd] *adj.* 深厚的；意义深远的；渊博的

Paragraph D

obscure [əb'skjʊə(r)] *v.* 掩盖；使含混；变得模糊

fragmentation [ˌfrægmen'teɪʃn] *n.* 破碎；分裂

enterprise ['entəpraɪz] *n.* 企业

underestimate [ˌʌndər'estɪmeɪt] *v.* 低估；看轻

amorphous [ə'mɔːfəs] *adj.* 无定型的；无组织的

Paragraph E

institutional [ˌɪnstɪ'tjuːʃənl] *adj.* 制度的；制度上的

commodity [kə'mɒdəti] *n.* 商品，货物；日用品

rank [ræŋk] *v.* 把……排列起来   quote [kwəʊt] *v.* 引用，引证

statistical [stə'tɪstɪkl] *adj.* 统计的；统计学的

precise [prɪ'saɪs] *adj.* 精确的；明确的；严格的

Questions

mass tourism 大众旅游   promote recreation 促进娱乐

ascertain [ˌæsə'teɪn] *v.* 确定；查明；探知

真题考点词替换清单

题号	题目——原文
3	difficulty in recognising—hidden/obscured
	effects—impact
5	figures—measure
8	significant—difficult to ascertain—hidden/obscured

题号	题目——原文
10	affects—impact
	individual—domestic
	not possible—easy【反】
11	most important—the major
12	major—number one
13	reflected—similar

⬆ *Reading Passage 2: Autumn leaves*

Paragraph A

captivating ['kæptɪveɪtɪŋ] *adj.* 迷人的；有魅力的

magnificent [mæg'nɪfɪsnt] *adj.* 高尚的；壮丽的；华丽的；宏伟的

Paragraph B

convert [kən'vɜːt] *v.* 使转变；转换　　　　hemisphere ['hemɪsfɪə(r)] *n.* 半球

decline [dɪ'klaɪn] *v.* 下降

considerably [kən'sɪdərəblɪ] *adv.* 相当地；非常地

evergreen conifers 常绿针叶树

redundant [rɪ'dʌndənt] *adj.* 多余的，过剩的

discard [dɪs'kaːd] *v.* 丢弃　　　　dismantle [dɪs'mæntl] *v.* 拆除；取消

twig [twɪg] *v.* 细枝

deplete [dɪ'plɪt] *v.* 使减少；弄空；耗尽……的资源

dominate ['dɒmɪneɪt] *v.* 控制，支配

unmasking [ˌʌn'maːskɪŋ] *v.* 脱去假面具；暴露

sumac ['ʃuːmæk] *n.* 漆树；漆树木料

Paragraph C

anthocyanin [ˌænθəˈsaɪənɪn] *n.* 花青素

water-soluble [ˈwɔːtə(r)ˈsɒljəbl] *adj.* 可溶于水的

pigment [ˈpɪgmənt] *n.* 色素   visible spectrum 可见光谱

compound [ˈkɒmpaʊnd] *n.* 混合物，化合物

flavonoid [fˈleɪvənɔɪd] *n.* 类黄酮   scrambling [ˈskræmblɪŋ] *v.* 争夺

Paragraph D

fungi [ˈfʌŋgiː] *n.* 真菌   anti-fungal [ˈæntɪˈfʌŋgl] *n.* 抗真菌

anti-herbivore [ˈæntɪˈhɜːbɪvɔː(r)] *n.* 抗食草动物

Paragraph E

vivid [ˈvɪvɪd] *adj.* 鲜艳的   robust [rəʊˈbʌst] *adj.* 强健的；健康的

mount [maʊnt] *v.* 挂载   defence [dɪˈfens] *n.* 防御

infestation [ˌɪnfeˈsteɪʃn] *n.* 感染；侵扰   resistant [rɪˈzɪstənt] *adj.* 抵抗的，反抗的

intensity [ɪnˈtensətɪ] *n.* 强度

Paragraph F

plausible [ˈplɔːzəbl] *adj.* 似合理的   hypothesis [haɪˈpɒθəsɪs] *n.* 假设

paradoxical [ˌpærəˈdɒksɪkl] *adj.* 矛盾的；诡论的

salvage [ˈsælvɪdʒ] *v.* 抢救

Paragraph G

exquisitely [ɪkˈskwɪzɪtlɪ] *adv.* 精致地；精巧地；敏锐地

nutrient deficiency 养分缺乏   acute [əˈkjuːt] *adj.* 严重的

dismantling [dɪsˈmæntlɪŋ] *v.* 拆除   unstable [ʌnˈsteɪbl] *adj.* 不稳定的

intact [ɪnˈtækt] *adj.* 完整的；原封不动的；未受损伤的

destructive [dɪˈstrʌktɪv] *adj.* 破坏的；毁灭性的

Paragraph H

susceptible [sə'septəbl] *adj.* 易受影响的　　excess [ɪk'ses] *adj.* 过量的

Paragraph I

disposal [dɪ'spəʊzl] *n.* 处理；支配；清理；安排

overexposure [ˌəʊvərɪk'spəʊʒə(r)] *n.* 感光过度

真题考点词替换清单

题号	题目——原文
14	responsible for—be created by
15	drop their leaves—discards them
	autumn—fall
16	some evidence—clues
18	serve—to convince
	warning signal—advertisements
19	facing—get
20	surfaces of leaves—side of the leaf
21	abundant—intense
22	increase—redder
	go further—the more
23	help to protect sth.—increase one's tolerance
25	sunlight—sunny

🔺 *Reading Passage 3: Beyond the blue horizon*

Paragraph 1

seafaring ['siːfeərɪŋ] *adj.* 航海的

derelict ['derəlɪkt] *adj.* 被抛弃了的，废弃的

burial ['berɪəl] *adj.* 埋葬的

harbor ['hɑːbə] *n.* 海港；海湾；避难所；躲藏处

Paragraph 2

daring ['deərɪŋ] *adj.* 大胆的，勇敢的

livestock ['laɪvstɒk] *n.* 牲畜；家畜

taro seedling 芋头苗

jungle-clad ['dʒʌŋglklæd] *n.* 丛林密布

coral ['kɒrəl] *n.* 珊瑚

outlier [aʊt'laɪə] *n.* 离群值

Paragraph 3

urn [ɜːn] *n.* 坟墓；骨灰瓮

modeled birds 模仿鸟

rim [rɪm] *n.* 边，边缘

peering down 俯身

sealed [siːld] *adj.* 密封的；未知的

conclusively [kən'kluːsɪvlɪ] *adv.* 最后地；决定性地

Paragraph 4

teased from 嘲笑的

spring from 起源于，发源（于）……；来自……

outward ['aʊtwəd] *adj.* 向外的

descendant [dɪ'sendənt] *n.* 后裔；子孙

Paragraph 5

equivalent [ɪ'kwɪvələnt] *adj.* 等价的，相等的；同意义的

rigging ['rɪgɪŋ] *n.* 索具；装备，传动装置

Paragraph 6

voyage ['vɔɪɪdʒ] *n.* 航行

launch out 出航

Paragraph 7

thrust [θrʌst] *n.* 推力

eastward ['iːstwəd] *adv.* 向东

prevailing [prɪ'veɪlɪŋ] *adj.* 流行的；主流的

headwind [hed'waɪnd] *n.* 逆风；顶头风

seafarer ['siːfeərə(r)] *n.* 船员　　　　　tide [taɪd] *n.* 潮汐

indicate ['ɪndɪkeɪt] *v.* 表明；指示，显示

Paragraph 8

eternity [ɪ'tɜːnətɪ] *n.* 来世，来生；不朽；永世

trend [trend] *n.* 趋势

Paragraph 9

presuppose [ˌpriːsə'pəʊz] *v.* 假定；预料；以……为先决条件

Paragraph 10

scatter ['skætə(r)] *v.* 分散　　　　　coral ['kɒrəl] *n.* 珊瑚

Paragraph 11

quits [kwɪts] *adj.* 对等的；两相抵消的　　vast emptiness 空荡荡

encounter [ɪn'kaʊntə(r)ː] *v.* 遇到；曾遭遇

Questions

colonise ['kɒlənaɪz] *v.* 在……开拓殖民地；移于殖民地

excavation [ˌekskə'veɪʃn] *n.* 挖掘，发掘　　not relied upon 不足为凭

withstand [wɪð'stænd] *v.* 抵挡，经得起

navigational [ˌnævɪ'geɪʃnəl] *adj.* 航行的，航运的

relatively ['relətɪvlɪ] *adv.* 相当地；相对地，比较地

habitable ['hæbɪtəbl] *adj.* 可居住的；适于居住的

prevailing [prɪ'veɪlɪŋ] *adj.* 流行的；盛行很广的

真题考点词替换清单

题号	题目——原文
27&28	3000-year-old—ancient/some 30 years old
	found—revealed traces of
	abandoned—derelict
	significant—important
29	took—carried
30&31	found—uncovered
32	little information—no-one has found
34	be able to—could
35	navigational aid—a safety net
36	could—against【反】
37	played a role in—helped
39	halt—quits
	expansion—spread

Test 4

🔺 *Reading Passage 1: The megafires of California*

megafires ['megə'faɪə(r)s] *n.* 特大火灾　　tinder ['tɪndə(r)] *n.* 易燃物

Paragraph 1

menace ['menəs] *n.* 威胁　　　　　　squad [skwɒd] *n.* 小队；小组

battling ['bætlɪŋ] *n.* 斗争　　　　　　blaze [bleɪz] *n.* 火焰；地狱

preparedness [prɪ'peərɪdnəs] *n.* 有准备；已准备

fan [fæn] *v.* 煽动；刺激

Paragraph 2

siege [siːdʒ] *n.* 围攻

Paragraph 3

precipitation [prɪˌsɪpɪ'teɪʃn] *n.* 降水；沉淀

unintentional [ˌʌnɪn'tenʃənl] *adj.* 非故意的；无意识的

halt [hɔːlt] *v.* 使停止

eradication [ɪˌrædɪ'keɪʃn] *n.* 消灭，扑灭；根除

underbrush ['ʌndəbrʌʃ] *n.* 林下灌木丛；矮树丛

Paragraph 4

wooded areas 树木繁茂的地区

Paragraph 5

fire-prone ecosystems 易燃的生态系统　　adjunct ['ædʒʌŋkt] *adj.* 兼任的

Paragraph 6

residential [ˌrezɪ'denʃl] *adj.* 住宅的

Paragraph 7

scorch [skɔːtʃ] *v.* 使烧焦　　　　　　　sting [stɪŋ] *v.* 刺

bungling ['bʌŋglɪŋ] *n.* 拙劣的工作

peculiar [pɪ'kjuːlɪə(r)] *adj.* 特殊的；独特的；奇怪的；罕见的

Paragraph 8

dilapidated [dɪ'læpɪdeɪtɪd] *adj.* 荒废的，要塌似的；破坏的

insufficient blueprints 不足的蓝图　　　praising [preɪzɪŋ] *n.* 赞美；溢美之词

proactive [ˌprəʊ'æktɪv] *adj.* 先行一步的；积极主动的

budgetary ['bʌdʒɪtəri] *adj.* 预算的

infrastructure ['ɪnfrəstrʌktʃə(r)] *n.* 基础设施；公共建设；下部构造

Paragraph 9

traverse [trə'vɜːs] *v.* 穿过；反对；遍历

mammoth ['mæməθ] *adj.* 巨大的，庞大的

serpentine ['sɜːpəntaɪn] *adj.* 蜿蜒的；阴险的；弯弯曲曲的

jurisdiction [ˌdʒʊərɪs'dɪkʃn] *n.* 司法管辖区；行政辖区

mutual-aid ['mjuːtʃʊəleɪd] *n.* 互济

adequately ['ædɪkwətlɪ] *adv.* 充分地；足够地；适当地

revamped [ˌriː'væmpt] *adj.* 修订的；修补的

procedure [prə'siːdʒə(r)] *n.* 程序；规程

coordination [kəʊˌɔːdɪ'neɪʃn] *n.* 协调，调和

Paragraph 10

evacuation [ɪˌvækjʊ'eɪʃn] *n.* 疏散；撤离；排泄

procurement [prə'kjʊəmənt] *n.* 采购；获得，取得

endure [ɪn'djʊə(r)] *v.* 忍耐

Questions

characteristic [ˌkærəktə'rɪstɪk] *n.* 特性，特征；特色；特质

occurrence [ə'kʌrəns] *n.* 发生；出现；事件；发现

vulnerable ['vʌlnərəbl] *adj.* 易受攻击的，易受……的攻击；易受伤害的；有
弱点的

diminish [dɪ'mɪnɪʃ] *v.* 减少；削弱

mishandling [ˌmɪs'hændlɪŋ] *n.* 违反运行规程；不正确运转

containment [kən'teɪmmənt] *n.* 抑制，遏制

capacity [kə'pæsətɪ] *n.* 能力

真题考点词替换清单

题号	题目——原文
1	unpredictably—erratically
2	two decades ago—20 years ago
3	rainfall—precipitation
	average—normal
4	today—now
	the primary…for—sth. to act as…
5	extended—longer than
6	vulnerable place—on the side of active volcano
8	in reading—in state history
	fight fires—on preparedness
9	mishandling—bungling
10	firefighting tools—sth. to fight fires
12	work together—coordination
	disapprove—dedication/coordination/greater efficiency【反】
13	notwithstanding—despite
	continue—no longer【反】

🔺 *Reading Passage 2: Second nature*

Paragraph A

trait [treɪt] *n.* 特性，特质

habitual [həˈbɪtʃʊəl] *adj.* 习惯的；惯常的；习以为常的

Paragraph B

cite [saɪt] *v.* 援引；引用　　　　inherently [ɪnˈhɪərəntlɪ] *adv.* 天性地

introverted [ˈɪntrəvɜːtɪd] *adj.* 内向的　　reticence [ˈretɪsns] *n.* 沉默寡言

disastrous [dɪˈzɑːstrəs] *adj.* 灾难性的；损失惨重的；悲伤的

extroverted [ˈekstrəvɜːtɪd] *adj.* 性格外向的；外向性的；喜社交的

Paragraph C

rehabilitation [ˌriːəˌbɪlɪ'teɪʃn] *n.* 复原

Paragraph D

cultivate ['kʌltɪveɪt] *v.* 培养

Paragraph E

pursuit [pə'sjuːt] *n.* 追赶，追求   freediving [friː'daɪvɪŋ] *n.* 自由潜水

plunge [plʌndʒ] *v.* 使陷入

stamina ['stæmɪnə] *n.* 毅力；精力；活力；持久力

untangle [ˌʌn'tæŋgl] *v.* 解开……纠结

Paragraph G

compatible [kəm'pætəbl] *adj.* 兼容的；能共处的；可并立的

cerebrospinal [ˌserɪbrəʊ'spaɪnəl] *adj.* [解剖] 脑脊髓的

nourish ['nʌrɪʃ] *v.* 滋养；怀有；使健壮

Paragraph H

executive [ɪg'zekjətɪv] *n.* 总经理；执行者；经理主管人员

ethically ['eθɪklɪ] *adv.* 伦理上   intimidating [ɪn'tɪmɪdeɪtɪŋ] *adj.* 吓人的

mitigate ['mɪtɪgeɪt] *v.* 使缓和，使减轻

allegation [ˌælə'geɪʃn] *n.* 主张，断言；辩解

Questions

rational ['ræʃnəl] *adj.* 理性的

真题考点词替换清单

题号	题目——原文
14 — 15	traditional believed—long hold
	impossible—cannot
	fixed—determined
17	necessary—requires
	learn—mastering
	a wide variety of—a range of
	different—diverse
18	understand and feel—open to experiencing
	increase—more
	happiness—joy and passion
19	they do not know much—your own ignorance
	first trying—newcomer
20	good things—favourable outcomes
21	learned—acquire
	responsibility—obligation
22	shyness—inherently introverted/reticence
23	physical goals—untangle her fear
26	risk—security would be threatened

Reading Passage 3: When evolution runs backwards

Paragraph 1

throwback ['θrəʊbæk] *n.* 返祖

reluctant [rɪ'lʌktənt] *adj.* 不情愿的；勉强的；顽抗的

march [mɑːtʃ] *n.* 行进，前进

Paragraph 2

atavism ['ætəvɪzəm] *n.* 返祖现象；隔代遗传

primitive ['prɪmətɪv] *adj.* 原始的，远古的

sub-human [ˌsʌb'hjuːmən] *n.* 非人性

Paragraph 3

irreversible [ˌɪrɪ'vɜːsəbl] *adj.* 不可逆的；不能取消的；不能翻转的

probability [ˌprɒbə'bɪlətɪ] *n.* 概率；可能性

irreversibility ['ɪrɪˌvɜːsə'bɪlɪtɪ] *n.* 不可逆性；不可改变性

Paragraph 4

cropping up 突然出现

humpback ['hʌmpbæk] *n.* 驼背；座头鲸

appendage [ə'pendɪdʒ] *n.* 附加物

Paragraph 5

reverse [rɪ'vɜːs] *n.* 倒退　　　　　reappear [ˌriːə'pɪə(r)] *v.* 再出现

Paragraph 6

mutation [mjuː'teɪʃn] *n.* 突变；变化　　reason ['riːzn] *v.* 说服；推断

rendering ['rendərɪŋ] *n.* 呈现

Paragraph 7

salamander ['sæləmændə(r)] *n.* 蝾螈　　amphibian [æm'fɪbɪən] *n.* 两栖动物

tadpole ['tædpəʊl] *n.* 蝌蚪

metamorphose [ˌmetə'mɔːfəʊz] *v.* 变质；变形；使变成

axolotl ['æksə'lɒtl] *n.* 蝾螈　　　　lineage ['lɪnɪɪdʒ] *n.* 血统

time frame 时间框架；时间范围

Paragraph 8

minuscule ['mɪnəskjuːl] *adj.* 极小的　　hind [haɪnd] *adj.* 后部的

differ ['dɪfə(r)] *v.* 相异；意见分歧；不同

digit ['dɪdʒɪt] *n.* 位数

Paragraph 9

dorsal ['dɔːsl] *adj.* 背部的；背的，背侧的

intriguing [ɪn'triːgɪŋ] *adj.* 有趣的；迷人的

Paragraph 10

timescale ['taɪmskeɪl] *n.* 时标；时间尺度　　　embryo ['embrɪəʊ] *n.* 胚胎；晶胚

ancestral feature 祖先的特征　　　sprout hind 发芽后

Questions

exemplify [ɪg'zemplɪfaɪ] *v.* 例证；例示

extensive [ɪk'stensɪv] *adj.* 广泛的；大量的；广阔的

assertion [ə'sɜːʃn] *n.* 断言，声明；主张，要求；坚持

真题考点词替换清单

题号	题目——原文
29	re-emergence—reappear
	certain—long-lost
	traits—certain characteristics
30	correct—fits with
32	rejected—have been reluctant
	possibility—controversial
33	criminals—convictions
34	traits—characteristics
	disappeared millions of years ago—long lost
35	particular feature—similar structures
	different—unrelated
36	existence—survived
39	long-lost traits—ancestral features
	rare—many species【反】
40	evolutionary throwbacks—silent genes degrade

General Training: Reading and Writing
Test A

♠ Section 1

Smoke alarms in the home

presence ['prezns] *n.* 存在；出席；参加；风度；仪态

emit [ɪ'mɪt] *v.* 发出，放射；发行；发表

ionization ['aɪənaɪzeɪʃən] *n.* 离子化　　fiercely [fɪəslɪ] *adv.* 猛烈地；厉害地

thick [θɪk] *adj.* 厚的；浓的

photoelectric [ˌfəʊtəʊɪ'lektrɪk] *adj.* 光电的

installation [ˌɪnstə'leɪʃn] *n.* 安装，装置；就职

sensitivity [ˌsensə'tɪvətɪ] *n.* 敏感；敏感性；过敏

真题考点词替换清单

题号	题目——原文
1	must—required
	new—recently
2	cost less—the cheapest
4	must—require/need
	fitted—installed
	specialist technician—professional installation/ licensed professional
5	get in touch with—contact
	placing—disposed
	household rubbish—domestic waste
6	warning sound—short beep
	low—running out
7	checked—tested
	once a month—every month

Sydney Opera House Tours

interactive audio-visual technology 交互式视听技术

baton ['bætɒn] *n.* 指挥棒；接力棒；警棍；司令棒

orchestra pit 乐池   past and present 过去与现在

真题考点词替换清单

题号	题目——原文
8	discount—concession
	young visitor—seniors/ students/children
9	footwear—rubber-soled shoes
10	pretend—imagine
	concert—performance
11	restriction—limited
	participants—people per tour
12	reduction—not essential
13	in advance—two days prior
14	length—duration

⬆ *Section 2*

Using direct mail to sell your product

compiled [kəm'paɪld] *adj.* 编译的

crucial ['kruːʃl] *adj.* 重要的；决定性的；定局的；决断的

brochure ['brəʊʃə(r)] *n.* 手册，小册子   enclose [ɪn'kləʊz] *v.* 封闭；围合

amend [ə'mend] *v.* 修订；改进

promptly ['prɒmptlɪ] *adv.* 迅速地；立即地；敏捷地

真题考点词替换清单

题号	题目——原文
15	sent—address
16	as much as possible—maximum

题号	题目——原文
17	be caught by—attract
18	letters—mailing
19	two or more colours—at least two- colour
20	more than—much greater than
	effective—incentive
	picture—photographs

Job Specification: Communications Manager

implement ['ɪmplɪment] *v.* 实施，执行；实现，使生效

distribute [dɪ'strɪbjuːt] *v.* 分配；散布；分开；把……分类

enquiry [ɪn'kwaɪərɪ] *n.* 询问；打听　　mainstream ['meɪnstriːm] *n.* 主流

demonstrable [dɪ'mɒnstrəbl] *adj.* 可论证的；显而易见的

interpersonal [ˌɪntə'pɜːsənl] *adj.* 人际的；人与人之间的

sustainability [səˌsteɪnə'bɪlətɪ] *n.* 持续性；永续性；能维持性

真题考点词替换清单

题号	题目——原文
22	improve—raise
23	wider—internal and external
24	make sure—ensure
	current—up to date
25	high—excellent
26	specific—particular

 Section 3

KAURI GUM—a piece of New Zealand's history

vast [vɑːst] *adj.* 广阔的　　　　　harden into gum 变硬成胶

rips [rɪps] *abbr.* 放射性同位素电源　　bark [bɑːk] *n.* 树皮

sap [sæp] *n.* 树液　　　　　　　　lumps of gum 树胶肿块

bewildering [bɪ'wɪldərɪŋ] *adj.* 使人困惑的；令人产生混乱的

transparency [træns'pærənsɪ] *n.* 透明，透明度

chalky ['tʃɔːkɪ] *adj.* 白垩的　　　　　swamp [swɒmp] *n.* 湿地

ignited [ɪɡ'naɪtɪd] *adj.* 烧灼的　　　　expedition [ˌekspə'dɪʃn] *n.* 探险队

established [ɪ'stæblɪʃt] *adj.* 确定的；已制定的，已建立的

spade [speɪd] *n.* 铁锹，铲子　　　　settler ['setlə(r)] *n.* 移居者；殖民者

varnish ['vɑːnɪʃ] *n.* 清漆，亮光漆

favoured ['feɪvəd] *adj.* 喜爱的；受优惠的；有特权的

pale [peɪl] *adj.* 苍白的；暗淡的　　　linoleum [lɪ'nəʊliəm] *n.* 油布；油毡；漆布

carve [kɑːv] *v.* 雕刻；切开　　　　　beads [biːdz] *n.* 玻璃粉

occasional [ə'keɪʒənl] *adj.* 偶然的；临时的；特殊场合的

peak [piːk] *v.* 达到高点

真题考点词替换清单

题号	题目——原文
28	high-quality gum—the best and purest gum
29	factors—buried/ health of the original tree and the areas of the bleeding
31	gathered—collected
32	main industrial—main commercial
33	recent—over the years
34	first used—original
35	peaked—maximum
36	farmers—settlers
37	jewellery—amber/prized/necklaces and bracelets
38	string instruments—violins
39	most—majority
39	underground—digging

General Training: Reading and Writing
Test B

⬆ *Section 1*

Passport application

enclose [ɪnˈkləʊz] *v.* 围绕；装入；放入封套

contactable [kɒntæktˈeɪbl] *adj.* 可接触

真题考点词替换清单

题号	题目——原文
1	for his wife—your own【反】
2	for his wife—your own【反】
3	incomplete application—miss information
6	have a passport—the holder of a valid passport
7	sign—write/sign

Auckland International Airport Services

terminal [ˈtɜːmɪnl] *adj.* 末端的；终点的；晚期的

situate [ˈsɪtʃʊeɪt] *v.* 使位于；使处于

pharmacy [ˈfɑːməsɪ] *n.* 药房；配药学，药剂学；制药业；一批备用药品

departure lounge 候机室；启程处   polythene [ˈpɒlɪθiːn] *n.* 聚乙烯

transit passenger 过境旅客

storage [ˈstɔːrɪdʒ] *n.* 存储；仓库；贮藏所

seminar [ˈsemɪnɑː(r)] *n.* 研讨会；专题讨论会

adjacent [əˈdʒeɪsnt] *adj.* 邻近的，毗连的

真题考点词替换清单

题号	题目——原文
8	observation—a view of
10	healthcare—medical/pharmacy
11	baggage—luggage or packages
12	fees—payments
14	departure—leaving the country
14	meeting—seminars or business gathering

 Section 2

Planning a Gap Year

yacht [jɒt] *n.* 游艇

reap [ri:p] *v.* 收获，获得

permanent ['pɜːmənənt] *adj.* 永久的，永恒的；不变的

thought-out plan 周全的计划

真题考点词替换清单

题号	题目——原文
15	young—between school and work or higher education
16	catering industry—washing up in a restaurant
18	easy—very soon
18	the sort of work—jobs
18	want—dream
19	check out—research
19	vacancies—job opportunities
19	before—in advance

Succeeding at Interviews

hurdle ['hɜːdl] *n.* 障碍

crucial ['kruːʃl] *adj.* 重要的；决定性的；定局的；决断的

vary from 不同

possess [pəˈzes] *v.* 控制；使掌握；持有；迷住；拥有，具备

adequate ['ædɪkwət] *adj.* 充足的；适当的；胜任的

punctual ['pʌŋktʃʊəl] *adj.* 准时的，守时的；精确的

真题考点词替换清单

题号	题目——原文
21	good—advantage/friendly/ polite
22	contacts—speak/ask
23	adequate responses—answer questions as fully as you can
24	get on well with—friendly and approachable
25	information—why…/whether…/what…/which…
26	honest—don't exaggerate
27	punctual—never...arriving late

⬆ *Section 3*

Serendipity: accidental discoveries in science

dynamite ['daɪnəmaɪt] *n.* 炸药

insulin ['ɪnsjəlɪn] *n.* [生化] [药] 胰岛素

artificial sweetener 人造甜味剂

serendipity [ˌserən'dɪpətɪ] *n.* 意外发现珍奇事物的本领；有意外发现珍宝的运气

iodine vapour 碘蒸气

cupboard ['kʌbəd] *n.* 碗柜；食橱

store [stɔ:(r)] *v.* 储存；容纳

intensify [ɪn'tensɪfaɪ] *v.* 使加强，使强化；使变激烈

systematically [ˌsɪstə'mætɪklɪ] *adv.* 有系统地；有组织地

mercury ['mɜ:kjərɪ] *n.* 汞，水银

vapour ['veɪpə(r)] *n.* 蒸汽（等于 vapor）；水蒸气

nitroglycerine [ˌnaɪtrəʊ'glɪsəri:n] *n.* [有化] 硝化甘油（等于 nitroglycerin），炸药

volatile ['vɒlətaɪl] *adj.* 挥发性的；不稳定的；爆炸性的

fibrous ['faɪbrəs] *adj.* 纤维的，纤维性的；纤维状的

sawdust ['sɔ:dʌst] *n.* 锯屑

stabilise ['steɪbəlaɪz] *v.* 使……坚固；使……安定

combustible [kəm'bʌstəbl] *adj.* 易燃的；易激动的；燃烧性的

brick dust 炭灰

tame [teɪm] *v.* 制服

spring a leak 出现漏洞

soaked into 侵入

ignite [ɪg'naɪt] *v.* 点燃；使燃烧；使激动

perseverance [ˌpɜːsɪ'vɪərəns] *n.* 坚持不懈；不屈不挠；耐性；毅力

grasp of the significance 理解的意义

pacifist ['pæsɪfɪst] *n.* 和平主义者

deterrent [dɪ'terənt] *n.* 威慑

warfare ['wɔːfeə(r)] *n.* 战争；冲突

bestow [bɪ'stəʊ] *v.* 使用；授予；放置；留宿

fraternity [frə't3ːnətɪ] *n.* 友爱；兄弟会；互助会；大学生联谊会

depend [dɪ'pend] *v.* 依赖，依靠；取决于；相信，信赖

真题考点词替换清单

题号	题目——原文
28	unworkable—impractical
29	flammability—catch fire
30	decreased—reduced
	energy—power
	explosion—explosive
31	safer—entirely safe
34	different method—add chemicals/sawdust and paper/brick dust
36	award—Nobel Prize Winners
38	take full advantage of lucky discovery—chance favours
39	exposure—exposing
	limited extent—weak
40	removal—removed
	did not affect—good

Cambridge
IELTS
11

Test 1

Reading Passage 1: Crop-growing skyscrapers

Paragraph 1

conservative [kən's3:vətɪv] *adj.* 保守的   estimate ['estɪmət] *n.* 估计

demographic [ˌdemə'græfɪk] *adj.* 人口的，人口统计学的

hectares ['hekteə(r)s] *n.* 公顷   raise [reɪz] *v.* 种植

Paragraph 2

indoor farming 温室种植   hothouse ['hɒthaʊs] *n.* 温室

produce [prə'djuːs] *n.* 农产品   vogue [vəʊg] *n.* 时尚，流行

urgent ['ɜːdʒənt] *adj.* 进击的，急迫的

accommodate [ə'kɒmədeɪt] *v.* 容纳，供应，使适应

entirely [ɪn'taɪəlɪ] *adv.* 完全地，彻底地   required [rɪ'kwaɪə(r)d] *adj.* 必需的

proposal [prə'pəʊzl] *n.* 提议，建议   situate ['sɪtʃʊeɪt] *v.* 使位于

drastically ['dræstɪklɪ] *adv.* 彻底地   construct [kən'strʌkt] *v.* 建造，构造

proponent [prə'pəʊnənt] *n.* 支持者   repair [rɪ'peə(r)] *v.* 修理，修复

sacrificed ['sækrɪfaɪst] *v.* 牺牲   vertical ['vɜːtɪkl] *adj.* 垂直的，直立的

horizontal [ˌhɒrɪ'zɒntl] *adj.* 水平的

Paragraph 3

grant [grɑːnt] *v.* 允许，承认   take for grant 理所应当

despoil [dɪ'spɔɪl] *v.* 掠夺，剥夺   verdant ['vɜːdnt] *adj.* 青翠的

ecozones ['iːkəʊzəʊns] *n.* 生态带   semi-arid deserts 半干旱的沙漠地带

shelter ['ʃeltə(r)] *n.* 庇护   rigours ['rɪgə(r)s] *n.* 严格，严厉，苛刻

hurricane ['hʌrɪkən] *n.* 飓风，暴风   monsoon [ˌmɒn'suːn] *n.* 季风

toll [təʊl] *n.* 代价，伤亡人数   ton [tʌn] *n.* 吨，大量，很多

Paragraph 4

optimum ['ɒptɪməm] *adj.* 最适宜的

organically [ɔː'gænɪklɪ] *adv.* 有机地

pesticides ['pestɪsaɪdz] *n.* 杀虫剂

infectious [ɪn'fekʃəs] *adj.* 传染的，传染性的

interface ['ɪntəfeɪs] *v.* 接触，相互作用

methane ['miːθeɪn] *n.* 沼气

non-edible 非食用

fossil fuel 化石燃料

tractors ['træktə(r)s] *n.* 拖拉机

pests [pests] *n.* 害虫

herbicides ['hɜːbɪsaɪds] *n.* 除草剂

incidence ['ɪnsɪdəns] *n.* 发生率

grid [grɪd] *n.* 网格，输电网

compost ['kɒmpɒst] *n.* 混合，合成

dramatically [drə'mætɪklɪ] *adv.* 戏剧性地

cut out 停止

ploughs [plaʊs] *n.* 犁

Paragraph 5

drawback ['drɔːbæk] *n.* 缺点，劣势

overhead [ˌəʊvə'hed] *adv.* 在头顶上，顶部

facility [fə'sɪlətɪ] *n.* 设备

prohibitively ['prɒhɪbɪtɪvlɪ] *adv.* 过分地

aspiration [ˌæspə'reɪʃn] *n.* 渴望，愿望

Paragraph 6

variation [ˌveərɪ'eɪʃn] *n.* 变化

tray [treɪ] *n.* 托盘

stacked [stækt] *adj.* 堆叠的

Paragraph 7

undoubted [ʌn'daʊtɪd] *adj.* 无疑的，确实的

detrimental [ˌdetrɪ'mentl] *adj.* 不利的，有害的

skyscraper ['skaɪskreɪpə(r)] *n.* 摩天大楼

rooftop ['ruːftɒp] *adj.* 屋顶上的

真题考点词替换清单

题号	题目——原文
1	food, …grown indoors—indoor farming
2	located in—situated in; less—reduce

题号	题目——原文
3	use—via; methane—methane generation
4	tractors—agricultural vehicles; cut—reduce
5	disadvantage—drawback
6	not fixed—not certain
7	probable—possible; towns and cities—urban
9	food producing food—the land that is suitable for raising crops; destruction—waste; some—15%
10	【反】the season—through year-round production
11	changing climate—climate change
12	【反】need—eliminating
13	less likely to—reduce

 Reading Passage 2: THE FALKIRK WHEEL

Paragraph 1

rotate [rəʊ'teɪt] *v.* 旋转

ambitious [æm'bɪʃəs] *adj.* 有雄心的；有野心的

millennium [mɪ'lenɪəm] *n.* 千年

navigability [ˌnævɪgə'bɪlətɪ] *n.* 适航性

waterways ['wɔːtəweɪs] *n.* 水路，水道

canals [kə'næls] *n.* 运河

Paragraph 2

sequence ['siːkwəns] *n.* 顺序

enclose [ɪn'kləʊz] *v.* 围绕

dismantled [dɪs'mæntld] *v.* 拆卸

commemoration [kə,memə'reɪʃn] *n.* 纪念

symbol ['sɪmbl] *n.* 象征

Paragraph 3

submit [səb'mɪt] *v.* 提交

roll [rəʊl] *v.* 滚动

tilt [tɪlt] *v.* 倾斜

tanks [tæŋks] *n.* 水槽

see-saw [siː sɔː] *n.* 跷跷板

monorails ['mɒnəʊreɪls] *n.* 单轨

manmade [mænmeɪd] *adj.* 人造的

notably ['nəʊtəblɪ] *adv.* 尤其

axe [æks] *n.* 斧

propeller [prə'pelə(r)] *n.* 螺旋桨

ribcage ['rɪbkeɪdʒ] *n.* 胸腔 | spine [spaɪn] *n.* 脊椎

Paragraph 4

assembled [ə'sembld] *v.* 装配，组装 | tonnes [tʌns] *n.* 吨

accuracy ['ækjərəsɪ] *n.* 精确度，准确性 | crane [kreɪn] *n.* 起重机

withstand [wɪð'stænd] *v.* 禁得起 | robust [rəʊ'bʌst] *adj.* 强健的

bolted [bəʊltɪd] *adj.* 用螺栓栓的 | welded [weldɪd] *adj.* 焊接的

hand-tightened 手动拧紧

Paragraph 5

opposing [ə'pəʊzɪŋ] *adj.* 相反的 | axe-shaped 斧子形状的

diametrically [ˌdaɪə'metrɪklɪ] *adv.* 完全地 | weigh [weɪ] *n.* 重量

displacement [dɪs'pleɪsmənt] *n.* 位移 | floating ['fləʊtɪŋ] *adj.* 漂浮的

roughly ['rʌflɪ] *adv.* 概略地

Paragraph 6

hydraulic [haɪ'drɔːlɪk] *adj.* 液压的，水力的

clamp [klæmp] *n.* 夹钳 | docked [dɒkt] *v.* 停驻(dock 的过去式)

an array of 一排 | axle ['æksl] *n.* 轴

upright ['ʌpraɪt] *adj.* 垂直的 | gear [gɪə(r)] *n.* 齿轮

cog [kɒg] *n.* 钝齿 | aqueduct ['ækwɪdʌkt] *n.* 沟渠

Paragraph 7

lock [lɒk] *n.* 水闸 | elevate ['elɪveɪt] *v.* 升起

owing to 由于

真题考点词替换清单

题号	题目——原文
14	【反】the first time—reconnect, historic
16	manufactured—constructed; put together—assemble

题号	题目——原文
18	【反】varies—the same
19	ancient monument—historically important Antonine Wall
20	a pair of—two; lift—raised; in order to—so as to
21	taken out—removed; enabling—allowing; rotate—turn
22	drive—rotate
23	remain level—keep upright
24	move—pass; directly—straight
26	raise—lift

Reading Passage 3: Reducing the Effects of Climate Change

Paragraph A

fossil fuels 化石燃料

carbon dioxide 二氧化碳

release [rɪ'liːs] v. 释放

inevitable [ɪn'evɪtəbl] adj. 必然的

carbon emissions 碳排放

stride [straɪd] n. 大步，进展

reverse [rɪ'vɜːs] v. 扭转

intentional [ɪn'tenʃənl] adj. 故意的，蓄意的

proponent [prə'pəʊnənt] n. 支持者

equivalent [ɪ'kwɪvələnt] n. 等价物

grand [grænd] adj. 宏伟的

Paragraph B

decade ['dekeɪd] n. 十年

May Day 五一劳动节

parade [pə'reɪd] n. 阅兵

cement [sɪ'ment] n. 水泥

disperse [dɪ'spɜːs] v. 分散，使散开

eye-catching ideas 受人关注的想法

scheme [skiːm] n. 方案

transparent [træns'pærənt] adj. 透明的

sunlight-refracting ['sʌnlaɪt rɪ'fræktɪŋ] adj. 太阳光折射的

sunshade ['sʌnʃeɪd] n. 太阳光遮光板

gram [græm] n. 克

Paragraph C

carry out 完成

depositing [dɪ'pɒzɪtɪŋ] *n.* 沉淀

algae ['ældʒiː] *n.* 藻类

melt [melt] *v.* 融化

replenish [rɪ'plenɪʃ] *v.* 补充，再装满

latitude ['lætɪtjuːd] *n.* 纬度

Paragraph D

aerosol sprays 喷雾剂

stratosphere ['strætəsfɪə(r)] *n.* 平流层

propose [prə'pəʊz] *v.* 提出

dimming [dɪmɪŋ] *n.* 变暗

model ['mɒdl] *v.* 以······为模型

scrutinize ['skruːtənaɪz] *v.* 详细检查

reinforced [ˌriːɪn'fɔːst] *adj.* 强化的

high-tension cable 高压电缆

pine [paɪn] *n.* 松树

absorb [əb'sɔːb] *v.* 吸收

radiation [ˌreɪdi'eɪʃn] *n.* 辐射

birch [bɜːtʃ] *n.* 桦树

shed [ʃed] *v.* 脱落

Paragraph E

implement ['ɪmplɪment] *v.* 实施

cautious ['kɔːʃəs] *adj.* 严谨的

substitute ['sʌbstɪtjuːt] *n.* 替代

permanent ['pɜːmənənt] *adj.* 永久的

guarded ['gɑːdɪd] *adj.* 谨慎的

Paragraph F

proposal [prə'pəʊzl] *n.* 建议

inject [ɪn'dʒekt] *v.* 注入；注射

rainfall ['reɪnfɔːl] *n.* 降雨

tropics ['trɒpɪks] *n.* 热带地区

seed [siːd] *v.* 播种（制造）

the extent of ······的范围

distribution [ˌdɪstrɪ'bjuːʃn] *n.* 分布

precipitation [prɪˌsɪpɪ'teɪʃn] *n.* 降雨

Paragraph G

pre-industrial [priː ɪn'dʌstrɪəl] *adj.* 工业化之前的

scenario [sə'nɑːriəʊ] *n.* 情景，情节

Paragraph H

scientific community 科学界人士   faith [feɪθ] *n.* 信仰，信念

thoroughly ['θʌrəlɪ] *adv.* 彻底地

真题考点词替换清单

题号	题目——原文
27	earlier—historic; volcanic explosions; phenomenon
28	successful—has been shown
29	definition—a term which generally refers to
30	a large number of—16 trillion; tiny—minute
31	place—depositing; sea—ocean
32	encourage—stimulate
33	create—form
34	strong—reinforced
35	allow—enabling
36	change—rerouting
39	limit the effectiveness—operate at half strength
40	replace—substitute; non-fossil-based fuels—renewable energy

Test 2

🔺 *Reading Passage 1: Raising the Mary Rose*

Paragraph 1

fleet [fliːt] *n.* 舰队   vessel ['vesl] *n.* 船，舰

warship ['wɔːʃɪp] *n.* 战船，军舰   maintain [meɪn'teɪn] *v.* 认为；主张

outdated [ˌaʊt'deɪtɪd] *adj.* 过时的，旧式的

undisciplined [ˌʌn'dɪsəplɪnd] *adj.* 无训练的，混乱无纪律的

crew [kruː] *n.* 全体人员，全体船员

undisputed [ˌʌndɪ'spjuːtɪd] *adj.* 无可争议的，无疑义的

sank [sæŋk] *v.* 沉陷   recover [rɪ'kʌvə(r)] *v.* 寻找

Paragraph 2

sand [sænd] *n.* 沙土

mud [mʌd] *n.* 淤泥

erode [ɪ'rəʊd] *v.* 侵蚀

mechanical degradation 机械降解

a layer of 一层

clay [kleɪ] *n.* 黏土

Paragraph 3

obstruction [əb'strʌkʃn] *n.* 障碍

timber ['tɪmbə(r)] *n.* 木材，木料

slightly ['slaɪtlɪ] *adv.* 轻微地

uncover [ʌn'kʌvə(r)] *v.* 发现

bronze [brɒnz] *adj.* 青铜制的

intermittently [ˌɪntə'mɪtəntlɪ] *adv.* 间歇地

bow [baʊ] *n.* 弓

Paragraph 4

fade [feɪd] *n.* 淡出

obscurity [əb'skjʊərətɪ] *n.* 默默无闻

amateur ['æmətə(r)] *adj.* 业余的

conjunction [kən'dʒʌŋkʃn] *n.* 结合

wreck [rek] *n.* 残骸

unsatisfactory [ˌʌnˌsætɪs'fæktərɪ] *adj.* 不令人满意的

collaboration [kəˌlæbə'reɪʃn] *n.* 合作

reveal [rɪ'viːl] *v.* 揭露；发现

Paragraph 5

excavation [ˌekskə'veɪʃn] *n.* 挖掘，发掘

stray [streɪ] *adj.* 离群的

climax ['klaɪmæks] *n.* 高潮，顶点

house [haʊs] *v.* 把……藏于房中

treasure ['treʒə(r)] *n.* 财宝

trove [trəʊv] *n.* 被发现的东西，收藏的东西

artefacts ['ɑːtɪfækts] *n.* 手工艺品

hull [hʌl] *n.* 船体

feasible ['fiːzəbl] *adj.* 可行的，可能的

go-ahead 前进

Paragraph 6

salvage ['sælvɪdʒ] *v.* 打捞

shell [ʃel] *n.* 空壳

namely ['neɪmlɪ] *adv.* 即，也就是

suck [sʌk] *v.* 吸吮

centimeter ['sentɪmi:tə(r)] *n.* 厘米(cm) hang [hæŋ] *v.* 悬挂

suction ['sʌkʃn] *n.* 吸，吸力 hook [hʊk] *n.* 挂钩

transfer [træns'fɜ:(r)] *n.* 转移 cradle ['kreɪdl] *n.* 摇篮

cushion ['kʊʃn] *v.* 缓冲 delicate ['delɪkət] *adj.* 脆弱的，易碎的

真题考点词替换清单

题号	题目——原文
1	some doubt—while witnesses agree that..., some maintain that..., others that...
3	undamaged—survived
4	【反】knew—unaware
5	launched—initiated
6	stopped—faded into obscurity
9	attached to hull—the attached to a lifting frame
10	prevent—overcome
11	place—locate
13	extra protection—additional cushioning

⬆ Reading Passage 2: What destroyed the civilisation of Easter Island?

Paragraph A

carve [ka:v] *v.* 雕刻 platform ['plætfɔ:m] *n.* 平台

identity [aɪ'dentətɪ] *n.* 身份 statues ['stætʃu:s] *n.* 雕像

bestselling [,best'selɪŋ] *adj.* 畅销的 stranded [strændɪd] *adj.* 搁浅的；滞留的

extraterrestrial [,ekstrətə'restrɪəl] *n.* 外星人

definitively [dɪ'fɪnətɪvlɪ] *adv.* 确定地 folklore ['fəʊklɔ:(r)] *n.* 民间传说

assume [ə'sju:] *v.* 假设 drag [dræg] *v.* 拉；拽

somehow ['sʌmhaʊ] *adv.* 以某种方式 rope [rəʊp] *n.* 绳索

log [lɒg] *n.* 原木

Paragraph B

scrawny ['skrɔːnɪ] *n.* 小树木

sediment ['sedɪmənt] *n.* 沉积物

palm [pɑːm] *n.* 棕榈树

wreck [rek] *n.* 破坏

windblown [wɪnd'bləʊn] *adj.* 被风吹的

yield [jiːld] *n.* 产量

cannibalism ['kænɪbəlɪzəm] *n.* 自相残杀

scenario [sə'nɑːrɪəʊ] *n.* 情节

pollen ['pɒlən] *n.* 花粉

lush [lʌʃ] *adj.* 苍翠繁茂的

descendent [dɪ'sendənt] *n.* 后裔

fragile ['frædʒaɪl] *adj.* 脆的，易碎的

volcanic ash 火山灰

civil war 内战

collapse [kə'læps] *v.* 倾倒；坍塌

Paragraph C

interpret [ɪn'tɜːprɪt] *v.* 解释

remote [rɪ'məʊt] *adj.* 遥远的

dominance ['dɒmɪnəns] *n.* 统治

toppling ['tɒplɪŋ] *v.* 推翻

chieftains ['tʃiːftəns] *n.* 首领

assert [ə'sɜːt] *v.* 维护，坚持

sledge [sledʒ] *n.* 雪橇

Paragraph D

catastrophe [kə'tæstrəfɪ] *n.* 灾难

excavations [ˌekskə'veɪʃns] *n.* 挖掘，发掘

heroic [hə'rəʊɪk] *adj.* 英雄的，英勇的

circular ['sɜːkjələ(r)] *adj.* 圆形的，循环的

windbreaks ['wɪndbreɪks] *n.* 防风林

prehistoric [ˌpriːhɪ'stɒrɪk] *adj.* 史前的

blame [bleɪm] *n.* 责备

moist [mɔɪst] *n.* 潮湿

Paragraph E

contend [kən'tend] *v.* 主张

back up 支持

handler ['hændlə(r)] *n.* 操作者

upright ['ʌpraɪt] *n.* 垂直，竖立

manoeuvre [mə'nuːvə(r)] *v.* 操纵

Paragraph F

wholly ['həʊllɪ] *adv.* 完全地

grooves [gru:vs] *n.* 凹槽

doom [du:m] *v.* 注定

slave traders 奴商

nuts [nʌts] *n.* 坚果

overrun [ˌəʊvə'rʌn] *n.* 泛滥成灾

immunity [ɪ'mju:nətɪ] *n.* 免疫力

shriveled ['ʃrɪvld] *adj.* 皱缩的

Paragraph G

vision ['vɪʒn] *n.* 观点

stewards ['stju:rədz] *n.* 管理员

reckless ['rekləs] *adj.* 鲁莽的，不计后果的

whichever [wɪtʃ'evə(r)] *pron.* 无论

ingenious [ɪn'dʒi:nɪəs] *adj.* 有独创性的

真题考点词替换清单

题号	题目——原文
14	undisputed answer—definitively proved
15	diminishing—decreased
16	worse—self-destruction
18	support—back up; belief—folklore
19	outside the control—not wholly responsible
21	cutting down its trees for fuel—firewood
22	able to—could; built—construct
23	food source—ate
24	both...and...—not only...but also...

🔺 *Reading Passage 3: Neuroaesthetics*

Paragraph 1

discipline ['dɪsəplɪn] *n.* 学科

masterpieces ['mɑ:stəpi:sɪs] *n.* 杰作

impressionist [ɪm'preʃənɪst] *n.* 印象派作家

crucial ['kru:ʃl] *adj.* 至关重要的

objectivity [ˌɒbdʒek'tɪvətɪ] *n.* 客观性

moving ['mu:vɪŋ] *adj.* 生动的

Paragraph 2

shed [ʃed] *v.* 阐释

abstract ['æbstrækt] *adj.* 抽象的

geometrical [ˌdʒiːə'metrɪkl] *adj.* 几何的

haphazard [hæp'hæzəd] *adv.* 偶然地，随意地

splashed [splæʃt] *v.* 泼

canvas ['kænvəs] *n.* 画布

sceptics ['skeptɪks] *n.* 怀疑论者

inclination [ˌɪnklɪ'neɪʃn] *n.* 倾向

perceptual [pə'septʃʊəl] *adj.* 有知觉的

mentality [men'tælətɪ] *n.* 心态

fuzzy ['fʌzɪ] *adj.* 模糊的

appreciation [əˌpriːʃɪ'eɪʃn] *n.* 欣赏

Paragraph 3

doodle ['duːdl] *n.* 涂鸦

captions ['kæpʃns] *n.* 说明

labeled ['leɪbld] *adj.* 标注的

acclaim [ə'kleɪm] *n.* 称赞

trial ['traɪəl] *n.* 试验

renowned [rɪ'naʊnd] *adj.* 著名的

Paragraph 4

ambiguous [æm'bɪgjʊəs] *adj.* 模糊不清的，引起歧义的

representational [ˌreprɪzen'teɪʃnl] *adj.* 具象派的

collaborators [kə'læbəreɪtə(r)s] *n.* 合作者

familiar [fə'mɪlɪə(r)] *adj.* 熟悉的

scrutiny ['skruːtənɪ] *n.* 细看

neural ['njʊərəl] *adj.* 神经的

puzzle ['pʌzl] *n.* 谜题

decipher [dɪ'saɪfə(r)] *v.* 破解

Paragraph 5

encasing [ɪn'keɪsɪŋ] *v.* 包含

deceptively [dɪ'septɪvlɪ] *adv.* 迷惑地

meticulously [mə'tɪkjələslɪ] *adv.* 细致地

flit [flɪt] *v.* 掠过

Paragraph 6

still life 静物

composition [ˌkɒmpə'zɪʃn] *n.* 组成

activation [ˌæktɪ'veɪʃn] *n.* 激活

interpretation [ɪnˌtɜːprɪ'teɪʃn] *n.* 理解

Paragraph 7

intricacy ['ɪntrɪkəsɪ] *n.* 复杂

what's more 除此之外

appealing [ə'piːlɪŋ] *adj.* 吸引人的

fractals ['fræktls] *n.* 分形学

motif [məʊ'tiːf] *n.* 图形

recurring [rɪ'kɜːrɪŋ] *adj.* 循环的，重现的

scale [skeɪl] *n.* 尺寸

branches [brɑːntʃɪz] *n.* 树枝

Paragraph 8

intriguing [ɪn'triːgɪŋ] *adj.* 有趣的

wonder ['wʌndə(r)] *v.* 猜想

dynamic [daɪ'næmɪk] *adj.* 生动的

energetic [ˌenə'dʒetɪk] *adj.* 精力充沛的，生动的

mimic ['mɪmɪk] *v.* 模仿

hypothesis [haɪ'pɒθəsɪs] *n.* 假设

longevity [lɒn'dʒevətɪ] *n.* 经久不衰

linger ['lɪŋgə(r)] *v.* 留下

Paragraph 9

early day 初级阶段

foolish ['fuːlɪʃ] *adj.* 愚蠢的

constantly ['kɒnstəntlɪ] *adv.* 不间断地，一直

decode [ˌdiː'kəʊd] *v.* 解读

真题考点词替换清单

题号	题目——原文
27	tendency—inclination; others—the crowd
28	perceive—sense; intention behind works—the artist's vision
29	a painting represents—decipher the meaning; satisfying—rewarding
30	more carefully put together—meticulously composed
31	emotions—feelings
32	complexity—a key level of detail
33	pleasing works—appealing pieces; images—motifs
35	further verification—the hypothesis will need to be thoroughly tested
36	depend on—adapted to
37	【反】should seek—foolish

Test 3

🔺 *Reading Passage 1: THE STORY OF SILK*

Paragraph 1

smooth [smu:ð] *adj.* 光滑的

shells [ʃels] *n.* 外壳

silkworms ['sɪlkwɜ:mz] *n.* 蚕

Yellow Emperor 黄帝

unravel [ʌn'rævl] *v.* 散开，解开

wind [waɪnd] *v.* 缠绕

persuade [pə'sweɪd] *v.* 说服

grove [grəʊv] *n.* 树丛

reel [ri:l] *n.* 卷轴

woven [wəʊvn] *v.* 纺织

millennia [mɪ'lenɪə] *n.* 一千年

cocoon [kə'ku:n] *n.* 蚕茧

mulberry ['mʌlbərɪ] *n.* 桑树

larvae ['lɑ:və] *n.* 幼虫

sipping [sɪpɪŋ] *v.* 小口啜饮

thread [θred] *n.* 线

subsequently ['sʌbsɪkwəntlɪ] *adv.* 接下来

rear [rɪə(r)] *v.* 养育

devised [dɪ'vaɪzd] *v.* 设计

fibres ['faɪbə(r)s] *n.* 纤维

cultivation [ˌkʌltɪ'veɪʃn] *n.* 培养，栽培

Paragraph 2

solely ['səʊllɪ] *adv.* 单独地

weave [wi:v] *v.* 纺织

royalty ['rɔɪəltɪ] *n.* 皇族

peasants ['peznts] *n.* 农民

prized [praɪzd] *adj.* 被看作重要的，有价值的

a unit of ……的单位

diplomatic [ˌdɪplə'mætɪk] *adj.* 外交的

bowstrings ['bəʊstrɪŋs] *n.* 弓弦

noble ['nəʊbl] *n.* 贵族

harvest ['hɑ:vɪst] *n.* 收获

symbol ['sɪmbl] *n.* 标志，象征

entitled [ɪn'taɪtld] *adj.* 有资格的

caste [kɑ:st] *n.* 阶层

grain [greɪn] *n.* 谷物

emperor ['empərə(r)] *n.* 皇帝

tomb [tu:m] *n.* 坟墓

Paragraph 3

exotic [ɪg'zɒtɪk] *adj.* 奇异的

fabric ['fæbrɪk] *n.* 织物

lucrative ['lu:krətɪv] *adj.* 获利多的，赚钱的

westward [westwəd] *adv.* 向西

commodity [kə'mɒdəti] *n.* 商品

stretched [stretʃt] *v.* 绵延

merchandise ['mɜːtʃəndaɪs] *n.* 商品

merchant ['mɜːtʃənt] *n.* 商人

entire [ɪn'taɪə(r)] *adj.* 整个的

middlemen ['mɪdlmæn] *n.* 中间商

Paragraph 4

native ['neɪtɪv] *n.* 原产于

monks [mʌŋks] *n.* 和尚，僧侣

smuggled ['smʌgld] *v.* 走私，偷运

concealed [kən'siːld] *adj.* 隐蔽的

hollow ['hɒləʊ] *adj.* 空心的

canes [keɪns] *n.* 手杖

strict [strɪkt] *adj.* 严格的

monopoly [mə'nɒpəli] *n.* 垄断

conquered ['kɒŋkə(r)d] *v.* 征服

capture ['kæptʃə(r)] *v.* 俘获

magnificent [mæg'nɪfɪsnt] *adj.* 华丽的

sweep [swiːp] *v.* 扫荡

extensively [ɪk'stensɪvlɪ] *adv.* 广泛地

province ['prɒvɪns] *n.* 省

esteemed [ɪ'stiːmd] *adj.* 受人尊敬的

reputation [ˌrepjʊ'teɪʃn] *n.* 名誉，声望

Paragraph 5

downfall ['daʊnfɔːl] *n.* 衰落

facilitated [fə'sɪlɪteɪtɪd] *v.* 推动，促进

nylon ['naɪlɒn] *n.* 尼龙

parachute ['pærəʃuːt] *n.* 降落伞

interrupted [ˌɪntə'rʌptɪd] *v.* 中断，打扰

stifled ['staɪfld] *v.* 扼杀

silk yarn 丝线

metric tons 公吨

真题考点词替换清单

题号	题目——原文
1	fell into—land in
2	invented—devised
3	only—solely

题号	题目——原文
4	be allowed to—be entitled to; wear—clothes
5	a suit of—a unit of
6	evidence—indication
7	gold and silver—precious metal
8	hide—smuggled
9	decline—stifled
10	gold was the most valuable—worth more than gold
11	merchant—tradesmen; go along—travel
12	【反】spread—secretive

Reading Passage 2: Great Migrations

Paragraph 1

interval ['ɪntəvl] *n.* 间隔

instinct ['ɪnstɪŋkt] *n.* 本能

prolonged [prə'lɒŋd] *adj.* 旷日持久的

linear ['lɪnɪə(r)] *adj.* 直线的

overfeeding ['əʊvəfiːdɪŋ] *n.* 过度进食

intense [ɪn'tens] *adj.* 强烈的

temptations [temp'teɪʃns] *n.* 诱惑

undistracted [ʌndɪ'stræktɪd] *adj.* 注意力集中的

inherit [ɪn'herɪt] *v.* 遗传

identified [aɪ'dentɪfaɪd] *v.* 总结

habitats ['hæbɪtæts] *n.* 栖息地

zigzaggy ['zɪgzægɪ] *adj.* 曲折迂回的

allocation [ˌælə'keɪʃn] *n.* 分配，配置

undeterred [ˌʌndɪ't3ːd] *adj.* 未受阻的

Paragraph 2

tern [t3ːn] *n.* 燕鸥

herring ['herɪŋ] *n.* 鲱鱼

voraciously [və'reɪʃəslɪ] *adv.* 贪婪地

handouts ['hændaʊts] *n.* 免费发的材料（这里指"馈赠"）

distraction [dɪ'strækʃn] *n.* 分神

undivided [ˌʌndɪ'vaɪdɪd] *adj.* 专一的

nice smelly 美味

gulls [gʌls] *n.* 海鸥

destination [ˌdestɪ'neɪʃn] *n.* 目的地

intent [ɪn'tent] *n.* 目的

gravelly ['grævəlɪ] *adj.* 砂砾遍地的

coastline ['kəʊstlaɪn] *n.* 海岸线

converged [kən'vɜːdʒd] *v.* 集结

hatch [hætʃ] *n.* 孵化

rear [rɪə(r)] *v.* 培养

offspring ['ɒfsprɪŋ] *n.* 后代

Paragraph 3

pronghorn ['prɒŋhɔːn] *n.* 叉角羚

terrestrial [tə'restrɪəl] *adj.* 陆生的

beast [biːst] *n.* 野兽（这里指"大型动物"）

back-and-forth movement 季节性来回移动

Paragraph 4

zooplankton [zuː'plæŋktən] *n.* 浮游动物

upward ['ʌpwəd] *adv.* 上浮

downward ['daʊnwəd] *adv.* 下潜

predator ['predətə(r)] *n.* 捕食者

aphids ['eɪfɪdz] *n.* 蚜虫类

depleted [dɪ'pliːtɪd] *v.* 耗尽

onward ['ɒnwəd] *adv.* 向前

host plant 寄主植物

Paragraph 5

intricate ['ɪntrɪkət] *adj.* 错综复杂的

cite [saɪt] *v.* 引用

sensitive ['sensətɪv] *adj.* 敏感的

take off 起飞

tender ['tendə(r)] *adj.* 柔软，嫩

wildebeest ['wɪldəbiːst] *n.* 牛羚

Paragraph 6

detrimental [ˌdetrɪ'mentl] *adj.* 有害的

range [reɪndʒ] *n.* 牧场

plain [pleɪn] *n.* 平原

wait out 熬过

sagebrush ['seɪdʒbrʌʃ] *n.* 蒿丛

notable ['nəʊtəbl] *adj.* 值得注意的

invariance [ɪn'veərɪəns] *n.* 不变性

severity [sɪ'verətɪ] *n.* 严重性

bounty ['baʊntɪ] *n.* 慷慨馈赠，奖金

grazing ['greɪzɪŋ] *n.* 放牧

windblown [wɪnd'bləʊn] *adj.* 被风吹的

overwinter [ˌəʊvə'wɪntə(r)] *v.* 过冬

distance vision 远视能力

traverse [trə'vɜːs] *v.* 穿过

corridor ['kɒrɪdɔː(r)] *n.* 走廊

crisis ['kraɪsɪs] *n.* 危机

choke off 阻塞　　　　　　　　passageway ['pæsɪdʒweɪ] *n.* 通道

Paragraph 7

complicated ['kɒmplɪkeɪtɪd] *adj.* 复杂的

vastly ['vɑːstlɪ] *adv.* 极大地，广大地，深远地

jurisdictions [ˌdʒʊərɪs'dɪkʃns] *n.* 管辖权　　borders ['bɔːdəz] *n.* 边界

wisdom ['wɪzdəm] *n.* 智慧　　　　resoluteness [ˌrezə'lutnɪs] *n.* 决心

真题考点词替换清单

题号	题目——原文
15	according to—depend on
17	perceive—sensitive
18	【反】distinguish—share
19	straight line—linear, not zigzaggy
20	prepare—preparation; eat more than they need—overfeeding
21	be unlikely to be discouraged by difficulties—undeterred by challenges
22	ignore distractions—resist distraction
23	eyesight—vision
24	winter—frozen months
26	narrow—150 metres wide

🔺 *Reading Passage 3: Preface to 'How the other half thinks: Adventures in mathematical reasoning'*

Paragraph A

occasionally [ə'keɪʒnəlɪ] *adv.* 偶尔；偶然

musical compositions 音乐的乐章　　advanced mathematics 高等数学

algebra ['ældʒɪbrə] *n.* 代数　　　　geometry [dʒɪ'ɒmətrɪ] *n.* 几何

trigonometry [ˌtrɪɡə'nɒmətrɪ] *n.* 三角函数

arithmetic [ə'rɪθmətɪk] *n.* 算术　　sum [sʌm] *n.* 总合

odd [ɒd] *n.* 奇数　　　　　　　　even ['iːvn] *adj.* 偶数的

common sense 常识　　　　　　　elementary [ˌelɪ'mentrɪ] *adj.* 基本的

logical ['lɒdʒɪkl] *adj.* 有逻辑的　　intuitive [ɪn'tjuːɪtɪv] *adj.* 直觉的

Paragraph B

reveal [rɪ'viːl] *v.* 展示　　　　　fascinating ['fæsɪneɪtɪŋ] *adj.* 引人入胜的

respect [rɪ'spekt] *n.* 方面　　　　application [ˌæplɪ'keɪʃn] *n.* 应用

adept [ə'dept] *n.* 内行；能手　　procedure [prə'siːdʒə(r)] *n.* 过程

Paragraph C

notorious [nəʊ'tɔːrɪəs] *adj.* 臭名昭著的　　right brain 右脑

left brain 左脑　　　　　　　　alleged [ə'ledʒd] *adj.* 所谓的

Paragraph D

omit [ə'mɪt] *v.* 省略　　　　　　foundation [faʊn'deɪʃn] *n.* 地基；基石

tantalized ['tæntəlaɪzd] *adj.* 被逗弄的　　spectator [spek'teɪtə(r)] *n.* 旁观者

subatomic [ˌsʌbə'tɒmɪk] *adj.* 亚原子的　　chromosomes ['krəʊməsəʊmz] *n.* 染色体

broad outline 大致轮廓　　　　　sketched [sketʃt] *v.* 大致勾勒

Paragraph E

insight ['ɪnsaɪt] *n.* 洞察力；深入了解

Paragraph F

aficionado [əˌfɪʃə'nɑːdəʊ] *n.* 疯狂爱好者　　sharpen ['ʃɑːpən] *v.* 加强

career [kə'rɪə(r)] *n.* 职业

extended [ɪk'stendɪd] *adj.* 全面的；广泛的

testimonials [ˌtestɪ'məʊnɪəls] *n.* 证明信

Paragraph G

physician [fɪ'zɪʃn] *n.* 内科医生　　lawyer ['lɔːjə(r)] *n.* 律师

theorems ['θɪərəmz] *n.* 定理　　　delight [dɪ'laɪt] *n.* 喜悦

naive [naɪˈiːv] *adj.* 天真的

unanticipated [ˌʌnænˈtɪsɪpeɪtɪd] *adj.* 没有预料到的

真题考点词替换清单

题号	题目——原文
27	lack of—have necessarily had to omit
28	not a typical book—differs from most books
32	this book and reading other kinds of publication—novel or a newspaper
33	accessible—understand
34	different—two; categories—types
35	both...and...—so it is...as well
36	a limit—a little
38	leave out—omit
39	while reading—turn these pages; perform—carry out

Test 4

🔺 *Reading Passage 1: Research using twins*

Paragraph 1

biomedical [ˌbaɪəʊˈmedɪkl] *adj.* 生物医药学的

untangle [ˌʌnˈtæŋgl] *v.* 解开，整理，解决

nurture [ˈnɜːtʃə(r)] *v./n.* 养育

fertilised egg 受精卵

virtually [ˈvɜːtʃʊəli] *adv.* 事实上；几乎

identical [aɪˈdentɪkl] *adj.* 完全相同的

split [splɪt] *v.* 分裂

Paragraph 2

alternatively [ɔːlˈtɜːnətɪvli] *adv.* 或者

quantify [ˈkwɒntɪfaɪ] *v.* 量化

vulnerability [ˌvʌlnərəˈbɪləti] *n.* 易损性

fraternal [frəˈtɜːnl] *adj.* 双胞胎的

ailment [ˈeɪlmənt] *n.* 小病

heredity [həˈredəti] *n.* 遗传，遗传性

Paragraph 3

pinpoint ['pɪnpɔɪnt] *v.* 确定

interplay ['ɪntəpleɪ] *n.* 互相影响，互相作用

Paragraph 4

twist [twɪst] *n./v.* 转换

Paragraph 5

colleague ['kɒliːg] *n.* 同事

mountain of data 海量的数据

makeup [meɪkʌp] *n.* 组成

in broad terms 从广义上来说

invisible [ɪn'vɪzɪb(ə)l] *adj.* 无形的；看不见的

Paragraph 6

conclusion [kən'kluːʒn] *n.* 结论；推论

epigenetics [ˌepɪdʒ'netɪks] *n.* 表现遗传学

Paragraph 7

tied to 相关联

component [kəm'pəʊnənt] *n.* 部件；组成；部分

weakened ['wiːkənd] *adj.* 削弱的

Paragraph 8

segment ['segmənt] *n.* 片段

struck [strʌk] *v.* 弹响

tune [tjuːn] *n.* 曲调

Paragraph 9

mechanism ['mekənɪzəm] *n.* 机制

pregnancy ['pregnənsɪ] *n.* 怀孕

fetus ['fiːtəs] *n.* 胎儿

rodent ['rəʊdnt] *n.* 啮齿动物

embryonic cells 胚胎细胞

Paragraph 10

hardwired ['haːdwaɪəd] *adj.* 电路的

Paragraph 11

surge [sɜːdʒ] *n.* 汹涌澎湃

schizophrenia [ˌskɪtsəˈfriːnɪə] *n.* 精神分裂症

reflective [rɪˈflektɪv] *adj.* 反射的；沉思的

真题考点词替换清单

题号	题目——原文
4	be different from both… and…—third factor
5	invent—coin; term—nature and nurture
6	increase our knowledge—take our understanding further
7	mathematical method—statistical concept
8	pioneered—first
9	lived apart—reared apart
10	activity—expressed
11	internal organs—parts of our bodies
12	be affected by—impact

⬆ *Reading Passage 2: An Introduction to Film Sound*

Paragraph 1

essentially [ɪˈsenʃəlɪ] *adv.* 本质上

sound track 音轨

sound effects 音效

dialogue [ˈdaɪəlɒg] *n.* 对话；对白

asynchronous sound 不同步音效

ultimately [ˈʌltɪmətlɪ] *adv.* 最后，根本

ingredient [ɪnˈgriːdɪənt] *n.* 原料，要素

so as to 以便……

synchronous sound 同步音效

Paragraph 2

stage drama 舞台戏剧

characterization [ˌkærəktəraɪˈzeɪʃn] *n.* 角色化

audience [ˈɔːdɪəns] *n.* 观众

motivation [ˌməʊtɪˈveɪʃn] *n.* 动机

the character 角色

merge [mɜːdʒ] v. 融合

texture ['tekstʃə(r)] n. 特质

Paragraph 3

physiognomy [ˌfɪzɪ'ɒnəmɪ] n. 相貌

gesture ['dʒestʃə(r)] n. 手势

realistic [ˌriːə'lɪstɪk] adj. 现实的

emerge [ɪ'mɜːdʒ] v. 出现

craft [krɑːft] n. 技术；技艺

struggle ['strʌgl] v. 挣扎

evident ['evɪdənt] adj. 明显的

banal [bə'nɑːl] adj. 平淡乏味的

intrinsic [ɪn'trɪnsɪk] adj. 内在的，本质的

portray [pɔː'treɪ] v. 扮演；描绘

inadequacy [ɪn'ædɪkwəsɪ] n. 不足

Paragraph 4

comedy ['kɒmədɪ] n. 喜剧

breakneck ['breɪknek] adj. 飞快的

underscore [ˌʌndə'skɔː(r)] v. 强调

dizzy ['dɪzɪ] adj. 头晕目眩的

absurdity [əb'sɜːdətɪ] n. 荒谬

humor ['hjuːmər] n. 幽默

bounced [baʊnst] v. 弹跳

gag [gæg] n. 噱头

whirlwind ['wɜːlwɪnd] n. 旋风

escapism [ɪ'skeɪpɪzəm] n. 逃避现实

frenetic [frə'netɪk] adj. 发狂的，狂乱的

Paragraph 5

realism ['rɪəlɪzəm] n. 现实主义

subconsciously [ˌsʌb'kɒnʃəslɪ] adv. 潜意识地

ominous ['ɒmɪnəs] adj. 预兆的

burglary ['bɜːglərɪ] n. 入室抢劫

volume ['vɒljuːm] n. 音量

suspense [sə'spens] n. 悬念

Paragraph 6

visible ['vɪzəbl] adj. 明显的

nuance ['njuːɑːns] n. 细微差别

opt [ɒpt] v. 选择

background sound 背景音乐

ambulance ['æmbjələns] n. 救护车

siren ['saɪrən] n. 汽笛

foreground ['fɔːgraʊnd] n. 前景

underscore [ˌʌndə'skɔː(r)] v. 强调

psychic ['saɪkɪk] *adj.* 精神上的 injury ['ɪndʒərɪ] *n.* 受伤

incur [ɪn'kɜː(r)] *v.* 引发

Paragraph 7

ubiquitous [juː'bɪkwɪtəs] *adj.* 普遍存在的

absence ['æbsəns] *n.* 缺席 tone [təʊn] *n.* 基调

depict [dɪ'pɪkt] *v.* 描绘 foreshadow [fɔː'ʃædəʊ] *v.* 预示

dissonant ['dɪsənənt] *adj.* 不协调的 menace ['menəs] *n.* 威胁

Paragraph 8

scene [siːn] *n.* 场景 salient ['seɪlɪənt] *adj.* 最重要的

motifs [məʊ'tiːfs] *n.* 主题，主旨

Paragraph 9

comprise [kəm'praɪz] *v.* 组成 chase [tʃeɪs] *v./n.* 追逐

horror film 恐怖电影 brilliantly ['brɪlɪəntlɪ] *adv.* 辉煌地

conceived [kən'siːvd] *v.* 感受，感知 subtle ['sʌtl] *adj.* 微妙的

foster ['fɒstə(r)] *v.* 培养 sprang [spræŋ] *v.* 跳跃

真题考点词替换清单

题号	题目——原文
14	overlook—underestimate
15	similar—no different
16	dull—banal, little intrinsic interest
17	emphasizes—underscore
18	manipulate—help to engage
20	anticipate—foreshadow; development—change
22	help the audience—aid viewer understanding
23	affecting—effects
24	combined appropriately—mixed and balanced
25	listen to the dialogue—dialogue serves to tell the story
26	appearance—physiognomy; moves—gesture; consistent—fit

Reading Passage 3: 'This Marvellous Invention'

Paragraph A

manifold ['mænɪfəʊld] adj. 多样的

material existence 物质存在

embarked [ɪm'bɑːkt] v. 登上

unparalleled [ʌn'pærəleld] adj. 不平行的

take pride of 有最重要的地位

pale [peɪl] adj. 苍白的；黯然失色的

ascent [ə'sent] n. 上升

Paragraph B

foremost ['fɔːməʊst] adj. 最重要的

ingenious [ɪn'dʒiːnɪəs] adj. 有独创性的

whilst [waɪlst] conj. 同时；当……的时候

stir [stɜː(r)] v. 激起

distilled [dɪ'stɪld] adj. 净化的

eloquently ['eləkwəntlɪ] adv. 极富表现力地

magnitude ['mægnɪtjuːd] n. 量级

homage ['hɒmɪdʒ] n. 尊敬

incongruity [ˌɪnkɒn'gruːətɪ] n. 不协调；不一致

paradox ['pærədɒks] n. 悖论

extraordinary [ɪk'strɔːdnrɪ] adj. 特别的

infinite ['ɪnfɪnət] adj. 无限的；无穷的

penetrate ['penɪtreɪt] v. 渗透

abbey ['æbɪ] n. 大修道院

celebrated ['selɪbreɪtɪd] adj. 有名的

hymns [hɪms] n. 赞美诗

conceal [kən'siːl] v. 隐藏

fascination [ˌfæsɪ'neɪʃn] n. 魅力

Paragraph C

handiwork ['hændɪwɜːk] n. 手工艺

morsel ['mɔːsl] n. 一口；（食物）少量

haphazard [hæp'hæzəd] adj. 偶然的

sigh [saɪ] v. 叹息

measly ['miːzlɪ] adj. 极少的

configuration [kən,fɪgə'reɪʃn] n. 结构

splutters ['splʌtə(r)s] n. 噼啪声

unravel [ʌn'rævl] v. 阐明

Paragraph D

forager ['fɒrɪdʒə] n. 抢劫者

subtropical [ˌsʌb'trɒpɪkl] adj. 亚热带的

exertion [ɪgˈzɜːʃn] *n.* 运用

victim [ˈvɪktɪm] *n.* 受害人

triumphs [ˈtraɪʌmfs] *n.* 凯旋

Paragraph E

estrangement [ɪˈstreɪndʒmənt] *n.* 疏远

exotic [ɪgˈzɒtɪk] *adj.* 异国的；外来的

outlandish [aʊtˈlændɪʃ] *adj.* 古怪的

town-dweller [taʊnˈdwelə(r)] *n.* 城镇人

monstrosity [mɒnˈstrɒsəti] *n.* 畸形

Paragraph F

freak [friːk] *n.* 怪胎

corresponding [ˌkɒrəˈspɒndɪŋ] *adj.* 相当的

convey [kənˈveɪ] *v.* 传达

slot [slɒt] *n.* 槽（空隙）

nifty [ˈnɪfti] *adj.* 漂亮的

contraption [kənˈtræpʃn] *n.* 奇妙的装置

真题考点词替换清单

题号	题目——原文
27	the most important—take pride of place
28	incompatible—incongruity
29	a huge range of—make so much out of; a few sounds—barely three dozen
30	universal—everybody
32	silence—the absence of the sound
33	life—existence
34	fundamental—depend on
35	a small number of sounds—twenty-five or thirty sounds
37	【反】might have—could never have embarked on
38	de justice to—celebrated eloquently the magnitude
40	recording of events—documentation of history

General Training: Reading and Writing Test 1

🔼 *Section 1*

Question 1—5

Are Your Children at school Today?

真题考点词替换清单

题号	题目——原文
2	all—a good reason

Introduction

punctually ['pʌŋktʃʊəlɪ] *adv.* 准时地，如期地

essential [ɪ'senʃl] *adj.* 必要的　　opportunity [ˌɒpə'tjuːnəti] *n.* 时机，机会

ensure [ɪn'ʃʊə(r)] *v.* 保证

regularly ['regjələlɪ] *adv.* 按计划地，定期地

registered ['redʒɪstə(r)d] *adj.* 注册的，登记过的

What you can do to help

encourage [ɪn'kʌrɪdʒ] *v.* 鼓励，激励　　habit ['hæbɪt] *n.* 习惯

record ['rekɔːd] *v.* 记录

unauthorized [ʌn'ɔːθəraɪzd] *adj.* 未被授权的

absence ['æbsəns] *n.* 缺席　　session ['seʃn] *n.* 学期

vital ['vaɪtl] *adj.* 至关重要的

preferably ['prefrəblɪ] *adv.* 最好，更适宜

policy ['pɒləsɪ] *n.* 政策　　dealt [delt] *v.* 处理

Authorised and Unauthorised Absence

absent ['æbsənt] *adj.* 缺席的　　consider [kən'sɪdə(r)] *v.* 考虑，认为

truancy ['truːənsɪ] *n.* 旷课　　acceptable [ək'septəbl] *adj.* 可接受的

sickness ['sɪknəs] *n.* 疾病

unavoidable [ˌʌnə'vɔɪdəbl] *adj.* 不可避免的，不能废除的

arrange [ə'reɪndʒ] *v.* 安排   prospective employer 潜在雇主

circumstances ['sɜːkəmstənsɪs] *n.* 情况   bereavement [bɪ'riːvmənt] *n.* 丧亲

religious observance 宗教活动

Question 6—14

HOLIDAY APRARTMENTS TO LET

真题考点词替换清单

题号	题目——原文
6	overlook—first floor（英国的二楼）
7	own parking space—private parking
8	centre—central location
9	seen—views
10	swimming pool for residents of the apartment complex—own pool
11	new—only just opened
12	own—for residents
13	private outdoor area—terrace
14	parking—garage

Paragraph A

uninterrupted [ˌʌnˌɪntə'rʌptɪd] *adj.* 一览无余的

well-established 完善的   resident ['rezɪdənt] *n.* 居民

Paragraph B

spacious ['speɪʃəs] *adj.* 宽敞的   unspoilt village 未被破坏的村庄

fabulous ['fæbjələs] *adj.* 难以置信的   championship ['tʃæmpɪənʃɪp] *n.* 锦标赛

Paragraph C

cottage ['kɒtɪdʒ] *n.* 小别墅   terrace ['terəs] *n.* 阳台

amenities [ə'miːnətɪs] *n.* 便利设施

Paragraph D

superb [suːˈpɜːb] *adj.* 极好的

Paragraph E

multi-storey [ˈmʌltiˈstɔːrɪ] *adj.* 多层的

Paragraph F

attractive [əˈtræktɪv] *adj.* 吸引人的，有魅力的

edge [edʒ] *n.* 边缘

Paragraph G

tennis courts 网球场

🔺 Section 2

Question 15—21

GZJ Travel - Recruitment Info

真题考点词替换清单

题号	题目——原文
15	education—academic background
20	way of working—working lifestyle
21	Meet a manager—introduced to the Area Leader

Paragraph 1

passionate [ˈpæʃənət] *adj.* 热情的   recruitment [rɪˈkruːtmənt] *n.* 招募

Paragraph 2

vacancy [ˈveɪkənsɪ] *n.* 空缺   role [rəʊl] *n.* 角色

evidence [ˈevɪdəns] *n.* 证明   solid [ˈsɒlɪd] *adj.* 可靠的

academic [ˌækəˈdemɪk] *n.* 大学生

Paragraph 3

effort [ˈefət] *n.* 努力   ceremonies [ˈserəmənɪs] *n.* 仪式

Paragraph 4

psychometric [ˌsaɪkə'metrɪk] *adj.* 心理测量的

characteristics [ˌkærəktə'rɪstɪks] *n.* 特征，特性

Paragraph 5

individual [ˌɪndɪ'vɪdʒʊəl] *adj.* 个人的　　career path 职业道路

Question 22—27

Hilton Laboratory

真题考点词替换清单

题号	题目——原文
22	avoid—Do not enter; certain places in the building—restricted areas
24	items which could cause injury—sharp objects; disposed of—into waste bins
25	not all departments have the same system— may vary

Personal safety

restricted [rɪ'strɪktɪd] *adj.* 受限制的

authorisation [ˌɔːθəraɪ'zeɪʃn] *n.* 授权，批准

observe [əb'zɜːv] *v.* 观察　　　　wedge [wedʒ] *v.* 挤进

tamper ['tæmpə(r)] *v.* 篡改　　　corridors ['kɒrɪdɔː(r)s] *n.* 走廊

How to dispose of rubbish safely

wrapped [ræpt] *v.* 包，覆盖，卷起　empty ['emptɪ] *v.* 使……成为空的

bin [bɪn] *n.* 箱子　　　　　　　　procedures [prə'siːdʒə(r)s] *n.* 程序

regard [rɪ'gɑːd] *n.* 注意

How to handle heavy objects

shelves ['ʃelvz] *n.* 架子　　　　capability [ˌkeɪpə'bɪlətɪ] *n.* 能力

trolley ['trɒlɪ] *n.* 手推车　　　manual ['mænjʊəl] *adj.* 体力的

posture ['pɒstʃə(r)] *n.* 姿势

Staying alert

drowsy ['draʊzɪ] *n.* 困倦的

concentrating ['kɒnsntreɪtɪŋ] *v.* 专心

Section 3

Question 28—40

The Zebras' long walk across Africa

真题考点词替换清单

题号	题目——原文
30	confusing information—the question
32	obstruction—the obstacle
33	three different ways—the first/second/final…
35	officially—experts call
36	male zebra—stallion; a number of—seven or eight
38	unsure—this raised the question
39	admiration—remarkable

Paragraph A

bush [bʊʃ] *n.* 灌木丛

terrain [tə'reɪn] *n.* 地带

obvious ['ɒbvɪəs] *adj.* 明显的

motivation [ˌməʊtɪ'veɪʃn] *n.* 动机

extraordinary [ɪk'strɔːdnrɪ] *adj.* 非凡的，特别的

incredible [ɪn'kredəbl] *adj.* 难以置信的

Paragraph B

migration [maɪ'greɪʃn] *n.* 移民，迁移

harems ['hɑːriːms] *n.* 马群

Juvenile foals 未成年的小马驹

loyalty ['lɔɪəltɪ] *n.* 忠诚，衷心

Paragraph C

evaporates [ɪ'væpəreɪts] *v.* 蒸发

moisture ['mɔɪstʃə(r)] *n.* 水蒸气

despite [dɪspaɪt] *prep.* 尽管

plentiful ['plentɪfl] *adj.* 丰富的

salt pans 盐田

Paragraph D

wildebeest ['wɪldəbiːst] *n.* 牛羚

giant ['dʒaɪənt] *adj.* 巨大的

fence [fens] *n.* 栅栏

domestic [də'mestɪk] *adj.* 家养的

obstacle ['ɒbstəkl] *n.* 障碍

Paragraph E

generation [ˌdʒenə'reɪʃn] *n.* 一代

assumed [ə'sjuːmd] *adj.* 假定的

elephants ['elɪfənts] *n.* 大象

Paragraph F

struggle ['strʌgl] *v.* 努力

athlete ['æθliːt] *n.* 运动员

Paragraph G

food chain 食物链

interpret [ɪn'tɜːprɪt] *v.* 解释，说明

trigger ['trɪgə(r)] *v.* 触发

crucial ['kruːʃl] *adj.* 关键的

undoubtedly [ʌn'daʊtɪdlɪ] *adv.* 无疑

herbivores ['hɜːbɪvɔː(r)s] *n.* 食草动物

General Training: Reading and Writing Test 2

Section 1

Question 1—6

Sustainable School Travel Strategy

真题考点词替换清单

题号	题目——原文
3	every year—annually; gather—collect; information—data
4	disappointed—proud 【反】
5	children—pupil; risen—increase; in recent years—last three years

Paragraph 1

engaged [ɪnˈɡeɪdʒd] *adj.* 使用中的

pollution [pəˈluːʃn] *n.* 污染

alert [əˈlɜːt] *adj.* 思维更加敏捷的

Paragraph 2

council [ˈkaʊnsl] *n.* 委员会

sustainable [səˈsteɪnəbl] *adj.* 可持续发展的

annually [ˈænjʊəli] *adv.* 每年

pupils [ˈpjuːpls] *n.* 学生

proud [praʊd] *adj.* 自豪的

despite [dɪˈspaɪt] *prep.* 尽管

Paragraph 3

collaborate [kəˈlæbəreɪt] *v.* 合作，协作

encourage [ɪnˈkʌrɪdʒ] *v.* 鼓励

Question 7—14

Flu: the facts

真题考点词替换清单

题号	题目——原文
7	likely—greater risk; badly affected—implications can be serious
9	new—latest
10	how long—about a year
11	possibility—small chance; type—strain; different—not contained in
12	categories—groups
13	consists of—contains
14	signs—symptoms

Paragraph A

flu [fluː] *n.* 流感

acute [əˈkjuːt] *adj.* 急性的

viral [ˈvaɪrəl] *adj.* 病毒性的

respiratory [rəˈspɪrətri] *adj.* 呼吸的

infection [ɪnˈfekʃn] *n.* 感染

spread [spred] *v.* 传播

Paragraph B

sneezes [sniːzɪz] *n.* 喷嚏　　　　　droplets ['drɒpləts] *n.* 飞沫

virus ['vaɪrəs] *n.* 病毒

Paragraph C

symptoms ['sɪmptəms] *n.* 症状　　　chill [tʃɪl] *n.* 寒冷

headache ['hedeɪk] *n.* 头疼　　　　　muscle pain 肌肉疼痛

extreme fatigue 极度疲劳　　　　　　a dry cough 干咳

sore throat 咽喉痛　　　　　　　　　stuffy nose 鼻塞

estimated ['estɪmətɪd] *v.* 估计，估量　attributable to 由于

Paragraph D

asthma ['æsmə] *n.* 哮喘　　　　　　diabetes [ˌdaɪə'biːtiːz] *n.* 糖尿病

eligible ['elɪdʒəbl] *adj.* 有资格的　　vaccination [ˌvæksɪ'neɪʃn] *n.* 接种疫苗

Paragraph F

antibodies ['æntɪbɒdɪs] *n.* 抗体

Paragraph H

circulating ['sɜːkjəleɪtɪŋ] *v.* 使流通，使传播

constantly ['kɒnstəntlɪ] *adv.* 不断地

Paragraph I

predicted [prɪ'dɪktɪd] *adj.* 预料的 预测的

 Section 2

Question 15—22

Tips for giving an effective business presentation

真题考点词替换清单

题号	题目——原文
15	practising—go through; a family member—relative
16	such as—like

题号	题目——原文
17	less rapid—slow; overcome nerves—relax
18	acceptable—not be too obvious; reassure—secure
19	like—as; people...hear you—your audience
20	check for—look for ; points—ideas
21	plenty of—full of; communicate—presentation
22	like—such as; extra details—subsidiary information

Preparation

evaluate [ɪ'væljʊeɪt] v. 评价，估价

presentation [ˌprezn'teɪʃn] n. 演讲

relative ['relətɪv] n. 亲属

podium ['pəʊdɪəm] n. 讲台

disorientating [dɪs'ɔːrɪənteɪtɪŋ] v. 使迷惑

Dealing with presentation nervousness

nervousness ['nɜːvəsnəs] n. 神经质

adrenaline [ə'drenəlɪn] n. 肾上腺素

concentrate on 关注，集中

calmer [kɑːmə] adj. 更平静的

fiddling ['fɪdlɪŋ] v. 摆动

Structuring effective presentations

subsidiary [səb'sɪdɪərɪ] adj. 辅助的

Question 23—27

How to get a job in journalism

真题考点词替换清单

题号	题目——原文
23	apply for—request; temporary—short-term; local papers—newspapers in the area
24	acquire—reach
25	build up—creating; displaying—show off; ability—talent; progressed—developed
26	detailed—thorough
27	makes sense—clarity; without—no; short—brevity

Paragraph 1

qualification [ˌkwɒlɪfɪ'keɪʃn] *n.* 资格，学历

journalism ['dʒɜːnəlɪzəm] *n.* 新闻业　　practical ['præktɪkl] *adj.* 实际的

theoretical [ˌθɪə'retɪkl] *adj.* 理论的　　substitute ['sʌbstɪtjuːt] *n.* 代替品

internships ['ɪntɜːnʃɪps] *n.* 实习岗位

Paragraph 2

impressive [ɪm'presɪv] *adj.* 令人印象深刻的

portfolio [pɔːt'fəʊliəʊ] *n.* 文件夹　　talent ['tælənt] *n.* 资质

Paragraph 4

curriculum vitae 个人简历

Paragraph 5

essential [ɪ'senʃl] *adj.* 必要的　　conveys [kən'veiːs] *v.* 传递

 Section 3

Question 28—40

What is it like to run a large supermarket?

真题考点词替换清单

题号	题目——原文
30	early—since 1982; career—work
31	different way—new ideas
36	all—someone needs help 【反】
37	worried—thinks; before the store is already—on time
39	thrown away—scrapped

Paragraph A

identify [aɪ'dentɪfaɪ] *v.* 确定　　perplexed [pə'plekst] *adj.* 为难的

checkout assistant 收银助理　　amuse [ə'mjuːz] *v.* 娱乐

Paragraph B

enthusiastic [ɪnˌθjuːzɪˈæstɪk] *adj.* 热情的   overnight [ˌəʊvəˈnaɪt] *adv.* 通宵

grocery [ˈɡrəʊsərɪ] *n.* 食品杂货店

Paragraph C

trolley [ˈtrɒlɪ] *n.* 手推车   prioritise [praɪˈɒrətaɪz] *v.* 给……优先权

Paragraph D

disappointing [ˌdɪsəˈpɔɪntɪŋ] *adj.* 令人失望的

florist [ˈflɒrɪst] *n.* 花商；种花人

Paragraph E

turnover [ˈtɜːnəʊvə(r)] *n.* 营业额   layout [ˈleɪaʊt] *n.* 布局；设计

squashy [ˈskwɒʃɪ] *adj.* 熟透的

Paragraph F

wastage [ˈweɪstɪdʒ] *n.* 损耗；衰老   scrapped [skræpt] *adj.* 报废的

manually [ˈmænjʊəlɪ] *adj.* 手动地

Paragraph G

supervisor [ˈsuːpəvaɪzə(r)] *n.* 监督人

Paragraph H

shrink [ʃrɪŋk] *v.* 收缩；畏缩   perspective [pəˈspektɪv] *n.* 预期；期望

General Training: Reading and Writing
Test 3

🔺 *Section 1*

Question 1—6

Summer activities at London's Kew Gardens

真题考点词替换清单

题号	题目——原文
1	different—every; sections—part

题号	题目——原文
2	art showing—exhibition; a different part of the world—South American
3	work exhibited—show
4	need—depends on
5	daily at the same times—on the hour throughout the day
6	relationship—how they interact; creatures—birds and bats

A

spectacular [spek'tækjələ(r)] *adj.* 壮观的

B

conservatory [kən's3ːvətrɪ] *n.* 温室　　　　stunning ['stʌnɪŋ] *adj.* 极好的

wildlife ['waɪldlaɪf] *n.* 野生动物

biodiversity [ˌbaɪəʊdaɪ'vɜːsətɪ] *n.* 生物多样性

C

gigantic [dʒaɪ'gæntɪk] *adj.* 巨大的　　　　sculptures ['skʌlptʃə(r)s] *n.* 雕像

interact [ˌɪntər'ækt] *v.* 互相影响

D

extraordinary [ɪk'strɔːdnrɪ] *adj.* 非凡的　　plam house 棕榈树温室

dusk [dʌsk] *n.* 黄昏　　　　　　　　　　choruses ['kɔːrəsɪs] *n.* 合唱

E

category ['kætəgərɪ] *n.* 类型，种类

F

interactive [ˌɪntər'æktɪv] *adj.* 交互式的　　landscape ['lændskeɪp] *n.* 景观

tunnel ['tʌnl] *n.* 隧道　　　　　　　　　fungi ['fʌŋgaɪ] *n.* 真菌

G

breath [breθ] *n.* 呼吸

H

botanical [bə'tænɪkl] *adj.* 植物学的   exotic [ɪg'zɒtɪk] *adj.* 异国的

Question 7—14

City Park and Ride

真题考点词替换清单

题号	题目——原文
8	fallen—reducing
10	must—possible【反】
12	free—£1.10【反】

Paragraph 1

purpose-built ['pɜːpəsbɪlt] *adj.* 为特殊目的建造的

congestion [kən'dʒestʃən] *n.* 堵车

Paragraph 2

scheduled ['ʃedjuːld] *adj.* 预定的   vehicles ['viːəkls] *n.* 车辆，交通工具

Paragraph 3

individual [ˌɪndɪ'vɪdʒʊəl] *adj.* 个人的

Paragraph 4

fare [feə(r)] *n.* 费用

unaccompanied [ˌʌnə'kʌmpənɪd] *adj.* 无人陪同的

Paragraph 5

allocated ['æləkeɪtɪd] *adj.* 分配的

Paragraph 6

concessionary [kən'seʃənərɪ] *adj.* 优惠的

 Section 2

Question 15—20

How to organise a successful business conference

真题考点词替换清单

题号	题目——原文
15	times—periods
16	spaces—areas; smaller meetings—groups for discussions
17	such as—ample
19	identification—name
20	opinions—responses

To start with

hassle-free ['hæslfriː] *adj.* 没有麻烦的（指"成功的"）

delegates ['delɪgəts] *n.* 代表   identify [aɪ'dentɪfaɪ] *v.* 确定

tailor ['teɪlə(r)] *v.* 量身定制

Where and when

periods ['pɪərɪədz] *n.* 周期   lecture hall 讲堂

anticipated [æn'tɪsɪpeɪtɪd] *v.* 预期   potential [pə'tenʃl] *adj.* 潜在的

Who

ample ['æmpl] *adj.* 足够的

demanding [dɪ'mɑːndɪŋ] *adj.* 要求高的，苛刻的

Contacting people

distribution [ˌdɪstrɪ'bjuːʃn] *n.* 分布，分配

Final arrangements

approximately [ə'prɒksɪmətlɪ] *adv.* 大约

provisional [prə'vɪʒənl] *adj.* 临时的，暂时的

questionnaires [ˌkwestʃə'neə(r)s] *n.* 调查问卷

Question 21—27

真题考点词替换清单

题号	题目——原文
21	improve—increasing; chance—likelihood
22	think of—create
23	a good time—an excellent opportunity; ask—request; extra—additional
24	critisism—negative assessments
25	a number of—a list of; individual—personal; arising from—based on
26	half-way through the year—six months; request—ask for
27	work—job

How to deal with the annual performance appraisal

appraisal [ə'preɪzl] *n.* 评价，评估

critical ['krɪtɪkl] *adj.* 至关重要的

superiors [suː'pɪərɪə(r)s] *n.* 上级

likelihood ['laɪklɪhʊd] *n.* 可能性

Preparation

additional [ə'dɪʃənl] *adj.* 额外的

responsibilities [rɪˌspɒnsə'bɪlətɪs] *n.* 责任，职责

During the appraisal

assessments [ə'sesmənts] *n.* 评价，评估

attack [ə'tæk] *n.* 攻击

calmly ['kɑːmlɪ] *adv.* 平静地，冷静地

After the Apprisal

detailed ['diːteɪld] *adj.* 详细的，详尽的

measurable ['meʒərəbl] *adj.* 能够测量的

scores [skɔː(r)s] *n.* 成绩，得分

progress ['prəʊgres] *n.* 进步

criticisms ['krɪtɪsɪzəmz] *n.* 批评

⬆ Section 3

Question 28—40

Effects to save a special bird—he spoon-billed sandpiper

真题考点词替换清单

题号	题目——原文
28	unusual—special
30	long journey—great distances
32	disappointment—concern; desirable outcomes—joy
33	optimism—hope
34	main—primary; purpose—aim
38	known as—called
39	plentiful—abundance
40	lack—relatively few

Paragraph A

spoon-billed [spuːnbɪld] *adj.* 勺嘴型的

sandpiper ['sændpaɪpə(r)] *n.* 鹬

migratory ['maɪgrətri] *adj.* 迁移的

flattened ['flætnd] *adj.* 扁平的

serration [se'reɪʃn] *n.* 锯齿状

Paragraph B

imperilled [ɪmpe'rəld] *adj.* 处于危险中的

hatch [hætʃ] *n.* 孵化　孵

Paragraph C

tropical ['trɒpɪkl] *adj.* 热带的

hostile ['hɒstaɪl] *adj.* 敌对的

predator ['predətə(r)] *n.* 掠食者

chick [tʃɪk] *n.* 小鸡

Paragraph D

tidal ['taɪdl] *adj.* 潮汐的

subsistence [səb'sɪstəns] *n.* 生存；存在

hazard ['hæzəd] *v.* 冒……的危险

intervention [ˌɪntə'venʃn] *n.* 介入；调停

Paragraph E

expedition [ˌekspə'dɪʃn] n. 探险队　　　destination [ˌdestɪ'neɪʃn] n. 目的地

territory ['terətrɪ] n. 领土　　　incubation [ˌɪŋkjʊ'beɪʃn] n. 孵化

microphone ['maɪkrəfəʊn] n. 麦克风

Paragraph F

rubber ['rʌbə(r)] n. 橡胶　　　crucial ['kruːʃl] adj. 至关重要的

General Training: Reading and Writing Test 4

⬆ Section 1

Question 1—7

Visitor attractions in southern England

真题考点词替换清单

题号	题目——原文
1	animals—species
2	business conference—corporate events
3	the last century—a hundred years ago
4	all year round—whatever the season
5	light meals—snacks

Paragraph A

reconstructed [ˌriːkən'strʌktɪd] v. 重建，改造　atmosphere ['ætməsfɪə(r)] n. 气氛

Paragraph B

observatory [əb'zɜːvətrɪ] n. 天文台，气象台　corporate ['kɔːpərət] adj. 团体的

Paragraph C

admire [əd'maɪə(r)] v. 钦佩，赞美

Paragraph D

renowned [rɪ'naʊnd] adj. 著名的　　　painter ['peɪntə(r)] n. 画家

Paragraph E

Madagascar [ˌmædə'gæskə(r)] n. 马达加斯加岛

endangered [ɪn'deɪndʒə(r)d] *adj.* 濒临灭绝的

extinction [ɪk'stɪŋkʃn] *n.* 灭绝

Paragraph F

costumes ['kɒstjuːmz] *n.* 戏服

 Section 2

Question 8—14

Paragliding in Australia

真题考点词替换清单

题号	题目——原文
11	unaccompanied—independently
12	before...training—on your course【反】
13	any age—14【反】

What is paragliding?

paragliding ['pærəglaɪdɪŋ] *n.* 高崖跳伞运动，滑翔伞运动

metal ['metl] *adj.* 金属的　　　　wood [wʊd] *n.* 木材

nylon ['naɪlɒn] *n.* 尼龙　　　　polyester [ˌpɒliˈestə(r)] *n.* 聚酯

canopy ['kænəpi] *n.* 遮篷　　　　harness ['hɑːnɪs] *n.* 降落伞背带

parachute ['pærəʃuːt] *n.* 降落伞

Is it safe?

crash [kræʃ] *n.* 坠落

Where do I learn?

spectacular cliffs 壮观的悬崖　　　inflate [ɪn'fleɪt] *v.* 膨胀，充气

launch [lɔːntʃ] *v.* 出发，开始　　　licence ['laɪsns] *n.* 许可证

What do I need?

pilots ['paɪləts] *n.* 飞行员　　　helmet ['helmɪt] *n.* 钢盔

sophisticated [sə'fɪstɪkeɪtɪd] *adj.* 复杂的

Who can do it?

potential [pə'tenʃl] *adj.* 潜在的　　　muscles ['mʌslz] *n.* 肌肉

Question 15—21

How to prepare for an interview?

真题考点词替换清单

题号	题目——原文
15	gain—have more
16	documents—materials
17	involved in—go with; post—job
18	unpaid help—voluntary work
19	development—future
20	work record—career history

Why prepare?

candidate ['kændɪdət] *n.* 应试者   brilliant ['brɪlɪənt] *adj.* 出众的

obviously ['ɒbvɪəslɪ] *adv.* 明显地

What to prepare?

specification [ˌspesɪfɪ'keɪʃn] *n.* 规格，说明

voluntary ['vɒləntrɪ] *adj.* 志愿的   unrelated [ˌʌnrɪ'leɪtɪd] *adj.* 无关的

gained [geɪnd] *v.* 获得

Question 22—27

Setting up your own business

真题考点词替换清单

题号	题目——原文
23	market—promote; method—system
24	find—look for; buy—invest
25	in accordance with—regulates; other essentials—insurance and tax
26	how much to charge—prices; calculate—build in
27	consider—think

Know your market

competitors [kəm'petɪtə(r)s] *n.* 竞争者   persuade [pə'sweɪd] *v.* 说服

established [ɪ'stæblɪʃt] *adj.* 确定的

How will you reach the customers?

traders ['treɪdə(r)s] *n.* 交易员

How will your business work?

recruit [rɪ'kruːt] *n.* 招聘   essential [ɪ'senʃl] *adj.* 必要的

The money!

forecast ['fɔːkɑːst] *n.* 预报，预测   profit ['prɒfɪt] *n.* 利润，利益

Section 3

Question 28—40

真题考点词替换清单

题号	题目——原文
28	solution—key; falling—decline; numbers—populations
29	features—adaptations
30	reproductive—breeding
31	lonely—self-sufficient
32	fussy eater—selective feeders
34	a range of—a variety of
36	difficult—problems
37	increased—higher; running fast—superior speed
38	resemble—like（538 个核心考点词第一名！）
39	characteristics—physical adaptations; avoid capture—survive; all-round—360°
40	massive—large; separately—independently

Understanding hares

cousin ['kʌzn] *n.* 表亲

intensification [ɪnˌtensɪfɪ'keɪʃn] *n.* 密集化

Paragraph A

herbivore ['hɜːbɪvɔː(r)] *n.* 食草动物

fondness [fɒndnəs] *n.* 爱好；溺爱

unploughed [ʌn'plaʊd] *adj.* 未耕的

margin ['mɑːdʒɪn] *n.* 边缘

Paragraph B

stamina ['stæmɪnə] *n.* 毅力

Paragraph C

leverets ['levərəts] *n.* 小兔

pregnant ['pregnənt] *adj.* 怀孕的

mate [meɪt] *v.* 交配

Paragraph D

simultaneously [ˌsɪməl'teɪnɪəslɪ] *adv.* 同时

predator ['predətə(r)] *n.* 食肉动物；掠食者

Paragraph E

nutritious [njʊ'trɪʃəs] *adj.* 有营养的

injurious [ɪn'dʒʊərɪəs] *adj.* 有害的

Paragraph F

thwarted [θwɔːtɪd] *adj.* 挫败的

wildness [waɪldnəs] *n.* 野蛮；原始

Cambridge
IELTS
12

Test 5

🔺 *Reading Passage 1: Cork*

Paragraph 1

thick [θɪk] *adj.* 厚的

bark [bɑːk] *n.* 树皮

oak tree 橡树

remarkable [rɪ'mɑːkəbl] *adj.* 不同寻常的

elastic [ɪ'læstɪk] *adj.* 有弹性的

tough [tʌf] *adj.* 坚硬的

buoyant ['bɔɪənt] *adj.* 有浮力的

fire-resistant ['faɪə(r)rɪ'zɪstənt] *adj.* 耐高温的

millennia [mɪ'lenɪə] *n.* 千年

seal [siːl] *v.* 密封

beehive ['biːhaɪv] *n.* 蜜蜂箱

sandals ['sændlz] *n.* 凉鞋；便鞋

Paragraph 2

extraordinary [ɪk'strɔːdnrɪ] *adj.* 非同寻常的

insulate ['ɪnsjʊleɪt] *v.* 使隔绝

wrap [ræp] *v.* 包

trunk [trʌŋk] *n.* 树干

branches [brɑːntʃz] *n.* 树枝

constant ['kɒnstənt] *adj.* 恒定的

defence(defense) [dɪ'fens] *n.* 抵御

cellular structure 细胞结构

cubic centimeter 立方厘米

replicate ['replɪkeɪt] *v.* 复制

fill with 装满

elasticity [ˌiːlæ'stɪsətɪ] *n.* 弹力

squash [skwɒʃ] *v.* 挤压

spring back 回弹

shape [ʃeɪp] 形状

release [rɪ'liːs] *v.* 释放

Paragraph 3

Mediterranean [ˌmedɪtə'reɪnɪən] 地中海

flourish ['flʌrɪʃ] *v.* 茂盛生长

millimeter ['mɪlɪmiːtə(r)] *n.* 毫米

grape vines 葡萄藤

thrive [θraɪv] *v.* 茂盛生长

root [ruːt] *n.* 根

moisture ['mɔɪstʃə(r)] *n.* 水分   nutrient ['njuːtrɪənt] *n.* 养分

meet [miːt] *v.* 满足   account for 对……做出解释（导致）

roughly ['rʌflɪ] *adv.* 大约

Paragraph 4

family-owned ['fæməliəʊnd] *adj.* 家族持有的

patience ['peɪʃns] *n.* 耐心   sapling ['sæplɪŋ] *n.* 树苗

harvest ['hɑːvɪst] *v./n.* 收获   a gap of... ……的间隔

approximately [ə'prɒksɪmətlɪ] *adv.* 大约   decade ['dekeɪd] *n.* 十年

strip [strɪp] *v.* 剥   damp [dæmp] *adj.* 潮湿的

Paragraph 5

specialized ['speʃəlaɪzd] *adj.* 专业化的

profession [prə'feʃn] *n.* 工作（指专业技能强的工作）

vertical ['vɜːtɪkl] *adj.* 垂直的   axe [æks] *n.* 斧子

lever/prise ['liːvə(r)/praɪz] *v.* 撬

semi-circular ['semɪ'sɜːkjələ(r)] *adj.* 半圆形的

husk [hʌsk] *n.* 树皮   boil [bɔɪl] *v.* 煮沸

insects ['ɪnsekts] *n.* 昆虫   bottle stopper 瓶塞

ideal [aɪ'diːəl] *adj.* 理想的   thermal insulation 隔热

acoustic insulation 隔音   concrete ['kɒŋkriːt] *n.* 混凝土

Paragraph 6

virtual ['vɜːtʃʊəl] *adj.* 事实上的   monopoly [mə'nɒpəlɪ] *n.* 垄断

chemical compound 化合物   trillion ['trɪljən] *n.* 万亿

spoil [spɔɪl] *v.* 破坏   plastic ['plæstɪk] *adj.* 塑料的

aluminum screw caps 铝螺旋盖　　　substitute ['sʌbstɪtjuːt] n. 代替品

Paragraph 7

classic ['klæsɪk] adj. 经典的　　　　image ['ɪmɪdʒ] n. 形象

associate [ə'səʊʃieɪt] v. 联系　　　sustainable [sə'steɪnəbl] adj. 可持续的

recycle [ˌriː'saɪkl] v. 回收　　　　resource [rɪ'sɔːs] n. 资源

biodiversity [ˌbaɪəʊdaɪ'vɜːsəti] n. 生物多样性

desertification [dɪˌzɜːtɪfɪ'keɪʃn] n. 沙漠化　promising ['prɒmɪsɪŋ] adj. 有希望的

Question

synthetic [sɪn'θetɪk] adj. 人造的　　　natural ['nætʃrəl] adj. 天然的

真题考点词替换清单

题号	题目——原文
2	scientists—technology; synthetic—replicating 【反】; the same...as—never succeeded 【反】
3	first and second harvest—first harvest..., and a gap of...
4	dry—damp...damaged
5	by hand—no mechanical means...has been invented
6	bottle contents—the product contained in the bottle
7	produce—manufacture
8	use—for the user
9	suit—keep with
10	made from...material—product
11	easily—without difficulty
12	aid—support
13	stop—prevent

↟ *Reading Passage 2: COLLECTING AS A HOBBY*

Paragraph 1

psychologist [saɪ'kɒlədʒɪst] *n.* 心理学家

dignify ['dɪgnɪfaɪ] *v.* 被授予；使……高贵

teddy bears 泰迪熊

postcards ['pəʊstkɑːdz] *n.* 明信片

chocolate wrappers 巧克力包装纸

productive [prə'dʌktɪv] *adj.* 富有成效的

fascinating ['fæsɪneɪtɪŋ] *adj.* 吸引人的

technical ['teknɪkl] *adj.* 专门的

postage stamps 邮票

amass [ə'mæs] *v.* 积聚

take times 花费时间

Paragraph 2

instrumental [ˌɪnstrə'mentl] *adj.* 工具的

at a profit 获利

dear [dɪə(r)] *adj.* 高价的

that is 换言之；也就是说

psychological element 心理效应

sense of triumph 成就感

Paragraph 3

items ['aɪtəms] *n.* 物品

bridge club 桥牌社

like-minded [laɪk'maɪndɪd] *adj.* 志趣相投的

variant ['veərɪənt] *n.* 变体

gym [dʒɪm] *n.* 健身房

Paragraph 4

motive ['məʊtɪv] *n.* 动机；目的

particular examples（本文）特别收藏品

recording [rɪ'kɔːdɪŋ] *n.* 唱片

aimless ['eɪmləs] *adj.* 漫无目的的

desire [dɪ'zaɪə(r)] *n./v.* 渴望

rare [reə(r)] *adj.* 稀少的

otherwise ['ʌðəwaɪz] *adv.* 否则

celebrate ['selɪbreɪt] *v.* 庆祝

Paragraph 5

potential [pə'tenʃl] *adj.* 潜在的

fossils ['fɒslz] *n.* 化石

around the globe 全球

inferior to 不如；比不上

vast [vɑːst] *adj.* 大的

Paragraph 6

extent [ɪkˈstent] *n.* 程度

locomotive [ˌləʊkəˈməʊtɪv] *n.* 火车头

engine [ˈendʒɪn] *n.* 引擎

by-product [baɪˈprɒdʌkt] *n.* 随带产生的结果

practitioners [prækˈtɪʃənə(r)s] *n.* （本文）经常参与猜火车的人

specification [ˌspesɪfɪˈkeɪʃn] *n.* 规格

trainspotting [ˈtreɪnspɒtɪŋ] *n.* 猜火车

tick off 列举

Paragraph 7

dolls [dɒlz] *n.* 玩偶

wax [wæks] *n.* 蜡

plastic [ˈplæstɪk] *n.* 塑料

reflect [rɪˈflekt] *v.* 反映

enlarge [ɪnˈlɑːdʒ] *v.* 增加

porcelain [ˈpɔːsəlɪn] *n.* 陶瓷

be inspired to 有兴趣……

notions [ˈnəʊʃns] *n.* 想法；观点

Paragraph 8

insecurity [ˌɪnsɪˈkjʊərəti] *n.* 不安全感

albums [ˈælbəms] *n.* 相册

commonplace [ˈkɒmənpleɪs] *n.* 普遍

depict [dɪˈpɪkt] *v.* 描述

arrange [əˈreɪndʒ] *v.* 排列

neatly [niːtlɪ] *adv.* 整洁地

alphabetical order 字母顺序

Paragraph 9

conscious [ˈkɒnʃəs] *adj.* 意识到的

individualism [ˌɪndɪˈvɪdʒʊəlɪzəm] *n.* 个人特征（个性）

convey [kənˈveɪ] *v.* 传达

Paragraph 10

mildly ['maɪldlɪ] *adv.* 温和地

fulfillment [fʊl'fɪlmənt] *n.* 实行

engross [ɪn'grəʊs] *v.* 全神贯注

eccentric [ɪk'sentrɪk] *adj.* 反常的

Question

completely [kəm'pliːtlɪ] *adv.* 完全地

object ['ɒbdʒɪkt] *n.* 目标；物体

真题考点词替换清单

题号	题目——原文
14	example—they'll look for, say
15	feeling—sense
16	share—exchange
17	similar interests—like-minded
18	life-long—whole lives; special item—recording
19	prevent—give...otherwise
20	different countries—other countries
21	male—among boys and men
25	unusual objects—unexpected as dog collars
26	unlikely to inspire—more than...

Reading Passage 3: *What's the purpose of gaining knowledge?*

Paragraph A

found [faʊnd] *v.* 建立

instruction [ɪn'strʌkʃn] *n.* 用法；指示；命令（本文：学科内容）

motto ['mɒtəʊ] *n.* 座右铭

philosophy [fə'lɒsəfɪ] *n.* 哲学

resort management 度假村管理

law enforcement 法律执行

I kid you not 不开玩笑

institution [ˌɪnstɪ'tjuːʃn] *n.* 机构

apt [æpt] *adj.* 恰当的

career [kə'rɪə(r)] *n.* 职业生涯

interior design 室内设计

arson ['ɑːsn] *n.* 纵火（罪）

meet [miːt] *v.* 满足

academic requirement 学术要求   sign up for 注册；选课

program ['prəʊɡræm] *n.* 大纲

Paragraph B

intend for 打算成为……   prospective [prə'spektɪv] *adj.* 未来的

investigator [ɪn'vestɪɡeɪtə(r)] *n.* 调查员   tricks [trɪks] *n.* 技巧

trade [treɪd] *n.* 行业   deliberately [dɪ'lɪbərətli] *adv.* 故意地

chain of evidence 证据链   prosecution [ˌprɒsɪ'kjuːʃn] *n.* 起诉

court of law 法庭；法院   arsonist ['ɑːsənɪst] *n.* 纵火犯人

professionalization [prəˌfeʃənəlaɪz'eɪʃn] *n.* 职业化

occupation [ˌɒkjʊ'peɪʃn] *n.* 职业   torch [tɔːtʃ] *v.* 放火烧   *n.* 火炬

creep [kriːp] *v.* 慢慢地移动   aspect ['æspekt] *n.* 方面

Paragraph C

anew [ə'njuː] *adv.* 重新   degree [dɪ'ɡriː] *n.* 学位

regular ['reɡjələ(r)] *adj.* 正式的   colleague ['kɒliːɡ] *n.* 同事

ethical ['eθɪkl] *adj.* 伦理的   perspective [pə'spektɪv] *n.* 观点；视角

assignment [ə'saɪnmənt] *n.* 功课   cue [kjuː] *n.* 线索

principled ['prɪnsəpld] *adj.* 有原则的   codify ['kəʊdɪfaɪ] *v.* 编纂

assume [ə'sjuːm] *v.* 假定（认为）   everything under the sun 在世界上

Paragraph D

downright ['daʊnraɪt] *adv.* 完全地   inspiration [ˌɪnspə'reɪʃn] *n.* 灵感

means [miːnz] *n.* 方法

Paragraph E

apply [ə'plaɪ] *v.* 使用   term [tɜːm] *n.* 术语

attitude ['ætɪtjuːd] *n.* 态度

acquisition [ˌækwɪ'zɪʃn] *n.* 获得某物

proposal [prə'pəʊzl] *n.* 建议

a field of knowledge 知识领域

hence [hens] *adv.* 因此

scrutiny ['skruːtənɪ] *n.* 仔细审查

irrelevant [ɪ'reləvənt] *adj.* 不相干的

expertise [ˌekspɜː'tiːz] *n.* 专业技能

capture ['kæptʃə(r)] *v.* 抓住

a professional endeavor 专业技能

deserve [dɪ'zɜːv] *v.* 值得

Paragraph F

supremely [su:'priːmlɪ] *adv.* 非常

prosecute ['prɒsɪkjuːt] *v.* 起诉

presumably [prɪ'zjuːməblɪ] *adv.* 可能；大概

articulate [ɑː'tɪkjʊleɪt] *v.* 明确地表达

welfare of society 社会福利

destructive [dɪ'strʌktɪv] *adj.* 破坏性的

unprincipled [ʌn'prɪnsəpld] *adj.* 没有原则的

fraud [frɔːd] *n.* 欺骗

divergent [daɪ'vɜːdʒənt] *adj.* 不同的

murder ['mɜːdə(r)] *n.* 谋杀

relevant ['reləvənt] *adj.* 相关的

generalize ['dʒenrəlaɪz] *v.* 概括

via ['vaɪə] *prep.* 通过

reckless ['rekləs] *adj.* 鲁莽的

identical [aɪ'dentɪkl] *adj.* 完全相同的

practice medicine 行医

Question

commitment [kə'mɪtmənt] *n.* 承诺

attracting [ə'træktɪŋ] *n.* 吸引

expectation [ˌekspek'teɪʃn] *n.* 预期 (未来的结果)

criminal intent 犯罪目的

equal ['iːkwəl] *adj.* 平等的

outcomes ['aʊtkʌmz] *n.* 结果

intend to 打算……

真题考点词替换清单

题号	题目——原文
27	surprising—I kid you not,...
28	wrong—dishonest and illegal
29	two meanings—codified; ethical
30	unexpected—crazy
31	two key issues—achieve (means); what X is (purpose)
32	different—divergent
33	study—sign up for the course
34	expectation—prospective; specializing—learn all the tricks of the trade
35	find—establish
36	lead to—for; successful—effective
39	too...to—criticize
40	detailed definition—seem; like 【反】

Test 6

↑ *Reading Passage1: The risks agriculture faces in developing countries*

Paragraph A

synthesis ['sɪnθəsɪs] *n.* 综合

distinguish [dɪ'stɪŋgwɪʃ] *v.* 区别

productive [prə'dʌktɪv] *adj.* 生产的

right [raɪt] *n.* 权利

hugely ['hjuːdʒlɪ] *adv.* 非常

unique [jʊ'niːk] *adj.* 独特的

political [pə'lɪtɪkl] *adj.* 权益的

cultural values 文化价值

entrench [ɪn'trentʃ] *v.* 确立；牢牢建立

Paragraph B

smallholder ['smɔːlhəʊldə(r)] *n.* 小农

adverse ['ædvɜːs] *adj.* 不利的

in terms of 在……方面

rainfall ['reɪnfɔːl] *n.* 降雨

infrastructure ['ɪnfrəstrʌktʃə(r)] *n.* 基础设施

counter-intuitively ['kaʊntə(r)ɪn'tjuːɪtɪvlɪ] *adv.* 让人意想不到的是

prevalent ['prevələnt] *adj.* 普遍的

Paragraph C

participant [pɑː'tɪsɪpənt] *n.* 参与者

online debate 在线讨论

address [ə'dres] *v.* 处理

underlying [ˌʌndə'laɪɪŋ] *adj.* 潜在的；根本的

inability [ˌɪnə'bɪlətɪ] *n.* 无能力

identify [aɪ'dentɪfaɪ] *v.* 确定；辨认

driver ['draɪvə(r)] *n.* 驱动力

Paragraph D

mitigating ['mɪtɪɡeɪtɪŋ] *n.* 减轻

call for 提倡

intervention [ˌɪntə'venʃn] *n.* 介入

storage facilities 储存设备

holding ['həʊldɪŋ] *n.* 持有

wild swings 猛烈震动

essayist ['eseɪɪst] *n.* 分析者

state [steɪt] *n.* 州

produce [prə'djuːs] *n.* 农产品

procurement [prə'kjʊəmənt] *n.* 采购

stock [stɒk] *n.* 股票

alleviate [ə'liːvɪeɪt] *v.* 缓和

Paragraph E

held up 提出（举起）

poverty ['pɒvətɪ] *n.* 贫穷

commentator ['kɒmənteɪtə(r)] *n.* 评论员

security [sɪ'kjʊərətɪ] *n.* 安全

compensate for 赔偿

landowner ['lændəʊnə(r)] *n.* 地主

social safety nets 社会保障

shock [ʃɒk] *n.* 危机（震动）

translate [træns'leɪt] *v.* 转化

subsidy ['sʌbsədɪ] *n.* 津贴；补助金

stranglehold ['stræŋglhəʊld] *n.* 束缚

Paragraph F

insurance [ɪn'ʃʊərəns] *n.* 保险

commodity futures markets 商品期货市场

rural ['rʊərəl] *adj.* 乡村的

adoption [ə'dɒpʃn] *n.* 采用

excessively [ɪk'sesɪvlɪ] *adv.* 过度地

emphasize ['emfəsaɪz] *v.* 强调

evident ['evɪdənt] *adj.* 一目了然的

scheme [skiːm] *n.* 计划

practice ['præktɪs] *n.* 方法

price volatility 价格波动

transparency [træns'pærənsɪ] *n.* 透明度

contend [kən'tend] *v.* 主张；争论

Paragraph G

mention ['menʃn] *v.* 提到

yield [ji:ld] *n.* 产量

magnitude ['mægnɪtjuːd] *n.* 量级（大小）

resilient [rɪ'zɪlɪənt] *adj.* 有弹性的（强适应性的）

co-founder ['koʊ 'faʊndə(r)] *n.* 联合创始人

peasant ['peznt] *n.* 农民

make up 补足

menu ['menjuː] *n.* 菜单（本文指有更多的选择）

Paragraph H

autonomous [ɔː'tɒnəməs] *adj.* 自主的

enhance [ɪn'hɑːns] *v.* 提高

synchronize ['sɪŋkrənaɪz] *v.* 同时发生

bargaining ['bɑːgənɪŋ] *n.* 议价

as a free good 唾手可得

stakeholders ['steɪkhəʊldə(r)s] *n.* 利益相关者

Paragraph I

presence ['prezns] *n.* 存在

intermediary [ˌɪntə'miːdɪərɪ] *adj.* 中间的

dictate [dɪk'teɪt] *v.* 命令（操纵）

subscription [səb'skrɪpʃn] *n.* 签署

guarantee [ˌgærən'tiː] *n.* 保证

fair [feə(r)] *adj.* 合理的

distribution [ˌdɪstrɪ'bjuːʃn] *n.* 分销

Question

assistance [ə'sɪstəns] *n.* 援助

collaborate [kə'læbəreɪt] *v.* 合作

standard ['stændəd] *n.* 标准

variation [ˌveərɪ'eɪʃn] *n.* 变异；变化

irrigation programmes 灌溉项目

真题考点词替换清单

题号	题目——原文
1	only—unique
2	challenges—risks; certain parts of the world—developing country
3	difficulties—does not...good
4	does not—...not poor, but rich...non-farmer traders
5	benefit—enhance; reduce
6	improve the standard of living—held up social safety nets and public welfare programmes...
9	infrastructure—basic services

🔺 *Reading Passage 2: The Lost City*

Paragraph A

encounter [ɪnˈkaʊntə(r)] *n.* 偶然碰见

icon [ˈaɪkɒn] *n.* 代表

remote [rɪˈməʊt] *adj.* 遥远的

capital [ˈkæpɪtl] *n.* 首都

plateau [ˈplætəʊ] *n.* 高原

valley [ˈvælɪ] *n.* 山谷

route [ruːt] *n.* 线路

ruined [ˈruːɪnd] *adj.* 毁灭的

academic [ˌækəˈdemɪk] *n.* 学者

hinterland [ˈhɪntəlænd] *n.* 内陆；内地

empire [ˈempaɪə(r)] *n.* 帝国

elevation [ˌelɪˈveɪʃn] *n.* 海拔

circuitous [səˈkjuːɪtəs] *adj.* 绕行的

canyon [ˈkænjən] *n.* 峡谷

Paragraph B

set off 出发

precede [prɪˈsiːd] *v.* 领先；在……之前

blast [blɑːst] *v.* 开辟

mule [mjuː] *n.* 骡子

rubber [ˈrʌbə(r)] *n.* 橡胶

previous [ˈpriːvɪəs] *adj.* 早先的

substantial [səb'stænʃl] *adj.* 大量的　　corner ['kɔːnə(r)] *n.* 偏僻处

Paragraph C

descent [dɪ'sent] *n.* 下降　　trek [trek] *n.* 艰苦跋涉

companions [kəm'pænɪəns] *n.* 同伴；同事

dull [dʌl] *adj.* 阴暗的　　damp [dæmp] *adj.* 潮湿的

keen on 热衷于……　　prospect ['prɒspekt] *n.* 期待

relate [rɪ'leɪt] *v.* 提到　　expectation [ˌekspek'teɪʃn] *n.* 期待

Paragraph D

vivid style 栩栩如生的风格

ever-present ['evə(r) 'preznt] *adj.* 经常存在的

deadly snakes 致命毒蛇

spring [sprɪŋ] *v.* 弹起（文中用 spring 表示蛇起得快的含义）

pursuit [pə'sjuːt] *v.* 追　　prey [preɪ] *n.* 猎物

mounting ['maʊntɪŋ] *adj.* 逐渐增加的　　terrace ['terəs] *n.* 梯田

mausoleum [ˌmɔːsə'liːəm] *n.* 陵墓　　monument ['mɒnjʊmənt] *adj.* 壮观的

grand [grænd] *adj.* 宏伟的　　ceremonial [ˌserɪ'məʊnɪəl] *adj.* 仪式的

spellbound ['spelbaʊnd] *adj.* 着迷的

Paragraph E

hindsight ['haɪndsaɪt] *n.* 过后被认可　　reveal [rɪ'viːl] *v.* 揭露

dimension [daɪ'menʃn] *n.* 尺寸　　at this stage 眼下；在那时

extent [ɪk'stent] *n.* 程度

Paragraph F

make a name 有声望　　birthplace ['bɜːθpleɪs] *n.* 诞生地

chronicler ['krɒnɪklə(r)] *n.* 年代史编者

flee [fliː] *v.* 逃走

invade [ɪn'veɪd] *v.* 侵略

desperate ['despərət] *adj.* 不顾一切的

magnificent [mæg'nɪfɪsnt] *adj.* 壮丽的

jungle ['dʒʌŋgl] *n.* 丛林

Paragraph G

perplex [pə'pleks] *v.* 使困惑

archaeologist [ˌɑːkɪ'ɒlədʒɪst] *n.* 考古学家

alike [ə'laɪk] *adj.* 相似的

conquest ['kɒŋkwest] *n.* 征服；占领

country estate 庄园

emperor ['empərə(r)] *n.* 皇帝

elite [eɪ'liːt] *n.* 社会精英阶层

custom ['kʌstəm] *n.* 传统

descendant [dɪ'sendənt] *n.* 后代

Question

particular route 特定的路线

enthusiasm [ɪn'θjuːzɪæzəm] *n.* 热情

真题考点词替换清单

题号	题目——原文
14	aim—greatest achievement
15	new—particular route; blast
16	lack—least
17	dramatic—unbelievable dream; spellbound
18	different accounts—said little
19	publish—broke the story
20	common—gained wide acceptance; belief—idea
23	as soon as he saw it—nor did he realize…
25	transportation—brought up

↑ *Reading Passage 3: The Benefits of Being Bilingual*

Paragraph A

figure ['fɪgə(r)] *n.* 数字；数据

bilingual [ˌbaɪ'lɪŋgwəl] *adj.* 双语的

multilingual [,mʌltɪ'lɪŋgwəl] *adj.* 多语的

peer [pɪə(r)] *n.* 同龄人

deeply ['diːplɪ] *adv.* 深入地

interact [,ɪntə'rækt] *v.* 相互影响

cognitive ['kɒgnətɪv] *adj.* 认知的

neurological system 神经系统

Paragraph B

active ['æktɪv] *adj.* 激活的；积极的

entire [ɪn'taɪə(r)] *adj.* 全部的

sequential [sɪ'kwenʃl] *adj.* 有顺序的；连续的

order ['ɔːdə(r)] *n.* 顺序；命令

activate ['æktɪveɪt] *v.* 刺激

recognition [,rekəg'nɪʃn] *n.* 感知；分辨

activation [,æktɪ'veɪʃn] *n.* 激活

auditory ['ɔːdətrɪ] *adj.* 听觉的

corresponding [,kɒrə'spɒndɪŋ] *adj.* 一致的

compelling [kəm'pelɪŋ] *adj.* 引人注目的

phenomenon [fə'nɒmɪnən] *n.* 现象

objects ['ɒbdʒɪkts] *n.* 物品

map [mæp] *v.* 映射

Paragraph C

persistent linguistic competition 持续语言选择

name [neɪm] *v.* 选中；指定

tip-of-the-tongue states 话在嘴边说不出来

quite [kwaɪt] *adv.* 完全

constant ['kɒnstənt] *adj.* 经常的

juggling ['dʒʌglɪŋ] *n.* 杂耍（本文：使用）

conflict management 冲突管理

classic ['klæsɪk] *adj.* 经典的

font [fɒnt] *n.* 字形

excel [ɪk'sel] *v.* 擅长

tap [tæp] *v.* 采用

competing [kəm'piːtɪŋ] *adj.* 干扰的；相互矛盾的

perceptual [pə'septʃʊəl] *adj.* 感知的

switch [swɪtʃ] *v.* 转换

categorize ['kætəgəraɪz] *v.* 分类

Paragraph D

extend to 延伸

sensory ['sensərɪ] *adj.* 感觉的

adolescent [ˌædə'lesnt] *n.* 青少年

intervening [ˌɪntə'viːnɪŋ] *adj.* 介入的；干扰的

brain stem 脑干

encoding [ɪn'kəʊdɪŋ] *n.* 编码

fundamental [ˌfʌndə'mentl] *adj.* 基本的

frequency ['friːkwənsɪ] *n.* 频率

pitch [pɪtʃ] *n.* 高音

perception [pə'sepʃn] *n.* 感觉；知觉

Paragraph E

interference [ˌɪntə'fɪərəns] *n.* 干扰

Paragraph F

recruiting [rɪ'kruːtɪŋ] *n.* 招募

degenerative [dɪ'dʒenərətɪv] *adj.* 退化的

initial [ɪ'nɪʃl] *adj.* 最初的

symptom ['sɪmptəm] *n.* 症状

severity [sɪ'verətɪ] *n.* 严重

outward ['aʊtwəd] *adj.* 肉体的；外面的

Paragraph G

tinkling ['tɪŋklɪŋ] *adj.* 清脆的

puppet ['pʌpɪt] *n.* 木偶

halfway [ˌhɑːf'weɪ] *n.* 中途

opposite ['ɒpəzɪt] *adj.* 相反的

infants ['ɪnfənts] *n.* 婴幼儿

navigate ['nævɪgeɪt] *v.* 操纵；航行

impart [ɪm'pɑːt] *v.* 给予；传授

Question

observe [əb'zɜːv] *v.* 观察；看

engage [ɪn'geɪʒ] *v.* 参与

simultaneous [ˌsɪml'teɪnɪəs] *adj.* 同时的

mechanism ['mekənɪzəm] *n.* 途径

handle ['hændl] *v.* 操作

superior [suː'pɪərɪə(r)] *adj.* 出众的；更好的

consistently [kən'sɪstəntlɪ] *adv.* 一贯地   non-verbal [nɒn 'vɜːbl] *adj.* 非语言的

真题考点词替换清单

题号	题目——原文
27	certain objects—stamp; observe—study
28	known as—called
30	handle—perform; more—better
31	superior—better
35	all situations—when.... . when...
37	non-verbal auditory input—background noise
38	before we learn to speak—start very early
40	negative—difficulties

Test 7

Reading Passage 1: Flying tortoises

Paragraph A

spiny ['spaɪnɪ] *adj.* 多刺的

uneven [ʌn'iːvn] *adj.* 不均匀的

plain [pleɪn] *n.* 平原

distinct [dɪ'stɪŋkt] *adj.* 分布各处的；不同的

lunar ['luːnə(r)] *adj.* 月亮上的

vegetation [ˌvedʒə'teɪʃn] *n.* 植被

peak [piːk] *n.* 山顶

terrain [tə'reɪn] *n.* 地带

give rise to 产生

absence ['æbsəns] *n.* 无

weighing [weɪɪŋ] *n.* 体重

cacti ['kæktaɪ] *n.* 仙人掌（复数）

lava ['lɑːvə] *n.* 熔岩

landscape ['lændskeɪp] *n.* 土地

skirt [skɜːt] *v.* 绕过

respite ['respaɪt] *n.* 缓解

inhospitable [ˌɪnhɒ'spɪtəbl] *adj.* 荒凉的

subspecies [sʌb'spiːʃiːz] *n.* 亚种

predator ['predətə(r)] *n.* 捕食者

Paragraph B

archipelago [ˌɑːkɪ'peləgəʊ] *n.* 群岛

whaling ships 捕鲸船

exploitation [ˌeksplɔɪ'teɪʃn] *n.* 开发（本文：捕猎）

exponentially [ˌekspə'nenʃəlɪ] *adv.* 成倍地

passage ['pæsɪdʒ] *n.* 航程

high-grade [haɪ greɪd] *adj.* 优质的

clear [klɪə(r)] *v.* 清理

pirate ['paɪrət] *n.* 海盗

capable ['keɪpəbl] *adj.* 有能力的

process ['prəʊses] *v.* 加工

exacerbate [ɪg'zæsəbeɪt] *v.* 加重

alien species 外来物种

cattle ['kætl] *n.* 牛   goat [gəʊt] *n.* 羊

rat [ræt] *n.* 鼠

Paragraph C

captive-breeding ['kæptɪv 'briːdɪŋ] *n.* 圈养（人工养殖）

overpopulation [ˌəʊvəˌpɒpjʊ'leɪʃn] *n.* 数量过剩

Paragraph D

pressing ['presɪŋ] *adj.* 紧迫的   reintroduce [ˌriːɪntrə'djuːs] *v.* 再引入

hardened ['hɑːdnd] *adj.* 变硬的   shell [ʃel] *n.* 壳

Paragraph E

repatriation [ˌriːˌpeɪtrɪ'eɪʃn] *n.* 遣送回国（本文：放归）

on the backs of men 人背着

treacherous ['tretʃərəs] *adj.* 暗藏危险的

trail [treɪl] *n.* 小路   motor yacht captain 机动游艇长

helicopter pilot 直升机长

Paragraph F

unprecedented [ʌn'presɪdentɪd] *adj.* 前所未有的

logistical [lə'dʒɪstɪkl] *adj.* 物流的   air ambulance 空中救援机

rear [rɪə(r)] *n.* 后开门   custom ['kʌstəm] *adj.* 定做的

crate [kreɪt] *n.* 箱   hold up 装

payload ['peɪləʊd] *n.* 承重   around the clock 夜以继日地

park wardens 公园管理员   remote [rɪ'məʊt] *adj.* 遥远的

Paragraph G

release [rɪ'liːs] *v.* 释放

juvenile ['dʒuːvənaɪl] *adj.* 青少年的　*n.* 青少年

territory ['terətrɪ] *n.* 领土

feed on 品尝

tiny ['taɪnɪ] *adj.* 小的

lumber ['lʌmbə(r)] *v.* 慢慢地移动

side by side 并肩

symbol ['sɪmbl] *n.* 标志

regeneration [rɪˌdʒenə'reɪʃn] *n.* 重获新生

Question

carry out 实行

conservation [ˌkɒnsə'veɪʃn] *n.* 保护

destruction [dɪ'strʌkʃn] *n.* 破坏

<h3 style="text-align:center">真题考点词替换清单</h3>

题号	题目——原文
3	start—begin
4	timing—point
7	young—juvenile/tiny tortoise; old—fully grown giant/around a hundred years
8	small numbers—few; taken onto ships—on boards
9	kept—act as
10	produce—be processed into
11	hunted—exploitation
12	destruction—destroy; various—range from... to...; not native—alien
13	fed on—prey on; baby—young

🔺 *Reading Passage 2: The Intersection of Health Sciences and Geography*

Paragraph A

eradicate [ɪ'rædɪkeɪt] *v.* 根除

vaccination [ˌvæksɪ'neɪʃn] *n.* 接种疫苗

availability [əˌveɪlə'bɪlətɪ] *n.* 实用性

healthcare [helθkeə] *n.* 医疗

prevalent ['prevələnt] *adj.* 盛行的

super-viruses ['su:pə(r) 'vaɪrəsɪz] *n.* 超级病毒

infection [ɪn'fekʃn] *n.* 感染　　　　　resistant [rɪ'zɪstənt] *n.* 抵抗（能力）

Paragraph B

malaria-prone areas 疟疾高发地区　　　tropical ['trɒpɪkl] *adj.* 热带的

foster ['fɒstə(r)] *v.* 培养；造就　　　mosquitos [mə'ski:təʊs] *n.* 蚊子

Paragraph C

well-being [wel 'bi:ɪŋ] *n.* 幸福　　　smog [smɒg] *n.* 雾霾

asthma ['æsmə] *n.* 哮喘　　　　　　lung [lʌŋ] *n.* 肺

expansion [ɪk'spænʃn] *n.* 扩张

Paragraph D

polio ['pəʊlɪəʊ] *n.* 小儿麻痹　　　re-emerge [reɪɪ'mɜ:dʒ] *v.* 重新出现

respiratory [rə'spɪrətrɪ] *adj.* 呼吸的　interpret [ɪn'tɜ:prɪt] *v.* 解读；说明

hybrid ['haɪbrɪd] *adj.* 混合的　　　be prone to 易于……

Paragraph E

overlay [əʊvə'leɪ] *v.* 叠加　　　　correlation [ˌkɒrə'leɪʃn] *n.* 联系

epidemiology [ˌepɪˌdi:mɪ'ɒlədʒɪ] *n.* 传染病学

Paragraph F

interaction [ˌɪntər'ækʃn] *n.* 相互影响　asthma ['æsmə] *n.* 哮喘

global scales 全球范围　　　　　map [mæp] *v.* 绘图

Paragraph G

subcategory [sʌbˌkætɪˌgərɪ] *n.* 分支　provision [prə'vɪʒn] *n.* 供给

thereof [ˌðeər'ɒv] *adv.* 由此　　　discrepancy [dɪs'krepənsɪ] *n.* 差异

income brackets 收入水平　　　　frontline [frʌntlaɪn] *n.* 前线

Paragraph H

overlook [ˌəʊvə'lʊk] *v.* 忽略　　　constitute ['kɒnstɪtjuːt] *v.* 构成

Question

acceptance [ək'septəns] *n.* 承认　　classify ['klæsɪfaɪ] *v.* 分类

extend [ɪk'stend] *v.* 延伸　　　　mixture ['mɪkstʃə(r)] *n.* 混合

rare [reə(r)] *adj.* 少的　　　　　barrier ['bærɪə(r)] *n.* 障碍

真题考点词替换清单

题号	题目——原文
14	not all…totally eliminated—while…will always be prone to…; eliminated—eradication
15	human behaviors—cars; factories; industrialisation
16	classifying—categorising…into; geographically—local and global scales
17	vary—discrepancy; access to—available
18	mixture——combination
19	type of area—high-altitude deserts; rare—less
20	disappeared—eradicated; thanks to—due to; better—improvements
21	more contact—more common; losing their usefulness—resistant to
22	hot—warm
23	pollution—cars, factories; burn—run on; a particular fuel—coal
24	growth—expansion
25	growing after having been eradicated—re-emerging
26	prevent…from…—difficult

⬆ *Reading Passage 3: Music and emotions*

Paragraph 1

abstract ['æbstrækt] *n.* 摘要

explicit [ɪk'splɪsɪt] *adj.* 明确的；清楚的

symptom ['sɪmptəm] *n.* 症状；征兆

dilate [daɪ'leɪt] *v.* 扩张

conductance [kən'dʌktəns] *n.* 传导性

devoid [dɪ'vɔɪd] *adj.* 没有的；不包含的

betray [bɪ'treɪ] *v.* 背叛；出卖

arousal [ə'raʊzl] *n.* 激发；唤起

pulse [pʌls] *n.* 脉搏

cerebellum [ˌserə'beləm] *n.* 小脑

Paragraph 2

underpinning [ˌʌndə'pɪnɪŋ] *n.* 基础

stimulus ['stɪmjʊləs] *n.* 刺激

magnetic [mæg'netɪk] *adj.* 磁力的

emission [ɪ'mɪʃn] *n.* 排放

extract ['ekstrækt] *v.* 提取

genre ['ʒɑːnrə] *n.* 风格

methodology [ˌmeθə'dɒlədʒɪ] *n.* 方法论

trigger ['trɪgə(r)] *v.* 触发；激发

potent ['pəʊtnt] *adj.* 强有力的

fancy ['fænsɪ] *adj.* 精美的

resonate ['rezəneɪt] *v.* 共振；共鸣

request [rɪ'kwest] *n./v.* 请求

virtually ['vɜːtʃʊəlɪ] *adv.* 事实上

monitor ['mɒnɪtə(r)] *v.* 监控

portrait ['pɔːtreɪt] *n.* 画像

neutron ['njuːtrɒn] *n.* 神经元；神经细胞

Paragraph 3

anticipate [æn'tɪsɪpeɪt] *v.* 预测

precede [prɪ'siːd] *v.* 在……之前

cluster ['klʌstə(r)] *n.* 群；组

purpose ['pɜːpəs] *n.* 目的；意图

acoustic [ə'kuːstɪk] *adj.* 声学的

melodic [mə'lɒdɪk] *adj.* 旋律的

Paragraph 4

labyrinth ['læbərɪnθ] *n.* 迷宫

symphony ['sɪmfənɪ] *n.* 交响乐

intricate ['ɪntrɪkət] *adj.* 复杂的

composer [kəm'pəʊzə(r)] *n.* 作曲家

studious ['stju:dɪəs] *adj.* 不遗余力的   deny [dɪ'naɪ] *v.* 否定

Paragraph 5

flirtation [flɜ:'teɪʃn] *n.* 逗弄   submission [səb'mɪʃn] *n.* 让步；屈从

dissect [daɪ'sekt] *v.* 分解   masterpiece ['mɑːstəpiːs] *n.* 杰作

harmonic [hɑː'mɒnɪk] *adj.* 和谐的   ingenious [ɪn'dʒiːnɪəs] *adj.* 天才的

chord [kɔːd] *n.* 和弦

Paragraph 6

suspenseful [sə'spensfl] *adj.* 悬而未决的 tension ['tenʃn] *n.* 张力

connotative ['kɒnəʊteɪtɪv] *adj.* 暗示的；暗含的

unfolding [ʌn'fəʊldɪŋ] *adj.* 逐步展开的 arise from 由……引起

Question

substance ['sʌbstəns] *n.* 物质   intense [ɪn'tens] *adj.* 强烈的

innovative ['ɪnəveɪtɪv] *adj.* 有创造性的 recommend [ˌrekə'mend] *v.* 推荐

evoke [ɪ'vəʊk] *v.* 激起   poignant ['pɔɪnjənt] *adj.* 强烈的

sympathy ['sɪmpəθɪ] *n.* 共鸣

真题考点词替换清单

题号	题目——原文
27	stimulate—trigger; release—production
28	parts—regions; be linked with—be associated with; feeling—experience
29	area—region
30	known as—call
31	expectation—anticipating
37	prior to—before
38	decrease—adapt to
40	actual—real; pictures—images; events—experiences

Test 8

🔺 *Reading Passage 1: The History of Glass*

Paragraph 1

origin ['ɒrɪdʒɪn] *n.* 起源

form [fɔːm] *n.* 形式　*v.* 形成

eruption [ɪ'rʌpʃn] *n.* 喷发；爆发

archaeologist [ˌɑːkɪ'ɒlədʒɪst] *n.* 考古学家

bead [biːd] *n.* 珠子

container [kən'teɪnə(r)] *n.* 容器

historian [hɪ'stɔːrɪən] *n.* 历史学家

volcano [vɒl'keɪnəʊ] *n.* 火山

spear [spɪə(r)] *n.* 矛

date back 追溯

hollow ['hɒləʊ] *adj.* 空心的

molten ['məʊltən] *adj.* 熔化的

Paragraph 2

impurity [ɪm'pjʊərəti] *n.* 杂质

tint [tɪnt] *v.* 着色

empire ['empaɪə(r)] *n.* 帝国

reputation [ˌrepjʊ'teɪʃn] *n.* 名望

raw material 原料

guard [gɑːd] *v./n.* 保卫

collapse [kə'læps] *v.* 倒塌

craftsmen ['krɑːftsmən] *n.* 工匠

Paragraph 3

milestone ['maɪlstəʊn] *n.* 里程碑

crystal ['krɪstl] *n.* 水晶；晶体

optical ['ɒptɪkl] *adj.* 光学的

astronomical [ˌæstrə'nɒmɪkl] *adj.* 天文学的

microscope ['maɪkrəskəʊp] *n.* 显微镜

occur [ə'kɜː(r)] *v.* 发生

invaluable [ɪn'væljʊəbl] *adj.* 无价的

lenses [lensɪz] *n.* 镜头；镜片

telescope ['telɪskəʊp] *n.* 望远镜

Paragraph 4

levy ['levɪ] *v.* 征税

revolutionary [ˌrevə'luːʃənərɪ] *adj.* 革命性的

exhibition [ˌeksɪ'bɪʃn] *n.* 展览；展示

domestic [də'mestɪk] *adj.* 家庭的；国内的（本文：私家的）

horticultural [ˌhɔːtɪ'kʌltʃərəl] *adj.* 园艺的 architecture ['ɑːkɪtektʃə(r)] *n.* 建筑

technique [tek'niːk] *n.* 技巧；方法

Paragraph 5

semi-automatic ['semɪ ˌɔːtə'mætɪk] *adj.* 半自动的

previous ['priːvɪəs] *adj.* 先前的   install [ɪn'stɔːl] *v.* 安置

Paragraph 6

fiercely [fɪəslɪ] *adv.* 激烈地   competitive [kəm'petətɪv] *adj.* 竞争的

maintain [meɪn'teɪn] *v.* 维持；保留   package ['pækɪdʒ] *n.* 包装

foodstuff ['fuːdstʌf] *n.* 食品；食物   cosmetics [kɒz'metɪks] *n.* 化妆品

Paragraph 7

ideal [aɪ'diːəl] *adj.* 完美的；理想的   recycling [ˌriː'saɪklɪŋ] *n.* 回收；再利用

landfill ['lændfɪl] *n.* 垃圾填埋地   quarry ['kwɒrɪ] *v.* 开采

Question

fully-automated ['fʊlɪ 'ɔːtəmeɪtɪd] *adj.* 全自动的

真题考点词替换清单

题号	题目——原文
1	material—natural glass
2	sharp points—tips
4	because of—due to
6	developed—invention
7	avoid—counter
10	hire—founder【反】
12	environment—green; containers—bottles and jars

🔺 *Reading Passage 2: Bring back the big cats*

Paragraph 1

vanish ['vænɪʃ] *v.* 消失

presume [prɪ'zjuːm] *v.* 估计；以为

compelling [kəm'pelɪŋ] *adj.* 强有力的

roughly ['rʌflɪ] *adv.* 大约

spotted ['spɒtɪd] *adj.* 有斑点的

inhabitant [ɪn'hæbɪtənt] *n.* 居民

extinction [ɪk'stɪŋkʃn] *n.* 灭绝

Paragraph 2

glimpse [glɪmps] *n.* 一瞥；一眼

pursue [pə'sjuː] *v.* 追逐

speckled ['spekld] *adj.* 有斑点花纹的

totemic [təʊ'temɪk] *adj.* 图腾的

boar [bɔː(r)] *n.* 野猪

mounted ['maʊntɪd] *adj.* 骑马的

stubby ['stʌbɪ] *adj.* 粗短的

transform [træns'fɔːm] *v.* 改变；转换

Paragraph 3

restoration [ˌrestə'reɪʃn] *n.* 恢复

seabed ['siːbed] *n.* 海床

striking ['straɪkɪŋ] *adj.* 令人震惊的

dynamic [daɪ'næmɪk] *n.* 动力　*adj.* 有活力的

retain [rɪ'teɪn] *v.* 保留；保有

resonate ['rezəneɪt] *v.* 共鸣；共振

denude [dɪ'njuːd] *v.* 使变得光秃

dredge [dredʒ] *v.* 捕捞　*n.* 捕捞船

niches [niːʃɪz] *n.* 生态位；一席之地

Paragraph 4

conservation [ˌkɒnsə'veɪʃn] *n.* 保护；保存

assemblage [ə'semblɪdʒ] *n.* 集合

pickle ['pɪkl] *n.* 泡菜

merely ['mɪəlɪ] *adv.* 仅仅

arbitrary ['ɑːbɪtrərɪ] *adj.* 随机的

preserve [prɪ'zɜːv] *v.* 保护；保存

arrest [ə'rest] *v.* 逮捕

dynamism ['daɪnəmɪzəm] *n.* 活力；动态

Paragraph 5

potential [pə'tenʃl] adj. 潜在的；n. 潜力

literature ['lɪtrətʃə(r)] n. 文学

chase [tʃeɪs] v. 追逐

boost [buːst] v. 促进　n. 推动

insistence [ɪn'sɪstəns] n. 坚持；执着

scour ['skaʊə(r)] v. 冲洗；清除

breed [briːd] v. 繁殖

reserve [rɪ'zɜːv] v./n. 储存；保留

Paragraph 6

rare [reə(r)] adj. 稀少的

articulate [ɑː'tɪkjʊleɪt] v. 大声表达

enthusiasm [ɪn'θjuːzɪæzəm] n. 热情

inspiring [ɪn'spaɪərɪŋ] adj. 有启发性的

promise ['prɒmɪs] n./v. 允诺

otherwise ['ʌðəwaɪz] adv. 否则(表转折)

Paragraph 7

explode [ɪk'spləʊd] v. 爆炸；激增

intensive [ɪn'tensɪv] adj. 加强的；集中的

browse [braʊz] v. 吃草

winkle ['wɪŋkl] v. 追逐

exotic [ɪg'zɒtɪk] adj. 外来的；异域的

hide [haɪd] v. 隐藏

impenetrable [ɪm'penɪtrəbl] adj. 无法穿透的

plantation [plɑː'teɪʃn] n. 种植园

bare [beə(r)] adj. 无遮蔽的

barren ['bærən] adj. 荒芜的

livestock ['laɪvstɒk] n. 牲畜

subsidy ['sʌbsədɪ] n. 补贴；津贴

Paragraph 8

extraordinary [ɪk'strɔːdnrɪ] adj. 非凡的；显著的

proposal [prə'pəʊzl] n. 提议

perspective [pə'spektɪv] n. 观点

triple ['trɪpl] v. 翻三倍

lucrative ['luːkrətɪv] adj. 有利可图的

charismatic [ˌkærɪz'mætɪk] adj. 超凡魅力的

Paragraph 9

hint [hɪnt] n./v. 暗示

catalyse ['kætəlaɪz] v. 催化

294

Question

reveal [rɪ'viːl] *v.* 揭示

direction [də'rekʃn] *n.* 方向

practical benefits 现实的好处

opposition [ˌɒpə'zɪʃn] *n.* 反对

environmental campaigns 环保活动

appealing [ə'piːlɪŋ] *adj.* 有吸引力的

真题考点词替换清单

题号	题目——原文
19	no evidence—no known instance; in danger—threat
20	reduce the number—predator; increased enormously—exploded; roe deer—wild animals
21	a minimal threat—little risk; kept away from habitats—kept out of the woods; farm animals—sheep and other livestock
22	reintroduction—reintroduce; link with—marries with; return—bring

🔺 *Reading Passage 3: UK companies need more effective boards of directors*

Paragraph A

governance ['gʌvənəns] *n.* 控制；管理

radical ['rædɪkl] *adj.* 彻底的；激进的

meltdown ['meltdaʊn] *n.* 暴跌

prolong [prə'lɒŋ] *v.* 延长

downturn ['daʊntɜːn] *n.* （经济）衰退

post-mortem [ˌpəʊst 'mɔːtəm] *n.* 事后分析

crisis ['kraɪsɪs] *n.* 危及

auditor ['ɔːdɪtə(r)] *n.* 审计师

frame [freɪm] *n.* 框架

inquiry [ɪn'kwaɪərɪ] *n.* 询问

commentary ['kɒməntrɪ] *n.* 评论

Paragraph B

knock-on [nɒk ɒn] *adj.* 连锁的

scrutiny ['skruːtənɪ] *n.* 监视；细看

fulfill [fʊl'fɪl] *v.* 履行；实现

directorship [də'rektəʃɪp] *n.* 管理者

corporate ['kɔːpərət] *adj.* 公司的；企业的

agenda [ə'dʒendə] *n.* 议程   overload [ˌəʊvə'ləʊ] *n./v.* 过重负担

constructive [kən'strʌktɪv] *adj.* 建设性的 in favor of 支持；有利于

Paragraph C

devolve [dɪ'vɒlv] *v.* 移交；委托   committee [kə'mɪtɪ] *n.* 委员会

cope with 应对   workload ['wɜːkləʊd] *n.* 工作量

efficient [ɪ'fɪʃnt] *adj.* 高效率的   address [ə'dres] *v.* 解决

at the expense of 以……为代价   collaboration [kəˌlæbə'reɪʃn] *n.* 合作

tick [tɪk] *v.* 做记号   tackle ['tækl] *v.* 处理；应对

Paragraph D

extensive [ɪk'stensɪv] *adj.* 广泛的   complex ['kɒmpleks] *adj.* 复杂的

dedicated ['dedɪkeɪtɪd] *adj.* 致力于的   establish [ɪ'stæblɪʃ] *v.* 建立

guidelines ['ɡaɪdlaɪns] *n.* 方针   engage in 从事

recruitment [rɪ'kruːtmənt] *n.* 招聘   remuneration [rɪˌmjuːnə'reɪʃn] *n.* 薪酬

appropriate [ə'prəʊprɪət] *adj.* 合适的   executive [ɪɡ'zekjətɪv] *n.* 总经理

comprehend [ˌkɒmprɪ'hend] *v.* 理解   anticipate [æn'tɪsɪpeɪt] *v.* 预测

Paragraph E

criticism ['krɪtɪsɪzəm] *n.* 批评   sufficiently [sə'fɪʃntlɪ] *adv.* 充足地

strategy ['strætədʒɪ] *n.* 策略

sustainability [səˌsteɪnə'bɪlətɪ] *n.* 可持续发展性

concentrate on 集中   metrics ['metrɪks] *n.* 度量

requirement [rɪ'kwaɪəmənt] *n.* 需求；要求 tyranny ['tɪrənɪ] *n.* 独裁

quarterly ['kwɔːtəlɪ] *adv.* 按季度   distort [dɪ'stɔːt] *v.* 扭曲

appetite ['æpɪtaɪt] *n.* 胃口

·automated ['ɔːtəmeɪtɪd] *adj.* 自动化的

profile ['prəʊfaɪl] *n.* 概述；轮廓

incentivize [ɪn'sentɪvaɪz] *v.* 激励

Paragraph F

compensation [ˌkɒmpen'seɪʃn] *n.* 补偿

frequently ['friːkwəntlɪ] *adv.* 频繁地

shareholder ['ʃeəhəʊldə(r)] *n.* 股东

expose [ɪk'spəʊz] *v.* 揭露；曝光

irony ['aɪrənɪ] *n.* 讽刺

combat ['kɒmbæt] *n./v.* 战斗；对抗

transparency [træns'pærənsɪ] *n.* 透明

vote [vəʊt] *n./v.* 投票；选举

bonus ['bəʊnəs] *n.* 津贴

privacy ['prɪvəsɪ] *n.* 隐私

Paragraph G

stimulate ['stɪmjʊleɪt] *v.* 激励；刺激

ethics ['eθɪks] *n.* 道德规范

encompass [ɪn'kʌmpəs] *v.* 包围；环绕

awareness [ə'weənəs] *n.* 意识

erode [ɪ'rəʊd] *v.* 腐蚀；侵蚀

realignment [ˌriːə'laɪnmənt] *n.* 整改

Question

scrutiny ['skruːtənɪ] *n.* 仔细审查

non-executive [nɒnɪg'zekjətɪv] *adj.* 非执行性的

board [bɔːd] *n.* 董事会

economic downturn 经济低迷

relevance ['reləvəns] *n.* 关联性

真题考点词替换清单

题号	题目——原文
27	external bodies—government, regulators, central banks and auditors
32	financial arrangements—compensation, bonus to be paid; senior managers —chief executives
34	economic downturn—financial meltdown
39	emphasis on—concentrate on; considerations—metrics
40	pay—compensation

General Training: Reading and Writing
Test 5

⬆ Section 1

A Bath International Music Festival

folk [fəʊk] *n.* 民谣

classical ['klæsɪkl] *adj.* 古典的

renowned [rɪ'naʊnd] *adj.* 著名的

musician [mjʊ'zɪʃn] *n.* 音乐家

exception [ɪk'sepʃn] *n.* 例外，异议

B The Great Escape

refer to 提及，称呼，参考

perform [pə'fɔːm] *v.* 表演

venue ['venjuː] *n.* 地点

C Springwatch Festival

celebrate ['selɪbreɪt] *v.* 庆祝

wood carving 木雕

demonstration [ˌdemən'streɪʃn] *n.* 示范，表达

insect ['ɪnsekt] *n.* 昆虫

accompany [ə'kʌmpənɪ] *v.* 陪同，伴随

sort [sɔːt] *n.* 种类

produce [prə'djuːs] *n.* 农产品

D Wychwood Music Festival

nominate ['nɒmɪneɪt] *v.* 提名，任命，指定

genre ['ʒɑːnrə] *n.* 体裁

featuring ['fiːtʃə(r)ɪŋ] *adj.* 有特点的

comedy ['kɒmədɪ] *n.* 喜剧

selection [sɪ'lekʃn] *n.* 挑选

amazing [ə'meɪzɪŋ] *adj.* 使人惊奇的

E Love Food Festival

educate ['edjʊkeɪt] *v.* 教育

sample ['sɑːmpl] *v.* 品尝，抽样调查

tasty ['teɪstɪ] *adj.* 美味的

F The 3 Wishes Faery Festival

magical ['mædʒɪkl] *adj.* 有魔力的，奇妙的

surrounding [sə'raʊndɪŋ] *n.* 环境   fancy ['fænsɪ] *v.* 想要

resident ['rezɪdənt] *n.* 居民

G Bath International Dance Festival

champion ['tʃæmpɪən] *n.* 冠军   promise ['prɒmɪs] *v.* 承诺，希望

attempt [ə'tempt] *n.* 尝试

真题考点词替换清单

题号	题目——原文
1	help—join in; one particular event—a world record attempt
2	local musicians—artists from around the Wychwood area
3	lots of different places—30-plus venues
4	not necessary to pay—free music; one of the events—party in the city
5	stay overnight—three-day festival, taking a rent, put visitors up
6	children—family festival
7	get advice—educate visitors
8	watch craftspeople at work—sheep herding, wood carving demonstrations, insect hunt…

BIG ROCK CLIMBING CENTRE

climb [klaɪm] *v.* 爬

professionally [prə'feʃənəlɪ] *adv.* 专业地，娴熟地

fantastic [fæn'tæstɪk] *adj.* 非常棒的   fit [fɪt] *adj.* 健康的

harness ['hɑːnɪs] *n.* 保护带   thrill [θrɪl] *n.* 兴奋

arena [ə'riːnə] *n.* 场所

foam [fəʊm] *n.* 泡沫

cushion ['kʊʃn] *v.* 缓冲

真题考点词替换清单

题号	题目——原文
9	compulsory—without【反】
10	watch—overlook
11	climbing session—mobile wall, climbing faces; garden—outdoors
12	clothing—scarves; forbidden— remove
13	used—operated; dry—light rain【反】; calm weather—winds up to 50 kph【反】
14	afraid of heights—feel nervous

Who is Big Rock for?

previous ['priːvɪəs] *adj.* 之前的

specialist ['speʃəlɪst] *adj.* 专业的，专门的

equipment [ɪ'kwɪpmənt] *n.* 设备

alternative [ɔːl'tɜːnətɪv] *n.* 选择

overlook [ˌəʊvə'lʊk] *v.* 俯瞰

Mobile Climbing Wall

available [ə'veɪləbl] *adj.* 可获得的

enhance [ɪn'hɑːns] *v.* 加强

design [dɪ'zaɪn] *v.* 设计

simultaneously [ˌsɪml'teɪnɪəslɪ] *adv.* 同时地

qualified ['kwɒlɪfaɪd] *adj.* 有资格的，合格的

instructor [ɪn'strʌktə(r)] *n.* 教官，教练

ideal [aɪ'diːəl] *adj.* 理想的

remove [rɪ'muːv] *v.* 移除

scarf [skɑːf] *n.* 围巾

adaptable [ə'dæptəbl] *adj.* 适应的

operate ['ɒpəreɪt] *v.* 操作

condition [kən'dɪʃn] *n.* 条件

What about hiring the Mobile Climbing Wall for my school or college?

participate [pɑːˈtɪsɪpeɪ] v. 参加

concern [kənˈsɜːn] v. 关注

nervous [ˈnɜːvəs] adj. 紧张的

assure [əˈʃʊə(r)] v. 确认

benefit [ˈbenɪfɪt] v. 受益

Section 2

Marketing advice for new business

set up 建立

真题考点词替换清单

题号	题目——原文
15	most effective places—right places
17	forms—print, press, direct mail, telemarketing, email and the internet; more likely—increase your chances; find out—seen
18	can—possible; provide—send; useful— helpful
19	improve your business—change your business for the better
20	success—great asset; new customers—others; largely depends on—more likely to be influenced

Know where your customers look

customer [ˈkʌstəmə(r)] n. 消费者

advertise [ˈædvətaɪz] v. 广告

contact [ˈkɒntækt] v. 联系

information [ˌɪnfəˈmeɪʃn] n. 信息

Always think like a customer

survey [ˈsɜːveɪ] n. 调查

invaluable [ɪnˈvæljʊəbl] adj. 无价值的

Make sure customers know you are there

loads of 大量

promote [prəˈməʊt] v. 提升，促进

telemarketing [ˈtelɪmɑːkɪtɪŋ] n. 电话推销

Ignore your customers and they'll go away

obvious ['ɒbvɪəs] *adj.* 明显的

retention [rɪ'tenʃn] *n.* 保留

transaction [træn'zækʃn] *n.* 交易，数据处理

update [ˌʌp'deɪt] *n.* 更新

relevant ['reləvənt] *adj.* 相关的

Know what works (and what doesn't)

professional [prə'feʃənl] *n.* 业内人士

room [ruːm] *n.* 空间

improvement [ɪm'pruːvmənt] *n.* 改善，提高

Remember word-of-mouth: the best advertising there is

influence ['ɪnfluəns] *v.* 影响

recommendation [ˌrekəmen'deɪʃn] *n.* 推荐

reputation [ˌrepjʊ'teɪʃn] *n.* 声誉

asset ['æset] *n.* 资产，优势

incline [ɪn'klaɪn] *v.* 倾向于

complain [kəm'pleɪn] *v.* 抱怨

Working Time Regulations for Mobile Workers

crew [kruː] *n.* 工作人员

vehicle ['viːəkl] *n.* 机动车

define [dɪ'faɪn] *v.* 界定

真题考点词替换清单

题号	题目——原文
21	don't apply to—not covered by
22	maximum—up to; provided—maintained
23	more than 10 hours—work longer
24	include—count as; vehicle—transport operation
25	with—accompanying
26	some—reasonable amount of; count as—satisfy the requirements
27	cause—due to; delays—hold-ups

What are the limits

average ['ævərɪdʒ] *adj.* 平均的

workforce ['wɜːkfɔːs] *n.* 劳动力

statutory ['stætʃʊtəri] *adj.* 法定的

sick leave 病假

maintain [meɪn'teɪn] *v.* 维持

agreement [ə'griːmənt] *n.* 协议

annual leave 年假

maternity/paternity leave 产假

What counts as work

count [kaʊnt] *v.* 算作

normal ['nɔːml] *adj.* 正常的

delay [dɪ'leɪ] *n.* 耽搁，延期

specific [spə'sɪfɪk] *adj.* 具体的

reasonable ['riːznəbl] *adj.* 合理的

queue [kjuː] *n.* 排队

brake [breɪk] *n.* 刹车

foreseeable [fɔː'siːəbl] *adj.* 可预见的

duty ['djuːtɪ] *n.* 职责，关税

accompany [ə'kʌmpəni] *v.* 伴随

congestion [kən'dʒestʃən] *n.* 拥堵

Section 3: A brief history of automata

Paragraph 1

automata [ɔː'tɒmətə] *n.* 自动控制

construct [kən'strʌkt] *v.* 建立

be reputed to 被认为

activate ['æktɪveɪt] *v.* 启动，触发

resemble [rɪ'zembl] *v.* 相像

stretch back 追溯

assist [ə'sɪst] *v.* 帮助

intend [ɪn'tend] *v.* 意指，计划

Paragraph 2

experiment [ɪk'sperɪmənt] *v.* 做实验

wink [wɪŋk] *v.* 眨眼

principle ['prɪnsəpl] *n.* 原则，原理

Paragraph 3

treatise ['triːtɪs] *n.* 论文

fountain ['faʊntən] *n.* 喷泉

mechanical [mə'kænɪkl] *adj.* 机械的

elaborate [ɪ'læbərət] *adj.* 精细的，复杂的

link [lɪŋk] *v.* 联系

remarkable [rɪ'mɑːkəbl] *adj.* 出色的，非凡的

artificial [ˌɑːtɪ'fɪʃl] *adj.* 人工的

perch [pɜːtʃ] *v.* 暂栖

honour ['ɒnə(r)] *n.* 荣誉

salute [sə'luːt] *v.* 欢迎，致敬

Paragraph 4

royal ['rɔɪəl] *adj.* 皇家的

aristocratic [ˌærɪstə'krætɪk] *adj.* 贵族的

patron ['peɪtrən] *n.* 赞助人

wealth [welθ] *n.* 财富

Paragraph 5

contribute to 导致

investigate [ɪn'vestɪgeɪt] *v.* 调查

simulate ['sɪmjʊleɪt] *v.* 模拟

gearing ['gɪərɪŋ] *n.* 转动装置

cog [kɒg] *n.* 齿轮

repertoire ['repətwɑː(r)] *n.* 全部节目

flute [fluːt] *n.* 长笛

Paragraph 6

swan [swɒn] *n.* 天鹅

rotate [rəʊ'teɪt] *v.* 旋转

bend [bend] *v.* 弯曲

mechanism ['mekənɪzəm] *n.* 机制

Paragraph 7

wonder ['wʌndə(r)] *n.* 奇迹

legibly ['ledʒəbli] *adv.* 清晰地，易辨认地

Paragraph 8

stunning ['stʌnɪŋ] *adj.* 令人震惊的

complete [kəm'pliːt] *v.* 完成

depict [dɪ'pɪkt] *v.* 描绘

nobility [nəʊ'bɪləti] *n.* 贵族

figure ['fɪgə(r)] *n.* 人物

manner ['mænə(r)] *n.* 方式

court life 宫廷生活

butcher ['bʊtʃə(r)] *n.* 屠夫

slaughter ['slɔːtə(r)] *v.* 屠杀   barber ['bɑːbə(r)] *n.* 理发师

guard [gɑːd] *n.* 警卫   march [mɑːtʃ] *v.* 行进

Paragraph 9

technique [tek'niːk] *n.* 技术   amusement [ə'mjuːzmənt] *n.* 娱乐，消遣

export [ek'spɔːt] *v.* 出口   favour ['feɪvə(r)] *n.* 喜爱

真题考点词替换清单

题号	题目——原文
28	a number of—several; concerning—interested in
29	worked by—powered by; human operators—human action
30	designed—intended; educational principle—demonstrating basic scientific principles
31	a bird—swan; interacting—turn its head, bend down, catch fish
32	performed—play; musical instrument—flute
33	produced—wrote; documents—treatises; create—build
34	require a human—work by turning a handle
35	air—air pressure
37	various—all manners of; the time—period
39	reduced the cost—made cheaply and easily
40	intended—became

General Training: Reading and Writing Test 6

↑ Section 1

Lost, Damaged or Delayed Inland Mail Claim Form

claim [kleɪm] v./n. 索赔

delayed [dɪ'leɪd] adj. 延时的

alternatively [ɔ:l't3:nətɪvlɪ] adv. 或者

booklet ['bʊklət] n. 小册子

checklist ['tʃeklɪst] n. 核对表

issue ['ɪʃuː] n. 问题

真题考点词替换清单

题号	题目——原文
1	learn about—find out; or—alternatively; relevant information—details
2	refer to—use; ensure—make sure; all—full
3	use—visit; request action—investigate an issue; proof—evidence
4	in the case of—if claiming for; prove—proof
5	showing the damage—as evidence
6	keep—retain
7	claim—submitted

Lost items

compensation [ˌkɒmpen'seɪʃn] n. 补偿

item ['aɪtəm] n. 一件物品，项目

receipt [rɪ'siːt] n. 收据

reference number 查询号码

bank statement 银行结单

Damaged items

retain [rɪ'teɪn] v. 保留

original [ə'rɪdʒənl] adj. 原始的

packaging ['pækɪdʒɪŋ] n. 包装

inspect [ɪn'spekt] v. 检查，审查

Time restrictions

accept [ək'sept] v. 接受

loss [lɒs] n. 损失

submit [səb'mɪt] *v.* 提交 recipient [rɪ'sɪpɪənt] *n.* 接受者

Days out for the family

Paragraph A

military ['mɪlətrɪ] *adj.* 军事的 occupation [ˌɒkjʊ'peɪʃn] *n.* 占领，职业

foundation [faʊn'deɪʃn] *n.* 基础，地基 feast [fiːst] *n.* 盛宴，节日

attraction [ə'trækʃn] *n.* 吸引 exhibit [ɪg'zɪbɪt] *v./n.* 展出，展览

Paragraph B

rumour ['ruːmə(r)] *v./n.* 谣言，传闻 chamber ['tʃeɪmbə(r)] *n.* 私室，洞穴

castle ['kɑːsl] *n.* 城堡 ghost tales 鬼故事

associate [ə'səʊʃɪeɪt] *v.* 与……相关

Paragraph C

cliff [klɪf] *n.* 悬崖 legendary ['ledʒəndrɪ] *adj.* 传说中的

reception [rɪ'sepʃn] *n.* 接待处 visualise ['vɪʒʊəlaɪz] *v.* 使形象化

shuttle bus 班车

Paragraph D

special ['speʃl] *adj.* 特殊的 come along 出现

worth [wɜːθ] *v.* 值得

Paragraph E

a range of 一系列 combat ['kɒmbæt] *n.* 战斗，争论

dungeon ['dʌndʒən] *n.* 地牢 scary ['skeərɪ] *adj.* 害怕的

Paragraph F

moat [məʊt] *n.* 护城河，壕沟 armour ['ɑːmə(r)] *n.* 装甲，护面

真题考点词替换清单

题号	题目——原文
8	certain times—summer; special meals—traditional feasts
9	get dressed up—try on armour
10	another castle—Helmsley Castle; the same area—nearby
11	stories—ghost tales; told about—associated with
12	part of the castle—dungeon; frightening—scary
13	perform—put on; part of the year—during the summer month
14	particularly—especially; suitable for children—designed with younger visitors

⬆ Section 2

North Sydney Council

Paragraph 1

council ['kaʊnsl] *n.* 议会，委员会   recognised ['rekəgnaɪzd] *v.* 认出，识别出

balance ['bæləns] *v./n.* 平衡

Paragraph 2

employee [ɪm'plɔɪiː] *n.* 员工   staff [stɑːf] *n.* 员工

access ['ækses] *n.* 入口，机会   *v.* 进入，访问，存取

flexi [fleksɪ] *adj.* 灵活的   occasionally [ə'keɪʒnəlɪ] *adv.* 偶尔

initiative [ɪ'nɪʃətɪv] *n.* 主动行为，主动性 career [kə'rɪə(r)] *n.* 事业

Paragraph 3

entitle [ɪn'taɪtl] *v.* 使享有权利   parental leave 育婴假

maternity leave 产假　　　　　　　　　provision [prə'vɪʒn] *n.* 提供

Paragraph 4

annual ['ænjʊəl] *adj.* 每年的　　　　　entitlement [ɪn'taɪtlmənt] *n.* 权利

pro-rata [prəʊ'rætə] *adj.* 成比例的

Paragraph 5

conduct ['kəndʌkt] *v.* 处理，安排，进行　partnership ['pɑːtnəʃɪp] *n.* 合伙关系

pension ['penʃn] *n.* 养老金　　　　　　induction [ɪn'dʌkʃn] *n.* 入门

process ['prəʊses] *n.* 过程，进程

Paragraph 6

charge [tʃɑːdʒ] *n.* 费用　　　　　　　register ['redʒɪstə(r)] *v.* 注册

psychologist [saɪ'kɒlədʒɪst] *n.* 心理学家

confidentially [ˌkɒnfi'denʃəlɪ] *adv.* 机密地，秘密地

self assessment 自我评价　　　　　　　eapdirect [ɪ-eɪ-p-də'rekt] *n.* 企业应用平台

真题考点词替换清单

题号	题目——原文
15	not to work regular hours— flexi time
16	look after a relative—carer's leave
17	two alternative periods—9 weeks, 18 weeks
18	without a break— continuous service; additional holidays—6.5 weeks LSL
19	about—specialise in
20	talk about—discuss; job—work; in private—confidentially

Registering As An Apprentice

be keen to 渴望做某事　　　　　　　　apprenticeship [ə'prentɪsʃɪp] *n.* 学徒工作

option ['ɒpʃn] *n.* 选择   contract ['kɒntrækt] *n.* 合同

acknowledge [ək'nɒlɪdʒ] *v.* 承认，认可

commitment [kə'mɪtmənt] *n.* 承诺，责任感

approve [ə'pruːv] *v.* 批准，赞成

真题考点词替换清单

题号	题目——原文
21	you—apprentice
22	requirements—ask for; regarding—about
23	each industry—apprenticeable occupation
24	relevant—related to
25	a member of—part of; during the apprenticeship—as an apprentice
26	supervised—under the guidance; known as—called
27	consulted—consultation; deciding—set up; schedule—times

How Do I Qualify

minimum ['mɪnɪməm] *n.* 最小化

qualification [ˌkwɒlɪfɪ'keɪʃn] *n.* 资格，素质，先决条件

diploma [dɪ'pləʊmə] *n.* 文凭   equivalent [ɪ'kwɪvələnt] *adj.* 相等的

prior ['praɪə(r)] *adj.* 之前的

What Is My Training Like

outline ['aʊtlaɪn] *n.* 轮廓，大纲   standardized ['stændədaɪzd] *adj.* 标准化的

award [ə'wɔːd] *v./n.* 奖励   credential [krə'denʃl] *n.* 资格

aptitude ['æptɪtjuːd] *n.* 资质，能力   definite ['defɪnət] *adj.* 明确的

progress ['prəʊgres] *v.* 发展，进步

guidance ['gaɪdns] *n.* 指导，引导

productive [prə'dʌktɪv] *adj.* 多产的

agent ['eɪdʒənt] *n.* 代理人

track [træk] *v.* 追踪

previous ['priːvɪəs] *adj.* 之前的

craft [krɑːft] *n.* 工艺

attend [ə'tend] *v.* 参加

consultation [ˌkɒnsl'teɪʃn] *n.* 商讨，查阅

certificate [sə'tɪfɪkət] *n.* 合格证

🔺 *Section 3: Crossing the Humber estuary*

Paragraph A

estuary ['estʃʊərɪ] *n.* 河口

major ['meɪdʒə(r)] *adj.* 主要的

bulk [bʌlk] *adj.* 大宗的

situate ['sɪtʃʊeɪt] *v.* 位于

settlement ['setlmənt] *n.* 定居

obstacle ['ɒbstəkl] *n.* 障碍物

arrival [ə'raɪvl] *n.* 到达

freight [freɪt] *n.* 货物，运费

prosperity [prɒ'sperətɪ] *n.* 繁荣

obstruct [əb'strʌkt] *v.* 阻碍，妨碍

Paragraph B

cater for 满足……的需要

stream [striːm] *n.* 水流

threaten ['θretn] *v.* 威胁

speculator ['spekjʊleɪtə(r)] *n.* 投机者

competition [ˌkɒmpə'tɪʃn] *n.* 竞争

hovercraft ['hɒvəkrɑːft] *n.* 气垫船

ferry ['ferɪ] *n.* 渡轮

integrate ['ɪntɪgreɪt] *v.* 融入，成为一体

encourage [ɪn'kʌrɪdʒ] *v.* 鼓励，促进

cope with 处理，应对

passenger ['pæsɪndʒə(r)] *n.* 乘客

Paragraph C

outcome ['aʊtkʌm] *n.* 成果

tunnel ['tʌnl] *n.* 隧道

scheme [skiːm] *n.* 计划

campaign [kæm'peɪn] *n.* 战役，运动

proposal [prə'pəʊzl] *n.* 提议

promote [prə'məʊt] *v.* 租金，提出

merchant ['mɜːtʃənt] *n.* 商人

woe [wəʊ] *n.* 麻烦，问题

financial [faɪ'nænʃl] *adj.* 财政的，金融的

depression [dɪ'preʃn] *n.* 大萧条

Paragraph D

approval [ə'pruːvl] *n.* 赞成

twofold ['tuːfəʊld] *adj.* 双重的，两倍的

pier [pɪə(r)] *n.* 桥墩

topography [tə'pɒɡrəfɪ] *n.* 地形

excessive [ɪk'sesɪv] *adj.* 过高的，过重的

suspension [sə'spenʃn] *n.* 暂停，悬挂

navigable ['nævɪɡəbl] *adj.* 可通航的

geology [dʒɪ'ɒlədʒɪ] *n.* 地质学

Paragraph E

proceed [prə'siːd] *v.* 继续，进展

concrete ['kɒŋkriːt] *n.* 混凝土

peak [piːk] *n.* 山峰，巅峰　*adj.* 最高的，最佳的

calculator ['kælkjʊleɪtə(r)] *n.* 计算器

steel [stiːl] *n.* 钢筋

blend [blend] *v.* 混合

Paragraph F

recall [rɪ'kɔːl] *v.* 记起

opposite ['ɒpəzɪt] *adj.* 对立的

astonishment [ə'stɒnɪʃmənt] *n.* 惊讶

Paragraph G

remote [rɪ'məʊt] *adj.* 遥远的

insular ['ɪnsjələ(r)] *adj.* 狭隘的，与世隔绝的

commercial [kə'mɜːʃl] *adj.* 商业的

outstrip [ˌaʊt'strɪp] *v.* 超过

destination [ˌdestɪ'neɪʃn] *n.* 目的地

elegance ['elɪɡəns] *n.* 优雅

真题考点词替换清单

题号	题目——原文
28	disadvantage—cut off, obstruct
29	rising demand—wider needs
30	alternative—a bridge or a tunnel
31	advantage—not obstruct the estuary
32	build—construct
33	growing popularity—children, people
34	growth—improvement
35	operating—establish; other forms of transport —overland transport system
36	mid-19th—1851; greater—increased
37	failed—didn't last long
38	moves—changing
39	grounds—because

General Training: Reading and Writing Test 7

↑ *Section 1*

Evening Courses

Paragraph A

recipe ['resəpɪ] *n.* 食谱

imagination [ɪˌmædʒɪ'neɪʃn] *n.* 想象力

discover [dɪ'skʌvə(r)] *v.* 发现

trick [trɪk] *n.* 诡计，绝技

confident ['kɒnfɪdənt] *adj.* 自信的

Paragraph B

entertain [ˌentə'teɪn] *v.* 使快乐，款待

plenty of 许多

adaptable [ə'dæptəbl] *adj.* 适应的

current ['kʌrənt] *adj.* 目前的

Paragraph C

tasty ['teɪstɪ] *adj.* 美味的

snack [snæk] *n.* 小吃

well [wel] *adj.* 身体健康的

Paragraph D

jewelry ['dʒuːəlrɪ] *n.* 珠宝

project ['prɒdʒekt] *n.* 项目

introductory [ˌɪntrə'dʌktərɪ] *adj.* 入门的

supply [sə'plaɪ] *v.* 提供

suitable ['suːtəbl] *adj.* 适合的

Paragraph E

take advantage of 利用

portrait ['pɔːtreɪt] *n.* 肖像，描绘

landscape ['lændskeɪp] *n.* 风景

still-life [stɪl laɪf] *adj.* 静物的

effective [ɪ'fektɪv] *adj.* 有效的

lenses [lensɪz] *n.* 镜头

benefit ['benɪfɪt] *v.* 受益

session ['seʃn] *n.* 学期，学年

Paragraph F

technique [tek'niːk] *n.* 技术

foundation [faʊn'deɪʃn] *n.* 基础

provided [prə'vaɪdɪd] *conj.* 假如

真题考点词替换清单

题号	题目——原文
1	teach their skills—show how to cook; others— kids
2	prepare at home—read ahead
3	certain materials—base metals; included in the course fee—supplied free
4	prepare meals for guests—special occasions that…
5	make the best use of—include effective use of; certain item—lenses and lighting
6	follow instructions—keep strictly to a simple recipe
7	improve—get; health—fit and well

The Bike Foundry

foundry ['faʊndrɪ] *n.* 铸造车间

environmentally-friendly [ɪnˌvaɪrən'mentlɪ 'frendlɪ] *adj.* 环境友好的

leisure ['leʒə(r)] *n.* 休闲

真题考点词替换清单

题号	题目——原文
8	second-hand—hand-restored
9	held—provide , offer
11	snacks—tea-and-coffe-making facilities and a bridge
12	books—manuals
14	one week—seven days; get their money back—refundable

Our Bikes

restore [rɪ'stɔ:(r)] v. 修复

affordable [ə'fɔ:dəbl] adj. 买得起的

gratefully ['greɪtfəlɪ] adv. 感激

donation [dəʊ'neɪʃn] n. 捐赠

Training

maintenance ['meɪntənəns] n. 保养，维持

premise ['premɪs] n. 假定，前提

workshop ['wɜ:kʃɒp] n. 车间，研讨班

Maintenance Training

brake [breɪk] v./n. 刹车

gear [gɪə(r)] n. 排挡，装备

puncture ['pʌŋktʃə(r)] n. 穿孔，刺破

specialist ['speʃəlɪst] adj. 专业的

compatible [kəm'pætəbl] adj. 相符的，兼容的

replacement [rɪ'pleɪsmənt] n. 代替

prior ['praɪə(r)] adj. 之前的

mechanics [mə'kænɪks] n. 力学，机械部件

facility [fə'sɪlətɪ] n. 设备，设施

reference manual 参考手册

Cycling Training

qualified ['kwɒlɪfaɪd] adj. 合格的

instructor [ɪn'strʌktə(r)] n. 教官

negotiate [nɪ'gəʊʃɪeɪt] v. 谈判，商定，解决

Booking Information

deposit [dɪ'pɒzɪt] n. 定金

confirm [kən'fɜ:m] v. 确认

refundable ['ri:fʌndəbl] adj. 可退还的

▲ *Section 2*

Benefits for staff of Hamberton Hospital

contribution [ˌkɒntrɪ'bju:ʃn] n. 贡献

provision [prə'vɪʒn] n. 提供

extensive [ɪk'stensɪv] adj. 广泛的

真题考点词替换清单

题号	题目——原文
15	recognition—acknowledge; work—high quality patient care
17	available—assist with; buy—purchase
18	not restricted to—not just
19	help—support; a long absence—a long illness or injuries
20	large—ample
21	reduce—discounts; using—provides

Financial Benefits

insurance [ɪnˈʃʊərəns] *n.* 保险

occupational [ˌɒkjʊˈpeɪʃənl] *adj.* 职业的

loan [ləʊn] *n.* 贷款

injury [ˈɪndʒərɪ] *n.* 伤害

entitlement [ɪnˈtaɪtlmənt] *n.* 权利

purchase [ˈpɜːtʃəs] *v./n.* 购买

Work-Life Balance

be committed to 承诺

recruit [rɪˈkruːt] *v.* 招聘

asset [ˈæset] *n.* 资产，优势

balance [ˈbæləns] *v.* 平衡

motivate [ˈməʊtɪveɪt] *v.* 促进，激励

Health

confidential [ˌkɒnfɪˈdenʃl] *adj.* 机密的

phase [feɪz] *n.* 阶段

counsel [ˈkaʊnsl] *v.* 咨询，劝告

Other Benefits

facility [fəˈsɪlətɪ] *n.* 设施

retail [ˈriːteɪl] *n.* 零售

ample [ˈæmpl] *adj.* 充分的

outlet [ˈaʊtlet] *n.* 商店，市场

NHS Discounts

discount ['dɪskaʊnt] v./n. 折扣

utility [juːˈtɪləti] n. 实用，公用事业

Performance-related pay

compete [kəmˈpiːt] v. 竞争

talent [ˈtælənt] n. 天赋，天才

disturb [dɪˈstɜːb] v. 弄乱，搅乱

measurable [ˈmeʒərəbl] adj. 可计量的，显著的

appraisal [əˈpreɪzl] n. 评价

真题考点词替换清单

题号	题目——原文
22	existing employees—current staff
23	agree on—based on; measured—measurable
24	related to—achieved
25	offered—used; employees—staff
26	records—copies
27	specific—particular; less money—smaller bonuses

Short-term schemes

bonus [ˈbəʊnəs] n. 奖金

commission [kəˈmɪʃn] n. 佣金

performance [pəˈfɔːməns] n. 成绩，表现

Long-term schemes

reward [rɪˈwɔːd] n. 奖金

loyalty [ˈlɔɪəlti] n. 忠诚

senior [ˈsiːnɪə(r)] adj. 年长的，级别较高的

What to do if you have problems

handbook [ˈhændbʊk] n. 手册

owe [əʊ] v. 欠，归因于

misunderstanding [ˌmɪsʌndəˈstændɪŋ] n. 误解

set out 摆放，陈述

calculate [ˈkælkjʊleɪt] v. 计算

breach [bri:tʃ] *n.* 违反   deduction [dɪ'dʌkʃn] *n.* 扣除，推论

discrimination [dɪˌskrɪmɪ'neɪʃn] *n.* 歧视

Deductions from wages/breach of contract

verbally ['vɜːbəlɪ] *adv.* 口头上   amount to 总计，相当于

Discrimination

particular [pə'tɪkjələ(r)] *adj.* 特定的   guideline ['gaɪdlaɪn] *n.* 指导方针

Section 3: Marine Ecosystems

Paragraph A

constant ['kɒnstənt] *adj.* 持续的   cod [kɒd] *n.* 鳕鱼

endangered [ɪn'deɪndʒə(r)d] *adj.* 濒临灭绝的

species ['spiːʃiːz] *n.* 物种   vessel ['vesl] *n.* 船

tuna ['tunə] *n.* 金枪鱼   ruin ['ruːɪn] *v.* 毁灭

terminal ['tɜːmɪnl] *adj.* 终点的，晚期的，不可救药的

decline [dɪ'klaɪn] *n.* 下降   stock [stɒk] *n.* 存货

Paragraph B

conclusion [kən'kluːʒn] *n.* 结论   bury ['berɪ] *v.* 埋葬

headline ['hedlaɪn] *n.* 大标题，重要新闻

survival [sə'vaɪvl] *n.* 生存   upset [ʌp'set] *v.* 打乱，搅乱

delicate ['delɪkət] *adj.* 易损的，易碎的

community [kə'mjuːnətɪ] *n.* 群落，团体，社会

collapse [kə'læps] *v.* 倒塌   ecosystem ['iːkəʊsɪstəm] *n.* 生态系统

extinct [ɪk'stɪŋkt] *adj.* 灭绝的   highlight ['haɪlaɪt] *v.* 突出，强调

revolutionise [ˌrevə'luːʃənaɪz] *v.* 使发生革命性改变

quota ['kwəʊtə] *n.* 限额，定额

biodiversity [ˌbaɪəʊdaɪˈvɜːsətɪ] *n.* 生物多样性

debate [dɪˈbeɪt] *v./n.* 争论

conduct [kənˈdʌkt] *v.* 处理，安排，经营

domain [dəˈmeɪn] *n.* 领域

Paragraph C

shrinking [ˈʃrɪŋkɪŋ] *adj.* 缩水的

glacier [ˈglæsɪə(r)] *n.* 冰川

pulsate [pʌlˈseɪt] *v.* 搏动，震颤

marsh [mɑːʃ] *n.* 沼泽

creature [ˈkriːtʃə(r)] *n.* 生物

disappear [ˌdɪsəˈpɪə(r)] *v.* 消失

mammal [ˈmæml] *n.* 哺乳动物

severely [sɪˈvɪə(r)lɪ] *adv.* 严重地

fishery [ˈfɪʃərɪ] *n.* 渔业

Paragraph D

assume [əˈsjuːm] *v.* 假定

combination [ˌkɒmbɪˈneɪʃn] *n.* 联合

exploitation [ˌeksplɔɪˈteɪʃn] *n.* 利用，开发，剥削

habitat [ˈhæbɪtæt] *n.* 栖息地

destruction [dɪˈstrʌkʃn] *n.* 毁坏

eutrophication [ˌjuːtrəfɪˈkeɪʃn] *n.* 富营养化

nutrient [ˈnjuːtrɪənt] *n.* 营养物

nitrogen [ˈnaɪtrədʒən] *n.* 氮

phosphorus [ˈfɒsfərəs] *n.* 磷

promote [prəˈməʊt] *v.* 促进

phytoplankton [ˈfaɪtəʊˌplæŋktən] *n.* 浮游植物

over-enrichment [ˈəʊvə(r)ɪnˈrɪtʃment] *n.* 富营养

ultimately [ˈʌltɪmətlɪ] *adv.* 最终

capacity [kəˈpæsətɪ] *n.* 产能，能力

absorb [əbˈsɔːb] *v.* 吸收

remove [rɪˈmuːv] *v.* 消除，移除

coastal [ˈkəʊstl] *adj.* 海岸的

filter [ˈfɪltə(r)] *n.* 过滤器

Paragraph E

recover [rɪˈkʌvə(r)] *v.* 修复

by contrast 相反

withstand [wɪðˈstænd] *v.* 承受住，经受住

substantially [səb'stænʃəlɪ] *adv.* 相当，可观地

robust [rəʊ'bʌst] *adj.* 强壮的，结实的　back up 支持

react [rɪ'ækt] *v.* 反应

Paragraph F

positive ['pɒzətɪv] *adj.* 积极的

reveal [rɪ'viːl] *v.* 揭露

disturbance [dɪ'stɜːbəns] *n.* 打扰，弄乱

function ['fʌŋkʃn] *v.* 起作用

reverse [rɪ'vɜːs] *v.* 逆转，反转

reserve [rɪ'zɜːv] *n.* 保留，储备

crucial ['kruːʃl] *adj.* 关键的

ecology [ɪ'kɒlədʒɪ] *n.* 生态学

Paragraph G

tendency ['tendənsɪ] *n.* 倾向，趋势

widespread ['waɪdspred] *adj.* 分布广泛的

marine wildlife 海洋生物

nematode ['nemətəʊd] *n.* 线虫类

resource [rɪ'sɔːs] *n.* 资源

emotional [ɪ'məʊʃənl] *adj.* 情绪的

aesthetically [iːs'θetɪklɪ] *adv.* 美观地

vital ['vaɪtl] *adj.* 重要的

真题考点词替换清单

题号	题目——原文
35	main concern—more serious point; completely—entire; break down—collapse
36	the public—human nature; less likely to help—support little; unattractive creatures—worm, nematodes
38	consequence—resulting; contracting—shrinking
39	full of—a high level of; different species— biodiversity; large numbers of—millions of; wetland—salt marshes and mud flats; shore—coast
40	destroy—collapse; marine creatures and vegetation—entire system; deprive—starvation

General Training: Reading and Writing
Test 8

⬆ *Section 1*

Music Clubs

Paragraph A

intend [ɪnˈtend] *v.* 意图

membership [ˈmembəʃɪp] *n.* 会员

intermediate [ˌɪntəˈmiːdɪət] *adj.* 中级的

rehearsal [rɪˈhɜːsl] *n.* 排练

perform [pəˈfɔːm] *v.* 表演

concert [ˈkɒnsət] *n.* 音乐会

instrument [ˈɪnstrəmənt] *n.* 乐器

Paragraph B

district [ˈdɪstrɪkt] *n.* 地区

buffet [ˈbʊfeɪ] *n.* 自助餐

precede [prɪˈsiːd] *v.* 先于

composer [kəmˈpəʊzə(r)] *n.* 作曲家

radius [ˈreɪdɪəs] *n.* 半径

enjoyable [ɪnˈdʒɔɪəblː] *adj.* 愉快的，有趣的

recording [rɪˈkɔːdɪŋ] *n.* 唱片

background [ˈbækgraʊnd] *n.* 背景

coach trip 长途汽车旅行

Paragraph C

amateur [ˈæmətə(r)] *n.* 业余爱好者

appreciative [əˈpriːʃətɪv] *adj.* 赞赏的，感激的

finance [ˈfaɪnæns] *v.* 为……提供资金

orchestra [ˈɔːkɪstrə] *n.* 管弦乐队

marketing experience 市场经验

Paragraph D

primarily [praɪˈmerəlɪ] *adv.* 主要

seek [siːk] *v.* 寻找

professional [prəˈfeʃənl] *adj.* 专业的

earn [ɜːn] *v.* 赚钱

contain [kənˈteɪn] *v.* 包含

fundraising [fʌndˈreɪzɪŋ] *adj.* 筹集资金的

sponsorship [ˈspɒnsəʃɪp] *n.* 资助，支持

musician [mjuˈzɪʃn] *n.* 音乐家

newsletter [ˈnjuːzletə(r)] *n.* 业务通讯

opera [ˈɒprə] *n.* 歌剧

真题考点词替换清单

题号	题目——原文
1	need—welcome; ways—marketing experience; increasing audience numbers—build sales
2	all—every member
3	distributes information—receive newsletter; musical events—concerts, operas and other performances
4	a certain level—intermediate standard
5	not be familiar with—not so well-known
6	children—anyone aged between 6 and 14; develop—improve; musical skills—playing
7	popular—appreciative; local people—audiences from the area
8	help—support; in financial need—earning a living

Biological Research Institute

Paragraph 1

institute ['ɪnstɪtjuːt] *n.* 机构

campus ['kæmpəs] *n.* 校园

comply with 遵守，服从

instruction [ɪn'strʌkʃn] *n.* 指示

Paragraph 2

arrival [ə'raɪvl] *n.* 到达

entrance ['entrəns] *n.* 入口

issue ['ɪʃuː] *v.* 分发，发放

visible ['vɪzəbl] *adj.* 可见的

Paragraph 3

vehicle ['viːəkl] *n.* 机动车辆

security [sɪ'kjʊərəti] *n.* 保安部门

identify [aɪ'dentɪfaɪ] *v.* 辨认，认出

ensure [ɪn'ʃʊə(r)] *v.* 确保

designate ['dezɪgneɪt] *v.* 指派，命名，指定

risk [rɪsk] *n.* 风险

Paragraph 4

display [dɪ'spleɪ] *v.* 陈列，公布   authorised ['ɔ:θəraɪzd] *adj.* 经授权的

personnel [ˌpɜːsə'nel] *n.* 员工，人事部门

restricted [rɪ'strɪktɪd] *adj.* 有限的，受控制的

machinery [mə'ʃiːnərɪ] *n.* 机器   accompany [ə'kʌmpənɪ] *v.* 伴随

Paragraph 5

require [rɪ'kwaɪə(r)] *v.* 要求   clothing ['kləʊðɪŋ] *n.* 衣服

appropriate [ə'prəʊprɪət] *adj.* 适合的

Paragraph 6

permission [pə'mɪʃn] *n.* 许可，允许   obtain [əb'teɪn] *v.* 获得

management ['mænɪdʒmənt] *n.* 管理

Paragraph 7

nursery ['nɜːsərɪ] *n.* 儿童室   facility [fə'sɪlətɪ] *n.* 设施

Paragraph 8

accident ['æksɪdənt] *n.* 事故   request [rɪ'kwest] *v./n.* 要求

assistance [ə'sɪstəns] *n.* 帮助   first-aid [fɜːsteɪd] *n.* 急救

真题考点词替换清单

题号	题目——原文
9	car—vehicle; tell—identify; where—area
10	advice—instructions; seen—displayed
11	authorisation—authorised
12	require—obtain
13	provide—available
14	phone—call

⬆ *Section 2*

Negotiating a better salary package for your new job

Paragraph 1

recruitment [rɪ'kruːtmənt] *n.* 招聘   nitty-gritty [ˌnɪtɪ'grɪtɪ] *n.* 基本事实

Paragraph 2

graduate training schemes 大学毕业生职业培训计划

loads of 许多，大量   exercise ['eksəsaɪz] *v.* 运用，行使

negotiate [nɪ'ɡəʊʃɪeɪt] *v.* 谈判   asset ['æset] *n.* 资产

remuneration [rɪˌmjuːnə'reɪʃn] *n.* 酬金   accordingly [ə'kɔːdɪŋlɪ] *adv.* 相应地

Paragraph 3

general ['dʒenrəl] *adj.* 普遍的，通常的   sensitive ['sensətɪv] *adj.* 敏感的

essential [ɪ'senʃl] *adj.* 必要的   practical ['præktɪkl] *adj.* 实际的，实用的

position [pə'zɪʃn] *v.* 摆放，部署   familiarise [fə'mɪlɪəraɪz] *v.* 使了解，使通晓

prior to 在……之前   package ['pækɪdʒ] *n.* 包裹，一组事物

comparable ['kɒmpərəbl] *adj.* 可比较的   advert ['ædvɜːt] *n.* 广告

approach [ə'prəʊtʃ] *v.* 接近，处理   *n.* 方法

union ['juːnɪən] *n.* 工会   profession [prə'feʃn] *n.* 职业

Paragraph 4

review [rɪ'vjuː] *n.* 审查，审核   criteria [kraɪ'tɪərɪə] *n.* 标准

include [ɪn'kluːd] *v.* 包括   contract ['kɒntrækt] *n.* 合同

Paragraph 5

payslip ['peɪslɪp] *n.* 工资单   benefit ['benɪfɪt] *n.* 好处，额外待遇

contributory [kən'trɪbjətərɪ] *adj.* 需要定期缴费的

mention ['menʃn] v. 提到，涉及   attach [ə'tætʃ] v. 固定，归属

persuasive [pə'sweɪsɪv] adj. 有说服力的

consistent [kən'sɪstənt] adj. 一贯的，持续的

compromise ['kɒmprəmaɪz] v. 妥协

Paragraph 8

term [tɜːm] n. 条款   confirm [kən'fɜːm] v. 确认，批准，证实

真题考点词替换清单

题号	题目——原文
15	view—see; useful—valuable
16	important—essential; be aware of—be sensitive to; company—organization
17	monitor—look at; similar positions— comparable jobs
18	belong to=a number of; what is the norm for payment—acceptable salary ranges; field—profession
19	arrange for—negotiate; salary—pay; initial period—the first six month
20	accept—agree to; getting nowhere—really want the job

How to run a successful project

project ['prɒdʒekt] n. 项目   completion [kəm'pliːʃn] n. 完成

budget ['bʌdʒɪt] n. 预算   veer off 偏离

track [træk] n. 路径，行踪   disruption [dɪs'rʌpʃn] n. 打断

1. Prepare the framework

framework ['freɪmwɜːk] n. 框架   inevitable [ɪn'evɪtəbl] adj. 不可避免的

maintain [meɪn'teɪn] v. 保持   critical ['krɪtɪkl] adj. 关键的

avoid [ə'vɔɪd] *v.* 避免

scope creep 范围蔓延 (指产品等在开发过程中超出计划目标的倾向)

repeat [rɪ'piːt] *v.* 重复

unmanageable [ʌn'mænɪdʒəbl] *adj.* 难管理的，难控制的

2. Select the team

human resources 人力资源

align with 校准，结盟

assign [ə'saɪn] *v.* 分配，指派

clarify ['klærəfaɪ] *v.* 澄清，净化

communication [kəˌmjuːnɪ'keɪʃn] *n.* 交流沟通

critical ['krɪtɪkl] *adj.* 关键的

grasp [grɑːsp] *v.* 抓住

in terms of 就……而言

outcome ['aʊtkʌm] *n.* 成果，结果

expectation [ˌekspek'teɪʃn] *n.* 期望

reasonable ['riːznəbl] *adj.* 合理的

3. Staying on track

interim ['ɪntərɪm] *adj.* 临时的，暂时的

milestone ['maɪlstəʊn] *n.* 里程碑，转折点

determine [dɪ'tɜːmɪn] *v.* 决定

stray [streɪ] *v.* 偏离正题

4. Manage project risks

define [dɪ'faɪn] *v.* 限定，界定

contingency [kən'tɪndʒənsɪ] *n.* 偶发事件，应急措施

occurrence [ə'kʌrəns] *n.* 发生，发生的事

imminent ['ɪmɪnənt] *adj.* 迫近的，即将作出的

preventive [prɪ'ventɪv] *adj.* 预防的

halt [hɔːlt] *v.* 暂停

5. Evaluate the project

evaluate [ɪ'væljʊeɪt] *v.* 评价，评估

internal [ɪn'tɜːnl] *adj.* 内部的

pinpoint ['pɪnpɔɪnt] *v.* 确定

establish [ɪ'stæblɪʃ] *v.* 建立

undertaking [ˌʌndəˈteɪkɪŋ] *n.* 任务，工作

真题考点词替换清单

题号	题目——原文
21	agreed deadline—on time
22	prevent—avoid; client—company paying for the project; more and more —repeatedly
23	choose—gather; team members—human resources; match— align with; duties— roles
24	promote—encourage; knows—clarify; require—expect
25	check—determine; running to schedule—staying on track
26	prepare—put...in place; activated—action; go wrong—risk
27	over—completed; strengths and weaknesses—right and wrong; future reference—future undertakings

🔺 *Section 3: Mass appeal of the manta rays*

Paragraph A

appeal [əˈpiːl] *n.* 呼吁，上述，吸引力

instant [ˈɪnstənt] *adj.* 立刻的

jaw [dʒɔː] *n.* 下颌

expend [ɪkˈspend] *v.* 付出，耗费

manta ray 蝠鲼

gaping [ɡeɪpɪŋ] *adj.* 张开的

cruise [kruːz] *v.* 徘徊于，巡航于

Paragraph B

silhouette [ˌsɪluˈet] *n.* 轮廓

peaceful [ˈpiːsfl] *adj.* 和平的，平静的

spine [spaɪn] *n.* 刺，脊椎

curious [ˈkjʊərɪəs] *adj.* 好奇的

venomous [ˈvenəməs] *adj.* 有毒的

company [ˈkʌmpənɪ] *n.* 陪伴

enthusiastically [ɪnˌθjuːzɪˈæstɪklɪ] *adv.* 热情地

twitch [twɪtʃ] *v.* 抽动

alarm [əˈlɑːm] *n.* 惊恐

ashamed [əˈʃeɪmd] *adj.* 惭愧的

fright [fraɪt] *n.* 惊吓

Paragraph C

lagoon [ləˈguːn] *n.* 环礁湖

uninhabited [ˌʌnɪnˈhæbɪtɪd] *adj.* 无人居住的

congregate [ˈkɒŋɡrɪɡeɪt] *v.* 聚集

monsoon [ˌmɒnˈsuːn] *n.* 雨季

tide [taɪd] *n.* 潮汐

shallow [ˈʃæləʊ] *adj.* 浅的

cul-de-sac [ˈkʌldəsæk] *n.* 死胡同

reef [riːf] *n.* 礁

plankton [ˈplæŋktən] *n.* 浮游生物

nutrition [njʊˈtrɪʃn] *n.* 营养

bay [beɪ] *n.* 海湾

Paragraph D

marine [məˈriːn] *adj.* 海洋的

resort [rɪˈzɔːt] *n.* 度假胜地

catalogue [ˈkætəlɒɡ] *v.* 将……编入目录

distinctive [dɪˈstɪŋktɪv] *adj.* 不同的

guarantee [ˌɡærənˈtiː] *v.* 保证

spot [spɒt] *v.* 看到

surface [ˈsɜːfɪs] *n.* 表面

accessible [əkˈsesəbl] *adj.* 容易到达的

snorkeller [ˈsnɔːklə(r)] *n.* 浮潜的人

competition [ˌkɒmpəˈtɪʃn] *n.* 竞争

giant [ˈdʒaɪənt] *adj.* 巨大的

Paragraph E

community [kəˈmjuːnətɪ] *n.* 社区，群落

safari [səˈfɑːrɪ] *n.* 游猎

monitor [ˈmɒnɪtə(r)] *v.* 监督

declare [dɪˈkleə(r)] *v.* 宣布

regulation [ˌreɡjʊˈleɪʃn] *n.* 规定

Paragraph F

receive [rɪˈsiːv] *v.* 收到

cabinet meeting 内阁会议

urge [ɜːdʒ] v. 竭力主张

combat ['kɒmbæt] v. 战斗

objective [əb'dʒektɪv] n. 目标

preserve [prɪ'zɜːv] v. 保护

coincide [ˌkəʊɪn'saɪd] v. 同时发生，相符

Paragraph G

pause [pɔːz] v. 暂停

coral ['kɒrəl] n. 珊瑚

outcrop ['aʊtkrɒp] n. 岩石露出的部分

parasite ['pærəsaɪt] n. 寄生虫

adapt for 适应

accelerate [ək'seləreɪt] v. 加速

gaze [geɪz] v. 凝视

remark [rɪ'mɑːk] v. 议论

capture ['kæptʃə(r)] v. 俘获

convince [kən'vɪns] v. 确信

Paragraph H

harass [hə'ræs] v. 烦扰

crowd [kraʊd] v. 挤

ranger ['reɪndʒə(r)] n. 护林员，巡逻队

permit ['pəmɪt] n. 许可

真题考点词替换清单

题号	题目——原文
28	record—identified more than 2000 individual manta rays
29	regrets—ashamed
30	reason—to see manta rays; visit— come
31	distinguish—catalogue
32	at short notice—spot; arranged— be brought by
33	presence of people—human competition; appear to object to—seem not to mind【反】
34	increasing interest—word is out that Hanifaru is a top manta spot
35	protect—preserve

题号	题目——原文
36	control—limit; has now been established—working to get
37	certain times—south-west monsoons; weather conditions—wind; collect—congregate; look for—hunt for
38	keep free from—remove
39	get up speed—accelerate rapidly; move quickly—fast swimming
40	scientists—researchers

Note

附录
全书词汇总表

A

a bed of 一层	a doctoral student 博士生	a dry cough 干咳	a field of knowledge 知识领域
a gap of... ……的间隔	a handful of 少量的，一小部分	a host of 一大群，众多	a large volume of 大量的
a layer of 一层	a matter of ……的问题	a mere 仅仅	a package of 一系列
a panel of 一组	a professional endeavor 专业技能	a quick look 快速一瞥	a range of 一系列
a rash of 大量	a rush of joy 一阵欢乐	a sea of 许多，大量	a series of 一系列
a short attention span 不能长久集中注意 力；分心	a spectrum of 连续的，连串的	a table alphabetically 一个按字母顺序排 列的表	a unit of ……的单位
a wide range of 各式各样的	abandon v. 放弃，遗弃	abandoned adj. 被抛弃的；无约 束的	abbey n. 大修道院
abdomen n. 腹部	abide by 遵守；履行	abnormal adj. 反常的	abnormally adv. 反常地；不规 则地
abolish v. 彻底废除；摧毁	above-average adj. 异乎寻常的，超 常的	abrupt adj. 突然的	absence n. 缺席；无
absent adj. 缺席的	absolute adj. 绝对的，无条件 的，完全的	absorb v. 吸收	abstract adj. 抽象的 n. 摘要，抽象概念
absurdity n. 荒谬	abundance n. 充裕，丰富	abundant adj. 丰富的	abuse n. 虐待，辱骂
academic adj. 学术的，理论的 n. 大学生；学者	academic requirement 学术要求	academic year 学年	academics n. 学术
academy n. 学会，学院	accelerate v. 加速，促进；强调	accept v. 接受	acceptability n. 可接受性

acceptable *adj.* 可接受的	acceptance *n.* 接受；赞同；承认	access *n.* 进入；使用权； 通路；入口，机会 *v.* 进入，访问，存取	access to 接近，进入
accessible *adj.* 可理解的；能取 得的；易接近的；容 易到达的	accessory *n.* 配件，配饰	accident *n.* 事故	acclaim *n.&v.* 喝彩，欢呼； 赞扬，称赞
accommodate *v.* 适应，容纳，供应	accommodation *n.* 住处，膳宿	accompany *v.* 陪同，陪伴，伴随	accompanying *adj.* 附随的
accomplished *adj.* 熟练的	accomplishment *n.* 成就	accordingly *adv.* 因此；相应地	account *n.* 记录，叙述；账目， 账单
account card 记账卡	account for 占到；对……负有责 任；对……做出解释 （导致）	account number 账号	accountability *n.* 责任
accountancy *n.* 会计工作	accounting *n.* 账单	accredit *v.* 委托，授权	accredited *adj.* 公认的，可信 任的
accrual *n.* 应计项目；自然 增长	accrue *v.* 产生	accumulate *v.* 积累，堆积	accumulate up 积聚
accuracy *n.* 准确性，精确度	accurate *adj.* 精确的	accurately *adv.* 精确地	accuse of 控告，谴责
ache *n.* 疼痛	achievable *adj.* 可完成的，可有 成就的	achieve *v.* 达到目的，完成	achievement *n.* 成就
achiever *n.* 获得成功的人	acid rain 酸雨	acidification *n.* 酸化，土地酸化	acknowledge *v.* 承认，认可
acknowledgement *n.* 感谢	Acoma *n.* 阿科马	acoustic *adj.* 听觉的，声学的	acoustic insulation 隔音
acquire *v.* 获得	acquisition *n.* 获得某物	acre *n.* 英亩	acrobatics *n.* 特技飞行

activate	activation	active	actively
v. 激活；刺激，使活动；启动，触发	*n.* 激活	*adj.* 活跃的；激活的；积极的	*adv.* 积极地
actual	acupuncture	acupuncturist	acute
adj. 真实的	*n.* 针刺疗法，针刺	*n.* 针灸医生	*adj.* 敏锐的，急性的
adage	adapt	adapt for	adapt to
n. 格言，谚语	*v.* 适应	调整，使适应于，适应	使适应
adaptability	adaptable	adaptation	adaptive
n. 适应性，可变性	*adj.* 能适应的，适应的	*n.* 适应	*adj.* 适合的
additional	address	adenosine	adept
adj. 附加的，额外的	*n.* 服装，致辞 *v.* 解决，处理；演讲	*n.* 腺苷，腺苷酸	*n.* 内行；能手
adequate	adequately	adherent	adjunct
adj. 充足的；适当的；胜任的	*adv.* 充分地；足够地；适当地	*n.* 支持者，拥护者 *adj.* 邻近的，毗连的	*n.* 附件；助手；附属物 *adj.* 兼任的
adjust	adjust to	adjustment	administer
v. 调整，使适合	调整，使适应	*n.* 调整，调节	*v.* 给予；施行；执行
administration	administrative charge	administrative staff	administrator
n. 管理，行政	管理附加费，手续费	管理人员	*n.* 管理人
admiration	admire	admittance	admittedly
n. 钦佩，赞赏	*v.* 钦佩，赞美	*n.* 进入，进入权	*adv.* 公认地
adobe	adolescent	adopt	adoption
n. 土砖	*n.* 青少年	*v.* 采取，接受，采纳，决定	*n.* 采用
adrenaline	adult fish	advanced	advanced mathematics
n. 肾上腺素	成鱼	*adj.* 高级的，先进的	高等数学
advancement	advantageous	advent	adventure tourism
n. 提升	*adj.* 有利的	*n.* 到来；出现；基督降临；基督降临节	探险游

adventurous *adj.* 充满危险的	adverse *adj.* 不利的	adverse effect 副作用	adversely *adv.* 不利地，有害地
adversity *n.* 逆境，不幸	advert *n.* 广告	advertise *v.* 做广告；广告	advice *n.* 建议
advisable *adj.* 可取的，适当的， 明智的	advise *v.* 建议	advocate *v.* 提倡，主张，拥护 *n.* 支持者	aerodynamic *adj.* 空气动力的
aeronautical *adj.* 航空学的	aeronautics *n.* 航空学	aeroplane *n.* 飞机	aeroplane pilot 飞行员
aerosol sprays 喷雾剂	aesthetic *adj.* 美学的，审美的	aesthetically *adv.* 审美地；美学 观点上地；美观地	affiliation *n.* 合作；联盟
afflict *v.* 折磨，使痛苦	affluent *adj.* 富裕的；丰富的	afford *v.* 负担得起，给予	affordable *adj.* 负担得起的；买 得起的
aficionado *n.* 疯狂爱好者	after-effect *n.* 后果	afterwards *adv.* 后来	Agatha Christie 阿加莎·克里斯蒂
aged support 老年人赡养	ageing *n.* 老化	agency *n.* 机构，中介	agenda *n.* 议程
age-norm *n.* 年龄常模	agent *n.* 药剂；代理人	agent technology 代理技术	age-related *adj.* 与年龄相关的
aggression *n.* 侵犯，侵害	aggressive *adj.* 侵略性的	agreement *n.* 协议，同意	agriculture *n.* 农业，农学
agristudy *n.* 农业研究	agrochemical *adj.* 农用化学品的	agroecologist *n.* 农业生态学家	aid *n.* 援助，帮助
aid agency 援助机构	ailment *n.* 小病	aimless *adj.* 漫无目的的	air ambulance 空中救援机
air network 飞航网络	air quality 空气质量	air tour 空中游览	air traffic control 空中交通管制
airborne *adj.* 空运的	aircraft *n.* 飞机	airline *n.* 航空公司	airport transfer 机场接送
airspace *n.* 领空，空间	air-traffic *adj.* 空中交通的	air-water interface 水天交接处	alarm *n.* 惊恐

alarming	alarming rate	Alaska	Alaska Native Language Centre
adj. 令人担忧的	惊人的速度	*n.* 阿拉斯加	阿拉斯加原住民语言中心
albeit	albums	aldehyde	alert
conj. 虽然；即使	*n.* 相册	*n.* 乙醛	*v.* 使警觉 *adj.* 思维更加敏捷的
Aleut	algae	algebra	alien
n. 阿留申人	*n.* 藻类，海藻	*n.* 代数	*adj.* 国外的；相异的
alien species	alienation	alight	align
外来物种	*n.* 疏远，疏远感，脱离	*v.* 下来；飞落	*v.* 使成一线；排列
align with	alike	alive	all sorts of
校准，结盟	*adj.* 相似的 *adv.* 相似地	*adj.* 活泼的，有生气的	各种各样的
all works of life	allegation	allege	alleged
各行各业	*n.* 主张，断言；辩解	*v.* 宣称，断言，辩称	*adj.* 所谓的
all-encompassing	allergic reaction	allergy	alleviate
adj. 无所不包的	过敏反应	*n.* 过敏症	*v.* 缓和
allocate	allocated	allocation	allot
v. 分配	*adj.* 分配的	*n.* 分配，配置	*v.* 分配
allotype	alloy	all-smelling	along with
n. (同种) 异型抗免疫球蛋白	*n.* 合金	*adj.* 嗅的	(除……之外) 还，以及
alongside	alpha	alphabetical order	alphabetically
adv. 在旁边	*n.* 最初	字母顺序	*adv.* 按照字母顺序地
Alpine	alter	alteration	alternate
adj. 阿尔卑斯山的	*v.* 变化，改变	*n.* 修改	*v.* 交替，轮流
alternative	alternatively	altitude	altruistic
adj. 供替代的，供选择的 *n.* 替代品；二中择一；选择	*adv.* 可选择地；或者	*n.* 高度；海拔	*adj.* 利他的，无私心的

aluminium	aluminum screw	amass	amateur
n. 铝	caps	v. 积聚	adj. 业余的
	铝螺旋盖		n. 业余爱好者
amazed	amazing	ambience	ambiguity
adj. 吃惊的，惊奇的	adj. 令人惊异的；使	n. 周围环境，气氛	n. 含糊，不明确
	人惊奇的		
ambiguous	ambition	ambitious	ambivalent
adj. 模糊不清的，引	n. 抱负，雄心	adj. 有雄心的，野心	adj. 矛盾的
起歧义的		勃勃的，有野心的	
ambulance	amend	amenities	American boutu
n. 救护车	v. 修订；改进	n. 便利设施	美洲亚马孙河豚
Amex	ammonia	amongst	amorphous
n. 运通卡	n. 氨	prep. 在……之中	adj. 无定形的；无组
			织的
amount	amount to	amphibian	ample
n. 数量，总额	合计，总计，相当于	n. 两栖动物	adj. 宽敞的，足够的;
			充分的
amplify	Amsterdam	amuse	amused
v. 扩大	n. 阿姆斯特丹	v. 娱乐	adj. 愉快的，有趣的
amusement	amusement park	an abundance of	an array of
n. 娱乐，消遣	游乐场	大量的	一排
an avalanche of	an extra fee	analogous	analogy
突然一阵的，蜂拥而	额外的费用	adj. 类似的	n. 类比
来的，如雪片飞来的			
analyse	analysis	analyst	analytical
v. 分析	n. 分析	n. 分析者	adj. 善于分析的
anatomist	ancestor	ancestral	ancestral feature
n. 解剖学家	n. 祖先	adj. 祖先的，祖传的	祖先的特征
ancestry	anchor	Anchorage	anecdotal evidence
n. 祖先	n. 锚	n. 安克雷奇	传闻证据
anecdote	anew	angle	animated film
n. 轶事，奇闻	adv. 重新	n. 角度	动画片
animation	annexe	announce	annoying
n. 卡通片绘制	n. 附加物	v. 宣布	adj. 讨厌的，恼人的
annual	annual leave	annually	annum
adj. 每年的	年假	adv. 每年	n. 年，岁

ant n. 蚂蚁	Antarctica n. 南极洲	anthocyanin n. 花青素	anthropological adj. 人类学的；人类学上的
anthropologist n. 人类学家	anthropology n. 人类学	anti-ageing adj. 抗衰老的	antibiotics n. 抗生素
antibodies n. 抗体	anticipate v. 预料	anti-competitive adj. 反竞争的	anti-fungal n. 抗真菌
anti-herbivore n. 抗食草动物	antiquated adj. 过时的，陈旧的	antiseptic adj. 防腐的,抗菌的;非常整洁的	anti-social adj. 反社会的
anxious adj. 急切的	apart adj. 分离的	apart from 除……之外，除去	ape n. 猿猴
apex n. 顶	aphid n. 蚜虫	apparatus n. 设备，仪器	apparent adj. 明显的，表面上的
apparently adv. 显然地，明显地	appeal v. 有吸引力，迎合……的爱好 n. 呼吁，上述，吸引力	appealing adj. 吸引人的；有吸引力的	appeasement n. 缓和，平息
appendage n. 附加物	appetite n. 胃口	applicable adj. 可适用的	applicant n. 申请人
application n. 应用；申请	application form 申请表	applied adj. 应用的	applied science 应用科学
apply n. 应用 v. 申请；使用	apply for 申请	apply to 适用于	appoint v. 任命，约定
appointment n. 约定	apportion v. 分配，分派	appraisal n. 评价；估价（尤指估价财产，以便征税）；估计	appreciably adv. 明显地，相当地
appreciate v. 领会；赏识，为……表示感激	appreciation n. 感激，感谢，欣赏	appreciative adj. 赞赏的，感激的	apprehensive adj. 忧虑的，不安的

apprentice *n.* 学徒	apprenticeship *n.* 学徒身份；学徒 工作	approach *n.* 方法，途径 *v.* 接近，靠近，处理	appropriate *adj.* 适当的，合适的， 适合的
approval *n.* 批准；赞成	approve *v.* 批准，赞成	approximate *v.* 接近	approximately *adv.* 大约，近似地
apt *adj.* 恰当的；有…… 倾向的；聪明的	aptitude *n.* 才能，资质，天资， 能力	aquaculture *n.* 水产业	aquatic *adj.* 水生的
aqueduct *n.* 沟渠	aquifer *n.* 蓄水层	arable *adj.* 可开垦的	arbitrary *adj.* 随机的
arc *n.* 弧（度）	arch *n.* 拱桥	archaeological *adj.* 考古学的	archaeologist *n.* 考古学家
archaeology *n.* 考古学	archipelago *n.* 群岛，列岛	architect *n.* 建筑师	architecturally *adv.* 建筑上地；关 于建筑地
architecture *n.* 建筑	Arctic *n.* 北极圈	Arctic land *n.* 北极土地	arduous *adj.* 费力的
arena *n.* 场所	Argentina *n.* 阿根廷	arguably *adv.* 可论证地	argue for 赞成，支持
arise *v.* 出现，上升	arise from 起因于；由……引起	aristocrat *n.* 贵族	aristocratic *adj.* 贵族的
Aristotle *n.* 亚里士多德（古希 腊哲学家）	arithmetic *n.* 算术	Arizona *n.* 亚利桑那	armchair *n.* 扶手椅
armour *n.* 装甲，护面	armoury *n.* 兵工厂	aroma *n.* 芳香	around the clock 夜以继日地
around the globe 全球	arousal *n.* 觉醒，激励；激发； 唤起	arouse *v.* 引起，唤醒	arrange *v.* 安排，排列
arrangement *n.* 布置，安排	array *n.* 数组；大批	arrest *v.* 逮捕	arrival *n.* 到达者，抵达者， 到达
arson *n.* 纵火（罪）	arsonist *n.* 纵火犯人	art form 艺术形式	artefact *n.* 人工制品，加工品

arteriosclerosis n. 动脉硬化	arthritis n. 关节炎	articulate v. 大声表达，明确地 表达	artifact n. 人工制品
artificial adj. 人造的，仿造的， 人工的	artificial flood 人造洪水	artificial intelligence 人工智能	artificial light 人造光
artificial sweetener 人造甜味剂	artificially adv. 人为地	artistic adj. 艺术的	artistically adv. 在艺术上地
artwork n. 艺术品	as a free good 唾手可得	as per 按照，根据	as to 关于，就……而论
asbestos n. 石棉	ascent n. 上升	ascertain v. 确定；查明；探知	ascribe v. 把……归因于
ashamed adj. 惭愧的	Asian Development Bank 亚洲开发银行	aside adv. 撇开	aspect n. 方面
aspiration n. 渴望，愿望	aspirator n. 抽吸器	assemblage n. 集合	assembled v. 装配，组装
assembly n. 装配；集会，集合	assert v. 坚持，主张，维护	assertion n. 断言，声明；主张， 要求；坚持	assertiveness n. 自信
assess v. 评定，估计	assessment n. 评定，评价，评估	asset n. 有价值的或有用 的人；财富；资产， 优势	assign v. 分配；指派
assignment n. 功课；任务，作业	assist v. 帮助	assist with 帮助，协助	assistance n. 帮助
assistant n. 助手	associate n. 同事，伙伴 v. 联系；与……相关	associate professor 副教授	associate with 联合
associated adj. 关联的	assortment n. 搭配，分类	assume v. 猜想，假定，假设 （认为）	assumed adj. 假定的
assumption n. 假定，设想	assurance n. 保险	assure v. 保证；使确信， 确认	asthma n. 哮喘

astonishing adj. 惊人的	astonishment n. 惊讶	astounding adj. 令人震惊的	astrology n. 占星术
astronaut n. 宇航员	astronomer n. 天文学家，天文 学者	astronomical adj. 天文的	astronomy n. 天文学
Aswan n. 阿斯旺（埃及一 城市）	asynchronous sound 不同步音效	at a bit 一点儿，有点儿	at a good height 在一个非常合适的 高度
at a profit 获利	at all costs 不惜一切代价	at first glance 乍一看，一看就	at greater distances 在更远的距离
at hand 在手边	at its broadest 最广义上来讲	at its most intense 以它最大的强度	at one's fingertip 近在手边，随时可使 用的
at stake 处于危险中，在紧要 关头	at the expense of 以……为代价	at the mercy of 受……支配	at the turn of the 20th century 在 20 世纪之交
at the very least 至少，起码	at this stage 眼下；在那时	atavism n. 返祖现象；隔代 遗传	athlete n. 运动员
Atlantic n. 大西洋	atlas n. 地图集	atmosphere n. 气氛	atmospheric adj. 大气的，大气 层的
atom n. 原子	attach v. 附加，贴上；固定， 归属	attach to 依附	attachment n. 附件，附属物
attack n. 袭击，攻击	attain v. 实现；获得	attainable adj. 可达到的，可得 到的	attainer n. 取得成就者
attainment n. 成绩，成就	attempt n. 试图，尝试	attempt to 试图做	attend v. 上（学）；参加
attentional adj. 注意的	attenuate v. 减弱，衰弱，变小	attitude n. 看法，态度	attracting n. 吸引
attraction n. 吸引	attractive adj. 吸引人的，有魅 力的	attributable to 由于	attribute n. 特质 v. 导致，引起

attribute to 导致	audience *n.* 读者；观众	audio-visual *adj.* 视听的，视听教学的	audit *n.&v.* 审计，查账
auditor *n.* 审计师	auditorium *n.* 观众席	auditory *adj.* 听觉的	auditory comprehension 听力理解
Australian Journal of Public Health 澳大利亚公共健康杂志	authentic *adj.* 真正的，真实的；可信的	authenticity *n.* 可靠性，真实性	authorisation *n.* 授权，批准
authorised *adj.* 经授权的	authorised student travel office 被授权的学生旅游办公室	authoritarian *adj.* 权力主义的，独裁主义的	authority *n.* 当局，权威
authorisation *n.* 授权，批准	authorise *v.* 批准	autistic *n.* 自闭症患者，孤僻症患者	autocratic *adj.* 专制的
auto-dependent *adj.* 依赖汽车的	automata *n.* 自动控制	automated *adj.* 自动化的	automatic *adj.* 自动的，无意识的
automatically *adv.* 自动地，无意识地	autonomous *adj.* 自主的，独立的	autonomy *n.* 自治，自治权	availability *n.* 可用性，有效性；实用性
available *adj.* 可得到的；空闲的	avant-garde *n.* 前卫派，先锋派	average *adj.* 平均的；普通的	aviation *n.* 航空
avid *adj.* 狂热的	avidly *adv.* 贪心地，热心地	avoid *v.* 避免，消除	avoidable *adj.* 可避免的
award *v.* 授予；奖励 *n.* 奖励	aware *adj.* 意识到的,知道的	awareness *n.* 意识；明白	awe *n.* 敬畏
awkward *adj.* 笨拙的，不适合的	axe *n.* 斧	axe-shaped 斧子形状的	axis *n.* 轴，轴线
axolotl *n.* 蝾螈	Ayers Rock 艾尔斯山		

B

Babylonian *n.* 巴比伦人	back *v.* 支持	back up 支持，援助	back-and-forth movement 季节性来回移动
backdrop *n.* 背景	background *n.* 背景	background sound 背景音乐	backlash *n.* 反击，后坐
backless shoes 露脚背的鞋	backpack *n.* 双肩背包	backwards *adv.* 向后	bacteria *n.* 细菌
bad press 在报上名声不好	badge *n.* 徽章	baggage *n.* 行李	bait *n.* 诱饵
bakelite *n.* 人造树胶	baker *n.* 面包工人，面包师	balance *v./n.* 平衡	balance due 尚欠余额
balanced *adj.* 平衡的	balancing *n.* 平衡	baldness *n.* 秃头	baleen species 长须鲸，须鲸类
balk at 不惜做某事	bamboo *n.* 竹子	ban *v.* 禁止，取缔	banal *adj.* 平淡乏味的
Bangkok *n.* 曼谷（泰国首都）	Bank Holiday 银行假日（在英国指法定节假日）	bank statement 银行结单	barber *n.* 理发师
bare *adj.* 无遮蔽的	barely *adv.* 几乎不；仅仅	bargain *n.* 物美价廉的商品	bargaining *n.* 议价
barge *n.* 游艇	bark *n.* 树皮 *v.* 犬吠	baroque *adj.* 巴洛克式的，复杂的	barren *adj.* 荒芜的
barrier *n.* 障碍	basalt *n.* 玄武岩	base *n.* 基地	base on 基于，在……的基础上
basement *n.* 底层	basin *n.* 盆	basis *n.* 基础	bask *v.* 沐浴于
basket weaving 篮子编织	Basque *n.* 巴斯克人	bat *n.* 蝙蝠	batch *n.* 一炉，一批
bathing *n.* 沐浴；游泳	baton *n.* 指挥棒；接力棒；警棍；司令棒	batter *v.* 猛击	battery *n.* 电池；层架式鸡笼

battlefield n. 战场	battling n. 斗争	bay n. 海湾	be around the corner 即将来临
be bound to 一定，必然	be committed to 承诺	be defined as 被定义为	be dispensed with 被免除
be home to 是……的家；为……的居所	be inspired to 有兴趣……	be keen to 渴望做某事	be liable to 易于……
be prone to 易于……	be reputed to 被认为	be similar to 相似	be struck by 被……感动，被……触动，被……打动
be subject to 受……支配；遭受	be up to 最……的职责	beach n. 海滩	beach towel 海滩浴巾
beacon n. 灯塔	bead n. 珠子	beads n. 玻璃粉	beak n. 鸟嘴，鸟喙
beam v. 发出，发送	bear v. 具有；生子	bear up 支持	bearing n. 方位
beast n. 野兽	beat v. 打败；有节奏地敲打	Bedfordshire n. 贝德福德郡	bedside adj. 床旁的，枕边的
bee n. 蜜蜂	beef n. 牛肉	beehive n. 蜜蜂箱	beetle n. 甲虫
beforehand adv. 事先，预先	beg v. 乞求，乞讨	begetter n. 父；生产者；初学者，新手	behavioural adj. 行为的
behavioural psychology 行为心理学	Belgian adj. 比利时的	Belgium n. 比利时	belief n. 信念
believable adj. 可信的	belong to 属于	belongings n. 财产，所有物；行李	bend v. 弯曲
beneath prep. 在……之下，在……下面	beneficial adj. 有益的	benefit n. 好处；额外待遇 v. 对……有益，使……得益；受益	benevolent adj. 慈善的

benzodiazepine n. 苯二氮	bereavement n. 丧亲	Bering Strait 白令海峡	berth n. (轮船、火车的) 卧铺
besiege v. 包围	bestow v. 使用；授予；放置； 留宿	bestselling adj. 畅销的	beta n. 第二
betray v. 背叛；出卖	better off 情况好	better-constructed adj. 更好地创造的	better-educated adj. 受过良好教育的
beverage n. 饮料	bewildering adj. 使人困惑的；令 人产生混乱的	Bhutan n. 不丹	bias v. 使有偏见
big-bang n. 大爆炸	bilingual adj. 双语的	bilingualism n. 双语，双语教育， 双语现象	bill n. 账单 v. 开账单
bin n. 箱子	bind v. 约束	bind up 结合	binding n. 装订
Bingham Regional College 宾厄姆区域学院	biochemical adj. 生化的	bio-control n. 生物控制	biodiversity n. 生物多样性
biographer n. 传记作者	biological adj. 生物的	biological basis 生物学基础	biological clock 生物钟
biologically adv. 生物学上地	biologist n. 生物学家	biomechanical adj. 生物力学的	biomechanics n. 生物力学
biomedical adj. 生物医药学的	birch n. 桦树	birth certificate 出生证明	birthplace n. 诞生地
biscuits n. 饼干	bishop n. 主教	bit n. 少量	bitter adj. 激烈的
bitterly adv. 极其，非常	black-and-white film 黑白电影	blade n. 叶片，刀片	blame v. 责备，归咎于
blank adj. 空白的	blanket v. 覆盖	blast n. 爆炸 v. 开辟	blaze n. 火焰；地狱
blemish n. 瑕疵，缺点	blend n./v. 混合	blight n. 枯萎	blink n. 眨眼
blip n. 物体光点	block n. 大厦；街区；障 碍物	blood pressure 血压	blood test 验血

bloodstream	blotting paper	blow	blowhole
n. 血流	吸墨纸	v. (风) 吹	n. 喷水孔
blue-stocking	boar	board	body
n. 女才子	n. 野猪	n. 董事会 v. 登(车、船、飞机等)	n. 机构，组织
body language	body mass	boffin	boil
肢体语言	体重	n. 研究员，科学工作者	v. 煮沸
boiling point	bolt	bolted	bombard
沸点	n. 闪电 v. 拴住，用螺栓固定	adj. 用螺栓栓的	v. 轰炸，炮轰
bonding	bonus	book	booking
n. 结合，人与人之间的关系	n. 奖金，红利；津贴	v. 预订，预约	n. 预订
booking confirmation 预订订单	booklet	boom	boost
	n. 手册，小册子	n. 激增，繁荣 v. 急速发展	v. 促进，增加 n. 推动
border	boredom	borne	botanical
n. 边界 v. 与……接壤	n. 厌烦	v. 承担；携带	adj. 植物学的
bother with	bottle stopper	bottlenose dolphin	bottom line
为……操心	瓶塞	宽吻海豚	底线
Boulevard des Capucines 卡普西奈大街	bounce	bound	boundary
	v. 反射回，弹回	v. 束缚，捆绑	n. 边界；底线
bounty	bout	bow	bower
n. 丰富，慷慨，慷慨馈赠，奖金	n. 回合，一阵	n. 弓	n. 凉亭
bowhead whale	bowing	bowl	bowling
北极露脊鲸	n. 鞠躬	n. 碗，一碗	n. 保龄球戏
bowstrings	brain stem	brain-derived	brake
n. 弓弦	脑干	adj. 脑衍生的	n. 闸，刹车 v. 刹车；减速
Bramley College	branch	branches	brasserie
布拉姆里大学	n. 分支	n. 树枝	n. 啤酒店

brave v. 勇敢地面对	Brazilian Street Percussion 巴西街头打击乐	breach n. 违反	bread item 面包类食物
break n. 中断	break out 突然发生，爆发	break time 休息时间	breakdown n. 分裂；故障
breakneck adj. 飞快的	breakthrough n. 突破	breath n. 呼吸	breed n. 品种，种类 v. 繁殖，养育
breeder n. 饲养员	breeding n. 繁殖，饲养	brew v. 酿造，酝酿	bribe v. 贿赂，收买
brick dust 炭灰	bride n. 新娘	bridge club 桥牌社	bridge the gap 缩小差距
brief adj. 简洁的，简短的， 简要的	briefcase n. 公文包	briefly adv. 简短地	bright adj. 光明的
brilliant adj. 出众的	brilliantly adv. 辉煌地	brink n. 边缘	Britain's Foundation for Endangered Languages 英国濒危语言基金会
brittle adj. 脆弱的	broad outline 大致轮廓	broadband adj. 宽频的	broadcaster n. 广播员，广播公司
broadly adv. 明显地	brochure n. 手册，小册子	bronchitis n. 支气管炎	bronze adj. 青铜制的
brow n. 眉毛	browse v. 吃草	brute adj. 粗野的	bubble n. 气泡 v. 使冒泡，沸腾
bud n. 萌芽，蓓蕾	Buddhism n. 佛教	budding adj. 发育期的，萌 芽的	budget n. 预算
budgetary adj. 预算的	buffet n. 自助餐	bug n. 臭虫，小虫	built-in adj. 内在的；天生的
bulb n. 灯泡	bulging adj. 膨胀的	bulk adj. 大宗的	bulk supplies of 大量的
bulky adj. 庞大的	bully v. 欺负，威吓	bullying n. 恃强欺弱的行为	bump v. 碰撞

bun	bungling	bunting	buoyant
n. (圆形的) 小面包或点心	n. 拙劣的工作	n. 鹀	adj. 有浮力的
burden	bureaucratic	burger	burglary
n. 负担	adj. 官僚的	n. 汉堡包	n. 入室抢劫
burial	burst	bury	bus shelter
adj. 埋葬的	n. 爆发，突发 v. 爆炸	v. 埋葬	公交车候车亭
bush	bushfood	business model	business-related
n. 灌木	n. 招牌菜	商业模式	adj. 商务相关的
butcher	buzz	buzzing	by and large
n. 屠夫	n. 嗡嗡声	adj. 嘈杂的	大体上，总的来说
by contrast	by correspondence	by definition	bygone
相反	用写信的办法	当然地，明显地	adj. 过去的
bypass	by-product		
v. 绕开，忽视	n. 随带产生的结果		

C

cabin	cabinet	cabinet meeting	cable
n. 客舱	n. 橱柜	内阁会议	n. 电缆
cacti	cafe	Cairo	calamity
n. 仙人掌 (复数)	n. 小餐厅，小餐馆	n. 开罗	n. 灾难
calculate	calculated	calculation	calculator
v. 计算	adj. 计算出的，合适的	n. 计算，估算	n. 计算器
calendar	calendar year	calf	California State University
n. 日历	历年	n. (鲸等大型哺乳动物的) 幼崽；牛犊	加利福尼亚州州立大学
call for	call upon	call-sign	calmer
提倡；要求	要求	n. 呼叫标记	adj. 更平静的
calmly	caloric	Cambridge	camouflaged
adv. 平静地，冷静地	adj. 热量的	n. 剑桥 (英国城市)	adj. 伪装的
campaign	camper	campus	canal
n. 运动；战役	n. 露营者	n. 校园	n. 管道，灌溉水渠，运河

canary n. 金丝雀	cancel v. 取消	candida n. 念珠菌属	candidate n. 候选人，应试者
candle-wax n. 蜡烛	canes n. 手杖	cannibalism n. 自相残杀	canoe n. 独木舟，轻舟
canoeing n. 划独木舟	canopy n. 遮篷	Canterbury College 坎特伯雷大学	canvas n. 画布
canyon n. 峡谷	cap v. 加帽于	capability n. 才能，能力；性能	capable adj. 能够的，能胜任的，能干的；有能力的
capacity n. 容量，能力；产能	capital n. 首都	capriciousness n. 变幻莫测，变化无常	capsize v. 倾覆
capsule n. 胶囊	captions n. 说明	captivating adj. 迷人的；有魅力的	captive adj. 被俘获的，被迷住的
captive dolphin 圈养海豚	captive-breeding n. 圈养（人工养殖）	captivity n. 圈养	capture v. 俘获，抓住，获得
car-based adj. 基于汽车的	carbolic acid 石碳酸	carbon n. 碳	carbon dioxide 二氧化碳
carbon emissions 碳排放	car-dependent adj. 依靠汽车的	cardiovascular adj. 心血管的	career n. 职业；职业生涯；事业
career path 职业道路	carefree adj. 无忧无虑的	caregiver n. 照料者，护理者	carer n. 看护者
caretaker n. 看管者	Carey n. 凯里	cargo ship 货船	cargo-handling adj. 货物卸载的
carnival n. 狂欢节	carpenter n. 木匠	carry out 实行；完成	carry over 延期
cartography n. 制图学，地图制作	cartoon n. 卡通片，动画片	carve v. 雕刻；切开	case n. 案例
case design 案例设计	case study 个案研究	case-based adj. 基于案例的	cash management 现金管理

casing	cassette	cast	caste
n. 香肠的肠衣	*n.* 盒式磁带	*n.* 阵容，成员	*n.* 阶层
casting	cast-iron	castle	casual
n. 铸造	*adj.* 铸铁的	*n.* 城堡	*adj.* 临时的，非正式的
casual clothes	catalogue	cataloguing	catalyse
休闲服	*n.* 目录 *v.* 编目录；将……编入目录	*n.* 编目	*v.* 催化
catalyst	catastrophe	catastrophic	catch
n. 催化剂	*n.* 灾难	*adj.* 灾难的	*n.* 捕捉；捕获物
catch fire	categorical	categorise	category
着火	*adj.* 绝对的	*v.* 分类	*n.* 种类，类型
caterer	cater for	catering	caterpillar
n. 备办食物者，承办酒席者	满足……的需要；提供饮食及服务；迎合，满足	*n.* 餐饮供应，酒席承办	*n.* 毛虫
cattle	cause	cautious	cavalcade
n. 牛，牲畜	*n.* 原因	*adj.* 严谨的	*n.* 骑兵队伍
cave	cave art	cave painting	cavort
n. 洞穴	洞穴艺术，洞穴壁画	洞穴壁画，洞窟画	*v.* 欢腾
CCSU (Canterbury College Students Union) 坎特伯雷大学学生会	CD player CD 音碟机	ceaselessly *adv.* 不停地	cedar *n.* 雪松，香柏
ceiling	celebrate	celebrated	celebration
n. 天花板	*v.* 庆祝	*adj.* 有名的	*n.* 庆典
cellular	cellular structure	cellulose	Celsius
adj. 细胞的	细胞结构	*n.* 纤维素	*n.* 摄氏度
cement	cent	centimeter	centralized
n. 水泥	*n.* 分	*n.* 厘米 (cm)	*adj.* 集中的；中央集权的
centrally	ceramic	cerebellum	cerebrospinal
adv. 在中心	*adj.* 陶瓷的	*n.* 小脑	*adj.* [解剖] 脑脊髓的

ceremonial *adj.* 仪式的	ceremonies *n.* 仪式	certificate *n.* 证书；执照；合格证	certification *n.* 证明，保证
certify *v.* 证明，保证	cetacean *n.* 鲸	chain of evidence 证据链	chair *v.* 担任主席，主持
chairman *n.* 董事长	chalky *adj.* 白垩的	challenge *n.* 挑战	chamber *n.* 房间，室；私室，洞穴
champion *n.* 冠军	championship *n.* 锦标赛，冠军赛	chance *n.* 可能性，概率	channel *n.* 通道
chant *n.* 圣歌	chaos *n.* 混乱	char *v.* 烧黑，熏黑	characterise *v.* 描绘；具有……特征
characteristic *n.* 特性，特征；特色；特质；特点	characterization *n.* 角色化	charcoal *n.* 木炭	charge *n.* 费用 *v.* 收费
charged *adj.* 充满感情的	charismatic *adj.* 超凡魅力的	charity *n.* 慈善，慈善团体	chart *n.* 图表
charter *v.* 租，包租	chartered *adj.* 受特许的	chase *v.* 追逐	check *v.* 检查
checklist *n.* 核对表	checkout assistant 收银助理	check-ups *n.* 检查	cheese *n.* 奶酪，干酪
chef *n.* 厨师	chemical compound 化合物	chemical-based *adj.* 依靠化学药品的	chemical-resistant *adj.* 抗化学药品的
cheque *n.* 支票	chess *n.* 国际象棋	chess playing 博弈	chest *n.* 胸部
chick *n.* 小鸡	chief *n.* 负责人	chieftains *n.* 首领	childcare *n.* 儿童保育
childhood *n.* 童年	chill *n.* 寒冷	chimpanzee *n.* 黑猩猩	Chinese beiji 中国白鳍豚
Chinook *n.* 切努克人	chiropractor *n.* 脊椎按摩师	chocolate wrappers 巧克力包装纸	choir *n.* 合唱队
choke off 阻塞	chord *n.* 和弦	chorus *n.* 合唱	chromosomes *n.* 染色体
chronic *adj.* 长期的，慢性的	chronically *adv.* 长期地，慢性地	chronicle *n.* 编年史，年代记	chronicler *n.* 年代史编者

chrysalis	chum	cider	cinema
n. 虫茧	n. 狗鲑 v. 搅拌	n. 苹果酒	n. 电影业
cinematic adj. 电影的，影片的	cinematograph n. 电影放映机	cipher n. 暗号	circuit n. 电路，线路
circuitous adj. 绕行的	circular adj. 圆的，循环的	circulate v. 流传，循环，传播	circulating adj. 循环的 v. 使流通，使传播
circulation n. 流通，循环	circumscribe v. 限制	circumstance n. 环境，境遇，情况	cite v. 援引；引用
civic adj. 市民的	civil engineering project 土木工程	civil war 内战	civilisation n. 文明
claim n. 要求；索赔 v. 声称，声明；索赔	clamour v. 大声地要求	clamp n. 夹钳	clarify v. 澄清，净化
classic adj. 经典的	classical adj. 古典的，经典的	classification n. 分类	classify v. 分类
clay n. 黏土	cleaner n. 保洁员，清洁工	clear v. 清理	clearance n. 空隙
clearing n. 清扫	clearing-house n. 信息交流中心	clearly adv. 清楚地	clerical adj. 办事员的
clerk n. 职员	click n. 滴答声；点击	client n. 客户	clientele n. 客户，诉讼委托人
cliff n. 悬崖	climate n. 气候	climatic adj. 气候的	climatic change 气候变化
climax n. 高潮，顶点	climb v. 爬	clime n. 地方	cling v. 坚持，附着
clinic n. 诊所	clipper n. 快速帆船；大剪刀；剪削者；理发剪	close by 在附近	close call 险象环生，死里逃生
clothing n. 衣服	cloud-zapper n. 击云器	clue n. 线索，情节，提示	cluster n. 群，簇；组
clutch n. 控制.	clutter up 胡乱地填满	cluttered adj. 混乱的	coach n. 教练 v. 指导

coach trip 长途汽车旅行	coal *n.* 煤	coarse *adj.* 粗糙的	coarsely *adv.* 粗糙地
coastal *adj.* 海岸的，沿海的	coastline *n.* 海岸线	coated *adj.* 上涂料的	coating zone 涂层区
co-author *n.* 合著者	cockpit *n.* 驾驶舱	coconut *n.* 椰子，椰子肉	cocoon *n.* 蚕茧
cod *n.* 鳕鱼	code *n.* 编码，代码	codename *n.* 代码	codify *v.* 编纂
co-founder *n.* 联合创始人	cog *n.* 齿轮，钝齿	cognition *n.* 认识，知识	cognitive *adj.* 认知的
coherent *adj.* 连贯的，一致的， 明了的，清晰的	coho *n.* 银大马哈鱼，银鲑	coil *v.* 盘绕，把……卷 成圈	coiled *adj.* 盘绕的
coin *n.* 硬币 *v.* 创造	coin meter 硬币收费表	coincide *v.* 一致，符合；同时 发生，相符	coincidence *n.* 巧合；一致；同 时发生
coincidental *adj.* 一致的，巧合的	coke *n.* 焦炭	cold-blooded *adj.* 冷血的	collaborate *v.* 合作，协作
collaboration *n.* 合作	collaborative *adj.* 合作的，协作的	collaborators *n.* 合作者	collapse *n.* 倒塌，失败 *v.* 倒塌，瓦解，倾倒
collate *v.* 核对，校对，比较； 对照	collateral *adj.* 附属的	colleague *n.* 同事	collection *n.* 采集，收集
collectively *adj.* 共同地	College Accommodation Service 大学住宿服务	collision *n.* 碰撞	cologne *n.* 古龙水
colonise *v.* 在……开拓殖民 地；移于殖民地， 居住	colonist *n.* 殖民者，移民者， 开拓者	colonizer *n.* 移民	colonnaded *adj.* 有柱廊的；有列 柱的
colony *n.* 聚居地，（动植物 的）群体	Colorado *n.* 科罗拉多	Colorado University 科罗拉多大学	colossal *adj.* 巨大的

colourfast *adj.* 不掉色的	combat *n.* 战斗，争论 *v.* 反对，与……战斗；战斗	combination *n.* 联合，组合	combination lock 暗码锁；号码锁
combine *v.* 使联合，使结合	combine with 联合，结合	combustible *adj.* 易燃的；易激动的；燃烧性的	come along 出现
come into force 生效，开始实施	come to light 真相大白	come up with 想出，提出	comeback *n.* 恢复
comedian *n.* 喜剧演员，滑稽人物	comedy *n.* 喜剧	comet *n.* 彗星	comfort *n.* 舒适
comic *adj.* 喜剧的	command *n.* 命令	commemoration *n.* 纪念	commence *v.* 开始
comment *n.* 评论；意见 *v.* 评论	comment on 发表评论，发表意见；评价	commentary *n.* 评论，评注	commentator *n.* （电台或广播的）时事评论员
commerce *n.* 贸易，商业	commercial *adj.* 商业的	commercialised *adj.* 商业化的	commercially *adv.* 商业上
commission *n.* 佣金 *v.* 委托制作；委任	commit *v.* 使……承担任务	commitment *n.* 承诺，责任感	committee *n.* 委员会
commodity *n.* 商品，货物；日用品	commodity futures markets 商品期货市场	common practice 惯例	common sense 常识
commonly *adv.* 通常地，一般地	commonplace *adj.* 平凡的 *n.* 普遍	Commonwealth Institute of Biological Control 英联邦生物防治研究所	communal *adj.* 公共的，公社的，公有的
communicate *v.* 沟通，交流，通讯，传达	communication *n.* 交流，通信，通讯；沟通	community *n.* 社会，社区，团体，群落	community-based *adj.* 基于社区的
commute *v.* 往返于两地之间	commuting *n.* 乘公交车上下班	compact *adj.* 紧凑的	compact disc 光盘

companion n. 同伴；同事	company n. 陪伴	comparable adj. 可比较的，比得 上的	comparatively adv. 比较地
compare v. 与……相比较	compare to 比喻为	comparison n. 比较；类似，对照	compass n. 指南针 v. 包围
compatible adj. 兼容的；能共处 的；可并立的；相 符的	compelling adj. 强有力的；引人 注目的；引人注意的	compensate v. 补偿；付报酬	compensate for 弥补；赔偿
compensation n. 补偿，赔偿金	compete v. 竞争	competing adj. 干扰的；相互矛 盾的	competition n. 竞争
competitive adj. 竞争的，有竞争 力的	competitors n. 竞争者	compile v. 编译，汇编	compiled adj. 编译的
complain v. 抱怨，投诉	complaint n. 疾病；抱怨，投诉	complaints handling team 投诉处理团队	complement n. 补充
complementary adj. 补足的，补充的	complete v. 完工，完成	completely adv. 完全地	completion n. 完成
complex adj. 复杂的 n. 复合体；综合设施	complexity n. 复杂 (性)	complicated adj. 复杂的	compliment n. 赞美，称赞，恭维
comply with 服从；照做，遵守	components n. 成分，要素，部件， 组成，部分 adj. 组成的	composer n. 作曲家	composite n. 混合物，合成物， 复合材料
composition n. 构成，组成	compost n. 混合物，合成物	compound n. 混合物，化合物 adj. 混合的	comprehend v. 理解
comprehensive adj. 广泛的；综合的	compression n. 压缩	comprise v. 包含；由……组成	compromise v. 危害；妥协
compulsory adj. 必需的	computational adj. 计算的	compute v. 计算，估算	computer lab 计算机实验室

computer science 计算机科学	computer-driven *adj.* 电脑驱动的	computing *n.* 计算，从事电脑 工作	comrade *n.* 伙伴
conceal *v.* 隐藏	concealed *adj.* 隐蔽的	conceive *v.* 构思；以为；持有， 设想	concentrate *v.* 集中，专注
concentrate on 集中精力于；关注， 集中	concentrating *v.* 专心	concentration *n.* 集中	concept *n.* 概念，理念
conceptual *adj.* 概念的，概念 上的	concern *n.* 关心；关心的事 *v.* 关系到；涉及； 关注	concert *n.* 音乐会	concession *n.* (对某类人) 减价
concessionary *adj.* 优惠的	concise *adj.* 简明的，简洁的	conclude *v.* 推断，得出结论	conclusion *n.* 结论；推论
conclusively *adv.* 最后地；决定 性地	Concordia University 康卡迪亚大学	concrete *n.* 混凝土	concur *v.* 同意
condemn *v.* 使……处于 (不利 的境况)	condense *v.* 浓缩，精简	condition *n.* 条件	conduct *v.* 进行，实施；导电； 处理，安排；经营
conductance *n.* 传导性	cone *n.* 球果	coneflower *n.* 金菊花	cone-shaped *adj.* 圆锥形的
confer *v.* 授予，给予	conference *n.* 会议；信心	conference room 会议室	confident *adj.* 自信的
confidential *adj.* 机密的，秘密的	confidentially *adv.* 机密地，秘密地	configuration *n.* 配置，结构	confirm *v.* 确定，证实；限制； 确认，批准
conflict *n.* 冲突，矛盾	conflict management 冲突管理	conform *v.* 符合，遵照	confront *v.* 面临，遭遇
confront with 使面临	Confucius *n.* 孔子	confuse *v.* 使混乱，使迷惑	confusion *n.* 混乱，困惑
congested *adj.* 拥挤的	congestion *n.* 拥挤，拥塞，堵车； 拥堵	congregate *v.* 聚集	conjunction *n.* 结合

connect with 与……有关	Connecticut *n.* 美国康涅狄格州	connection *n.* 关系，联系	connotative *adj.* 暗示的；暗含的
conquer *v.* 征服	conquest *n.* 征服；占领	conscious *adj.* 意识到的	consciously *adv.* 自觉地，有意识地
consciousness *n.* 意识	consecutive *adj.* 连贯的，连续不断的	consensus *n.* (意见等) 一致	consequence *n.* 后果，结果
consequent *adj.* 随之发生的	consequently *adv.* 因此，结果	conservation *n.* 保存，保护	conservative *adj.* 保守的
conservator *n.* 保护者，救护者	conservatory *n.* 温室	conserve *v.* 保存，保藏	consider *v.* 认为；考虑，思考
considerable *adj.* 相当大的，重要的	considerably *adv.* 相当地；非常地	consideration *n.* 考虑；关心	consistency *n.* 一致性
consistent *adj.* 始终如一的，一致的；一贯的，持续的	consistent with 符合，与……一致	consistently *adv.* 一贯地	conspicuous *adj.* 显而易见的
constant *adj.* 不变的；经常的；持续的；恒定的	constantly *adv.* 不断地，一直	constituent *n.* 成分	constitute *v.* 组成，构成
constrain *v.* 驱使，强迫，束缚，限制	constraint *n.* 限制，约束	construct *v.* 建造，构造	construction *n.* 建设；重建
constructive *adj.* 建设性的	consult *v.* 查阅，商量，请教，咨询	consultant *n.* 顾问	consultant engineer 顾问工程师
consultation *n.* 会诊，咨询；商讨，查阅	consulting *adj.* 咨询的，顾问的	consulting engineer 顾问工程师	consume *v.* 消耗
consumer *n.* 消费者	consumption *n.* 消费；消耗	contact *v.* 联系，接触	contactable *adj.* 可接触
contain *v.* 包含	container *n.* 容器	container crane 集装箱起重机	containerization *n.* 集装箱化

containment n. 抑制，遏制	contamination n. 污染物	contemporary adj. 当代的，同时代的	contend v. 主张；争论
content adj. 满意的	context n. 背景；上下文	continent n. 大陆，陆地	continental adj. 大陆的
continental breakfast 欧式早餐，英式早餐	continent-wide adj. 全大陆的	contingency n. 偶然性，可能性；偶发事件，应急措施	contingent adj. 因情况而异的
continued adj. 持久的	continuity n. 分镜头剧本，连续性	continuous adj. 持续的，连续的	continuum n. 连续
contract n. 合同 v. 使缩短	contractor n. 承包人，立契约者	contradict v. 与……抵触，与……相矛盾	contraption n. 奇妙的装置
contrast v. 对比	contribute to 导致	contributing adj. 起作用的，作贡献的	contribution n. 贡献
contributory adj. 需要定期缴费的	controller n. 控制员	controversial adj. 有争论的	controversy n. 争论
convection current （气象）对流	convenience n. 便利	convenient adj. 方便的	convention n. 惯例，手法，习俗
conventional adj. 传统的；惯例的	converged v. 集结	conversation n. 交谈，会话	converse n. 相反的事情，反面的说法
convert n. 皈依者 v. 转变，改变；使转变；转换	convert to 转换为	convey v. 表达，传达	conveyor belt 传送带
convict v. 证明有罪	conviction n. 信念	convince v. 说服，使确信；确信	cooked food 熟食
cool v. 使冷却	coolant-lined adj. 内衬冷却液的	cooling n. 冷却	cooperative adj. 合作的

coordinate v. 协调，调整	coordination n. 协调，调和	coordinator n. 协调人	cope v. 处理
cope with 处理，应对	Copenhagen n. 哥本哈根	Copernicus n. 哥白尼（波兰天文学家）	copper n. 铜
copy v. 抄袭	coral n. 珊瑚 adj. 珊瑚色的	core n. 核心	corner n. 偏僻处
cornerstone n. 基础，基石	corpora n. 全集，全部资料	corporal adj. 肉体的	corporate adj. 公司的; 企业的; 团体的
corporation n. 公司	correlation n. 联系; 相关，关联	correspond v. 符合，一致	corresponding adj. 相应的，相当的; 一致的
corridor n. 走廊	cortex n. 皮质，皮层	cortisol n. 皮质醇	cosmetics n. 化妆品
cosmic adj. 宇宙的	cost-effective adj. 划算的，成本效益好的，性价比高的	costly adj. 昂贵的，代价高的	costumes n. 戏服
cot n. 简易床，轻便小床	cottage n. 小别墅	cotton n. 棉线，棉布 adj. 棉制的	cough n. 咳嗽
council n. 议会，委员会	counsel v. 咨询，劝告	counseling service 咨询服务	count v. 计算，清点，算做
counter v. 反对 adj. 相反的	counter-intuitive adj. 反直觉的; 违反语感的	counter-intuitively adv. 让人意想不到的是	counterpart n. 对应物，极相似的事物
counter-productive adj. 产生相反效果的	counterproductive adj. 效率低下的	counting n. 计算	counting house 会计室
country estate 庄园	couple v. 结合	couple with 结合	courier n. 导游; 情报员
course n. 进程; 课程	course design 课程设计	coursework n. 修习，指定功课	court life 宫廷生活
court of law 法庭; 法院	courtship n. 求爱（时期）	cousin n. 远亲，表亲	cover v. 包括; 覆盖; 报道，采访

coverage	covering	cowboy	coyote
n. 新闻报道；覆盖范围	adj. 掩盖的	n. 牛仔	n.（一种产于北美大草原的）小狼，丛林狼
crack	cradle	craft	craftsman
v. 使破裂	n. 支架，摇篮	n. 技术；技艺；工艺	n. 工匠
cram	crane	crash	crash-land
v. 塞进，填满	n. 起重机	n. 碰撞；坠落	n. 紧急降落
crate	crater	creative	creativity
n. 箱	n. 火山口	adj. 创造性的	n. 创造力
creature	credence	credential	credibility
n. 生物	n. 证据，凭证	n. 信任状，文凭；资格	n. 可信性
credit	credit card	credit note	creep
n. 贷款；信誉 v. 归功于	信用卡	信用票据	v. 慢慢地移动
cretaceous	crew	criminal intent	crisis
adj. 白垩纪的	n. 全体人员，全体船员	犯罪目的	n. 危机；危及
crisps	criteria	criterion	critic
n. 薯片	n. 标准，条件	n. 标准	n. 评论家，批评家
critical	critical length	critically	criticism
adj. 鉴定的；批评的，爱挑剔的；危险的；决定性的；评论的，关键的，至关重要的	临界长度	adv. 危急地；批评性地	n. 批评
criticize	crocodile	crop	cropping up
v. 批评，挑剔，评论	n. 鳄鱼	n. 农作物，庄稼	突然出现
cross	cross-section	crowd	crucial
v. 横过	n. 横截面	n. 群众，一群 v. 挤	adj. 至关重要的；决定性的；定局的；决断的；关键的
cruise	crumple	crusade	crust
v. 巡航；漫游；徘徊于，巡航于	v. 弄皱，变皱	n. 改革运动	n. 外壳

crypt n. 土窖，地下室	cryptosporidium n. 隐孢子虫	crystal adj. 透明的 n. 水晶；晶体	crystalline adj. 透明的，水晶般的
cub n.（狮、虎等的）幼兽	cube n. 立方体	cubic adj. 立方体的	cubic centimeter 立方厘米
cubic metre 立方米	cue n. 提示；线索	cuisine n. 菜肴，烹饪	cul-de-sac n. 死胡同
culminate v. 达到极值；导致	culprit n. 重要原因，罪魁祸首；形成问题的事物	cult n. 祭仪	cultivate v. 培养，耕作
cultivation n. 耕作，培养，栽培	cultural adj. 文化的	cultural anthropology 文化人类学	cultural values 文化价值
cumulative adj. 累积的	cupboard n. 碗柜；食橱	curator n. 管理者	curb v. 控制；勒住
cure n. 治疗，治愈	cure-all n. 万灵药	curiosity n. 好奇心；奇人，奇物	curious adj. 好奇的
current adj. 目前的 n.（水，气，电）流	currently adv. 目前，普遍地	curriculum n. 课程	curriculum vitae 个人简历
curse n. 诅咒，咒骂	curtail v. 缩减	curve n. 曲线	cushion n. 垫子，缓冲 v. 缓冲
custom adj. 定做的 n. 传统；风俗	custom duty 关税	customer n. 消费者	cut n. 削减
cut back on 削减	cut out 停止	cutter n. 切割机	cybernetics n. 控制论
cycle n. 循环，周期	cyclist n. 骑自行车的人		

D

dab v. 轻拍；很快地涂抹	daily life 日常生活	dairy n. 牛奶场，牛奶	daisy n. 雏菊

dam	dam project	damp	dampen
n. 大坝，水坝	水坝工程	adj. 潮湿的	v. 抑制
dancer	daredevil	daring	dark side
n. 舞者	adj. 蛮勇的，不怕死的	adj. 大胆的，勇敢的	负面
darken	dashed	databank	database
v. 使变黑	adj. 画虚线的	n. 数据库	n. 数据库
date back	dawn	day length	daybreak
追溯（溯到）	n. 黎明，破晓	昼长	n. 黎明
day-neutral	dazzling	DDT	deadline
adj. 无论有无阳光均能生长的	adj. 耀眼的，眼花缭乱的	n. 滴滴涕（一种杀虫剂）	n. 最后期限
deadly	deadly snakes	deal table	dealt
adj. 致命的；殊死的	致命毒蛇	牌桌	v. 处理
dear	dearth	debate	debit
adj. 高价的	n. 缺乏	v./n. 论辩，争论	n. 借方
debris	debt	decade	decan
n. 碎片，残骸	n. 债务	n. 十年	n. 黄道十度分度
decay	decent	deceptively	decidedly
v. 衰退	adj. 像样的，大方的	adv. 迷惑地	adv. 果断地；断然地；明显；毫无疑问
decipher	decision-maker	decision-support	decisive
v. 破解	n. 决策者	adj. 决策支持的	adj. 决定性的
deck	declaration	declare	decline
n. 甲板	n. 宣布，宣告	v. 宣布，断言	n. 减少，下降；衰退 v. 下降
declining	decode	decorative	decreased
adj. 下滑的，衰退的	v. 解码，译码，解读	adj. 装饰性的；装潢用的	adj. 减少的
dedicate	dedicated	dedication	deduce
v. 致力，贡献	adj. 致力于的；专注的，有奉献精神的，献身的	n. 奉献	v. 推论，推断
deduction	deem	deepen	deeply
n. 扣除，减除；推论；减除额	v. 认为，视为	v. 使加深；使强烈	adv. 深入地

deep-sea	defective	defence (defense)	defender
adj. 深海的	adj. 有缺陷的	n. 抵御	n. 拥护者
defer	deficiency	deficit	define
v. 延期	n. 缺陷，缺点	n. 缺乏	v. 定义，明确；限定，界定
defined	definite	definitely	definitive
adj. 清晰的，明确的	adj. 确切的；明确的	adv. 清楚地，明确地	adj. 明确的
definitively	defoliant	deforestation	degenerate
adv. 确定地	n. 落叶剂，脱叶剂	n. 采伐森林	v. 退化，堕落
degenerative	degradation	degrade	degree
adj. 退化的	n. 退化	v. 降级	n. 学位
delay	delayed	delegates	deliberately
n. 延期，耽搁	adj. 延迟的；延时的	n. 代表	adv. 谨慎地，故意地
delicate	delight	delighted	delightful
adj. 微妙的；精美的，易碎的，纤弱的，脆弱的；易损的	n. 喜悦	adj. 高兴的	adj. 令人愉快的
deliver	delivery	delta	delude
v. 传送，递送，交付；实现，履行	n. 递送	n. 三角洲	v. 迷惑，使失望
demanding	dementia	democratic	demographer
adj. 苛求的，要求高的，苛刻的	n. 痴呆	adj. 民主的	n. 人口统计学家
demographic	demolish	demonstrable	demonstrate
adj. 人口统计学的；人口学的	v. 打败；推倒	adj. 可论证的；显而易见的	v. 显示，展示；表明，证明；示威
demonstration	denigration	Denmark	denomination
n. 示范，表达	n. 诋毁；贬义词	n. 丹麦	n. 面额
denote	denounce	dense	density
v. 表示，指示	v. 谴责，指责	adj. 稠密的	n. 密度
dental	dentist	denude	deny
adj. 牙科的，牙齿的	n. 牙医	v. 使变得光秃	v. 否定；否认；拒绝
deoxy	depart	department	departure
adj. 脱氧的	v. 出发，起程	n. 部门	n. 离开

departure lounge 候机室；启程处	depend on 依靠	depended v. 依赖，依靠；取决 于；相信，信赖	depict v. 描绘，描述
deplete v. 使减少；弄空；耗 尽……的资源	deposit n. 保证金；定金 v. 存放，存款；使 沉积	depositing n. 沉淀	depressed adj. 沮丧的
depression n. 抑郁，沮丧；大 萧条	deprivation n. 丧失	deprive v. 剥夺，使丧失	deprived adj. 缺少食物的；缺 乏足够教育的
depth n. 深度	deregulate v. 撤销，解除管制	deregulation n. 解除管制	derelict adj. 玩忽职守的；无 主的；被抛弃了的， 废弃的
derision n. 嘲笑	derive v. 源于，得自	derive from 由……起源，取自	desalination n. 脱盐作用
descend v. 下降	descend on 降临	descendant n. 后代；后裔；子孙	descending v. 下降
descent n. 下降	description n. 描述	descriptive adj. 叙述的，描写性 的	desert n. 荒原，沙漠
desert annuals 荒漠一年生植物	desertification n. 沙漠化	deserve v. 值得，应得	design v. 设计
designate v. 指定，指派，标出； 命名	designer n. 设计者	desirability n. 愿望，渴求	desirable adj. 合适的，值得 要的
desire n. 欲望 n./v. 渴望	desktop n. 台式机；桌面	desolate adj. 荒凉的，无人的	desperate adj. 不顾一切的
desperately adv. 非常，特别， 极其	despise v. 轻视	despite prep. 尽管	despoil v. 掠夺，剥夺
destination n. 目的地	destruction n. 破坏；毁坏	destructive adj. 破坏的；毁灭性 的；破坏性的	detail n. 细节，详情，详 细内容

detailed *adj.* 详细的，详尽的	detain *v.* 留住	detect *v.* 察觉，探测，发现	detective *n.* 侦探 *adj.* 侦探的
detector dog 缉毒犬	deter *v.* 制止，阻止；使打 消念头	deter-international *adj.* 反全球化的	deteriorate *v.* 恶化
deterioration *n.* 恶化；退化；堕落	determination *n.* 测定	determine *v.* 决定；确定	determined *adj.* 决定了的；坚 定的
deterrent *n.* 威慑	detrimental *adj.* 有害的，不利的	devastate *v.* 毁坏，毁灭	devastating *adj.* 毁灭性的
devastation *v.* 毁坏，摧毁	deviation *n.* 背离，偏离	device *n.* 装置	devious *adj.* 偏僻的，间接的
devise *v.* 设计，发明；想出	devoid *adj.* 没有的；不包含 的	devolve *v.* 移交；委托	devote *v.* 奉献
devote assist 投入协助	devote to 把……专用于，致 力于	devotion *n.* 忠诚；热爱；奉献	devour *v.* 吞噬
diabetes *n.* 糖尿病	diagnosis *n.* 诊断	dial *n.* 仪表盘	dial meter 刻度盘仪表
dialogue *n.* 对话；对白	diameter *n.* 直径	diametrically *adv.* 完全地	diarrhea *n.* 腹泻，痢疾
dice *n.* 骰子；概率	dictate *v.* 规定；命令(操纵)	differ *v.* 相异；意见分歧； 不同	differentiate *v.* 区别
diffraction *n.* 衍射，反射	digest *v.* 消化，吸收	digestive *adj.* 消化的，易消化的	digit *n.* 位数
digital camera 数码相机	digital display meter 数字显示仪表	digitise *v.* 数字化	dignify *v.* 被授予；使…… 高贵
dilapidated *adj.* 荒废的，要塌似 的；破坏的	dilate *v.* 扩张	dilemma *n.* 困境，进退两难	diligent *adj.* 勤勉的，用功的
dimension *n.* 尺寸；维	diminish *v.* 减少；削弱；使减 少；使变小	diminishing *adj.* 逐渐减少的	dimming *n.* 变暗

dine v. 进餐，用餐	dinosaur n. 恐龙	dip v. 蘸；浸入	diploma n. 文书；毕业证书；文凭
diplomatic adj. 外交的	direction n. 方向	director n. 主任，主管	directorship n. 管理者
directory n. 目录	disability n. 残疾	disabled adj. 残疾的，无自理能力的	disadvantaged adj. 处于不利地位的
disagreement n. 争论，不同意	disappear v. 消失	disappointing adj. 令人失望的	disaster area 灾区
disastrous adj. 灾难性的；损失惨重的；悲伤的	discard v. 抛弃，放弃	discharge v. 放出；免除；排放	disciplinary adj. 纪律的，训诫的
discipline n. 纪律；学科	disclosure n. 披露，揭发	discount v./n. 折扣	discounted adj. 已折扣的
discourage v. 阻止，阻碍，使气馁	discover v./n. 发现	discrepancy n. 不符，矛盾；差异	discrimination n. 歧视
discuss v. 论述，讨论	discussion n. 讨论	disease-spreading adj. 传播病菌的	disenchantment n. 不抱幻想，清醒
disguise v. 假装，掩饰	disgust n. 厌恶，嫌恶	disgusting adj. 令人厌恶的	dish n. 一道菜
disillusioned adj. 幻想破灭的	disjunction n. 分离	disk drive 磁盘驱动器，碟片驱动器	dismantle v. 拆开，拆卸，拆除取消
dismiss v. 解散	dismissive adj. 轻视的	disorder n. 混乱，紊乱；失调	disorderly adj. 无秩序的
disorganised adj. 紊乱的，无组织的	disorientated adj. 不知所措的	disorientating v. 使迷惑	disparate adj. 不同的
dispense v. 分发，分配；执行	dispersal n. 分散，传播	disperse v. 分散，使散开	displace v. 取代

displacement *n.* 位移	display *n.* 表现；显示 *v.* 显示，表现；陈列， 公布	disposable *adj.* 用完即可丢弃 的，一次性的	disposal *n.* 处理；支配；清理； 安排
dispose *v.* 处理	dispose of 处理	disproportionately *adv.* 不成比例地	dispute *n.* 争论
disputed *adj.* 有争议的	disrupt *v.* 破坏	disruption *n.* 打断	disruptive *adj.* 令人困扰的
dissect *v.* 分解	disseminate *v.* 传播，宣传	dissonant *adj.* 不协调的	distain *n.* 轻视，鄙视
distance vision 远视能力	distant *adj.* 遥远的	distaste *n.* 厌恶，讨厌	distilled *adj.* 净化的
distinct *adj.* 分布各处的；不 同的；明显的，独 特的	distinction *n.* 区别，差别；特性	distinctive *adj.* 有特色的，与众 不同的；不同的	distinctiveness *n.* 特殊性
distinguish *v.* 区别，辨别；使杰 出	distort *v.* 扭曲	distorted *adj.* 歪曲的，变形的	distortion *n.* 曲解
distract *v.* 转移，分心	distracted *adj.* 思想不集中的	distractibility *n.* 注意力分散	distractible *adj.* 易分心的
distraction *n.* 干扰，注意力分 散，分神	distressing *adj.* 使痛苦的；悲伤 的；使烦恼的	distribute *v.* 分配；散布；分开； 把……分类	distribution *n.* 分布，分配；分销
district *n.* 区域；地区	disturb *v.* 打扰；弄乱，妨碍； 搅乱	disturbance *n.* 打扰，弄乱	disturbing *adj.* 令人不安的
dive *v.* 潜水，跳水	divergent *adj.* 不同的	diverse *adj.* 不同的，多样的	diversity *n.* 多样性，差异
divert *v.* 转移	dividing line 分界线	divinity *n.* 神学；神	divulge *v.* 泄露
dizzy *adj.* 头晕目眩的	dock *n.* 码头	docked *v.* 停驻（dock 的过 去式）	dockside *n.* 坞边

doctoral student 博士生	document v. 用文件证明	documentary n. 纪录片 adj. 记录的	documentation n. 文件；文件材料
dodge v. 托词，避开	dolls n. 玩偶	dolphin n. 海豚	domain n. 领域; 域名; 产业; 地产
domestic adj. 国内的，家庭的， 家养的；国内的	domesticate v. 驯养，教化	dominance n. 统治	dominant adj. 主要的；支配的， 占优势的
dominant boss 占主导地位的老板	dominate v. 控制，支配；占 优势	Dominican Republic 多米尼加共和国	donate v. 捐赠
donation n. 捐赠	donkey n. 驴子	doodle n. 涂鸦	doom v. 注定
doomsday n. 世界末日	dorsal adj. 背部的；背的， 背侧的	dose n. 剂量，一剂	dot v. 点缀
dotted adj. 星罗棋布的；有 点的	double v. 使加倍	doughnut n. 炸面圈	downfall n. 衰落
download v. 下载	downright adv. 完全地	downside n. 下降趋势	downstream adj. 顺流的
downturn n. (经济) 衰退	downward adv. 下潜	downwind adj. 顺风的	dozen n. 一打，十二个
drab adj. 单调的	draft v. 起草，制定	drag v. 拖，拉，拽	drain v. 流出，排出
drama n. 戏剧	dramatic adj. (影响) 大的；戏 剧化的；激动人心 的；引人注意的	dramatic feature 戏剧性特点	dramatically adv. 剧烈地，戏剧 性的
dramatization n. 编剧，改编成戏剧	drastic adj. 严厉的	drastically adv. 大大地，彻底地	draw v. 吸引

draw to one's attention 引起某人的注意	drawback *n.* 缺点，不利因素，劣势	drawing *n.* 图画	drawn *adj.* 绘制的
dredge *v.* 捕捞 *n.* 捕捞船	dress heels 正装跟鞋	dress shoes 正装皮鞋	dressing *n.* 穿衣，装饰
drill *v.* 钻孔	drinking water 饮用水	drip *v.* 滴下，溢出	driver *n.* 驱动力
driving licence 驾驶证	drop *n.* 下降 *v.* 使降低	drop in 拜访，来访	droplets *n.* 飞沫
drought *n.* 干旱	drought-resistant *adj.* 抗旱的	drowsy *n.* 困倦的	drug *n.* 毒品
drumbeat *n.* 鼓声	dry out 变干	dual-purpose *adj.* 双重目的的，两用的	dub *v.* 把……称为，授予称号
Duke University 杜克大学	dull *adj.* 阴暗的	dump *v.* 倾倒	dungeon *n.* 地牢
duplex *adj.* 双重的	duplicate *n.* 副本 *v.* 复制，模仿	duplication *n.* 复制；副本	durable *adj.* 持久的
duration *n.* 期间，持续时间	dusk *n.* 黄昏	Dutch *n.* 荷兰人	duty *n.* 职责，关税
duvet cover 被套	dwelling *n.* 住所	dwindle *v.* 减少	dye *n.* 染料，颜色
dyke *n.* 岩脉	dynamic *n.* 动态；动力 *adj.* 有活力的，生动的	dynamics *n.* 动力学	dynamism *n.* 活力；动态
dynamite *n.* 炸药	dysentery *n.* 痢疾		

E

eagerly *adv.* 热切地，渴望地	eagle *n.* 鹰	eapdirect *n.* 企业应用平台	Early Childhood Care and Education Working Group 幼儿保育和教育工作小组
early children nursing 孩子早期看护	early day 初级阶段	earn *v.* 赚钱	earner *n.* 赚钱者
earning *n.* 收入，获利	earrings *n.* 耳环，耳饰	earthenware *n.* 陶器，土器	earth-moving *adj.* 惊天动地的
earthquake *n.* 地震	earth-shattering *adj.* 惊天动地的	ease *n.* 轻松	easterly wind 东风
eastward *adv.* 向东	eaves *n.* 屋檐	eccentric *adj.* 古怪的，反常的	eccentricity *n.* 反常，古怪
echinacea *n.* 紫锥花属	echinacin *n.* 海胆碱	echo *n.* 回声，回音	echolocation *n.* 回声测距，回声定位法
ecological *adj.* 生态学的	ecologist *n.* 生态学者	ecology *n.* 生态学	economic downturn 经济低迷
economical *adj.* 经济的，节约的	economist *n.* 经济学家	economy *n.* 节约，节俭	econopass *n.* 经济通行卡
ecosystem *n.* 生态系统	ecozones *n.* 生态带	edge *n.* 边缘	edible *adj.* 可食用的
Edinburgh *n.* 爱丁堡（英国城市名）	editorial *adj.* 编辑的，社论的	educate *v.* 教育	education institution 教育机构
educational *adj.* 教育的	effective *adj.* 有效的；实际的	effectively *adv.* 有效地	efficiency *n.* 效率；效能
efficient *adj.* 有效率的，有能力的；足够的	effort *n.* 努力	effortless *adj.* 不费力气的	effortlessly *adv.* 不费力地
egghead *n.* 受过高等教育的人，书呆子	egg-shaped *adj.* 蛋形的	eggshell *n.* 蛋壳	Egyptology *n.* 埃及古物学

Einstein	El Chichon	El Nino/La Nina	elaborate
n. 爱因斯坦	n. 萨尔瓦多奇诺	n. 厄尔尼诺 / 拉尼娜现象	v. 详细阐述，精心制作；从简单成分合成 adj. 精细的，复杂的
elaboration	elapse	elastic	elasticity
n. 详细阐述	v. 消逝	adj. 有弹性的	n. 弹力
elderly	elderly care	electricity	electricity supply
adj. 高龄的	养老服务	n. 电力	电力供应
electron	electronic	electronically	elegance
n. 电子	adj. 电子的	adv. 电子地	n. 优雅
element	elementary	elementary school	elephants
n. 元素，要素	adj. 基本的	小学	n. 大象
elevate	elevated	elevation	elicit
v. 升起	adj. 高尚的	n. 海拔	v. 抽出，引出
eligibility	eligible	eliminate	elite
n. 资格	adj. 合格的，符合条件的，有资格的	v. 消除，排除	n. 社会精英阶层
elitist	elixir	Elizabethan	eloquently
n. 精英，优秀人才	n. 长生不老药；万能药	n. 伊丽莎白时代	adv. 极富表现力地
elucidate	elusive	embark	embark on
v. 阐明，说明	adj. 难懂的，难捉摸的；行踪隐秘的	v. 开始或从事（尤指新的或难的事），乘船；登上	从事，着手
embarrassed	embarrassment	embed	embellish
adj. 尴尬的	n. 难堪	v. 植入，嵌入	v. 修饰；装饰
emblazon	embrace	embryo	embryonic cells
v. 用纹章装饰	v. 留住，吸引	n. 胚胎；晶胚	胚胎细胞
emerge	emergence	emergency	emergent
v. 浮现；摆脱；暴露，出现	n. 出现，发生	n. 紧急情况，突发事件	adj. 浮现的
emeritus	émigré	eminent	emission
adj. 退休的，名誉退休的	n. 流亡者，移居者	adj. 著名的，知名的，杰出的	n. 排放；发出，散发

emit	emotionally	empathy	emperor
v. 发出，放射；发行；发表	adv. 感情上地，情绪上地	n. 共鸣，同感	n. 皇帝
emphasis	emphasise	emphysema	empire
n. 重点，强调	v. 强调；加强……的语气	n. 肺气肿	n. 帝国
empirical	empirically	employ	employee
adj. 经验主义的	adv. 以经验为主地	v. 雇用	n. 雇员，员工
employer	employment	empty	emulate
n. 雇主，老板	n. 职业，雇用	v. 使……成为空的	v. 模仿
enable	encapsulate	encase	encasing
v. 使能够	v. 概述	v. 围绕	v. 包含
enclose	enclosure	encode	encoding
v. 围绕；装入；放入封套；封闭；围合	n. 附件	v. 编码，译码	n. 编码
encompass	encounter	encounter with	encourage
v. 包围；环绕	n. 偶然碰见 v. 遇到；曾遭遇	遭遇，遇到	v. 促进，鼓励，激励
encouragingly	encyclopedia	encyclopedic	endanger
adv. 鼓舞人心地	n. 百科全书	adj. 渊博的，知识广博的	v. 危及
endangered	Endangered Language Fund	ending	endurance
adj. 濒临灭绝的	濒危语言基金会	n. 结尾	n. 持久，耐久；耐力
endure	enduring	energetic	energetically
v. 持续，持久	adj. 持久的	adj. 充满活力的，精力充沛的，生动的	adv. 精力充沛地
energy cost	enervation	enforce	engage
能量消耗	n. 贫瘠	v. 施行，执行	v. 从事；使参加
engage in	engaged	engender	engine
从事于	adj. 忙碌的，使用中的	v. 产生，造成	n. 引擎
engineering	English-speaking country	engraving	engross
n. 工程，工程学	说英语的国家	n. 雕刻品	v. 全神贯注

engrossed in 全神贯注于	enhance v. 提高；加强	enhanced adj. 加强的	enigma n. 谜
enjoyable adj. 愉快的，有趣的	enlarge v. 增加	enlarged adj. 放大的；增大的； 扩展的	enormous adj. 庞大的，巨大的
enormously adv. 巨大地	enquiry n. 询问，盘问	enrich v. 使丰富，使富足	enroll v. 登记，入学；注册
enrollment n. 登记	ensue v. 接着发生	en-suite n. 套房	ensure v. 保证，确保
entanglement n. 纠缠	enterprise n. 企业	enterprising adj. 大胆的，有魄力 的	entertain v. 使快乐，款待
entertainment n. 娱乐	enthusiasm n. 热情；热心，热忱	enthusiast n. 狂热者，发烧友	enthusiastic adj. 狂热的，热心的， 热情的
enthusiastically adv. 充满激情地； 热情地	entice v. 诱使，怂恿	entire adj. 整个的，全部的	entirely adv. 完全地，彻底地
entitle v. 称做，定名为； 使……有权利	entitled adj. 有资格的	entitlement n. 应得权益；权利	entity n. 实体；存在
entrance n. 入口	entrench v. 确立；牢牢建立	entrepreneurial adj. 创业的	entrepreneurship n. 企业家精神
entwine v. 缠住，交织	environmental campaigns 环保活动	environmentalist n. 环境论者，研究 环境问题的专家	environmentally- friendly adj. 环境友好的
envy v. 嫉妒	epic adj. 史诗般的	epidemiologist n. 流行病学家	epidemiology n. 传染病学
epigenetics n. 表现遗传性	episode n. 片段，插曲；一 段情节	equable adj. 平静的	equal adj. 平等的
equation n. 等式	equator n. 赤道	equilibrium n. 平衡，均衡	equinox n. 春分，秋分
equip v. 装备，配备	equipment n. 设备	equitable adj. 公平的	equity n. 公平，公正

equivalent *n.* 对应物，等价物 *adj.* 等价的，相等的	equivalent to 等于，相当于	era *n.* 时代，年代	eradicate *v.* 根除
eradication *n.* 消灭，扑灭；根除	erect *v.* 建造 *adj.* 竖立的	erode *v.* 腐蚀；侵蚀	erosion *n.* 减少；侵蚀，磨损
erroneous *adj.* 错误的	error *n.* 错误	erupt *v.* 爆发，喷发	eruption *n.* 喷发；爆发
escalate *v.* 逐步上升	escalating *adj.* 上升的	escapement *n.* 擒纵机构棘轮装置	escapism *n.* 逃避现实
esoteric *adj.* 难懂的	essay *n.* 论文，散文，随笔	essayist *n.* 分析者	essence *n.* 本质，实质；精华； 香精
essential *adj.* 必要的，必不可 少的；本质的，基 本的 *n.* 要素	essential information 基本信息	essentially *adv.* 本质上，核心地	establish *v.* 建立
established *adj.* 确定的；已制定 的，已建立的	establishment *n.* 确立，制定；公司； 设施	estate *n.* 房地产	esteemed *adj.* 受人尊敬的
estimate *n.* 估计；预算	estimated *v.* 估计，估量	estrangement *n.* 疏远	estuary *n.* 河口
eternity *n.* 来世，来生；不朽； 永世	ethanol *n.* 乙醇	ethereal *adj.* 轻巧的，缥缈的	ethical *adj.* 伦理的，道德的
ethically *adv.* 伦理上	ethics *n.* 道德规范	Ethiopia *n.* 埃塞俄比亚	ethnicity *n.* 种族划分
ethnographer *n.* 人种志学者	ethnography *n.* 人种学	ethnology *n.* 人类文化学	ethylene *n.* 乙烯
European Renaissance 文艺复兴	European Union 欧盟	eutrophication *n.* 富营养化	evacuation *n.* 疏散，撤离；排泄
evaluate *v.* 评估，评价	evaluation *n.* 评价；[审计]评 估；估价；求值	evaluative *adj.* 可估价的	evaporate *v.* 蒸发

even	evening tuition	evenly	eventuality
adj. 偶数的	夜校，晚班	*adv.* 均匀地；平衡地	*n.* 可能发生的事
eventually	evergreen conifers	ever-present	ever-rising
adv. 最后地，总共	常绿针叶树	*adj.* 经常存在的	*adj.* 不断增长的
everything under the sun 在世界上	evidence *n.* 迹象；证据，证明	evident *adj.* 明显的；一目了然的	evidently *adv.* 显然，明显地；清楚地
evil *adj.* 有害的，不幸的	evoke *v.* 唤起，引起；博得；激起	evolution *n.* 进化，演变	evolutionary *adj.* 进化的，发展的，演变的
evolve *v.* 进化，发展；逐渐形成	exacerbate *v.* 加重；使……加剧	exaggerate *v.* 夸大，夸张	examination *n.* 检查
exam-orientated *adj.* 考试定向的，以考试为目标的	excavation *n.* 挖掘，发掘	exceed *v.* 超过	excel *v.* 擅长
exception *n.* 例外，异议	exceptional *adj.* 异常的，特别出色的	excess *adj.* 过量的	excessive *adj.* 过多的，过度的；专用的，独有的，专属的；过高的，过重的
excessively *adv.* 过度地	exchange *v.* 交换	exciting *adj.* 令人兴奋的	exclude *v.* 排除
exclusive of 不包括	exclusively *adv.* 专有地，唯一地	excretion *n.* 排泄，排泄物	excursion *n.* 短程旅行
executive *n.* 总经理；执行者；管理人员	Executive Committee 执政管理委员会	exemplify *v.* 例证；例示	exempt *adj.* 被免除的，被豁免的
exercise *v.* 运用，行使	exert *v.* 施以……影响；施加	exertion *n.* 运用	exhaust pipe 排烟管，排气管
exhausted *adj.* 疲惫的，耗尽的	exhaustible *adj.* 可被用尽的	exhaustive *adj.* 详尽的，彻底的	exhibit *v./n.* 展出，展览；呈现

exhibited	exhibition	existence	existent
adj. 展出的	*n.* 展览；展示	*n.* 存在	*adj.* 存在的，生存的
existing	exodus	exotic	expand
adj. 现存的	*n.* 大批离去，成群外出	*adj.* 外来的；异域的；奇异的，异国的	*v.* 扩张
expansion	expansive	expect	expectation
n. 发展，扩大；扩张	*adj.* 广阔的	*v.* 期望，指望	*n.* 期待；预期（未来的结果）
expected	expedition	expend	expense
adj. 预期的	*n.* 探险队	*v.* 付出，耗费	*n.* 损失，代价
experience	experienced	experiment	experimental
v. 体验	*adj.* 富有经验的	*n.* 实验，试验 *v.* 做实验	*adj.* 实验性的，试验性的
experimental theatre 试验剧院	experimentation *n.* 实验，试验	experimenter *n.* 实验者	expert *n.* 专家
expertise *n.* 专门知识；专门技术；专家的意见；专业技能	expletive *n.* 咒骂语	explicit *adj.* 明确的；清楚的	explode *v.* 爆发；爆炸；激增
exploit *v.* 开发，利用	exploitation *n.* 开发；利用；广告推销；剥削	exploitative *adj.* 剥削的	exploration *n.* 探究
explore *v.* 探索，探测	explorer *n.* 探险家	explosion *n.* 激增；爆发	explosive *adj.* 爆炸的
exponentially *adv.* 成倍地	export *n./v.* 出口	expose *v.* 暴露；（使）曝光；揭露	exposure *n.* 暴露
Express Delivery Service 快递服务	exquisitely *adv.* 精致地；精巧地；敏锐地	ex-smoker *n.* 已戒烟的人	extend *v.* 扩展，延伸，推广
extend to 延伸	extended *adj.* 全面的；广泛的	extension *n.* 延长，延期，伸展	extensive *adj.* 广泛的；大量的；广阔的
extensively *adv.* 广阔地，广泛地	extent *n.* 程度	external *adj.* 外部的；外观的	externality *n.* 外部效应

extinct v. 灭绝 adj. 灭绝的，绝种的	extinction n. 灭绝	extra adj. 额外的，另外的	extra work 额外的任务
extract n. 摘录 v. 提取	extraction n. 取出，抽出	extraordinary adj. 非凡的; 显著的; 离奇的	extrapolation n. 推断
extraterrestrial n. 外星人	extravagance n. 奢侈; 过度	extra-wide adj. 额外宽的	extreme fatigue 极度疲劳
extroverted adj. 性格外向的；外 向性的；喜社交的	extrusion n. 喷出	exuberant adj. 丰富的	ex-vessel n. 以前的船
eye-catching ideas 受人关注的想法	eye-witness n. 目击者		

F

fabric n. 织物，布	fabulous adj. 难以置信的	face-to-face adv. 面对面地	facial massage 面部按摩
facilitate v. 促进；使便利；使 更容易	facilitated v. 推动，促进	facilitator n. 服务商	facility n. 能力，设备；设 施
facsimile n. 复印本	factual film 纪实片	faculty n. 能力	fade n. 淡出
fade away 逐渐消失	faecal adj. 粪的	failure n. 故障	faint adj. 模糊的；微弱的
fair adj. 合理的	fair share 合理的份额	Fairbanks n. 菲尔班克斯	fairground n. 露天市场，游乐场
fairly adv. 相当地	faith n. 信念，信任，信仰	faith healing （靠祈祷等治病的） 信仰疗法	fake n. 假货
fall v. 变少	false dawn 假曙光	fame n. 名声，名望	familiar adj. 熟悉的
familiarise v. 使了解，使通晓	family-owned adj. 家族持有的	famine n. 饥荒	fan v. 煽动；刺激

fancy *adj.* 精美的 *v.* 想要	fantastic *adj.* 非常棒的；奇异的，奇妙的	fantasy *n.* 梦幻，幻想	fare *v.* 过活；经营 *n.* 票价；费用
far-flung *adj.* 遥远的；广泛的；广布的	farm output 农产品产量	farmland *n.* 农田	farm-work *n.* 农活
fascinate *v.* 使着迷	fascinating *adj.* 迷人的，吸引人的，引人入胜的	fascination *n.* 魅力	fashionable *adj.* 流行的
fast-growing *adj.* 高速发展的	fatigue *n.* 疲劳，疲乏	fault *n.* 错误	faulty *adj.* 出毛病的，有问题的
favour *v.* 赞成，喜欢，有助于 *n.* 喜爱	favourable *adj.* 有利的；赞成的；令人满意的	favoured *adj.* 喜爱的；受优惠的；有特权的	feasible *adj.* 可行的，可能的
feast *n.* 盛宴，节日	feat *n.* 成功，功绩，壮举	feature *v.* 由……主演 *n.* 特征，特点	feature film 正片，故事片
feature-length *adj.* 长篇的，达到正片长度的	featuring *adj.* 有特点的	federal *adj.* 联邦的	Federal Aviation Administration 联邦航空管理局
fee *n.* 费用	feeble *adj.* 虚弱的，微弱的	feed *v.* 喂养	feed on 品尝
feedback *n.* 反馈；成果	feeding *adj.* 供给食物的	female *n.* 女性	fence *n.* 栅栏
ferry *n.* 渡轮 *v.* 用渡船运送	fertile *adj.* 肥沃的	fertilisation *n.* 施肥	fertilise *v.* 使肥沃，施肥
fertilised egg 受精卵	fertiliser *n.* 肥料，化肥	fertility *n.* 肥沃，富饶	fetus *n.* 胎儿
few and far between 稀少的，不常发生的	fibres *n.* 纤维	fibrous *adj.* 纤维的，纤维性的；纤维状的	fiction *n.* 小说
fiddling *v.* 摆动	field *n.* 领域	field station 野外观测站，野外台	field test 现场试验

fierce *adj.* 凶猛的	fiercely *adv.* 激烈地; 猛烈地; 厉害地	figure *n.* 人物; 图表; 数字; 数据 *v.* 认为	figure out 理解, 想出
figure-of-eight *adj.* 8字形的	fill with 装满	filler *n.* 填充物	film *v.* 把……拍成电影
film fiction 电影小说	film-maker *n.* 电影摄制者	film-making *n.* 电影摄制	filter *n.* 滤波器, 滤色镜; 过滤器 *v.* 过滤
filth *n.* 污秽	finance *v.* 为……提供资金	financial *adj.* 财政的, 金融的	finding *n.* 发现; 结果
fine *n./v.* 罚款	fine ash 精细土	finest *adj.* 好的, 出色的	fingertip *n.* 指尖
finite *adj.* 有限的	finitude *n.* 有限, 界限	fire brigade 消防队	firefly *n.* 萤火虫
fire-prone ecosystems 易燃的生态系统	fire-resistant *adj.* 耐高温的	firewood *n.* 柴火, 木柴	firm *adj.* 牢固的
first aid 急救	first floor 【英】第二层	first frost 初霜	fisherman *n.* 渔人, 渔夫
fishery *n.* 渔业, 水产业	fishing fleet 渔船队	fit *adj.* 健康的 *n.* 匹配	fit together 组合
fitness *n.* 健康	fitting *adj.* 适合的	fixed *adj.* 固定的	fixed asset 固定资产
fixed charge 固定支出	flag *v.* 标记	flaming *adj.* 燃烧的	flap *n.* 襟翼
flashing light 闪光灯	flashy *adj.* 闪光的, 俗丽的	flat *adj.* 平坦的, 扁平的	flatten *v.* 摧毁, 夷平
flattened *adj.* 扁平的	flatter *v.* 使高兴, 使荣幸; 奉承, 恭维	flavonoid *n.* 类黄酮	flaw *n.* 瑕疵, 缺点
flawed *adj.* 有缺陷的	fledgling *n.* 刚会飞的鸟	flee *v.* 消失; 逃走, 逃离	fleet *n.* 舰队

flex	flexi	flexibility	flexible
v. 折曲，弯曲	adj. 灵活的	n. 灵活性，适应性，弹性	adj. 机动的，灵活的
flexibly	flight	flimsy	flip
adv. 灵活地	n. 飞行，航班	adj. 脆弱的，易损坏的	v. 蹦跳
flirtation	flit	float	float process
n. 逗弄	v. 掠过	v. 使……漂浮	浮法玻璃生产法
floating	flock	flood	flood with
adj. 漂浮的	n. 群	v. 充满	充满
flooded	flooding	floor-standing	floppy disk
adj. 洪水泛滥的	n. 洪汛，泛滥	adj. 落地的	软盘；软式磁碟片
floret	florist	flourish	flourishing
n. 小花	n. 花商；种花人	v. 繁荣，兴旺；茂盛；活跃	adj. 旺盛的
flow	flow of trade	flower	flowering top
n. 流动	贸易流量	v. 开花	开花顶部
flu	fluctuate	fluent	fluid
n. 流感	v. 使波动	adj. 流利的，流畅的	n. 液体 adj. 流动的
flush away	flush out	flustered	flute
冲去，冲走	排出	adj. 慌张的，恐惧的	n. 长笛
flying fish	foam	focus	focused
飞鱼	n. 泡沫	v. 使集中	adj. 聚焦的；专心的
fodder	foe	foldable	folk
n. 饲料	n. 敌人，危害物	adj. 可折叠的	n. 民谣
folk medicine	folk remedy	folklore	follow-up
民间医学	偏方	n. 民间传说	adj. 后续的 n. 后续工作
fondness	font	food chain	food reserve
n. 爱好；溺爱	n. 字形	食物链	食物储备
food source	food-gathering	food-growing	foodstuff
食物来源	n. 采集食物	n. 种植粮食作物	n. 食品；食物
foolish	footbridge	footing	footwear
adj. 愚蠢的	n. 人行桥	n. 基础，立足处	n. 鞋类

for certain 肯定地	for the sake of 为了……	forage v. 觅食	forager n. 觅食者；强征队员；抢劫者
foraging adj. 觅食的	foraging column 觅食队伍	forcep n. 钳子	fore n. 前部
forecast v. 预报，预测	foreground n. 前景	foreign exchange 外汇	foremost adj. 最重要的
foreseeable adj. 可预知的	foreshadow v. 预示	forestry n. 林业	forgo v. 放弃，对……断念，锻造，伪造
fork n. 叉子	form n. 形式 v. 形成	formal adj. 正式的	formaldehyde n. 甲醛
formality n. 仪式，礼节	format n. 格式	formation n. 形成	formative adj. 形成的
formatted adj. 格式化的	formula n. 公式	formulate v. 制定，规划；提出	forthcoming adj. 即将来临的
fortuitous adj. 偶然的	fortunate adj. 幸运的	fortune n. 财富	forum n. 论坛
forward v. 转寄	forwards adv. 向前	Fosbury flop 背越式跳高	fossil adj. 化石的 n. 化石
fossil fuel 矿物燃料，化石燃料	fossilisation n. 石化	fossilise v. 使……成化石	foster v. 培养，促进；造就
foul adj. 污秽的	found v. 建立	foundation n. 基金会；地基；基石；基础	foundry n. 铸造车间
fountain n. 喷泉	fourfold adj. 四倍的	fractals n. 分形学	fraction n. 部分
fracture v. 使破裂	fragile adj. 脆弱的，脆的，易碎的	fragment n. 碎片	fragmentation n. 破碎；分裂
fragrant adj. 芳香的，愉快的	frame n. 画面；结构，框架	framework n. 框架，结构；体系	fraternal adj. 双胞胎的

fraternity	fraud	frayed	freak
n. 友爱；兄弟会；互助会；大学生联谊会	n. 欺骗	adj. 磨破的，磨损的	n. 怪胎
free	free compulsory education	freediving	free-feeding
v. 释放，解放	免费义务教育	n. 自由潜水	adj. 自由喂养的
free-flowing	freely	free-ranging	free-standing
adj. 自由流淌的	adv. 自由地	adj. 自由放养的	adj. 独立的，自立的
freeze	freezer	freezing	Freiburg University
n. 冻结	n. 冰箱	adj. 冰冻的，严寒的	弗赖堡大学
freight	frenetic	frequency	frequent
n. 货运；船货；运费	adj. 发狂的，狂乱的	n. 频率	adj. 频繁的
frequently	fresh water	freshly	freshwater lagoon
adv. 频繁地，经常地	淡水	adv. 新鲜地	淡水泻湖
Freud	friction	fright	frightened
n. 弗洛伊德（奥地利神经学家、精神病医学家、精神分析的创始人）	n. 摩擦	n. 惊吓	adj. 受惊的
frightening	fringe	fro	frontier
adj. 令人恐惧的	n. 边缘	adv. 向后	n. 前沿，边界
frontline	frost	froth	frugally
n. 前线	n. 冰冻，严寒	v. 起泡沫	adv. 节约地
fruit	fruit fly	fruition	frustration
v. 结果	果蝇	n. 完成	n. 挫折
fuel	fulfill	fulfillment	full fare
n. 燃料 v. 给……提供燃料	v. 履行；实现；满足	n. 实行	全额
Fullerton	full-free	full-length feature	full-scale
n. 富勒顿州	adj. 全免的	完整长度的电影	adj. 全面的
full-time	fully-automated	function	functional
adj. 全职的	adj. 全自动的	v. 起作用	adj. 有功能的，起作用的

functioning	fund	fundamental	funded
n. 运作；功能	*v.* 投资，资助	*adj.* 基本的，根本的	*adj.* 提供资金的
funding	fundraising	fungi	fungus
n. 资金，经费	*adj.* 筹集资金的	*n.* 真菌，菌类	*n.* 真菌
funnel	fur	fur hunter	furnace
n. 漏斗	*n.* 毛皮	毛皮猎人	*n.* 火炉，熔炉
furniture	further	furthermore	fury
n. 家具	*adj.* 更远的，更深的	*adv.* 此外，而且	*n.* 狂怒
fuse	fusee	fuzzy	
v. 混合	*n.* 引信	*adj.* 模糊的	

G

gadget	gag	gain	galaxy
n. 小玩意，小器具	*n.* 噱头	*v.* 获得	*n.* 银河，银河系；星系
ganzfeld	gaping	garret	gas
adj. 超感官知觉全域试验的	*adj.* 张口状的；张开的	*n.* 阁楼，顶楼	*n.* 气体
gather	Gaza	gaze	GDP (Gross Domestic Product)
v. 收集，聚集	*n.* 加沙（地中海岸港市）	*v.* 凝视	国内生产总值
gear	gear wheel	gearing	gene
n. 排挡，装备，齿轮 *v.* 开动；使……准备好	齿轮	*n.* 转动装置	*n.* 基因
gene pool	general	generalize	generate
基因库	*adj.* 普遍的，通常的	*v.* 概括	*v.* 生产，生成
generation	generative	generator	genetic
n. 一代	*adj.* 有生产力的	*n.* 发电机	*adj.* 基因的，遗传的
genetically	geneticist	genetics	genius
adv. 从遗传角度讲	*n.* 遗传学者	*n.* 遗传学	*n.* 天才，天赋
genre	gens	gently	genuine
n. 类型；体裁；风格	*n.* 来源；氏族	*adv.* 轻轻地	*adj.* 真实的

genuinely *adv.* 真诚地	geographic *adj.* 地理的，地理学的	geographical *adj.* 地理（学）的	geography *n.* 地理，地形
geologist *n.* 地质学家	geology *n.* 地质学	geometrical *adj.* 几何的	geometry *n.* 几何
germ-free *adj.* 无菌的	germinate *v.* 发芽，生长	gesture *n.* 姿势，手势	get about 移动
get anywhere 有进展	get by 过活	get in touch with 与……取得联系	get off to 走进；陷入
Ghana *n.* 加纳	ghost tales 鬼故事	giant *adj.* 巨大的	gift *n.* 天赋
gifted *adj.* 有天赋的，有才华的	gigantic *adj.* 巨大的	gill *n.*（鱼）鳃	gimmick *n.* 骗人的玩意儿
give birth to 生孩子	give rise to 产生	give way to 给……让路，让步	given *adj.* 确定的
giver *n.* 提供者	glacial *adj.* 冰冷的，冰河时代的	glacier *n.* 冰川	glaring *adj.* 明显的
Glass and Glazing Federation 玻璃和玻璃装配联合会	glassmaker *n.* 玻璃工人	glass-sided *adj.* 玻璃面的	glide *v.* 滑翔
glider *n.* 滑翔机	gliding *n.* 滑翔	glimpse *n.* 一瞥；一眼	global *adj.* 全球的
Global Positioning System 全球定位系统	global scales 全球范围	global warming 全球变暖	globalisation *n.* 全球化
global-trotter *n.* 环球旅行者	glorious *adj.* 极好的	glossy *adj.* 有光泽的	glow *v.* 发光
glow signal 发光信号	glow-worm *n.* 萤火虫	glucose *n.* 葡萄糖	glycol *n.* 乙二醇，甘醇
go back 追溯	go-ahead 前进	goal-post *n.* 目标位置	goal-setting *adj.* 设定目标的
goat *n.* 羊	golf *n.* 高尔夫	golf course 高尔夫球场	golfer *n.* 打高尔夫的人

good-quality *adj.* 质量好的	goods *n.* 货物	good-sized *adj.* 大型的，相当 大的	govern *v.* 支配，控制
governance *n.* 控制；管理	gown *n.* 长袍，长外衣	grab *v.* 攫，握	grace *n.* 优惠
graceful *adj.* 优雅的	grade *n.* 级别	graduate trainee 毕业实习生，毕业培 训生	graduate training schemes 大学毕业生职业培 训计划
grain *n.* 粮食，谷物	gram *n.* 克	grammar *n.* 语法	grammarian *n.* 语法家，文法家
Grand Canyon 大峡谷 (美)	grand *adj.* 宏伟的	granite *n.* 花岗岩	grant *v.* 拨款；授予；允许， 承认
granular *adj.* 颗粒状的	grape vines 葡萄藤	graph *n.* 图表，曲线图	graphic *adj.* 文字的; 形象的; 图表的
graphic artist 图形艺术家	grapple *v.* 抓住	grasp *n./v.* 领会	grasp of the significance 理解的意义
grass seed 草种	grassland *n.* 草地	grass-scale *adj.* 大规模的	grateful *adj.* 令人愉快的
gratefully *adv.* 感激	gratuity *n.* 小费；退职金	gravelly *adj.* 砂砾遍地的	gravity *n.* 引力
grazing *n.* 放牧	grease *n.* 油脂	Great Barrier Reef 大堡礁	greenhouse gas 温室气体
Greenland *n.* 格陵兰岛	greying *n.* 老年化	grid *n.* 输电网，网格	grim *adj.* 糟糕的
grimace *v.* 作苦相	grind *v.* 磨掉，磨	grinding *adj.* 刺耳的	grinding mill 磨坊
grip *n.* 紧握；柄；支配； 握拍方式；拍柄绷带	groan *n.* 呻吟	grocery *n.* 食品杂货店	grooves *n.* 凹槽
gross national product 国民生产总值	gross pay 工资总额	grossly *adv.* 很，非常	ground *n.* 范围

ground floor 【英】第一层	ground water 陆地水	groundfish n. 低栖鱼，低层鱼	grounding n. 基础
group project 团体项目	grove n. 果园，树丛	growing adj. 越来越多的，增多的	guarantee n. 保证；担保 v. 保证；担保
guard n. 警卫 v. 保卫	guarded adj. 谨慎的	guardian n. 监护人	guidance n. 指导，引导
guide n. 向导	guideline n. 指导方针	guiding adj. 引导的，控制的；领导性的	gulls n. 海鸥
gum n. 牙龈	gunfight n. 枪战	gush v. 喷出	gym n. 健身房

H

habit n. 习惯	habitable adj. 可居住的；适于居住的	habitat n. 栖息地，住处	habitual adj. 习惯的；惯常的；习以为常的
hail n. 冰雹 v. 致敬，向……欢呼	hailstone n. 冰雹	hairy adj. 多毛的	half-scale adj. 一半比例的
halfway n. 中途	hall n. 走廊	hallmark n. 印记	halt n./v. 停止，中止，暂停
halve v. 对半分开；均分；把……减半	Hampshire n. 汉普郡	hamster n. 仓鼠	hand collecting 徒手收集
hand down 宣布，把……传下去	hand out 分发	hand over 上交	handbook n. 手册
handful n. 少数，一把	handicap n. 障碍	handicraft n. 手工艺品	handiwork n. 手工艺
handle n./v. 处理；操作	handler n. 处理者，管理者；训练者；操作者	handout n. 救济品；免费发的材料（也可以指"馈赠"）	handrail n. 扶手

hands-on *adj.* 亲身实践的，亲自动手的	hand-tightened 手动拧紧	handy *adj.* 便利的，手边的	hang *v.* 悬挂
hanging in the air 未完成的	haphazard *adv.* 偶然地，随意地	harass *v.* 烦扰	harbour *v.* 心怀某种想法；庇护，藏匿 *n.* 海港；避难所
hard currency 硬通货	hard winter 严冬，寒冬	hardback *n.* 精装版	hard-core *adj.* 顽固不化的
harden *v.* 使变硬	harden into gum 变硬成胶	hardened *adj.* 变硬的	hardship *n.* 困苦；苦难
hardware *n.* 硬件；武器装备	hard-wearing *adj.* 耐磨的	hardwired *adj.* 电路的	hard-wired *adj.* 硬连线的，硬接线的，不可改变的
hard-won *adj.* 来之不易的，难得的	harems *n.* 马群	harmful *adj.* 有害的	harmonic *adj.* 和谐的
harmonise *v.* 使和谐	harness *v.* 使用，驾驭，利用 *n.* 降落伞背带；保护带	harsh *adj.* 艰难的；严酷的	Harvard University 哈佛大学
harvest *v./n.* 收获	harvesting *n.* 收获	hashish *n.* 印度大麻制剂	hassle-free *adj.* 没有麻烦的（指"成功的"）
hatch *n./v.* 孵化	haul *v.* 拖，拉	haulage *n.* 拖运；拖曳	haulier *n.* 承运人
haunt *v.* 困扰，时时萦绕心头	have far to go 还有很长的路要走	havoc *n.* 大破坏，浩劫	Hawaii *n.* 夏威夷
hazard *n.* 危险，冒险，冒……的危险	head *v.* 前进	head cover 头盖，头罩	head for 朝……方向去
headache *n.* 头疼	heading *n.* 标题	headlight *n.* 汽车等的前灯	headline *n.* 大标题，重要新闻
headphone *n.* 双耳式耳机，头戴式耳机	headstart *n.* 抢先，提前教育	headteacher *n.* 校长	headwind *n.* 逆风；顶头风

healing art	health care	health programs	healthcare
医术	医疗保健	健康措施	n. 医疗保健
hear from	heart disease	heart rate	heat
收到……的信	心脏病	心率	v. 加热
heat wave	heating	heat-resistant	heat-sealed
热浪，热波	n. 供暖	adj. 抗热的	adj. 热封的
heavy use	hectare	hedgehog	hedgerow
大量使用	n. 公顷	n. 刺猬	n. 灌木树篱
height	held up	helicopter pilot	helmet
n. 高度	提出（举起）	直升机长	n. 钢盔
helpline	hemisphere	hemlock	hence
n. 服务热线	n. 半球	n. 铁杉	adv. 因此
henceforth	herb	herbal	herbalism
adv. 从今以后，今后	n. 药草	adj. 草本的，草药的	n. 草药学
herbalist	herbicides	herbivore	herd
n. 草药医生	n. 除草剂	n. 食草动物	v. 放牧
herding	heredity	heritage	heritage-listed
n. 畜牧	n. 遗传，遗传性	n. 遗产，传统	adj. 被列为古迹的
heroic	heroin	herring	hesitation
adj. 史诗般的，英雄的，英雄的	n. 海洛因	n. 鲱鱼，青鱼；主要产品，主食	n. 犹豫
hexa	heyday	hibernation	hiccup
n. 糖醛酸	n. 全盛期	n. 冬眠，过冬	n. 小难题
hide	hieroglyph	high blood pressure	high jumper
v. 隐藏	n. 象形文字，图画文字	高血压	跳高运动员
highbrow	high-fidelity	highflier	high-grade
n. 卖弄知识的人，知识分子	n. 高保真；高保真度	n. 有抱负有能力的人	adj. 优质的
highlight	high-powered	high-quality	high-spending
v. 强调，使突出；突出	adj. 高性能的；强有力的	adj. 高质量的	adj. 高消费的
high-tension cable	high-volume	hiking	hill-farmer
高压电缆	adj. 大容量的	n. 徒步旅行	n. 山农

hill-region n. 山区	hillside n. 山坡	hilly adj. 丘陵的，多坡的	hind adj. 后部的
hinder v. 阻碍	hindrance n. 障碍	hindsight n. 过后被认可	hint n. 暗示，线索；一点，微量 v. 暗示
hinterland n. 内陆；内地	hire n. 租用 v. 雇用	historian n. 历史学家	historical adj. 历史的，基于史实的
hit v. 打击，袭击	hit the headline 上头条新闻	hit-list n. 重要名单	hit-rate n. 命中率
hive n. 蜂房，蜂巢	HNC Software HNC 软件公司	hold n. 船舱	hold back 抑制，阻止
hold mistaken views 持错误观点	hold responsibility for 对……负责	hold up 装；举起	holder n. 持有者
holding n. 持有	holistic adj. 整体的，全盘的	hollow adj. 凹的，中空的，空心的	hollow bone 空心骨
Hollywood n. 好莱坞	homage n. 尊敬	home delivery service 送货上门服务	home medical aid 家庭医疗救助
home tutoring 家庭教育	home visit 家访；出诊	homeland n. 故乡	homeopath n. 同种疗法医师
home-produced adj. 自家做的	homogeneity n. 同质，同种	homogenise v. 使均匀	honoraria n. 酬金，谢礼
honour n. 荣誉	hooded adj. 戴头巾的	hook n. 挂钩	Hopi groups 霍皮族人
horizon n. 视野，眼界；地平线	horizontal adj. 水平的，水平线的	horizontally adv. 水平地	hormonal adj. 荷尔蒙的，激素的
hormone n. 激素，荷尔蒙	horror film 恐怖电影	horse-riding n. 骑马	horticultural adj. 园艺的
horticulture n. 园艺学	hospitality n. 好客，殷勤	host plant 寄主植物	hostile adj. 不利的；敌对的，有敌意的

hot shower 热水淋浴	hothouse n. 温室	house v. 把……藏于房中	household n. 家庭 adj. 家庭的
housing n. 房屋	hovercraft n. 气垫船	hue n. 色彩，色调	hugely adv. 非常
hull n. 船体	human resources 人力资源	Human Resources 人力资源部	humanistic adj. 人文主义的，人道主义的
humanity n. 人类，人性；人文科学	humble v. 使谦恭	humor n. 幽默	humorous adj. 幽默
humpback n. 驼背；座头鲸	humpback whale 座头鲸	hunch n. 大块	hundredth adj. 第一百的，百分之一的
hunter n. 猎人	hunting n. 打猎	hurdle n. 障碍	hurl v. 猛投，投掷
hurricane n. 飓风，暴风	hurtful adj. 令人感到伤痛的	husk n. 树皮	hut n. 小屋
hyacinth n. 风信子	hybrid adj. 混合的	Hyderabad-based adj. 总部位于海德巴拉的	hydraulic adj. 液压的，水利的
hydrogen n. 氢	hydropower n. 水力发电	hygiene n. 卫生学，保健法	hymns n. 赞美诗
hype n. 大肆炒作	hypnosis n. 催眠	hypnotic adj. 催眠的	hypothesis n. 假设
hypothetical adj. 假设的			

I

I kid you not 不开玩笑	ice core 冰核	ice pack 流冰群，大片浮冰	ice-cap n. 冰帽，冰盖
ice-free adj. 不冻的，不会冰冻的	icon n. 代表；图标	iconoclastic adj. 打破旧习的	Idaho University 爱达荷大学
ideal adj. 完美的；理想的	ideally adv. 理想地，观念上地	identical adj. 完全相同的	identifiable adj. 可辨认的

identification	identify	idiom	idiosyncratic
n. 鉴定，识别	n. 身份；同一性，认同感 v. 确定，识别；辨认；认出	n. 成语，习语	adj. 特质的，与众不同的
igloo n. 冰屋；圆顶建筑	ignite v. 点燃；使燃烧；使激动	ignited adj. 烧灼的	ignorance n. 不知，不懂
ignore v. 忽视，不顾	illegal adj. 非法的	illiterate adj. 文盲的，不识字的，未受过教育的	ill-suited adj. 不适合的
illuminate v. 照亮	illusion n. 错误的观念或信仰	illustrate v. 阐明，说明	illustration n. 图解，插图
image n. 形象	image bank 图片库	imagery n. 意象，形象化	imagination n. 想象力
imaginative adj. 富有想象力的	imaginatively adv. 想象地	imagine v. 想象	imbalance n. 不平衡，不安定
imitate v. 模仿	immediate adj. 立即的；直接的；最接近的	immediately adv. 立刻	immense adj. 极大的，巨大的
immensely adv. 极大地，无限地	immigrant n. 移民	immigration n. 移民	imminent adj. 迫近的，即将作出的
immortality n. 不朽，长生不老	immune adj. 免疫的	immune-system n. 免疫系统	immunity n. 免疫力
immunization n. 免疫	immunoglobulin n. 免疫球蛋白	impact n. 影响	impair v. 削弱，减少
impairment n. 缺隙，损伤	impart v. 给予；传授	impartial adj. 公平的	impede v. 阻碍，阻止
impenetrable adj. 无法穿透的	imperative n. 命令；需要；规则 adj. 必要的，势在必行的	imperial adj. 帝国的，皇家的	imperilled adj. 处于危险中的
impersonal adj. 不受个人感情影响的，客观的	impetus n. 动力	impinge v. 冲击	implement v. 实施，执行；实现，使生效

implementation	implemented	implication	implicit
n. 实现	adj. 应用的	n. 含义，暗示	adj. 含蓄的；暗示的；盲从的
imply	import	import quota	impose
v. 意味着，表明	n. 进口	进口配额，进口限额	v. 利用；施加……影响；限制，强加
impoverished	impractical	impression	impressionist
adj. 贫穷的，赤贫的	adj. 不切实际的，不现实的	n. 效果，印象	n. 印象派作家
impressive	impressively	improve	improved
adj. 感人的；给人深刻印象的	adv. 令人难忘地	v. 提高	adj. 改良的
improvement	improvised	impurity	in addition to
n. 改进，改善，提高	adj. 即兴的	n. 杂质	除了……之外
in advance	in answer to	in broad terms	in case
预先，提前	作为对……的回答	从广义上来说	万一，以防
in comparison to	in contrast to	in earnest	in essence
与……相比	与……比起来	认真地，诚挚地	其实，实质上
in excess of	in exchange	in favor of	in flight
超过，多于	作为交换	支持；有利于	在飞行中
in good supply	in isolation	in keeping with	in line with
充足的	单独地，个别地	与……保持一致	符合，与……一致
in preparation	in reality	in short supply	in store
在准备中	事实上，实际上	供不应求	将要发生
in term of	in terms of	in the absence of	in the case of
就……而言；	在……方面；按照	在没有……的情况下	在……的情况下
in the face of	in the light of	inability	inaccessible
面对，尽管	基于，按照	n. 无能力	adj. 无法进入的
inactive	inadequacy	inadequate	in-air
adj. 不活跃的，不活动的	n. 缺乏，不适当，不足	adj. 不足的，不充分的	adj. 在空中的
inappropriate	inaugurate	inbox	incapable
adj. 不适当的	v. 开创	n. 收件箱	adj. 无能力的
incentive	incentivize	incidence	incidentally
n. 刺激，鼓励；动机	v. 激励	n. 发生率，影响	adv. 偶然地

incisor	inclination	incline	include
n. 切牙，门牙	*n.* 倾向	*v.* 倾向于	*v.* 包括
inclusion	inclusive	income	income brackets
n. 内含物	*adj.* 包括的	*n.* 收入	收入水平
incomparably	incompatible	incomplete	incongruity
adv. 无比地；无敌地	*adj.* 不相容的，不能并存的	*adj.* 不完整的	*n.* 不协调，不一致
incongruous	inconsistent	inconvenience	incorporate
adj. 不协调的	*adj.* 不一致的，前后矛盾的	*n.* 不便，麻烦	*v.* 吸收
incorporated	increasing	increasingly	incredible
adj. 合成一体的	*adj.* 越来越多的，渐增的	*adv.* 越来越多地	*adj.* 难以置信的
incredibly	increment	incubation	incur
adv. 难以置信地	*n.* 盈余，增额	*n.* 孵化	*v.* 引发
indeed	independence	independent of	in-depth
adv. 事实上；甚至	*n.* 自主	独立于……	*adj.* 彻底的，深入的
Indian susus	Indiana Jones	Indiana University	indicate
印度淡水豚	夺宝奇兵（电影名），印第安纳琼斯	印第安纳大学	*v.* 表明；指示，显示
indication	indicator	indigenous	indiscriminate
n. 表明	*n.* 指示器，指示物	*adj.* 本土的，土著的	*adj.* 任意的，不加选择的
indispensable	individual	individualism	individually
adj. 不可缺少的	*n.* 个人 *adj.* 个人的	*n.* 个人特征（个性）	*adv.* 单独地
indoor farming	induce	induction	indulge
温室种植	*v.* 引起，引诱	*n.* 入门	*v.* 沉溺（于）
industrial	industrial revolution	industrialisation	industrialise
adj. 工业的	工业革命	*n.* 工业化	*v.* 使工业化
industrialised	industrialising	industrially	inefficient
adj. 工业化的	*n.* 工业化	*adv.* 工业地	*adj.* 无效率的，效率低的

inequity *n.* 不公平，不公正	inevitable *adj.* 不可避免的，必然（发生）的	inevitably *adv.* 不可避免地	inexorable *adj.* 无法改变的
inexpensive *adj.* 便宜的	inextricably *adv.* 无法摆脱地，解不开地	infancy *n.* 婴儿期，幼年	infant *n.* 婴儿；幼儿；未成年人
infant mortality 婴儿死亡率	infect *v.* 传染	infection *n.* 感染	infection-fighting *adj.* 抗干扰的
infectious *adj.* 传染的，传染性的	inferior to 不如；比不上；比……差	infest *v.* 侵扰，寄生于	infestation *n.* 感染；侵扰
infinite *adj.* 无限的；无穷的	infirmity *n.* 虚弱，衰弱	inflate *v.* 膨胀，充气	inflation *n.* 通货膨胀
inflict *v.* 造成，遭受	influence *n./v.* 影响	inform *v.* 通知，告知	inform of 告知，通知
informant *n.* 被调查者	information *n.* 信息	informative *adj.* 提供有用信息的	informative text 信息文本
infrastructure *n.* 基础设施；公共建设；下部构造	infrequently *adv.* 稀少地	ingenious *adj.* 天才的；有独创性的	ingenuity *n.* 独创性；精巧；精巧的装置
ingredient *n.* 原料；要素；组成部分	inhabitant *n.* 居民；居住者	inherently *adv.* 天性地	inherit *v.* 继承，遗传
inhibit *v.* 抑制；禁止	inhospitable *adj.* 荒凉的	initial *adj.* 最初的	initial investment 初期投资
initially *adv.* 最初，首先	initiate *v.* 发起，开始实施	initiative *n.* 主动权（的行动），提倡；主动性	inject *v.* 注入；注射
injection *n.* 注射	injurious *adj.* 有害的	injury *n.* 受伤；伤害	inner *adj.* 内部的
inner layer 内层	inner wall 内壁	innermost *adj.* 最深处的，最里面的	innovation *n.* 创新，革新；新方法

innovative adj. 革新的，新颖的； 有创造性的	input n. 输入，学到的知识	inquiry n. 询问	insect n. 昆虫
insecticide n. 杀虫剂，农药	insecurity n. 不安全感	insider language 行话	insight n. 洞察力，洞悉； 深入了解
insignificant adj. 无关紧要的	insist v. 坚持	insistence n. 坚持；执着	insomnia n. 失眠症
insomniac n. 失眠症患者	inspect v. 检查，审查	inspection n. 检查	inspiration n. 灵感
inspirational adj. 鼓舞人心的	inspire v. 鼓舞，激励，启迪	inspiring adj. 有启发性的	install v. 安置；安装
installation n. 安装，装置；就职	instant adj. 立刻的	instinct n. 本能，直觉，天性	instinctively adv. 本能地
instinctual adj. 本能的	institute n. 机构 v. 开始	Institute for Science and Technology Policy 科学和技术政策研 究所	institution n. 机构；制度
institutional adj. 制度的；制度 上的	institutionalisation n. 制度化，体制化	institutionalise v. 使……制度化	instruct v. 指导；通知；命令； 教授
instruction n. 教导，指示；用 法说明；命令	instructional adj. 指导的，教育的	instructor n. 教官，教练	instrument n. 器具，仪器
instrumental adj. 工具的	instrumentation n. 使用仪器	instrument-rated adj. 用设备测评的	insufficient adj. 不足的
insufficient blueprints 不足的蓝图	insular adj. 狭隘的，与世隔 绝的	insulate v. 使隔绝	insulating adj. 绝缘的，隔热的
insulin n. [生化] [药] 胰 岛素	insurance n. 保险	insurance company 保险公司	insurance cover 保险金额

intact	intake	integral	integrate
adj. 完整的；原封不动的；未受损伤的	*n.* 摄入，摄取量	*adj.* 完整的	*v.* 融入，成为一体
integrated	integrity	intellectual	intellectual labour
adj. 综合的；完整的；互相协调的	*n.* 正直，诚实	*adj.* 理智的；智力的 *n.* 知识分子	脑力劳动
intelligence	intelligent	intend	intend for
n. 智力	*adj.* 聪明的，理解能力强的	*v.* 意图；意指，计划	打算成为……
intend to	intense	intensely	intensification
打算……	*adj.* 强烈的	*adv.* 极度地，强烈地	*n.* 密集化
intensify	intensity	intensive	intensively
v. 使加强，使强化；使变激烈	*n.* 强度；强烈	*adj.* 广泛的；集中的，加强的	*adv.* 强烈地，集中地
intent	intentional	Inter Exchange	interact
n. 目的	*adj.* 故意的，蓄意的	国际交流项目	*v.* 相互影响，相互作用
interaction	interactive	interactive audio-visual technology	interbreed
n. 相互作用，交流，互动	*adj.* 交互式的	交互式视听技术	*v.* 异种交配，品种杂交
interchange	interchangeable	intercity	interconnected
n. 互换；交换	*adj.* 可互换的，可交替的	*adj.* 城市之间的	*adj.* 相互连接的
interface	interfere	interfere with	interference
v. 接触，相互作用	*v.* 妨碍，干涉，介入，冲突	妨碍	*n.* 干扰；干涉
interim	interior	interior design	interiorise
adj. 临时的，暂时的	*n.* 内部 *adj.* 内部的	室内设计	*v.* 内化，使看法深入内心
inter-library loan	intermediary	intermediate	intermittently
馆际互借的图书	*adj.* 中间的	*adj.* 中级的 *n.* 中间体，中间物；调解人	*adv.* 间歇地

intermix	intermodal	internal	internal clock
v. 混合，混杂	adj. 联合运输的	adj. 内部的	生物钟
internal frontiers	internally	International Athletic Federation	international sporting event
内部边界	adv. 内部地	国际运动联合会	国际体育赛事
internet-only	internships	interpersonal	interplay
adj. 纯网络的	n. 实习岗位	adj. 人际的；人与人之间的	n. 互相影响，互相作用
interpret	interpretation	interpreting	interrupt
v. 解释，诠释；翻译（口译），说明	n. 说明，诠释，理解	n. 解释；口译	v. 中断
intertwine	interval	intervening	intervention
v. 缠结在一起，缠绕	n. 间隔，间距；幕间休息	adj. 介入的；干扰的	n. 干涉，调停；介入
interview	intimate	intimately	intimidating
v. 采访	adj. 亲密的	adv. 密切地; 熟悉地; 错综复杂地	adj. 吓人的
intolerable	intricacy	intricate	intricately
adj. 不能忍受的，无法容忍的	n. 复杂	adj. 复杂的，繁冗的; 错综复杂的	adv. 杂乱地
intrigue	intriguing	intrinsic	introductory
v. 激起……兴趣	adj. 有趣的；迷人的	adj. 内在的，本质的	adj. 引导的；入门的
introspection	introverted	intrusion	intrusive
n. 自省，反思	adj. 内向的	n. 侵入	adj. 打扰的，侵入的
intuition	intuitive	Inuit	inundation
n. 直觉（力）	adj. 直觉的	n. 因纽特人	n. 洪水，泛滥
invade	invalid	invaluable	invariably
v. 侵略	adj. 无效的	adj. 无价的；无价值的	adv. 总是；不变地；一定地
invariance	invasion	invective	invention
n. 不变性	n. 入侵，侵犯	n. 痛骂，猛烈抨击	n. 发明
inventor	inverted	inverted commas	invest
n. 发明家	adj. 倒转的，颠倒的	引号	v. 包围；投资；赋予

investigate	investigation	investigative	investigator
v. 调查，研究	n. 调查，研究	adj. 调查的，研究的	n. 研究者，调查员
investment	investor	invisible	inviting
n. 投资，投入	n. 投资者	adj. 看不见的，无形的	adj. 诱人的
invoke	involve	involve in	involvement
v. 调用	v. 包含，牵涉	卷入，参与	n. 投入；参与
iodine vapour	ion	ionization	iron
碘蒸气	n. 离子	n. 电离作用，离子化	adj. 铁的
iron product	Ironbridge Gorge World Heritage Site	iron-caster	ironically
铁产品	铁桥峡谷世界文化遗产	n. 铸工	adv. 讽刺地
ironing	ironworks	irony	irregular
n. 熨烫	n. 钢铁厂	n. 讽刺	adj. 无规律的
irrelevant	irresistible	irreversibility	irreversible
adj. 不相干的	adj. 无法抗拒的	n. 不可逆性；不可改变性	adj. 不可逆的；不能取消的；不能翻转的
irrigation	irrigation programmes	irritability	Irvine
n. 灌溉	灌溉项目	n. 易怒	n. 欧文
isolate	isolated	isolation	Israel
v. 使隔离，使孤立	adj. 孤立的，分离的	n. 隔离，孤立	n. 以色列
issue	item	ivory	
n. 问题 v. 发行，发布；排出	n. 条款，项目；一件物品	n. 象牙	

J

jacket	Jakarta	jam	Jamaica
n. 夹克	n. 雅加达	v. 拥挤	n. 牙买加
jam-packed	jar	jaw	jealously
adj. 拥挤不堪的	n. 罐子	n. 下颌	adv. 猜疑地
jean	jeopardize	jerk	jet
n. 牛仔裤	v. 危害，使陷危地	n. 猛拉，猛推 v. 急动，猛拉	n. 喷射

jet engine	jet lag	jewelry	jingle
喷射发动机	时差感综合征	*n.* 珠宝	*n.* 叮当声
jogging	Johnson's dictionary	joint	joint action
n. 慢跑	塞缪尔·约翰的词典	*n.* 结合处	联合行动
joint program	joke-telling	jolt	journal
联合计划	*n.* 讲笑话	*n.* 摇晃	*n.* 杂志
journalism	judgement	juggling	jungle
n. 新闻业	*n.* 判断力，评价	*n.* 杂耍	*n.* 丛林
jungle-clad	junior	Jupiter	jurisdiction
n. 丛林密布	*adj.* 后进的；下级的	*n.* 木星，朱庇特	*n.* 司法管辖区；行政辖区；管辖权
justice	justification	juvenile	juvenile foals
n. 正义，公平	*n.* 理由，辩护	*adj.* 青少年的；幼年的 *n.* 青少年	未成年的小马驹

K

kaleidoscope	Kant	Karoo	kayak
n. 万花筒	*n.* 康德(德国哲学家)	*n.* 卡鲁(南非干旱台地高原)	*n.* 皮船，木筏
keen	keen on	keenly	keep pace with
adj. 热切的；急迫的，强烈的	热衷于……	*adv.* 强烈地	跟上，与……齐步前进
keep up	Kepler	kettle	key
赶上	*n.* 开普勒	*n.* 壶	*adj.* 关键的，主要的
keycard	Khumbu Valley	kindergarten	kitchen goods
n. 出入证	昆布谷	*n.* 幼儿园	厨房用品
kite	kite-lifting	knock down	knock-on
n. 风筝	*adj.* 风筝升降的	拆除	*adj.* 连锁反应的
know-all	knowledgeable	Kotzebue	
n. 万事通	*adj.* 知识渊博的，有见识的	*n.* 科茨布	

L

label	labeled	laboratory	labor-intensive
v. 打上标签，分类	*adj.* 标注的	*n.* 实验室	*adj.* 劳动密集型的

labour intensive	labrador	labyrinth	lade
劳动集约	*n.* 纽芬兰猎犬	*n.* 迷宫	*v.* 装载
lagoon	lamp	lampyridae	lance-shaped
n. 环礁湖	*n.* 灯，照射器	*n.* 萤科	*adj.* 长矛状的
land	land mass	landfill	land-hungry
v. 着陆	大陆块	*n.* 垃圾填埋地	*adj.* 渴望占有土地的
landlord	landmark	landowner	landscape
n. 房东	*n.* 地标，里程碑	*n.* 地主	*n.* 风景，景观；土地
landscaped garden	lantern	lap	Lapland
园景花园	*n.* 灯笼，提灯；灯笼式天窗	*v.* 轻拍	*n.* 拉普兰
lapwing	larger-brained	large-scale	larva
n. 鸟头麦鸡	*adj.* 大脑袋的	*adj.* 大规模的，大范围的；大比例尺的	*n.* 幼体，幼虫
larval	laser	laser printer	laser-toting
adj. 幼虫状态的，潜在的	*n.* 激光	*n.* 激光印刷机	*adj.* 携带激光的
lash	lasting	last-minute	late-comer
n. 睫毛	*adj.* 持久的	*adj.* 最后的，紧要关头的	*n.* 晚到的人
latitude	latter	launch	launch out
n. 纬度	*adj.* 后者的	*v.* 发动，投入；发行；开始；出发	出航
launching	lava	law	law enforcement
n. 发射	*n.* 火山岩浆	*n.* 规律	法律执行
law firm	lawyer	lay	layer
法律事务所	*n.* 律师	*v.* 产卵 *adj.* 外行的	*n.* 层
layout	lead	leading	leaf litter
n. 布局，安排；设计	*n.* 铅	*adj.* 领导的，主要的	落叶层
leaflet	leaf-mining	leak	leakage
n. 传单	*adj.* 破坏叶子的	*n.* 泄漏	*n.* 泄漏
leap	learned	Learning Resources Centre (LRC)	lease
v. 跳跃，飞跃	*adj.* 博学的	学习资源中心	*n.* 租约
lecture hall	lecturer	left brain	legacy
讲堂	*n.* 讲师	左脑	*n.* 遗产

legendary *adj.* 传说中的	legibly *adv.* 清晰地，易辨认地	legion *adj.* 众多的	legislation *n.* 立法，法律
legitimacy *n.* 合法，合理	legitimate *adj.* 合法的	leisure *adj.* 业余的，空闲的 *n.* 休闲	leisure time 闲暇时间
leisurely *adv.* 悠闲地	lend support to 支持，支援	length *n.* (时间或距离的) 长短	lenses *n.* 镜头；镜片
lessen *v.* 使……减轻， 使……变少	lessons learned 经验教训	let *v.* 出租	let off 排放；放过
lethal *adj.* 致命的，致死的	lethargy *n.* 昏睡	Lethbridge University 莱斯布里奇大学	level *v.* 夷为平地
lever/prise *v.* 撬	lever-based *adj.* 基于杠杆原理的	leverets *n.* 小兔	levy *v.* 征税
lexical *adj.* 词汇的	lexicographer *n.* 词典编纂者	liberal *adj.* 自由主义的	liberalism *n.* 自由主义
liberty *n.* 自由	licence *n.* 许可证	license number 执照号码	licensed bar 有售酒许可证的酒吧
lid *n.* 眼睑	lieu *n.* 代替	life cycle 生存期	life expectancy 预期寿命，平均寿命
life-size *adj.* 与实物大小一 样的	lifespan *n.* 寿命	lifestyle *n.* 生活方式	lifter *n.* 升降机
light intensity 光强度	light meal 便餐	light organ 发光器官	light phase 光相
light rail 轻轨	light-colored *adj.* 浅色的	lighting *n.* 照明设备	lightning *n.* 闪电
lightning flash 电闪，闪光	lightweight *adj.* 重量轻的	likelihood *n.* 可能性	like-minded *adj.* 志趣相投的
liken *v.* 比拟，把……比做	likewise *adv.* 同样地，也	limb *n.* 四肢 *v.* 切断	lime *n.* 石灰

limestone	limitation	limited	lineage
n. 石灰岩	n. 限制	adj. 有限的	n. 血统
linear	linen	linger	lingua franca
adj. 直线的	n. 亚麻布，亚麻制品	v. 留下	通用语
linguist	linguistic	linguistically	linguistics
n. 语言学家	adj. 语言（学）的	adv. 语言地	n. 语言学
link	link to	link-up	linoleum
v. 连接；联系	与……有联系，相关	n. 连接	n. 油布；油毡；漆布
lipread	liquid	listener	literacy
v. 观唇辨意	n. 液体	n. 听众	n. 读写能力；精通文学
literal	literary	literate	literature
adj. 文字的	adj. 精通文学的，学术的	adj. 受过教育的	n. 文学，著作
litre	litter	live birth	live up to
n. 公升	n. 垃圾，枯枝落叶	婴儿安全出生	符合，达到预期标准
Liverpool School	livestock	living	lizard
利物浦学校	n. 牲畜；家畜	n. 生计	n. 蜥蜴
load	loads of	loafer	loan
v. 装载	许多，大量	n. 平底便鞋	n. 贷款，借款
loath	lobby	lobe	local firm
adj. 不愿的	n. 游说议员的团体 v. 游说	n. (脑、肺等的) 叶	当地公司
localisation	locality	loch	locomotive
n. 地方化；定位	n. 地点	n. 湖，海湾；水闸	n. 机车，火车头
lodge	log	logging	logic
n. 旅馆	n. 原木 v. 记录	n. 砍伐树木	n. 逻辑学
logical	logistical	logistics	logo
adj. 有逻辑的	adj. 物流的	n. 后勤；物流	n. 商标
London-based	lóng-day	longevity	longitudinal
adj. 总部位于伦敦的	adj. 长日照的	n. 长寿，长命，经久不衰	adj. 经度的，纵向的
long-term	look-in	looting	lopsidedness
adj. 长期的	n. 成功的机会	n. 抢劫，打劫	n. 不平衡

lorry n. 卡车，货车	loss n. 损失	lounge area 休息室	low frequency 低频率
low-calorie adj. 低卡路里的	low-cost adj. 低成本的	low-lying adj. 低地的	loyal adj. 忠诚的
loyalty n. 忠诚；忠心	lozenge n. 锭剂	lucrative adj. 获利多的，赚钱 的；有利可图的	ludicrousness n. 可笑，滑稽
luggage n. 行李	lumber v. 慢慢地移动	lump adj. 成块的	lumps of gum 树胶肿块
lunar adj. 月亮上的	lunar cycle 农历周期	lunar month 太阴月，农历月	lunatic adj. 疯狂的
lung n. 肺	lush adj. 苍翠繁茂的	luxury n. 奢侈，奢华 adj. 奢侈的	

M

macadamia n. 澳大利亚坚果， 夏威夷果	machinery n. 机器，机械	Madagascar n. 马达加斯加岛	madness n. 疯狂
magical adj. 有魔力的，奇 妙的	magma n. 岩浆	magnetic adj. 磁力的；有磁 性的	magnetic field 磁场
magnetism n. 磁学，磁力	magnificent adj. 高尚的; 壮丽的; 华丽的；宏伟的	magnified adj. 放大的	magnify v. 放大，夸大
magnitude n. 量级（大小）	mainspring n. 主要动力	mainstream n. 主流	maintain v. 维持；保留；维修， 认为；主张；保持
maintenance n. 维护，维持；维修， 保养	majestic adj. 庄严的，宏伟的	major adj. 主要的	majority n. 大多数
make a go 成功	make a name 有声望	make a profit 获利，赚钱	make do with 设法应付
make his fortune 发大财	makeup n. 组成	make-up n. 化妆	make up 补足

make way for 让步	make-believe adj. 虚假的，虚构的	malaria-prone areas 疟疾高发地区	Malaysia n. 马来西亚
male n. 男性	malevolent adj. 恶意的	malleable adj. 可塑的	malnourished adj. 营养不良的
malt n. 麦芽	mammal n. 哺乳动物	mammalian adj. 哺乳动物的	mammoth adj. 巨大的，庞大的
manage one's finance 理财	manageable adj. 易管理的	managed adj. 托管的	management n. 管理
manager n. 经理	managerial adj. 管理的	mandate v. 授权，托管	mangle n. 轧布机
manifest v. 出现，表现	manifestation n. 表现，显示	manifold adj. 多样的	Manila n. 马尼拉
manipulate v. 操纵；操作；巧妙 地处理；篡改	manipulative adj. 被操纵的	manmade adj. 人造的	manner n. 方式
mannerism n. 特殊习惯	manoeuvre n. 策略 v. 用策略，操纵	manta ray 蝠鲼	mantle n. 地幔
manual adj. 手动的；体力的	manually adv. 手动地	manufacturable adj. 可制造的	manufacture n./v. 制造
manufactured adj. 制造的	manufacturer n. 制造商，生产商	manufacturing n. 制造业	manuscript n. 手稿；原稿
Maori n. 毛利人，毛利语	Maori chief 毛利人首领	map v. 绘制地图；映射	mar v. 损毁，损坏
Marathon n. 马拉松	march n. 行进，前进 v. 行进	margin n. 边缘；页边空白	marginally adv. 少量地
marine adj. 海的，海洋的， 海中的	marine wildlife 海洋生物	mark v. 打分数；作记号	mark...out 划分，区分
marked adj. 显著的	markedly adv. 明显地，显著地	marker n. 标记，标示	marketable adj. 可销售的，市 场的
market-based adj. 基于市场的	market-driven economy 市场经济	marketing n. 行销，销售	marketing experience 市场经验

marketing people 营销人员	marketing specialist 营销专家	marketplace *n.* 市场，商场	marsh *n.* 沼泽
marshal *n.* 司仪 *v.* 整理	marshy *adj.* 沼泽的	martial *adj.* 军事的，战争的	Martinique *n.* 马提尼克
marvel *v.* 对……感到惊异	mass *n.* 大量	mass extinction 大量消亡，大灭绝	mass media 大众媒体
mass tourism 大众旅游	massive *adj.* 大量的，巨大的	mass-produced *adj.* 大量生产的，大批生产的	master *v.* 控制，征服
MasterCard *n.* 万事达信用卡	masterpiece *n.* 杰作	match *v.* 匹配	match to 把……相搭配
matchstick *n.* 火柴杆	mate *n.* 配偶 *v.* 交配	material existence 物质存在	materialise *v.* 实现
maternal *adj.* 母亲的，母性的	maternity/paternity leave 产假	mathematical *adj.* 数学的	mathematician *n.* 数学家
matinee *n.* 白天举行的音乐会	matter *n.* 事件；原因	mature *adj.* 成熟的，成年的，稳重的	mausoleum *n.* 陵墓
maximal *adj.* 最大的	maximize *v.* 最大化	maximum *n.* 最大化 *adj.* 最高的，最大的	May Day 五一劳动节
maze *n.* 迷宫	meager *adj.* 贫乏的	means *n.* 方法	measles *n.* 麻疹
measly *adj.* 极少的	measurable *adj.* 可测量的；重要的；能够测量的	measure *v.* 测量，估量	measurement *n.* 测量，度量
mechanical degradation 机械降解	mechanical *adj.* 机械的，呆板的	mechanics *n.* 力学，机械部件	mechanisation *n.* 机械化
mechanise *v.* 使机械化	mechanism *n.* 机制，原理；途径	medal *n.* 奖章，奖牌，勋章	media coverage 媒体报道，媒体覆盖率

medical	medical card	medical-diagnosis	medication
adj. 医学的	医疗卡	*n.* 医疗诊断	*n.* 药物，药物治疗
medieval	Medieval Warm Period	mediocre	meditation
adj. 原始的；仿中世纪的	中世纪暖期	*adj.* 普通的，平凡的	*n.* 冥想，沉思
Mediterranean	Mediterranean coast	Mediterranean Sea	medium
adj. 地中海的 *n.* 地中海	地中海沿岸	地中海	*n.* 方法；媒体；媒介；中间物
medium-sized	meet	megafires	megalopolis
adj. 中型的	*v.* 满足	*n.* 特大火灾	*n.* 特大城市
melatonin	Melbourne	Melksham	melodic
n. 褪黑激素	*n.* 墨尔本	*n.* 梅尔克舍姆	*adj.* 有旋律的
melt	meltdown	melt-water	membership
v. 熔化；融化	*n.* 暴跌	*n.* 冰川融水	*n.* 会员
memorable	memorise	menace	mental
adj. 显著的	*v.* 记忆，储存	*n.* 威胁，恐吓	*adj.* 神经的，心理的
mentality	mentally	mention	menu
n. 心态	*adv.* 智力上，精神上	*v.* 提到，涉及	*n.* 菜单
merchandise	merchant	mercury	mercy
n. 商品	*n.* 商人	*n.* 汞，水银	*n.* 宽容，怜悯
mere	merely	merge	meshed
adj. 仅仅的，只不过的	*adv.* 仅仅，只不过；只是	*v.* 合并，融合	*adj.* 网状的
Mesopotamian	mess	meta-analysis	metabolic
n. 美索不达米亚	*n.* 混乱	*n.* 荟萃分析，元分析	*adj.* 新陈代谢的，变化的
metacognition	metal	metamorphose	metaphor
n. 元认知；后设认知	*adj.* 金属的	*v.* 变质；变形；使变成	*n.* 隐喻
metaphorical	meteorite	meteorological	meteorology
adj. 隐喻(性)的，比喻(性)的	*n.* 陨石，流星	*adj.* 气象学的	*n.* 气象学
meter	meter reading	methane	methodology
n. 仪表	仪表读数	*n.* 甲烷，沼气	*n.* 方法论
meticulously	metric tons	metrics	metropolitan
adv. 细致地	公吨	*n.* 度量	*n.* 大都市

microfiche reader 缩微平片阅读器	Micrographia n. 显微图谱（书名）	microphone n. 麦克风	microscope n. 显微镜
microwave n. 微波	microwave oven 微波炉	middlemen n. 中间商	mighty adj. 强有力的
migrate v. 转移，迁移	migration n. 迁移，移民	migratory adj. 迁移的	mild adj. 温和的
mildly adv. 温和地	miler n. 一英里赛跑的运动员	milestone n. 里程碑，划时代事件	military adj. 军事的
milk v. 挤，榨取	millennia n. 一千年	millennium n. 千禧年，一千年	millimeter n. 毫米
mimic v. 模仿	mind set 思维定式	mineral n. 矿物	miniature adj. 微型的，小型的
minimal adj. 最少的	minimally adv. 最低限度地	minimize v. 最小化，使……减到最小	minimum n. 最小化，最小量
minimum fare 最低票价	minimum pay 最低工资	minister n. 部长	Ministerial Conference 部长大会
minor adj. 二流的，次要的	minority n. 少数，少数派 adj. 少数的	minuscule adj. 极小的	minute adj. 微小的
miraculous adj. 不可思议的，奇迹的	misconception n. 误解，错误想法	mishandle v. 处理不当	mishandling n. 违反运行规程；不正确运转
mislead v. 误导	mismanagement n. 管理不当，处理失当	mist n. 模糊不清之物	mistrust v. 不信任，怀疑
misunderstanding n. 误解，误会	misuse n. 滥用	mitigate v. 使缓和，使减轻	mitigating n. 减轻
mitochondrial adj. 线粒体的	mixed-ability adj. 学生能力不一的	mixture n. 混合，混合物	moat n. 护城河，壕沟
mobilise v. 调动，使流通	mobility n. 移动性	model n. 模型，样式 v. 以……为模型	modeled birds 模仿鸟

moderate	moderately	moderation	modest
adj. 适度的	*adv.* 适度地，相对地	*n.* 适度，适量	*adj.* 适度的
modification	modified	modify	module
n. 修改，修正	*adj.* 改良的	*v.* 修改	*n.* 模块
moist	moistened	moisture	molar
n. 潮湿	*adj.* 弄湿的	*n.* 水分，湿度，水蒸气	*n.* 臼齿，磨牙
molecular	molecule	mollusk	molten
adj. 分子的	*n.* 分子	*n.* 软体动物	*adj.* 炽热的，熔化的
molten rock	momentum	monetary	monitor
熔岩	*n.* 势头	*adj.* 货币的；财政的	*v.* 监控；监督
monitoring	monks	monoculture	monograph
n. 监视，监控；检验，检查	*n.* 和尚，僧侣	*n.* 单一品种种植	*n.* 专题论文
monolingual	monopoly	monorails	monotonous
adj. 仅用一种语言的	*n.* 垄断	*n.* 单轨	*adj.* 单调无聊的
monsoon	monstrosity	monument	Monument Valley
n. 季风，雨季	*n.* 畸形	*n.* 纪念碑	纪念谷
monumental	monuments	mood	moral
adj. 不朽的	*n.* 遗迹	*n.* 心情	*n.* 寓意；道德 *adj.* 道德上的
moral code	morale	morsel	mortality
道德准则	*n.* 士气，斗志	*n.* 一口；（食物）少量	*n.* 死亡率
mosaic	mosquitos	motifs	motion
n. 马赛克，镶嵌，拼接	*n.* 蚊子	*n.* 主题，主旨；图形	*n.* 运动，移动
motion line	motivate	motivation	motive
运动线条	*v.* 促进，激励	*n.* 动机；推动	*n.* 动机；目的
motive force	motor circuit	motor vehicle	motor yacht captain
动力	动力线路	机动车	机动游艇长
motorized	motor-skill	motorway	motto
adj. 机动化的	*n.* 运动技能	*n.* 高速公路	*n.* 座右铭
mould	mount	Mount Peelee	Mount Pinatubo
v. 模压，塑造；塑造成	*v.* 挂载	皮里岛	皮纳图博火山
Mount St Helen	Mount Tambora	mountain biking	mountain of data
神赫伦火山	坦博拉火山	山地车，山地自行车	海量的数据

mounted	mounting	move	movement
adj. 骑马的	*adj.* 逐渐增加的	*n.* 移居	*n.* 移动；乐章
moving	mud	muddle	muddy
adj. 生动的	*n.* 淤泥	*v.* 使混乱	*adj.* 泥泞的
mug	mulberry	mule	multifaceted
n. 杯子	*n.* 桑树	*n.* 骡子	*adj.* 多层面的
multilingual	multi-storey	multitude	mundane
adj. 多语的	*adj.* 多层的	*n.* 众多	*adj.* 世俗的，世界的
Munich University	municipal	murder	Murder in Mesopotamia
慕尼黑大学	*adj.* 地方的，市政的	*n.* 谋杀	古墓之谜（小说名），美索不达米亚谋杀案
Murdoch University	muscle	muscle pain	muscle strength
梅铎大学	*n.* 肌肉	肌肉疼痛	肌肉力量
musculo-skeletal	mushroom	musical	musical compositions
adj. 肌肉骨骼的	*n.* 蘑菇	*n.* 音乐剧，音乐片	音乐的乐章
musician	must	mutate	mutation
n. 音乐家	*n.* 必需品	*v.* 改变	*n.* 突变；变化
mutual	mutual-aid	myriad	mysterious
adj. 相互的，彼此的	*n.* 互济	*adj.* 无数的	*adj.* 神秘的；不可思议的
mystery	mystical	mystify	myth
n. 神秘，奥秘	*adj.* 神秘的	*v.* 使神秘化，使迷惑	*n.* 神话
mythology			
n. 神话			

N

nail	naive	name	namely
n. 指甲	*adj.* 天真的	*v.* 选中；指定	*adv.* 即，也就是
nanny	narration	narrative	narrow
n. 保姆	*n.* 叙述，讲述	*n.* 叙述，讲述 *adj.* 叙事的，叙述的	*adj.* 有限的，狭隘的
narrowly	nasal	nasty	National Literacy Crusade
adv. 一点，稍微	*adj.* 鼻的	*adj.* 凶险的，严重的，激烈的	全国扫盲运动

National Minimum Wage 国家最低工资标准	national park 国家公园	nationwide *adj.* 全国性的	native *n.* 原产于
native to 原产自……	natural *adj.* 天然的	natural enemy 天敌	naturalistic *adj.* 真实的，实际的
naturopath *n.* 理疗家	Navajo *n.* 纳瓦霍；纳瓦霍人（美国最大的印第安部落）	navigability *n.* 适航性	navigable *adj.* 可航行的，可通航的
navigate *v.* 操纵；航行；导航，定位	navigation *n.* 导航	navigational *adj.* 航行的，航运的	nearby *adj.* 附近的
neatly *adv.* 整洁地	necessitate *v.* 迫使，使成必要	needle *n.* 针	negligence *n.* 疏忽
negotiate *v.* 谈判，协商；商定，解决	nematode *n.* 线虫类	Nepal *n.* 尼泊尔	nerve *n.* 神经
nerve cell 神经细胞	nervous *adj.* 紧张的	nervousness *n.* 神经质	nest *n.* 巢穴；鸟巢
nesting site 筑巢区	netball *n.* 无网篮球	network *n.* 网络	neural *adj.* 神经的，神经中枢的
neural network 神经网络	neurobiologist *n.* 神经生物学家	neurobiology *n.* 神经生物学	neurological system 神经系统
neuroscientist *n.* 神经系统科学家	neurotrophic *adj.* 神经营养的	neutralize *v.* 中和	neutron *n.* 神经元；神经细胞
nevertheless *conj.* 然而，不过	New Haven 纽黑文市	New Yorker 纽约州人	New Zealander 新西兰人
newcomer *n.* 新手	newly-literate *adj.* 新受教育的	newsletter *n.* 实时通讯；业务通讯	newsreel *n.* 新闻影片
Nicaragua *n.* 尼加拉瓜	nice smelly 美味	niche *n.* 壁龛	niches *n.* 生态位；一席之地
nickel sulphide 硫化镍	nifty *adj.* 精巧的，漂亮的	Nigeria *n.* 尼日利亚（位于非洲）	nightclub *n.* 夜总会

night-flighting *adj.* 夜间飞行的	night-hunting *adj.* 夜间狩猎的	Nile 尼罗河	Nile delta 尼罗河三角洲
nitrate *n.* 硝酸盐	nitrogen *n.* 氮	nitroglycerine *n.* [有化] 硝化甘油 (等于 nitroglycerin)，炸药	nitty-gritty *n.* 基本事实
Nobel Prize 诺贝尔奖	nobility *n.* 贵族	noble *n.* 贵族	noble cause 崇高的事业
nobly *adv.* 高贵地；华丽地	nocturnal *adj.* 夜间的，夜间发生的	noisy *adj.* 嘈杂的	nomadic *adj.* 游牧的
nominate *v.* 提名，任命，指定	nominated beneficiary 被指定的受益人	non-biological *adj.* 非生物的	non-commercial *adj.* 非商业性的
non-contributory *adj.* 无须供款的，不必缴费的	nondescript *adj.* 难以区分的	non-edible 非食用	non-executive *adj.* 非执行性的
non-exempt employee 非免税员工	non-government *adj.* 非政府的	non-human *adj.* 非人类的	non-physical *adj.* 非物质的
non-polluting *adj.* 无污染的	non-porous *adj.* 无孔的	non-profit *adj.* 非营利的	non-refundable *adj.* 不可退款的
nonsense *n.* 胡说，废话	non-shrink *adj.* 不缩水的	non-smoking *adj.* 禁止吸烟的	non-targeted *adj.* 非针对性的，不是目标的
non-verbal *adj.* 非语言的	Nordic *adj.* 北欧的，日耳曼民族的	norm *n.* 规范	normal *adj.* 正常的
normally *adv.* 通常地	norm-referenced *adj.* 参照标准的	Norse *n.* 挪威人	North Coast College 北海岸大学
northern hemisphere 北半球	Northern Ireland 北爱尔兰	not in the same league as 不像……一样好	not relied upon 不足为凭
notable *adj.* 值得注意的，显著的	notably *adv.* 尤其	notational *adj.* 记数的	note *n.* 纸币 *v.* 注意

notice	notification	notify	notion
n. 注意	n. 通知	v. 通知	n. 概念，见解；观点
notoriety	notorious	notoriously	nourish
n. 名声	adj. 臭名昭著的	adv. 众所周知地	v. 滋养；怀有；使健壮，养育
nourishment	novelty	nuance	nuclear
n. 食物，营养品	n. 新颖，新奇	n. 细微差别	adj. 原子能的，原子核的
nuisance	numeracy	numerate	numeration
n. 讨厌的东西，麻烦事	n. 计算能力，识数	v. 数数，列举	n. 计算，计算法
numerous	Nunavut	nursery	nursery school
adj. 许多的，很多的	n. 努勒维特	n. 儿童室	幼儿园
nurture	nutrient	nutrient deficiency	nutrient-rich
v. 养育；赞成；养育 n. 养育	n. 养分；营养物	养分缺乏	adj. 营养丰富的
nutrition	nutritional	nutritionally	nutritious
n. 营养	adj. 营养的，滋养的	adv. 滋养地	adj. 有营养的
nuts	nylon		
n. 坚果	n. 尼龙		

O

oak tree	obedient	obesity	obey
橡树	adj. 顺从的	n. 肥胖症	v. 服从，按照……做，遵守
object	object to	objection	objective
n. 目标；物体	对……反对	n. 缺陷，缺点；异议，反对；妨碍	n. 目标，目的 adj. 客观的
objectively	objectivity	obligation	oblige
adv. 客观地	n. 客观性	n. 义务	v. 迫使；强制
obnoxious	obscure	obscurity	observation
adj. 讨厌的	v. 掩盖；使含混；变得模糊 adj. 晦涩的	n. 默默无闻，不出名	n. 观察，观察报告，检测
observatory	observe	observer	observer's paradox
n. 天文台，气象台	v. 观察，注意到，说，遵守；看	n. 观察者	调查者的矛盾

obsessive	obstacle	obstruct	obstruction
adj. 着迷的，急迫的	*n.* 妨碍，障碍；干扰；障碍物	*v.* 妨碍，阻碍，阻塞	*n.* 障碍
obtain	obvious	obviously	occasion
v. 获得	*adj.* 明显的	*adv.* 明显地	*n.* 时机，机会
occasional	occasionally	occupancy rate	occupant
adj. 偶然的；临时的；特殊场合的	*adv.* 偶尔；偶然地	租用率	*n.* 居住者，居民
occupation	occupational	occupy	occur
n. 占有，占领；职业	*adj.* 与职业有关的，职业的	*v.* 占据，占有	*v.* 出现，发生
occurrence	ocean floor	odd	odour
n. 发生；出现；事件；发现；发生的事	洋底	*adj.* 古怪的 *n.* 奇数	*n.* 气味
odourless	OECD (Organisation for Economic Cooperation and Development) 经济合作与发展组织	of consequence	of one's own making
adj. 无气味的		有意义的	自作自受
offence	offender	offensive	official
n. 犯罪	*n.* 罪犯	*adj.* 冒犯的，无礼的	*n.* 官员
officially	offing	off-peak	offspring
adv. 官方地，正式地	*n.* 在视野内的远处海面（即将到来）	*adj.* 非高峰时间的	*n.* 后代，子孙
oft-cited	ointment	olfaction	olfactory
adj. 经常引用的	*n.* 药膏	*n.* 嗅觉	*adj.* 嗅觉的，味道的
ominous	omit	on a daily basis	on target
adj. 预兆的	*v.* 省略	每天	切题，切中要害
on the backs of men	on the grounds	on the premises	oncoming
人背着	由于……原因	在……前提下	*adj.* 即将来临的
one line	one-off	online	online debate
一行	*adj.* 一次性的	*adj.* 在线的	在线讨论
onset	onslaught	on-the-job	onward
n. 开始	*n.* 猛攻，突击	在工作中的	*adj.* 向前的 *adv.* 向前

open to traffic 通车	open toe shoes 露脚背的鞋，鱼嘴鞋	open-air *adj.* 户外的	open-form *adj.* 开放式的
opera *n.* 歌剧	opera-house *n.* 剧院	operate *v.* 运转；操作	operation *n.* 操作
operations research 运筹学，作业研究	operator *n.* 操作员；经营者	opinion poll 民意测验	opportunism *n.* 机会主义，投机 主义
opportunity *n.* 机会，机遇，时机	oppose *v.* 反对	opposing *adj.* 相反的	opposite *adj.* 相反的；对立的
opposition *n.* 反对，敌对，对抗	opt *v.* 选择	opt out 决定退出；插播	optical *adj.* 光学的
optics *n.* 光学	optimal *adj.* 最佳的	optimism *n.* 乐观，乐观主义	optimistic *adj.* 乐观的
optimum *n.* 最佳效果 *adj.* 最佳的，最适宜 的，最有利的	option *n.* 选项，选择；选择	optional *adj.* 可选择的	opulence *n.* 富裕
oral *adj.* 口头的，口述的	orbit *n.* 轨道，眼眶	orbital *adj.* 眼窝的	orchestra *n.* 管弦乐队
orchestra pit 乐池	order *n.* 顺序；命令	ordinary *adj.* 普通的，平凡的， 平常的	ore *n.* 矿，矿石
Oregon *n.* 俄勒冈州	organic *adj.* 有机的	organic material 有机物	organically *adv.* 有机地
organism *n.* 有机体，生物体	organization *n.* 阻止，组织，机构	organizational *adj.* 组织的	orientation programme 迎新活动
orientation *n.* 情况介绍	origin *n.* 起源	original *adj.* 原始的	original science 原始科学
originality *n.* 创意，独创性	originally *adv.* 最初	ornate *adj.* 华丽的；装饰的	orthodox *adj.* 传统的
orthography *n.* 正确拼字	osteopath *n.* 整骨疗法家	otherwise *adv.* 否则（表转折）	ought to 应当，应该，理应
out of proportion 不成比例	outbreak *n.* 发作；爆发	outcome *n.* 成果，结果	outcrop *n.* 露出地面的岩层， 岩石露出的部分

outdated	outer edge	outer layer	outer skin
adj. 过时的，旧式的	外缘	外层	外壳
outlandish	outlay	outlet	outlier
adj. 古怪的	*n.* 费用，支出，经费	*n.* 商店，市场	*n.* 离群值
outline	outlook	outperform	output
n. 外形，略图；提纲；轮廓，大纲 *v.* 概述，略述	*n.* 观点；展望	*v.* 胜过，做得比……更好	*n.* 产量，输出量
outrageous	outright	outset	outsider
adj. 令人吃惊的	*adj.* 完全的	*n.* 开始，开端	*n.* 外人
outstanding	outstrip	outward	outward trip
adj. 杰出的，未偿付的	*v.* 超过，胜过	*adj.* 肉体的; 外面的; 向外的，外出的	旅程
oval	over the counter	overall	over-ambitious
adj. 椭圆形的	直接交易	*adj.* 全部的	*adj.* 野心过大的
overbearing	overcome	over-enrichment	overexposure
adj. 傲慢的；压倒一切的	*n.* 克服	*n.* 富营养	*n.* 感光过度
overfeeding	overfish	overhang	over-hanging
n. 过度进食	*v.* 过度捕捞	*n.*（房屋楼层的）悬挑部分，飞檐	*adj.* 悬伸的
overhead	overheat	overlap	overlapping
n. 经常费用 *adv.* 在头顶上，顶部	*v.* 使过热	*v.* 与……重叠	*adj.* 重叠的
overlay	overload	overlook	overly
v. 叠加	*n./v.* 超载；过重负担	*v.* 忽略；俯瞰	*adv.* 过度地
overlying	overnight	overpopulation	overrun
adj. 上覆盖的	*adv.* 通宵	*n.* 数量过剩	*n.* 泛滥成灾
overseas	oversee	oversimplified	overstate
adj. 海外的，国外的	*v.* 监视，监督	*adj.* 过于简单化的	*v.* 夸张（地叙述）
overtake	overtime	overwhelming	overwhelmingly
v. 赶上，超过	*adj.* 加班的，超时的	*adj.* 压倒性的，势不可当的	*adv.* 压倒性地，不可抵挡地
overwinter	owe	owe much to	owing to
v. 过冬	*v.* 欠，归因于	在很大程度上归功于，多亏了	由于

ownership	oxygen	oxygenated	
n. 所有权	n. 氧气，氧	adj. 氧化的	

P

pace	pacifist	pack	pack ice
n. 速度	n. 和平主义者	n. 包裹，背包	积冰
package	packaged	packaging	paddock
n. 包裹，一组事物；整套事务	adj. 包装过的	n. 包装	n. 小围场
paediatrics	pagoda	painstaking	paint brush
n. 儿科学	n. 宝塔	adj. 艰苦的	漆刷
painter	painting	palace	pale
n. 画家	n. 绘画	n. 宫殿，宅邸	adj. 苍白的；暗淡的；黯然失色的
palm	pamphlet	pancreatic	pane
n. 棕榈树	n. 小册子	adj. 胰的，胰腺的	n. 窗格，窗格玻璃
panel	panic	pant	paperwork
n. 小组	v. 惊慌，恐慌	v. 喘息，气喘吁吁地说	n. 文书工作
parachute	paraconsciously	parade	paradox
v. 用降落伞降落 n. 降落伞	adv. 超意识地	n. 阅兵	n. 悖论
paradoxical	paragliding	parallax	parallel to
adj. 矛盾的；诡论的	n. 滑翔伞运动，高崖跳伞运动	n. 视差	与……平衡
paralysed	parameter	paramotoring	parapsychologist
adj. 瘫痪的，无力的	n. 参数，系数	n. 动力滑翔伞运动	n. 通灵者
parapsychology	parasite	parcel	parched
n. 通灵学	n. 寄生虫	n. 包裹	adj. 炎热的，干旱的
parental leave	parent-educator	park wardens	parking
育婴假	n. 家长教育工作者	公园管理员	n. 停车
parking facility	parking zone	parkland	partially
停车设施	停车区	n. 有树丛的开阔草地，公用草地	adv. 部分地

participant	participate	participation	participatory
n. 参与者	*v.* 参加	*n.* 参与	*adj.* 供人分享的；吸引参与的
particular	particular examples	particular route	particularly
adj. 特定的	特别收藏品	特定的路线	*adv.* 特别地
partly	partnership	partridge	passage
adv. 部分地	*n.* 合伙关系	*n.* 鹧鸪	*n.* 航程
passageway	passenger	passing	passionate
n. 通道	*n.* 乘客	*adj.* 短暂的	*adj.* 热情的，热烈的
passivity	passport	passport-sized	password
n. 被动性；被动结构；无抵抗	*n.* 护照	*adj.* 护照尺寸的	*n.* 密码
past and present	pastime	pastry	pasture
过去与现在	*n.* 休闲，娱乐	*n.* 油酥点心，糕点	*n.* 草地，牧场
patch	patent	paterfamilias	paternal
n. 碎片；小块土地	*adj.* 新奇的，专利的 *v.* 获得专利权	*n.* 家长，一家之长	*adj.* 父亲的
pathway	patience	patron	patronage
n.（人身体里的）通路，脉络；途径	*n.* 耐心	*n.* 赞助人	*n.* 赞助
pattern	patterned belt	pattern-recognition	pause
n. 模式，方式，花样；图案；样品	带花纹的腰带	*n.* 模式识别	*v.* 暂停
pave	pavilion	pay cash	pay closer attention to
v. 为……铺平道路，铺设	*n.* 楼阁；大帐篷	付现金	密切注意
pay in installment	pay off	payable	paycheck
分期支付	得到好结果，取得成功	*adj.* 应付的	*n.* 付薪水的支票
payday	paying	payload	payment
n. 发薪日	*adj.* 支付的，付款的	*n.* 承重	*n.* 付款，支付
pay-off	payroll	payslip	peaceful
n. 回报	*n.* 工资单	*n.* 工资单	*adj.* 和平的，平静的

peak	peasant	pebble	peculiar
n. 最高峰，顶点； 山顶 v. 使……达到顶峰 adj. 最高的，最佳的	n. 农民	n. 卵石	adj. 特殊的；独特的； 奇怪的；罕见的
pedestrian n. 行人	pedigree n. 家谱，血统	peer n. 同龄人	peering down 俯身
peg n. 钉，桩	Peking n. 北京（旧称）	pelican n. 鹈鹕，塘鹅（一种 食鱼鸟）	pendulum n. 钟摆
penetrate v. 渗透	penetration n. 渗入	peninsula n. 半岛	pension n. 抚恤金，津贴； 养老金
pent up 被压抑的	pepper n. 胡椒	pepper with 使布满；在……上撒 （胡椒粉等）	per capita 人均
perceive v. 察觉，感觉，感知； 理解，认为	perception n. 观念；感知(能力)， 觉察（力），感觉， 知觉	perceptual adj. 知觉的，感觉的， 有知觉的	perch n. 鲈鱼 v. 暂栖
perennial adj. 常年的，四季不 断的，多年生的	perfect v. 使完美	perform v. 表演	performance n. 绩效，表演，表现； 成绩
peril n. 危险	perimeter n. 周界，边缘，周长	periodic adj. 周期的，定期的	periods n. 周期
peripheral adj. 外围的，次要的	perish v. 死亡	permafrost n. 永久冻土	permanent adj. 永久的，永恒的； 不变的
permanently adv. 永久地，长期 不变地	permission n. 允许，许可	permit n. 许可证，执照； 许可 v. 许可	perpetual adj. 永久的，不断的
perpetuate v. 保持，使……不朽	perplex v. 使困惑	perplexed adj. 为难的	perseverance n. 坚持不懈；不屈 不挠；耐性；毅力

persevere v. 坚持	persist v. 依旧存在，继续 存在	persistence n. 坚持	persistent adj. 坚持的，持久的
persistent linguistic competition 持续语言选择	personal preference 个人喜好	personality n. 个性，品格，名人	personalize v. 使个性化
personnel n. 全体人员，人员， 员工；人事部门	perspective n. 透视图；视角， 观点；预期；期望	persuade v. 说服	persuasive adj. 有说服力的
Perth n. 佩斯（澳大利亚城 市）	peruse v. 详细考察	Peruvian Andes 秘鲁的安第斯山脉	perversely adv. 倔强地
pessimistic adj. 悲观的	pest n. 害虫	pesticide n. 杀虫剂	phantom adj. 有名无实的；幽 灵的，幻觉的
pharmaceutical n. 药物，制药	pharmacist n. 药剂师	pharmacy n. 药房；配药学， 药剂学；制药业；一 批备用药品	phase n. 阶段
phenol n. 苯酚，石碳酸	phenolic adj. 酚的	phenomenal adj. 显著的；异常的	phenomenon n. 现象
Philippines n. 菲律宾	philosophy n. 哲学；指导思想	phosphate n. 磷酸盐	phosphorus n. 磷
photocopier n. 复印机	photocopy v. 复印	photoelectric adj. 光电的	photographer n. 摄影师
photographic adj. 摄影的	photographic paper 相纸	photography n. 摄影	photon n. 光子，光量子
photoperiodism n. 光周期现象	photosynthesis n. 光合作用	phrase n. 词汇	physical adj. 物质的
physical anthropology 人类体格学，身体人 类学	physician n. 医师，内科医生	physics n. 物理学	physiognomy n. 相貌
physiological adj. 生理（学）的	physiology n. 生理学	phytoplankton n. 浮游植物	pick up 获得
picking n. 采得物	pickle n. 泡菜	pier n. 桥墩	pierce v. 刺破

piercing	pigment	pillar	pillow case
n. 熔化穿孔	n. 色素	n. 柱子；柱状物	开口式枕套
pilot adj. 试点的，领先的 n. 飞行员	pilot plant 试验工厂	PIN (personal identification number) 个人身份证号码	pin down 使明确说明，确定
pine n. 松树	pineal gland 松果腺	pinpoint v. 确定	pinprick n. 针刺，针孔
pioneer n. 先锋 v. 开辟，做先驱	pioneering adj. 首创的	pipe n. 管，管道	piping hot 滚热的
pirate n. 海盗	pit n. 垫子	pitch n. 高音；调子	pitfall n. 陷阱
placebo n. 安慰剂	placement n. 人员配置	plagiarise v. 抄袭	plague v. 使得灾祸
plain n. 平原	plam house 棕榈树温室	planet n. 行星	plankton n. 浮游生物
plantation n. 种植园	planting n. 栽培，种植	plasterer n. 泥水匠，石膏匠	plastic adj. 塑料的 n. 塑料
plastic money 信用卡	plate n. 碟子	plateau n. 高原	platform n. 平台
plausible adj. 貌似合理的，貌似真实的	play-face n. 滑稽表演	play-fighting n. 打斗游戏	playfulness n. 嬉闹；玩笑
playmate n. 玩伴	pleased adj. 高兴的，喜欢的	pleasurable adj. 快乐的，令人愉悦的	plentiful adj. 丰富的
plenty adj. 足够的，很多的 n. 大量；充足，足够	plenty of 许多	plight n. 困境，苦境	plot n. 阴谋
ploughs n. 犁	plug n. 插头，塞子	plunge v. 使陷入	plyometric exercise 肌肉伸缩训练
pocket-sized adj. 袖珍的	podium n. 讲台	poetry n. 诗歌	poignant adj. 强烈的

point n. 要点	point out 指出	pointless adj. 无意义的，钝的	poise v. 保持……姿势
poison n. 毒物	poisoning n. 中毒	polar adj. 极地的，正好相反的	polemic n. 论战，争论，辩论
policy n. 政策	policy-making n. 决策	polio n. 小儿麻痹症	polish v. 磨光，擦亮
political adj. 权益的	political belief 政治信仰	politician n. 政治家	pollen n. 花粉
pollock n. 鳕鱼类	pollutant n. 污染物	polluted adj. 受污染的	pollution n. 污染
polyester n. 聚酯	polyester blend 聚酯混合物	Polynesian adj. 波利尼西亚(人)的	polythene n. 聚乙烯
pooter n. 吸虫管	popular science 大众科学	popularity n. 普及，流行	populated adj. 人口集中的
population n. 人口	population control 人口控制	population explosion 人口爆炸	porcelain n. 瓷，瓷器
porpoise n. 海豚 (鼠海豚)	portable adj. 便携的，轻便的	porter n. 搬运工	portfolio n. 文件夹
portion n. 部分，一份	Portland n. 波特兰	portrait n. 肖像，描绘	portray v. 扮演；描绘
portrayal n. 描绘	pose v. 提出，造成，形成	position v. 摆放，部署	positive adj. 积极的
positively adv. 当然，肯定地	possess v. 控制；使掌握；持有；迷住；拥有，具备	possibility n. 可能性	post n. 站，哨所
postage and packing charge 邮资和包装费	postage stamps 邮票	postcard n. 明信片	poster n. 海报，广告
posting n. 岗位，职位	post-mortem n. 事后分析	postpone v. 延期，延迟，延缓	posture n. 姿势
post-war adj. 战后的	pot n. 壶，罐	potent adj. 强有力的；有效的，强力的	potential n. 可能性，潜能 adj. 潜在的，可能的

potentially adv. 可能地，潜在地	pottery n. 陶器	poultice n. 膏药状	pound n. 兽栏
pounds sterling 英镑	pour v. 倒入，灌，灌注	pour into 倒入，灌入	poverty n. 贫穷
poverty-stricken adj. 非常贫困的	power grid 电力网	power plant 发电厂	power-based adj. 基于电的
power-distribution n. 配电	practicable adj. 可用的，行得 通的	practical adj. 实际的，实用 性的	practical benefits 现实的好处
practically adv. 实际上；几乎	practice n. 方法；惯例，实践， 实习，实施规定	practice medicine 行医	practitioner n. 开业者(尤指医生， 律师等)；经常参与 猜火车的人
pragmatic adj. 实用主义的	prairie n. 大草原	praise n. 赞扬	praising n. 赞美；溢美之词
pre-arranged adj. 预先准备好的	precarious adj. 危险的；不确 定的	precaution n. 预防，警惕	precede v. 领先；在……之前
precedent n. 先例，前例	preceding adj. 先前的	precipitation n. 降水；沉淀；冰雹； 沉淀物；降雨	precise adj. 精确的；明确的； 严格的
precisely adv. 精确地；恰恰	precision n. 精确	predator n. 捕食者，食肉动物； 食肉动物；掠食者	predecessor n. 前任，前辈
predicate on 以……为基础	predict v. 预测，预知	predict creativity 预测创造力	predictable adj. 可预测的，可预 言的
predicted adj. 预料的，预测的	prediction n. 预告，预测	predominate v. 占优势，支配	pre-existing adj. 先存在的
prefer v. 宁愿，更喜欢	prefer to 更喜欢	preferably adv. 更好地	preference n. 偏好，倾向
preferential adj. 优先的，特惠的	preferred adj. 首选的	prefrontal adj. 前额的	pregnancy n. 怀孕
pregnant adj. 怀孕的	prehistoric adj. 史前的	pre-history adj. 史前的	pre-industrial adj. 工业化以前的

prejudice *n.* 成见，偏见	preliminary *adj.* 初步的，开始的， 初级的	premature *adj.* 比预期早的	premier *adj.* 第一的，最初的
premise *n.* 店面，办公地； 假定，前提	premium *n.* 额外费用	premolar *n.* 前磨牙，前臼齿	prepaid *adj.* 先付的
preparatory *adj.* 预备的	preparedness *n.* 有准备；已准备	pre-plastic *adj.* 有塑料之前的	pre-school *n.* 学前教育
prescribe *v.* 开处方，开(药)， 吩咐用(疗法)	prescribed *adj.* 规定的	prescription *n.* 药方	prescriptivism *n.* 规定主义
presence *n.* 存在；出席；参加； 风度；仪态	presentation *n.* 介绍，描述；保留， 保存；演讲	preservative *n.* 防腐剂	preserve *v.* 保存，保护
preserving *n.* 保留，保存	pre-set *adj.* 预置的，提前设 定的	pre-sleep *adj.* 睡前的	press *n.* 新闻
press release 新闻稿	pressed *adj.* 熨平的，平展的	pressing *adj.* 紧迫的	pressure *n.* 压力 *v.* 迫使
pressured *adj.* 感受压力的	prestigious *adj.* 著名的，有声 望的	presumably *adv.* 大概,推测起来; 可能；大概	presume *v.* 估计；以为
presuppose *v.* 假定；预料； 以……为先决条件	pre-tax *adj.* 税前的	pretender *n.* 冒牌者，妄提要 求者	prevail *v.* 盛行
prevail upon 说服，劝说	prevailing *adj.* 流行的；盛行很 广的；主流的	prevalence *n.* 流行；普遍；广 泛	prevalent *adj.* 普遍的；盛行的
preventable *adj.* 可预防的	preventative *adj.* 预防性的	previous *adj.* 先前的；早先的； 之前的	previously *adv.* 以前，预先

pre-war *adj.* 战前的	prey *n.* 被捕食的动物， 猎物 *v.* 捕食	price *n.* 代价	price volatility 价格波动
prim *v.* 使整洁，整齐	primal *adj.* 原始的	primarily *adv.* 主要地	primary *adj.* 主要的
primary school 小学	primary school children 小学生	prime *adj.* 主要的	Prime Minister 首相，总理
primitive *adj.* 原始的，远古的； 简单的，粗糙的	principal *adj.* 首要的，最重要 的，主要的	principally *adv.* 大部分地	principia *n.* 基本原理
principle *n.* 原理，原则	principled *adj.* 有原则的	print out （打）印出	prior *adj.* 之前的
prior to 在……之前	prioritise *v.* 给予……优先权， 按优先顺序处理	priority *n.* 优先（权）	pristine *adj.* 原始的，古时的； 纯朴的
privacy *n.* 隐私	private hire car 私家出租汽车	privately-owned *adj.* 私有的	privileged *adj.* 享有特权的
prized *adj.* 被看作重要的， 有价值的	pro *abbr.* 自由职业者 （professional）	proactive *adj.* 先行一步的；积 极主动的	probability *n.* 概率；可能性
probe *n.* 探测器，探测仪； 探针	probing *n.* 探索，探查	problem-solving *n.* 解决问题，决策 *adj.* 解决问题的	procedure *n.* 程序，步骤，手续， 过程
proceed *v.* 进行下去，继续进 行，开始，发生； 进展	proceeding *n.* 程序，诉讼	process *n.* 过程，进程 *v.* 处理；加工	processed *adj.* 处理的，加工 过的
processed meat 加工肉	processor *n.* 处理器	procurement *n.* 采购；获得，取得	prodigious *adj.* 巨大的；异常的， 惊人的
prodigy *n.* 奇才	produce *n.* 农产品	producer *n.* 生产者	productive *adj.* 富有成效的；生 产的；多产的

productivity	profession	professional	professional image
n. 产量，生产力	n. 工作（指专业技能强的工作）；职业	n. 专业人员；业内人士 adj. 专业的	职业形象，专业形象
professionalization	professionally	professor	professorship
n. 职业化	adv. 专业地，娴熟地	n. 教授	n. 教授职位
profile	profit	profitable	profound
n. 概述；轮廓，档案，属性	v. 有益于 n. 利润，利益	adj. 赚钱的，有利可图的，有益的	adj. 深厚的；意义深远的；渊博的
program	progress	progression	progressively
n. 大纲	v./n. 进步；发展	n. 连续	adv. 渐进地
prohibit	prohibitive	prohibitively	project
v. 禁止	adj. 过高的	adv. 过高地，过分地	n. 计划，项目
proliferate	proliferation	prolong	prolonged
v. 使激增	n. 增殖	v. 拉长，延长	adj. 持续很久的，旷日持久的
prominence	promise	promising	promote
n. 突出，显著	n./v. 允诺；希望	adj. 有希望的，有前途的	v. 促进，推销；提升；租金，提出
promote recreation	promoter	promotion	promotional
促进娱乐	n. 发起人	n. 促销，提升，推广	adj. 奖励的
prompt	promptly	promulgate	prone
n. 提示 adj. 及时的 v. 促进，激起，提示	adv. 迅速地；立即地；敏捷地	v. 颁布，公布	adj. 有倾向的，易于的
pronghorn	proof	proofread	prop
n. 叉角羚	n. 证据，校样，证明	v. 校对	v. 支持
propagate	propel	propeller	properly
v. 传播，传送	v. 推进，推动	n. 螺旋桨	adv. 适当地
property	proponent	proportion	proposal
n. 财产，所有物，特性，性能，品质	n. 支持者	n. 比例，部分	n. 提议，建议
propose	propylene	pro-rata	prorated
v. 提出，打算，建议	n. 丙烯	adj. 成比例的	adj. 按比例分配的
prosecute	prosecution	prospect	prospective
v. 起诉	n. 起诉	n. 前途，期望，潜在客户	adj. 未来的

prospective employer 潜在雇主	prosper v. 使成功，使繁荣	prosperity n. 繁荣	prosperous adj. 繁荣的，兴旺的
protein n. 蛋白质	prototype n. 原型；模式，模范	prototyping n. 样机研究；原型设计	protozoa n. 原生细菌
proud adj. 自豪的	proverb n. 谚语，格言	provided conj. 假如，倘若	province n. 省
provision n. 规定；条款；准备；供应品，供应	provisional adj. 临时的，暂时的	prowess n. 本领；勇猛	proxy record 代用记录
psyche n. 灵魂	psychiatrist n. 神经病学家	psychic adj. 精神的，心灵的，精神上的	psychodrama n. 心理剧疗法
psychological adj. 心理上的	psychological element 心理效应	psychologist n. 心理学家	psychology n. 心理学
psychometric adj. 心理测量的	pterodactylus n. 翼手龙属	pterosaur n. 翼龙	public order 公共秩序
public transport 公共交通，公交车	publication n. 出版物	publicise v. 宣传，公布	publicity n. 宣传
publishing n. 出版	pueblo n. 印第安人村庄	pull n. 拉力	pulley n. 滑轮
pulsate v. 搏动，震颤	pulse n. 脉搏；脉冲	pumice n. 浮石，轻石	pump v. 抽出，抽水
pump down 排空	punchline n. 笑点	punctual adj. 准时的，守时的；精确的	punctually adv. 准时地，如期地
puncture n. 穿孔，刺破 v. 削弱	pup n. 幼崽，幼兽	pupa n. 蛹	pupil n. 小学生，学生
puppet n. 木偶	purchase n./v. 购买	purchase facility 购买设备	pure cotton 纯棉
purely adv. 纯粹地	purify v. 净化	purifying n. 净化；精制	purpose n. 目的；意图

purpose-built adj. 为特殊目的建 造的	purse n. 财源	pursue v. 从事，追求；追逐	pursuing n. 追逐；追赶
pursuit n. 追赶，追求；工作 v. 追	push to the wall 把……逼上绝路	put an end to 终止，结束	put another way 换句话说
put in 提出，提交	put into effect 实施，使生效	put off 推延，阻止	put sb. off 阻止，使……失去兴 趣，使……失去勇气
puzzle v. 使迷惑 n. 谜题	pyramid n. 金字塔		

Q

quadruple v. 翻两倍，使成四倍	qualification n. 任职资格，资格， 条件，学历；素质， 先决条件	qualified adj. 有资格的，合 格的	qualify v. 达到标准，证明 合格
qualitative adj. 定性的；质的， 性质上的	quantify v. 量化，确定数量	quantum n. 量子论	quarry v. 开采
quarter n. 四分之一	quarter-century n. 二十五年	quarterly adv. 按季度	quartz-crystal adj. 石英水晶的
query n. 疑问，质问	quest n. 追求，寻找	question-and- answer adj. 问答的	questioning adj. 疑问的
questionnaires n. 调查问卷	quetzalcoatlus n. 风神翼龙	queue n. 排队	quick-service n. 特快服务
quintet n. 五重奏	quite adv. 完全	quits adj. 对等的；两相抵 消的	quota n. 限额，定额
quotation n. 引文	quote v. 引用，引述，引证； 报价		

R

radar	radiation	radical	radically
n. 雷达	n. 辐射，放射物	n. 原子团 adj. 彻底的，根本的	adv. 彻底地
radio communication 无线电通信	radio wave 无线电波	radioactivity n. 放射性，辐射能	radium n. 镭
radius n. 范围，半径	raft n. 筏	rage n. 愤怒 v. 肆虐	rail-appointed travel agent 铁路运营方指定的旅行社
railpass n. 铁路通行卡	rainfall n. 降雨量，降雨	rainforest n. 热带雨林	raise v. 种植
raised-line adj. 加线条的	random adj. 随机的，任意的	range n. 牧场	ranger n. 护林员，巡逻队
rank v. 把……排列起来 排名	rapid eye movement 快速眼动	rapidly adv. 迅速地	rare adj. 稀有的，很少的
rarely adv. 很少；难得	rat n. 老鼠	rate n. 等级，价格	rating n. 等级，评级
ratio n. 比率，比例	rational adj. 理性的	raw material 原料	razor-sharp adj. 锋利的
RDF 无线电测向机	react v. 反应	reaction n. 反应	reactivity n. 反应
readily adv. 容易地，乐意地，很快地；欣然地，无困难地	realignment n. 整改	realisation n. 实现	realism n. 现实主义
realistic adj. 现实的	realistically adv. 现实地；实际地；逼真地	realm n. 领域，范围	reap v. 收获，获得
reappear v. 再出现	rear n. 后开门 v. 培养；树立，养育	rear light 尾灯，后灯	rearing n. 饲养

reason v. 说服；推断	reasonable adj. 合理的	reasonably adv. 合理地	reasoning n. 推理，论证
rebalance n. 再平衡；调整	rebound v. 弹回，反作用	rebuilding n. 重建	recalcitrant adj. 最难解决的
recall v. 回忆，回想；记起	recede v. 后退；减弱	receipt n. 收据	receive v. 获得，收到，受到
receiver n. 接收者	reception n. 接待，接收；接 待处	receptionist n. 接待员	recipe n. 食谱
recipe book 食谱	recipient adj. 容易接受的，接 受者	reciprocal adj. 互惠的	reciprocity n. 相互作用
reckless adj. 鲁莽的，不顾后 果的	reckon v. 估计，猜想，认为	re-clad v. 再包层，重新镀	re-cladding n. 重新喷镀，重新 电镀
reclaim v. 回收利用	reclining adj. 倾斜的	recognise v. 承认，认可，认识 到，认为是，意识到	recognition n. 感知；分辨；识别； 承认，认出；重视； 赞誉；公认
recollection n. 回忆，回忆起的 事物	recommend v. 推荐，建议	recommendation n. 推荐，建议	recommended adj. 被推荐的
reconstruct v. 重建，修复	record n./v. 记录	recorded adj. 记录的	recording n. 唱片
recover v. 修复；寻找	recreation n. 娱乐，消遣	recreational adj. 娱乐的，消遣的	recruit v./n. 招聘
recruiting n. 招募	recruitment n. 招聘；招募	rectangular adj. 矩形的	rectify v. 改正
recurring adj. 循环的，重现的	recycle v. 回收；使复循环， 重新利用	recycling n. 回收；再利用	Red Cross Society 红十字会
reduce v. 减少	reduced adj. 减少的	reduction n. 减少；下降；缩小	redundant adj. 多余的，过剩的； 被解雇的
reef n. 礁	reel n. 卷；胶卷，卷轴	re-emerge v. 重新出现	reenter v. 重新进入

re-examine	refectory	refer to	reference
v. 再检查	*n.* 食堂	提及，称呼，参考；指（的是），提及	*n.* 参考 *v.* 引用
reference manual	reference number	referendum	refine
参考手册	参考号；查询号码	*n.* 全民投票，公投	*v.* 改进，改善，使完善
refinement	refining	reflect	reflect off
n. 改良	*n.* 精炼	*v.* 反应，反映	倒映
reflect on	reflection	reflective	reflex
思考	*n.* 反映，反射	*adj.* 反射的；沉思的	*n.* 反应 *v.* 反射
refract	refrain	refreeze	refreshed
v. 使（光线）折射	*n.* 重复	*v.* 再冻结	*adj.* 恢复精神的
refreshment	refund	refundable	refurbishment
n. 点心	*n./v.* 退款，偿还	*adj.* 可退还的	*n.* 整修
refute	regard	regarding	regardless of
v. 反驳	*v.* 与……有关 *n.* 注意	*prep.* 关于	不管，不顾
regenerate	regeneration	regime	regimen
v. 再生	*n.* 再生，重建；重获新生	*n.* 体制，模式	*n.* 养生法，生活规则
regional	regional cohesion	register	registered
adj. 区域的	区域凝聚力	*v.* 记录；注册	*adj.* 注册的，登记过的
registration	registry	regret	regrettable
n. 登记，注册	*n.* 注册	*v.* 感到抱歉	*adj.* 令人遗憾的；可惜的；可悲的；抱歉的
regular	regularly	regulate	regulation
adj. 正式的	*adv.* 按计划地，定期地	*v.* 校准	*n.* 校准，规则，管理；规定
regurgitate	rehabilitation	rehearsal	rehearse
v. 反刍	*n.* 复原	*n.* 排练	*v.* 排练，预演
reign	reinforce	reinforced	reinforcement
n. 统治	*n.* 加固；加强	*adj.* 加强的，加固的，强化的	*n.* 加固，加强

reintroduce	reinvigorate	reiterate	reject
v. 再引入	*v.* 使复兴	*v.* 重申，反复地做	*v.* 抵制，拒绝，排斥，丢弃
rekindle	relate	relate to	related
v. 重新点燃，复燃	*v.* 涉及，有关；提到	与……相关	*adj.* 相关的
related field	relative	relatively	relaunch
相关领域	*adj.* 相对的 *n.* 亲属	*adv.* 相当地；相对地，比较地	*v.* 重新启动
relaxation	release	relentless	relevance
n. 放松，休息	*n.* 发布，提出 *v.* 释放	*adj.* 残酷的；不间断的	*n.* 关联性；相关
relevant	reliable	reliance	relic
adj. 相关的	*adj.* 可靠的，可信任的	*n.* 信赖，依靠	*n.* 遗迹，废墟
relief	religious observance	relish	relive
n. 减轻	宗教活动	*v.* 喜爱	*v.* 再生
relocate	reluctant	rely on	remaining
v. 重新安置	*adj.* 不情愿的；勉强的；顽抗的	依靠，依赖	*adj.* 剩余的
remains	remark	remark on	remarkable
n. 遗骸，残余	*v.* 评论	评论	*adj.* 不同寻常的；卓越的；出色的，非凡的
remarkably	remedial	remedy	remnant
adv. 非常地；显著地	*adj.* 治疗的	*n.* 药品，治疗法，补救，治疗	*n.* 剩余
remote	removal	remove	remuneration
adj. 偏僻的，遥远的	*n.* 挪用，移动，免职；移除，排除	*v.* 消除，移除	*n.* 报酬，酬劳
renaissance	render	rendering	rendition
n. 新生，再生；文艺复兴	*v.* 提出；描绘；放弃；报答；归还；宣布	*n.* 呈现	*n.* 解释；表演
renew	renewable	renewed	renowned
v. 复兴，使更新	*adj.* 可再生的	*adj.* 复兴的	*adj.* 著名的，有声望的

rent	rental	renting	rep
n. 租金	*n.* 租金	*n.* 出租	*abbr.* 代表
repair	repairing	repatriate	repatriation
n. 修理，恢复	*n.* 修复	*v.* 遣返，带回	*n.* 遣送回国
repeat	repeatedly	repel	repertoire
v. 重复	*adv.* 反复地	*v.* 击退	*n.* 全部才能；全部节目
repetition	repetitively	replace	replacement
n. 背诵，反复	*adv.* 重复地	*v.* 代替，替换	*n.* 代替
replenish	replenishment	replicate	replication
v. 补充，再填满，充注精力，再装满	*n.* 补充	*v.* 复制	*n.* 复制；回答；反响
reply to	report	report on	repository
回答，回复	*v.* 报道	就……作报告	*n.* 贮藏室，仓库；知识库；智囊团
represent	representation	representational	representative
v. 代表，表示，象征	*n.* 表现	*adj.* 具象派的	*n.* 代表
reprieve	reprint	reproduce	reproduction
v. 缓解，舒缓	*n.* 重印，翻版	*v.* 繁殖	*n.* 繁殖
reproductions	reptile	reputable	reputation
n. 复制品	*n.* 爬行动物	*adj.* 声誉好的	*n.* 名誉，声望
request	require	required	requirement
n./v. 请求，需要	*v.* 需要，要求	*adj.* 必需的，要求的	*n.* 需求；要求；必要条件
reroute	research	research paper	researcher
v. 重新定航线	*n.* 研究	研究报告	*n.* 研究员
resemble	resembling	reservation	reservation staff
v. 相似，像，类似于	*n.* 类似的	*n.* 预约；保留，居留地	票位预订员
reserve	reservoir	reshape	residence
n. 保留，储备 *v.* 储备，保留	*n.* 水库；蓄水池	*v.* 重新塑造	*n.* 住处
resident	residential	resilience	resilient
n. 居民	*adj.* 住宅的	*n.* 恢复力，顺应力	*adj.* 有弹性的（强适应性的）

resin n. 树脂	resist v. 抵制	resistance n. 抵抗力	resistant adj. 抵抗的，反抗的 n. 抵抗（能力）
resisted adj. 受到抵抗的	resoluteness n. 决心	resolve v. 解决	resonance n. 共振，共鸣
resonate v. 共鸣；共振	resort n. 度假村；度假胜地， 方法，凭借，手段	resort management 度假村管理	resource n. 资源
resourcefulness n. 足智多谋	respect n. 方面	respectively adv. 分别地，各自地	respiratory adj. 呼吸的
respite n. 缓解	respond to 作出反应	respondent n. 应答者	response n. 反应
responsibilities n. 责任，职责	responsibility n. 责任，义务	responsiveness n. 响应性，反应性	respray n. 重喷，重新喷漆
rest-and-repair theory 休息和修复理论	restoration n. 恢复；复位	restore v. 修复，恢复	restrict v. 限制
restricted adj. 保密的，有限的， 受限制的	restricting n. 整形，限制	restriction n. 限制	restrictively adv. 限制（性）地， 约束（性）地
result v. 产生	resulting adj. 作为结果的	retail n. 零售	retain v. 保持，记住
retard v. 阻止，延迟	retention n. 保留	rethink v. 反思	reticence n. 沉默寡言
retirement n. 退休	retreat n. 休息寓所	retrenchment n. 删除，修剪	retune v. 重新调整
returning adj. 返回的	revamped adj. 修订的；修补的	reveal v. 透露；显露；揭秘； 反映，展示；揭露； 发现	revelation n. 被揭露的真相； 出乎意料的事
revenue n. 收益	Revenue and Customs 税务及海关总署	reverberation n. 回声，回响	reverse n. 倒退 v. 扭转；逆转，反转
revert v. 使恢复原状	review n. 回顾；评论；审查， 审核	revise v. 修正	revision n. 修正

revitalise v. 使有新的活力	revival n. 复兴，苏醒	revive v. 使复苏，恢复	revolution n. 旋转
revolutionary adj. 革命的，革新的； 革命性的	revolutionise v. 变革；使发生革命 性改变	revolutionised adj. 革命化的；被彻 底改革的	revolve v. 循环
revulsion n. 厌恶，强烈反感	reward n. 报酬；奖金	rhesus n. 恒河猴	rhythm n. 节奏，韵律
rhythmic adj. 有节奏的，间 隙的	ribbon n. 带状	ribcage n. 胸腔	rice field 稻田
Richmond n. 里士满	rickety adj. 摇晃的，快散 架的	rift v. 使断裂，使分开	rig v. 操纵，装配
rigging n. 索具；装备，传 动装置	right n. 权利	right brain 右脑	rigid adj. 严格的
rigorous adj. 严密的	rigours n. 严格，严厉，苛刻	rim n. 边，边缘	ring of fire 太平洋火圈，火山带
ripen v. 成熟	ripple n. 波纹	rips abbr. 放射性同位素 电源	risk n. 风险
ritual n. 仪式	rival v. 竞争，与……相匹 敌，对手，比得上	river bed 河床	River Nile 尼罗河
River Severn 塞文河	riverbank n. 河岸	roam v. 流浪，漫游	roaring adj. 轰鸣的
robbery n. 抢劫	robust adj. 强健的；健康的； 稳固的；强壮的，结 实的	rocket n. 火箭	rodent n. 啮齿动物
role n. 角色	roll v. 滚动	roll in 滚滚而来，大量涌来	roller n. 滚子
Roman n. 罗马	Roman Empire 罗马帝国	roof n. 屋顶	rooftop adj. 屋顶上的

room	root	rope	rotate
n. 空间	n. 根	n. 绳索	v. 使转动，旋转
rotten	roughly	round	round up
adj. 腐烂的	adv. 大约，概略地	adj. 圆形的	使成整数
route	routine	routinely	rower
n. 线路	adj. 日常的，例行的	adv. 例行地，惯常地	n. 桨手
royal	royalty	rub	rubber
adj. 皇家的	n. 皇族	v. 摩擦	n. 橡胶
rubbish	rudimentary	ruin	ruined
n. 垃圾	adj. 未充分发展的，初步的，基本的	v. 毁灭	adj. 毁灭的
rumour	run out	run up	runny
v./n. 谣言，传闻	耗尽，用完	积欠	adj. 松软的，流动的
run-off	rural	rural business management	rushed
n. 利用；溢流	adj. 农村的，乡下的，乡村的	农村经济管理	adj. 匆忙的

S

sabbatical	sack	sacrifice	safari
n. 休假	n. 麻布袋	v. 牺牲；奉献	n. 游猎
safeguard	Safety Department	sagebrush	sail
v. 保护	安全部门	n. 蒿丛	n. 帆，篷 v. 航行
sail through	sailor	sailplane	salamander
顺利完成	n. 水手	n. 滑翔机	n. 蝾螈
salary	salary pension scheme	sale representative	sales manager
n. 薪水	薪酬抚恤金计划	销售代表	销售经理
salespeople	salient	saliva	salmon
n. 推销员，销售员	adj. 最重要的	n. 唾液	n. 鲑鱼
salon	salt pans	salute	salvage
n. 画廊，美术展览馆	盐田	v. 欢迎，致敬	n. 抢救，营救 v. 打捞

Salvinia molesta 槐萍	Samba n. 桑巴舞	sample n. 例子，样本，样品 adj. 试样的 v. 取样，尝试，抽样 调查，品尝	sampling n. 取样
sanction n. 处罚	sand n. 沙土	sand grain 沙粒	sandals n. 凉鞋；便鞋
sandpiper n. 鹬	sanitation n. 环境卫生；卫生 设备；下水道设施	sank v. 沉陷	sap n. 树液
sapling n. 树苗	satellite n. 卫星；人造卫星	satisfactorily adv. 令人满意地	satisfactory adj. 令人满意的
satisfy v. 令人满意	saturated arteries 饱和动脉	sauce n. 酱油	sausage n. 香肠，腊肠
saver n. 救助者	saving n. 节约	savings n. 储蓄，存款	sawdust n. 锯屑，锯末
scaffold n. 脚手架	scale n. 比例，范围，规模， 尺寸	scale-model n. 比例模块	scamper v. 蹦蹦跳跳，惊慌奔 跑
scan v. 浏览，扫描	Scandinavia n. 斯堪的纳维亚	scanned adj. 已扫描的	scanner n. 扫描仪
scarce adj. 缺乏的，不足的	scarcely adv. 几乎不	scare v. 使惊恐，使害怕	scarf n. 围巾
scary adj. 害怕的	scatter v. 分散	scattered adj. 分散的	scenario n. 方案；剧本，情节， 情景
scene n. 场景	scenic n. 风景胜地 adj. 风景优美的	scent n. 气味	sceptic n. 怀疑论者
sceptical adj. 怀疑的	scepticism n. 怀疑；怀疑论； 怀疑主义	sceptics n. 怀疑论者	schedule n. 时间表，计划表
scheduled adj. 预定的	scheme n. 方案，计划	schizophrenia n. 精神分裂症	scholar n. 学者
scholarly adj. 博学的	scholarship n. 奖学金	school v. 教育	schoolchildren n. 小学生

schoolmate	science-fiction	scientific community	scientific revolution
n. 同学	*n.* 科幻小说	科学界	科技革命
scoop	scope	scope creep	scorch
v. 挖掘	*n.* 范围；视野	范围蔓延（指产品等在开发过程中超出计划目标的倾向）	*v.* 使烧焦
score	scour	scout bee	scrambling
v. 得分，记分，分数，评价，成绩	*v.* 冲刷；侦查；冲洗；清除	侦察蜂	*v.* 争夺
scrap	scrapped	scratch	scrawny
v. 取消，放弃	*adj.* 报废的	*v.* 抓	*n.* 小树木
scream	screen	screen out	scrupulous
n./v. 尖叫	*v.* 拍摄；筛	筛选出	*adj.* 一丝不苟的，小心谨慎的
scrutinize	scrutiny	scuffle	sculpture
v. 详细检查，仔细钻研	*n.* 详细审查，监视，细看，仔细审查	*n.* 混战，扭打	*n.* 雕塑
seabed	seabird	seafarer	seafaring
n. 海底，海床	*n.* 海鸟	*n.* 船员	*adj.* 航海的
seal	sealed	searchlight	seasonal
n. 海豹，海狮 *v.* 密封	*adj.* 密封的；未知的	*n.* 探照灯	*adj.* 季节的
seasonality	seaweed	second-hand	secrecy
n. 季节性	*n.* 海藻，海草	*adj.* 二手的	*n.* 秘密
secretary	secretion	section	sector
n. 秘书，文秘	*n.* 分泌物	*n.* 截面，部门	*n.* 部门
secure	security	sediment	sediment-free
adj. 安全的 *v.* 保卫；获得，获取	*n.* 安全，保证，保安部门	*n.* 沉积物	*adj.* 无泥沙的
seed	seed-eating	seed-feeding	seedling
v. 播种（制造）	*adj.* 食种子的	*adj.* 以草种为食的	*n.* 幼苗
seek	seeming	seesaw	segment
v. 寻求，追求，寻找	*adj.* 表面上的	*n.* 跷跷板	*n.* 片段；段数；部分
seize	seldom	selected	selection
v. 抓住；夺取	*adv.* 很少，不常	*adj.* 挑出来的	*n.* 精选品，选择，挑选

selective	selective attention	self assessment	self-catering
adj. 选择性的	选择性注意力	自我评价	*adj.* 自供伙食的
self-conscious	self-determining	self-dispersing	self-drive
adj. 自觉的，自我意识清醒的	*adj.* 自己决定的	*adj.* 自行驱散的	*adj.* 租车自己驾驶的
self-esteem	self-evident	self-help	self-interested
n. 自尊	*adj.* 不言而喻的，不证自明的	*adj.* 自救的	*adj.* 自私的，利己主义的
selfless	self-observation	self-regulation	self-reliance
adj. 无私的	*n.* 自我观察，自我审查	*n.* 自动调节	*n.* 自力更生，依靠自己；自恃
self-reliant	self-sacrifice	self-sufficient	semantic
adj. 自力更生的；自恃的	*n.* 自我牺牲	*adj.* 自给自足的	*adj.* 语义的
semi-arid deserts	semi-automatic	semi-circle	semi-circular
半干旱的沙漠地带	*adj.* 半自动的	*adj.* 半圆的	*adj.* 半圆形的
semi-molten	seminar	semi-permanent	semi-synthetic
adj. 半熔化的	*n.* 研讨会；专题讨论会	*adj.* 半永久的	*adj.* 半合成的
sender	senior	senior citizen	sensation
n. 发出者，发送人	*adj.* 年长的，级别较高的	老年人，年长者	*n.* 感觉
sense of triumph	sensible	sensitive	sensitivity
成就感	*adj.* 明智的，通情达理的	*adj.* 敏感的，灵敏的；易受伤的	*n.* 敏感；敏感性；过敏
sensor	sensory	separated	sequence
n. 传感器	*adj.* 感觉的，知觉的	*adj.* 分开的	*n.* 顺序
sequential	serendipity	serial	seriously
adj. 有顺序的；连续的	*n.* 意外发现珍奇事物的本领；有意外发现珍宝的运气	*adj.* 连续的，连载的 *n.* 电视连续剧	*adv.* 真正地
serpentine	serration	serve	session
adj. 蜿蜒的；阴险的；弯弯曲曲的	*n.* 锯齿状	*v.* 可作⋯⋯用	*n.* 会话，会议，讲习会，时间；学期，学年

set	set a new world record	set aside	set off
n. 一套 *v.* 设置（问题）	创下新的世界纪录	留出	出发，动身
set out	set up	setting	settle
摆放，陈述，开始	建立	*n.* 布置，背景，环境	*v.* 定居，稳定，解决
settlement	settler	set-up	severe
n. 居住地；定居	*n.* 移居者；殖民者	*n.* 计划，安排	*adj.* 严峻的，严重的，苛刻的
severe limitation	severely	severity	sewage
严重缺陷	*adv.* 严重地；严格地	*n.* 严重，严重性	*n.* 下水道
sewer	shade	shade-intolerant	shade-tolerant
n. 下水道，阴沟	*n.* 少量，细微差别，阴暗	*adj.* 不耐阴的	*adj.* 耐阴的
shadow	shallow	shape	shard
n. 阴影	*adj.* 浅的	*n.* 形状	*n.* 碎片
shareholder	sharpen	shatter	shed
n. 股东	*v.* 加强	*v.* 碎裂，使粉碎	*v.* 阐释；脱落
shed new light on	sheer	shell	shellfish
为……提供更多线索	*n.* 偏航；透明薄织物 *adj.* 绝对的	*n.* 壳，空壳	*n.* 甲壳类动物
shelter	sheltered	shelves	Sherpa
n. 庇护	*adj.* 受保护的；掩蔽的	*n.* 架子	*n.* 夏尔巴人
shield	shift	shilling	shipment
n. 盾	*n./v.* 变化，改变	*n.* 先令	*n.* 运输
shipping	shock	shock absorber	shopping centre
n. 装运，运送	*n.* 震惊；危机（震动）	减震器	购物中心
short play	shortcut	short-day	short-lived
短剧	*n.* 捷径，近路	*adj.* 短日照的	*adj.* 短命的
shove	shovel	showcase	shower
v. 强使	*v.* 用铲子铲，用勺子舀	*n.* 玻璃柜台，玻璃陈列柜	*n.* 淋浴
shrine	shrink	shrinking	shriveled
n. 圣祠	*v.* 使缩小，使萎缩；收缩；畏缩	*adj.* 缩水的	*adj.* 皱缩的

shrub	shrunk	shudder	shun
n. 灌木	*v.* 减少；收缩，起皱	*n.* 发抖	*v.* 避开，回避
shutdown	shuttle bus	Siberia	sick leave
n. 停工	班车	*n.* 西伯利亚	病假
sickle	sickle-shaped	sickness	side by side
n. 镰刀	*adj.* 镰刀形的	*n.* 生病，疾病	并肩
side-effect	side-on	sideways	siege
n. 副作用	*adj.* 侧面的	*adj.* 向侧面的	*n.* 围攻
sift	sigh	sighted	sight-read
v. 过滤，筛选	*v.* 叹息	*adj.* 看得见的	*v.* 即兴演奏；即兴朗读
sign	sign up for	signal	signature
v. 签署，签名	注册；选课	*n.* 信号	*n.* 签名，签署
significance	significant	significantly	signify
n. 意义，重要性	*adj.* 重大的，有意义的	*adv.* 显著地，值得注目地	*v.* 表示；意味
silhouette	silk	silk yarn	silkworms
n. 轮廓	*adj.* 丝绸的	丝线	*n.* 蚕
silly	silt	Silva mind-control	silver
adj. 愚蠢的	*v.* 使淤塞；充塞 *n.* 泥沙	西瓦心灵术，控制法	*n.* 银
similarity	similarly	simplicity	simplistic
n. 类似，相似点	*adv.* 同样地	*n.* 简单	*adj.* 简单的
simulate	simulation	simultaneous	simultaneously
v. 假装；模拟	*n.* 仿真，模拟，模仿，仿真实验	*adj.* 同时的	*adv.* 同时地
Singapore	single event	single-handed	single-mindedness
n. 新加坡	单一事件	*adv.* 单独地，独力地	*n.* 专心；忠贞
single-parent	sink in	sipping	siren
adj. 单亲的	渗入，使完全理解	*v.* 小口啜饮	*n.* 汽笛
Sirius	site	situate	six-digit
n. 天狼星	*n.* 地点，场所	*v.* 使位于；使处于；位于	*adj.* 六位数字的
sizeable	skepticism	sketch	ski resort
adj. 相当大的	*n.* 怀疑	*n.* 梗概，素描，略图 *v.* 大致勾勒	滑雪胜地

skiing *n.* 滑雪运动	skim *v.* 略读	skirt *v.* 绕过	ski-slope *n.* 积雪的斜坡
skydiver *n.* 跳伞运动员	Skye *n.* 斯凯岛	skylark *n.* 云雀	sky-rocketing *adj.* 飞涨的
skyscraper *n.* 摩天大楼	slam *v.* 猛击	slapstick *n.* 低俗的闹剧	slaughter *v.* 屠杀
slave *n.* 奴隶	slave traders 奴商	sled *n.* 雪橇	sledge *n.* 雪橇
sleek *adj.* 圆滑的	sleep disorder 失眠	sleeper *n.* 卧车	sleep-walking *n.* 梦游
slender *adj.* 细长的	slice *v.* 切掉，减掉，划破	slide *v.* 滑动，滑落	slight shock 轻微的震动
slightly *adv.* 轻微地	slippery *adj.* 滑的	slit *n.* 狭长的口子，细长的缝	slither *n.* 滑动
slogan *n.* 标语	slop *v.* 溢出，使溅出	sloping side 斜边	slot *n.* 狭槽，槽（空隙）
slow-moving *adj.* 流动缓慢的	sludge *n.* 沉淀物；泥浆，烂泥	slurping *adj.* 发出响声的，巨响的	smallholder *n.* 小农
small-scale *adj.* 小规模的	smartcard *n.* 智能卡	smear *v.* 将……弄模糊，弄脏	smog *n.* 雾霾
smooth *adj.* 平滑的，光滑的	smuggled *v.* 走私，偷运	snack *n.* 小吃，快餐	snail *n.* 蜗牛
snakebite *n.* 蛇咬伤	snap *v.* 突然出现	snapshot *n.* 快照	sneezes *n.* 喷嚏
sniff *v.* 嗅，闻	snorkeller *n.* 浮潜的人	snowmobile *n.* 雪车，机动雪橇	so as to 以便……
soaked into 渗入	soapy *adj.* 涂有肥皂的	soar *v.* 高涨，激增，升高到；高飞，飞腾，急速上升	soaring *adj.* 激增的，猛增的
social safety nets 社会保障	socialise *v.* 使社会化	society *n.* 社团	socio-biologist *n.* 社会生物学家

sociobiology *n.* 社会生物学	socio-economic *adj.* 社会经济的	sock *n.* 短袜	sockeye *n.* 红鲑
soda ash 碳酸钠	soft drink 软饮料，不含酒精的饮料	soft foam 软质泡沫	soft furnishing 室内家装，室内装潢
soft-boiled *adj.* 半熟的	soften *v.* 使变柔软	soil imbalance 土壤失衡	solar day 太阳日
solar energy 太阳能	solar year 太阳年	sole *n.* 鳎目鱼 *adj.* 单独的，唯一的	solely *adv.* 单独地，唯一地
solemnly *adv.* 严肃地	solicitor *n.* 律师	solid *adj.* 可靠的	solid science 坚实的科学
solidify *v.* 凝固	soluble *adj.* 可溶的	solution *n.* 解决方法，答案	somatotropin *n.* 生长激素
somehow *adv.* 以某种方式	sonar *n.* 声呐	song-like *adj.* 像歌曲的	sophisticated *adj.* 复杂的，富有经验的，久经世事的
sophistication *n.* 复杂；老于世故	sore throat 咽喉痛	sorrow *n.* 悲伤	sort *n.* 种类，方式
sort out 解决	sought *v.* 寻找	sought-for *adj.* 寻求的	sound *adj.* 合理的，有效的，可靠的
sound effects 音效	sound track 音轨	soup *n.* 汤	Soviet Union 苏联
space *v.* 隔开	spacecraft *n.* 宇宙飞船，航天器	spacious *adj.* 宽敞的	spade *n.* 铁锹，铲子
spam *n.* 垃圾邮件	span *n.* 跨度，跨距，范围 *v.* 跨越	spare *n.* 备用零件；备用品 *v.* 节省，出让	spare land 空地
sparing *adj.* 节约的	spark *n.* 火光，痕迹 *v.* 鼓舞，激起，引起	spawn *v.* 产卵	spawner *n.* 已成熟的雌鱼
spear *n.* 矛	special *n.* 特价商品 *adj.* 特殊的	specialise in 主营，专营	specialised *adj.* 专业的

specialist n. 专家 adj. 专业的，专门的	species n. 物种	specific adj. 明确的; 特殊的; 具体的	specifically adv. 特别地
specification n. 规格，说明书， 说明	specify v. 指定	specimen n. 样本，样品	speckled adj. 有斑点花纹的
spectacle n. 奇观，壮观，景象	spectacular adj. 壮观的，惊人的	spectacular cliffs 壮观的悬崖	spectacularly adv. 壮观地，程度 大地
spectator n. 旁观者	spectrum n. 频谱，光谱，谱; 范围，幅度	speculate v. 推测	speculation n. 思索，推测
speculator n. 投机者	speech recognition 语音识别	spellbound adj. 着迷的	sphere n. 范围
spider n. 蜘蛛	spin v. 旋转，（使）旋转	spine n. 脊柱，脊椎; 刺	spiny adj. 多刺的
spiraling adj. 螺旋形的	spit v. 吐出	splashed v. 泼	splendor n. 壮丽，显赫
split v. 使分开，分裂	splutters n. 噼啪声	spoil v. 破坏	spoke n.（车轮上的）辐条
spokesman n. 发言人	sponge n. 海绵	sponsor n. 赞助者	sponsorship n. 资助，支持
spontaneous adj. 自发的; 自然的; 无意识的	spoon-billed adj. 勺嘴型的	spoon-feeding v. 用匙喂; 溺爱; 填 鸭式教育	sports science 运动科学，体育科学
spot n. 斑点，地点 v. 认出; 看到	spotted adj. 有斑点的	spouse n. 配偶	sprang v. 跳跃
sprawl n. 城市无计划扩张 v. 蔓延，延伸; 伸开	spray n. 喷雾	spraying n. 喷雾，喷洒	spread v. 传播
spreadsheet n. 电子数据表	spring n. 弹簧，泉水 v. 弹起	spring a leak 出现漏缝	spring back 回弹
spring flood 春汛，春洪	spring from 起源于，发源 (于)……; 来自……	spring to life 突然活跃起来	spring to mind 使人突然想起

sprint *n.* 冲刺，短跑	sprinter *n.* 短跑选手	sprout hind 发芽后	squad *n.* 小队；小组
square *adj.* 正方形的	squash *n.* 壁球 *v.* 挤压	squashy *adj.* 熟透的	squeak *n.* 吱吱声
squeeze *v.* 压榨，榨取	squirrel *n.* 松鼠	squishy *adj.* 湿软的，黏糊 糊的	stabilise *v.* 使……坚固； 使……安定
stability *n.* 稳定性	stable *adj.* 稳定的	stable atmosphere 稳定的大气	stack *v.* 堆积，堆叠
stacked *adj.* 堆叠的	staff *n.* 员工，职员	staffing *n.* 安置职工，人事	stage drama 舞台戏剧
staggering *adj.* 令人惊愕的	stain *v.* 给……染色，着色	staircase *n.* 楼梯	stakeholders *n.* 利益相关者
stall *n.* 货摊	stamina *n.* 毅力；精力；活力； 持久力	stamp *v.* 盖章，盖戳	stand back 退后，不介入
standard *n.* 标准	standard class 标准舱	standard committee 标准委员会	standardise *v.* 使……标准化
standardised *adj.* 标准化的	standby *adj.* 备用的	standing *n.* 身份	stare *v.* 凝视，注视
starkly *adv.* 严酷地；明显地	start off 开始	start up 开始，发动	starting point 起点
startling *adj.* 令人吃惊的	starve *v.* 挨饿	state benefit 政府补助金	state *n.* 州
state forest 国家森林	stated budget 规定的预算费	statehood *n.* 国家层面	statement *n.* 说法，陈述
statewide *adj.* 遍及全州的	static *adj.* 静态的	station *v.* 安置	stationary *adj.* 固定的
stationer *n.* 文具店	stationery *n.* 文具	statistical *adj.* 统计的；统计 学的	statistics *n.* 统计
statues *n.* 雕像	status *n.* 地位；状态；情形； 重要身份	statutory *adj.* 法定的	steadily *adv.* 稳定地

steak	stealing	steam	steel
n. 牛排，鱼排	n. 偷盗	n. 精力，蒸汽	n. 钢铁
steel-making	steep	steer	steer clear of
n. 炼钢	adj. 急剧上升的	v. 控制，引导	绕开，避开
steering	stem	stem from	Stephen Spielberg
n. 操纵，掌舵	n. 干，茎	起源于	史蒂芬·斯皮尔伯格
stereoscopic	sterilisable	steward	Stewart
adj. 立体的	adj. 杀菌的	n. 管家，管理员	n. 斯图尔特（男子名）
stick to	sticky	stifled	still
坚持	adj. 黏性的	v. 扼杀	adj. 静止的
still life	still-life	stilted	stimulate
静物	adj. 静物的	adj. 生硬的，死板的	v. 促进，刺激，激励，鼓励
stimulation	stimulus	sting	stir
n. 刺激；鼓励	n. 刺激，刺激物，促进因素（复数形式为 stimuli）	v. 刺痛，蛰 n. 蛰伤	v. 搅拌，激起
stitch	stock	Stockholm	stock-raising
n. 线迹	n. 贮备，库存；股票；存货	n. 斯德哥尔摩（瑞典城市）	n. 家畜饲养
stock-trading	stoke	stomach	stone column
adj. 股票交易的	v. 烧火	n. 胃，腹部	石柱
storage	storage facility	store	stored
n. 存储；仓库；贮藏所	存储设施	v. 储存；容纳	adj. 储存的
storey	storm drain	stormy	story-telling
n. 楼层；叠架的一层	雨水沟，雨水道	adj. 多风暴的	adj. 讲故事的
strain	stranded	stranglehold	strap
n. 血缘，品种，负担 v. 滥用	adj. 搁浅的；滞留的	n. 束缚	v. 捆绑，捆扎
strategy	stratosphere	stray	stream
adj. 战略，策略 n. 策略	n. 同温层，最上层；平流层	adj. 迷路的；离群的 v. 偏离正题	n. 一连串；水流
streamlined	streamside	Street Business Partnership	Street Kids International (SKI)
adj. 改进的	n. 河边地带	街头的业务伙伴关系	国际街童组织

street sign 路标	strength n. 力量	stretch n. 伸展，延伸；一片	stretch back 追溯
stretched v. 绵延	strict adj. 严格的	stride n. 进展，大步	strike v. 打击,冲击,使…… 惊讶，打劫
strike a dumb 哑口无言	striking adj. 令人震惊的; 显著 的，惊人的，突出的	string n. 线，细绳	strip v. 剥
stroke n. 划水，中风 v. 抚摸；划桨	stroke frequency 划频	stroke length 行程长度	struck v. 弹响
structural adj. 建筑的，结构的	structure n. 结构，构造	struggle n. 奋斗 v. 努力；挣扎	struggler n. 奋斗者，有困难 的人
stubby adj. 粗短的	Student Representative Council (SRC) 学生代表委员会	studio n. 电影制片厂；演 播室	studio camera 摄影棚用摄影机
studious adj. 不遗余力的	stuff n. 东西	stuffy nose 鼻塞	stumble upon 偶然发现
stumbling adj. 障碍的	stun v. 使震惊；给以深刻 的印象	stunned adj. 惊愕的，受惊的	stunning adj. 极好的； 令人 震惊的
stuntman n. 特技表演者	styrofoam n. 泡沫聚苯乙烯	subatomic adj. 亚原子的	subcategory n. 分支
subconsciously adv. 潜意识地	sub-cortical adj. 分皮质的	sub-discipline n. 分支学科	subdivide v. 把……细分
subgroup n. 子群	sub-human n. 非人性	subject n. 实验对象 v. 受……影响	subject to 取决于，依赖于
submarine n. 潜艇	submerge v. 淹没	sub-millimetre n. 亚毫米	submission n. 让步；屈从
submit v. 服从；提交	subscription n. 签署	subsequent adj. 后来的，随后的	subsequently adv. 接下来

subsidiary	subsidise	subsidised	subsidy
n. 子公司，附属公司 *adj.* 辅助的	*v.* 资助，给……补助金	*adj.* 资助的	*n.* 补贴，津贴；补助金
subsistence *n.* 生存，存在	subspecies *n.* 亚种	substance *n.* 物质，材料	substantial *adj.* 大量的；实质的 *n.* 本质
substantially *adv.* 实质上，大体上；相当，可观地	substitute *n.* 代替品；代替者，替补，替代 *adj.* 代替的	substitution *n.* 替换，代替	subtle *adj.* 微妙的
subtlety *n.* 微妙	subtropical *adj.* 亚热带的	suburb *n.* 郊区	successive *adj.* 接连的，连续的
succinctly *adv.* 简洁地；简便地	suck *v.* 吸吮	suckling *adj.* 尚未断奶的，哺乳的	suction *n.* 吸，吸力
suffice *v.* 足够	sufficient *adj.* 足够的；充分的	sufficiently *adv.* 充分地，足够地；充足地	sugar cane 甘蔗
suggestion *n.* 暗示	suggestopedia *n.* 暗示感应教学法	suicide *n.* 自杀	suit *v.* 适合
suit to 适合于	suitable *adj.* 适当的	suitable for 适合于	suitcase *n.* 手提箱
sulphur *n.* 硫	sulphur dioxide 二氧化硫	sum *n.* 金额，总和	sumac *n.* 漆树；漆树木料
summarise *v.* 总结，概括	sun-baked *adj.* 晒干的，日晒的	Sunda Straits 巽他海峡	sundial *n.* 日晷
sunlight *n.* 阳光	sunlight-refracting *adj.* 太阳光折射的	sunny *adj.* 晴朗的	sunset *n.* 日落，傍晚
sunshade *n.* 太阳光遮光板	superb *adj.* 华丽的；极好的	superbug *n.* 超级病菌	supercolony *n.* 巨大巢穴
superficially *adv.* 表面地；浅薄地；肤浅地	superior *adj.* 较高的，较好的，优先的；出众的；更好的	superiority *n.* 优越，优势；优越性	superiors *n.* 上级
supernatural *adj.* 超自然的	super-real 超真实	supersede *v.* 取代，代替	super-sniffer *n.* 超级嗅探

super-viruses n. 超级病毒	supervised adj. 有监督的	supervision n. 监督，管理	supervisor n. 监督人，监督者， 监管者
supplement n. 补充物 v. 补充	supplementary adj. 补充的，追加的	supplier n. 供应商	supply n. 供给 v. 提供
supply ship 供应船	supporter n. 支持者	supporting adj. 辅助性的	supportive adj. 支持的
suppose v. 假设，认为	supposed adj. 假定的	supposedly adv. 可能	suppress v. 抑制，镇压
supremacy n. 至高无上，很高 的地位	supremely adv. 非常	surface n. 表面	surge n.巨涌，涌动的气流， 激增；汹涌澎湃
surgery n. 手术	surpass v. 超越，超过	surprising adj. 令人惊讶的	surrender v. 放弃
Surrey University 瑟瑞大学	surrounding n. 环境 adj. 周围的	surveillance n. 监视，监督	survey n. 调查 v. 调查，研究
surveyor n. 测量员，检测员	survival n. 幸存；生存	survive v. 存活	survivor n. 幸存者
susceptible adj. 易受影响的	suspect v. 怀疑，猜想	suspend v. 吊，悬挂	suspense n. 悬疑，悬念
suspenseful adj. 悬而未决的	suspension n. 暂停，悬挂	sustain v. 承担，维持	sustainability n. 持续性；永续性； 能维持性；可持续发 展性
sustainable adj. 可持续的，可持 续发展的	sustainable development 可持续发展	sustained attention 持久性注意力	sustaining adj. 持续的
sustenance n. 生机	swamp n. 湿地 v. 使沉没	swan n. 天鹅	swap v. 交换，交易
sway v. 摇动，摇摆	sweating n. 发汗	Swedish adj. 瑞典的	sweep v. 席卷；扫荡
sweep up 清扫，清理	swiftly adv. 迅速地，敏捷地	swing v. 摆动，摇摆，摇晃	swing into action 立刻行动起来

switch *n.* 按钮 *v.* 转变，转换	swivel *v.* 旋转	symbol *n.* 标志，象征	symbolism *n.* 象征，符号化
sympathetic *adj.* 同情的	sympathy *n.* 同情（心），慰问； 共鸣	symphony *n.* 交响乐	symptoms *n.* 症状，征兆
synchronize *v.* 同时发生	synchronous sound 同步音效	syndrome *n.* 综合征；综合症状	synthesis *n.* 合成，综合，综 合（物）
synthetic *adj.* 合成的，人造的	syringing *n.* 注射（术）	syrup *n.* 糖浆	systematic *adj.* 系统的
systematically *adv.* 有系统地；有 组织地	systematization *n.* 系统化		

T

tackle *v.* 处理；应对	tadpole *n.* 蝌蚪	tail *n.* 尾巴	tailor *v.* 裁剪，使合适，量 身定制
tail-wagging *adj.* 摇尾巴的	take aback 使吃惊，使困惑	take advantage of 利用	take for grant 理所应当
take for granted 想当然，认为……是 理所当然	take its toll 造成损伤，损害	take legal action 提出诉讼，采取法律 行动	take off 起飞
take on 承担	take pride of 有最重要的地位	take times 花费时间	take up 开始从事；占据（地 方，时间）
takeaway service 外卖服务	takeoff 起飞	talent *n.* 资质；天赋，天才	talented *adj.* 有才能的
tame *v.* 制服	tamper *v.* 篡改	tanks *n.* 水槽	tannin *n.* 丹宁酸；鞣酸
tantalized *adj.* 被逗弄的	Tanzania *n.* 坦桑尼亚	tap *n.* 水龙头 *v.* 流入；激活；采用	tap into 接进
tape recorder 磁带录音机	taper *n.* 锥形物 *v.* 逐渐减少	tape-record *v.* 用录音带录音	target *n.* 目标，对象

tariff	taro seedling	task	Tasmania
n. 关税	芋头苗	*n.* 任务	*n.* 塔斯马尼亚岛
tasteful	tasty	taunt	tax year
adj. 雅致的	*adj.* 美味的	*v.* 嘲弄，讥讽	纳税年度
taxation	taxing	taxonomic	taxonomist
n. 征税；税款	*adj.* 费力的	*adj.* 分类学的	*n.* 分类学者
taxonomy	tea cloths	teacher-subject	tease
n. 分类法	吃茶点用的小台布	*n.* 教师为主体的教学模式	*v.* 戏弄，玩耍
tease out	teased from	tea-soaked	technical
找出，发现	嘲笑的	用茶浸泡后的	*adj.* 专门的
technical vocabulary	technically	technique	technological
科技词汇	*adv.* 技术上地	*n.* 技巧；方法；技术	*adj.* 技术的
technologically	tectonic	teddy bears	teen
adv. 技术上地	*adj.* 地壳构造的	泰迪熊	*n.* 青少年期
telecommunication	telemarketing	telepathic	telepathy
n. 电讯，电信	*n.* 电话推销	*adj.* 心灵感应术的	*n.* 心灵感应；传心术
telescope	teleservice	television set	teleworking
n. 望远镜	*n.* 远程服务	电视机	*n.* 电子办公；在家中上班
tell of	teller machine	temperate	temperature
讲述	出纳机	*adj.* 温和的，适度的	*n.* 温度
temperature zone	temporal	temporary	tempt
温带	*adj.* 时间的，暂时的	*adj.* 临时的，暂时的	*v.* 引诱，引起；使感兴趣
temptation	tend to	tendency	tender
n. 引诱，诱惑	趋向，倾向，倾向于，易于	*n.* 倾向，趋势	*v.* 提供；投标 *adj.* 柔软，嫩
tenet	tenfold	tennis court	tense
n. 原则，信条	*adv.* 十倍	网球场	*n.* 时态
tensile	tension	tent-shaped	term
adj. 可拉长的	*n.* 紧张，不安，拉力；张力	*adj.* 帐篷形状的	*n.* 术语；条款

terminal	tern	terrace	terrain
adj. 末端的；终点的；晚期的，不可救药的	*n.* 燕鸥	*n.* 阶地；露台；梯田，阳台	*n.* 地带；地理
terrestrial	terrifying	territory	test
adj. 陆地的，地球的，陆生的	*adj.* 令人恐惧的，骇人的	*n.* 范围，领域，领土	*v.* 考验
testament	testimonials	testimony	test-tube
n. 证据，证明	*n.* 证明信	*n.* 证据，证明	*n.* 试管
Texas	textbook	textile	texture
n. 得克萨斯	*n.* 教科书，课本	*n.* 纺织品，织物	*n.* 特质
Thailand	thankfully	that is	thaw
n. 泰国	*adv.* 感激地	换言之；也就是说	*n.* 融雪
the character	the elderly	the extent of	the Iron Bridge
角色	老年人，长者	……的范围	铁桥
the locals	the popular media	the tip of the iceberg	the United Nations Climate Change Panel
当地人	大众媒体	冰山一角	联合国气候变化专门委员会
the World Wide Fund for Nature	theatrical	theft	thence
世界自然基金会	*adj.* 戏剧性的	*n.* 盗窃，偷盗	*adv.* 因此
theorems	theoretical	theoretically	theory
n. 定理	*adj.* 理论上的，理论的	*adv.* 理论上地	*n.* 理论
therapist	therapy	thereby	thereof
n. 治疗学家，临床医学家	*n.* 治疗，疗法，理疗	*adv.* 因此	*adv.* 由此
thermal	thermal insulation	thermodynamics	thermoplastic
adj. 热的	隔热	*n.* 热力学	*n.* 热塑性塑料
thermosetting	thick	thickness	thinker
adj. 热固的，热硬化性的	*adj.* 厚的；浓的	*n.* 厚度	*n.* 思想家
thinly	thorough	thoroughly	thought-out plan
adv. 稀疏地	*adj.* 彻底的	*adv.* 彻底地	周全的计划

thread	threat	threaten	threefold
v. 穿线于 n. 线	n. 威胁，恐吓	v. 威胁	adj. 三倍的
three-stage	thrill	thrilled	thrive
adj. 三级的，三阶段的	n. 兴奋	adj. 非常兴奋的	v. 繁荣，兴旺，茁壮成长，茂盛生长
thriving	throat	throw some light	throwback
adj. 繁荣的	n. 喉咙	提供一些线索，给……照亮	n. 返祖
thrust	Thule	thundercloud	thunderstorm
n. 推力	n. 图勒（格陵兰岛西北部城镇）	n. 雷雨云	n. 雷暴雨
thwart	thwarted	tick	tick off
v. 阻挠，挫败	adj. 挫败的	v. 滴答地记录；标以记号；做记号	列举
ticket	tickle	tidal	tide
v. 对……开交通违规罚单	v. 使高兴，使满足	adj. 潮汐的，潮水的	n. 潮汐
tie up	tied to	tighten	tightrope walker
占用	相关联	v. 变紧	走钢丝者
tile	tilt	timber	time frame
n. 瓷砖，瓦片	v. 倾斜	n. 木材，木料	时间框架；时间范围
time travel	time-based	time-consuming	timekeeper
时间旅行	adj. 基于时间的，以时间为基准的	adj. 耗时的	n. 钟表
timescale	timing	tin	tincture
n. 时标；时间尺度	n. 时间选择	n. 锡	n. 酊剂
tinder	tinkling	tint	tinted
n. 易燃物	adj. 清脆的	v. 着色	adj. 着色的，带色彩的
tiny	tip	tip-of-the-tongue states	tissue
adj. 微小的；小的	v. 翻倒；倾覆 n. 建议，小费	话在嘴边说不出来	n. 组织
title	to a lesser extent	to be answered	to start
n. 题目 v. 把……称为，加标题于	在较小程度上	有待于解决，有待回答	首先

toil v. 辛苦工作	toilet n. 厕所	toilet seat 马桶座圈	tolerant adj. 抗……的，可忍受的
tolerate v. 忍受	toleration n. 忍受	toll n. 代价，伤亡人数	tomb n. 坟墓
ton n. 吨，大量，很多	tone n. 色调，语气，语调；基调	tonne n. 公吨，吨	toothed adj. 锯齿状的，有齿的
toothpaste n. 牙膏	top v. 超过……，达到……顶点	topic n. 主题，题目	topics of interest 感兴趣的话题
topography n. 地势，地形学；地形	topple v. 推翻	toppling v. 推翻	torch v. 放火烧 n. 火炬
torn adj. 破损的	Toronto n. 多伦多	torrential rain 暴雨，倾盆大雨	tortoise n. 乌龟
tortoise shell n. 龟甲	toss v. 投掷	totemic adj. 图腾的	touch v. 抚摸
tough adj. 坚硬的	toughen v. 使坚韧	toughened adj. 坚韧的	tourism n. 旅游业，游览
tourism venture 旅游企业	tout v. 兜售	town-dweller n. 城镇人	toxic adj. 有毒的
Toyota n. 丰田	trace n. 追溯; 痕迹; 微量; 描绘	trace back 追溯	track n. 路径，行踪 v. 追踪
trackage n. 轨道	tractors n. 拖拉机	trade n. 行业	trade association 贸易协会
trade barrier 贸易壁垒	trade fair 商品交易会，贸易展销会	trade union 工会	traders n. 交易员
traditionally adv. 习惯上，传统地	traffic jam 交通堵塞	trail n. 小径；小路 v. 追踪	trained adj. 受过培训的
traineeship n. 培训	trainer n. 训练员	training n. 训练	trainspotting n. 猜火车
trait n. 特性，特质	tram network 电车网络	trance n. 恍惚	tranquility n. 心神稳定

tranquilliser	transaction	transcend	transcribe
n. 镇静剂	*n.* 交易，数据处理	*v.* 胜过，超越	*v.* 转录，抄写
transcript	transcription	transfer	transferable
n. 文字记录；副本	*n.* 抄写	*n.* 转移	*adj.* 可转让的
transform	transformation	transient	transit
v. 转换，改变	*n.* 转化，转换	*adj.* 短暂的，路过的	*n.* 凌日
transit passenger	transition	translate	transmission
过境旅客	*n.* 转变	*v.* 转化	*n.* 传送，传递
transmit	transparency	transparent	transport
v. 传达，传输	*n.* 透明，透明度	*adj.* 透明的	*v.* 运输，运送；带领
transportation	trap	trapping	trash
n. 运输	*n.* 陷阱，圈套 *v.* 使……受限制，陷入	*n.* 俘获	*n.* 垃圾，废物
travel alarm clock	travel insurance	travelled	travelogue
旅行闹钟	旅游保险	*adj.* 有过旅行的	*n.* 旅行见闻讲演
traverse	tray	treacherous	treacle
v. 穿过；反对；遍历	*n.* 托盘	*adj.* 暗藏危险的	*n.* 糖浆
treadmill	treasure	treatise	treatment
n. 踏车，跑步机；单调的工作	*n.* 财产，遗产，财宝	*n.* 论文，专著	*n.* 治疗，疗法
tree ring	tree-dwelling	treeless	trek
树木的年轮	*adj.* 居住在树上的	*adj.* 不毛的，不长植物的	*n.* 艰苦跋涉
trekker	tremendous	tremor	trend
n. 登山者	*adj.* 巨大的，惊人的	*n.* 颤动	*n.* 趋势，趋向
trend-setting	trial	triangular	tribe
adj. 引领潮流的，决定方向的	*n.* 试验	*adj.* 三角形的；三方面的	*n.* 部落
tribunal	trick	tricycle	trigger
n. 裁决	*n.* 恶作剧；诀窍，花招，窍门；诡计，绝技	*n.* 三轮车	*n.* 触发，引发，引起 *v.* 触发；激发
triglyceride	trigonometry	trillion	triphosphate
n. 甘油三酸酯	*n.* 三角函数	*n.* 万亿	*n.* 三磷酸盐

triple	triple-rooted	triumph	triumphant
v. 翻三倍	三层的	*n.* 成功，胜利	*adj.* 成功的
trivial	trolley	tropical	tropical fruit growth
adj. 不重要的，琐碎的	*n.* 手推车	*adj.* 热带的	热带水果种植
tropics	trouble	troublesome	trove
n. 热带地区	*v.* 折磨	*adj.* 讨厌的，使人苦恼的	*n.* 被发现的东西，收藏的东西
truancy	trunk	trunk-like	Tsimshian
n. 旷课	*n.* 汽车行李箱；卡车；树干	*adj.* 像树干的	*n.* 钦西安人
tube	tuck	tuition	tuition fee
n. 管子；管，管状物	*v.* 挤进	*n.* 教学；学费；讲授	*n.* 学费
Tullamarine International Airport 图拉马莱恩国际机场	tuna *n.* 金枪鱼	tundra *n.* 苔原，冻原	tune *n.* 曲调
tune out	tunnel	turbid	turbine
关掉	*n.* 隧道	*adj.* 浑浊的，泥水的	*n.* 涡轮机
turboprop	Turkish	turn	turn down
n. 涡轮螺旋桨飞机	*adj.* 土耳其的	*n.* 转弯	拒绝
turn out	turn out to be	turn up	turnaround
结果是	结果是，证实是	到达，出现	*n.* 好转，转机
turning point 转折点	turnover *n.* 营业额，成交量	tutor *n.* 家庭教师，导师，助教	tutorial *n.* 个别指导 *adj.* 辅导的，家庭教师的
tweak	twig	twist	twitch
v. 用力拉，拧，开足马力	*v.* 细枝	*n./v.* 转换	*v.* 抽动
twofold	two-legged	two-parent	two-volume
adj. 双重的，两倍的	*adj.* 有两条腿的	*adj.* 双亲的	*adj.* 两卷的
typeface	typhoon	typically	tyranny
n. 字体	*n.* 台风	*adv.* 代表性地；作为特色地	*n.* 独裁

U

ubiquitous *adj.* 普遍存在的	ultimate *adj.* 终极的；最后的，最终的；最大的，极限的	ultimately *adv.* 根本；最终地；最后；最终	ultra-modern *adj.* 超现代化的
ultrasonic *adj.* 超声的	unaccompanied *adj.* 无人陪同的	unaccustomed *adj.* 不习惯的	unachievable *adj.* 不可完成的
unaided *adj.* 无帮助的，不需要帮助的	unaided eye （不借助设备的）肉眼	unanswered *adj.* 未回答的，未解决的	unanticipated *adj.* 没有预料到的
unappreciative *adj.* 不赏识的	unattended *adj.* 没人用的	unauthorized *adj.* 非法的，未被授权的	unavoidable *adj.* 不可避免的，不能废除的
unbeatable *adj.* 无与伦比的	unbelievably *adv.* 难以置信地，不可相信地	unbiased *adj.* 公正的，无偏见的	unblemished *adj.* 无瑕的
uncannily *adv.* 神秘地，不寻常地	uncanny *adj.* 神秘的，离奇的	uncertainty *n.* 不确定	unchanged *adj.* 不变的
uncommon *adj.* 不寻常的	unconscious *adj.* 无意识的	uncontested *adj.* 无竞争的	uncontrollable *adj.* 无法控制的
unconvince *v.* 使不信服，使不确信	uncoupling *n.* 解偶联	uncover *v.* 发现，揭开，揭露	under construction 在建设中
underachievement *n.* 低成就，学习成绩不良	under-achieving *adj.* 正在实现的	underbrush *n.* 林下灌木丛；矮树丛	underestimate *v.* 低估；看轻
undergo *v.* 经历，经受	underlie *v.* 成为……基础	underlying *adj.* 潜在的，根本的	underlying ideas 基本的想法
undermine *v.* 渐渐破坏	undernourished *adj.* 营养不良的	underpin *v.* 支持	underpinning *n.* 基础
underscore *v.* 强调	underside *n.* 底面	understandably *adv.* 可理解地	understanding *n.* 理解
understorey *n.* 下层林木	undertake *v.* 承担，从事	undertaking *n.* 任务，工作	undervalue *v.* 低估，看轻

undeterred *adj.* 未受阻的	undiagnosed *adj.* 未确诊的，尚未找到原因的	undisciplined *adj.* 无训练的，混乱无纪律的	undisputed *adj.* 无可争议的，无疑义的
undistinguished *adj.* 平凡的；混杂的	undistracted *adj.* 注意力集中的	undivided *adj.* 专一的	undoubted *adj.* 无疑的，确实的
undoubtedly *adv.* 毋庸置疑地 *adj.* 无疑的	undue *adj.* 过度的	uneven *adj.* 不均匀的	unexpected *adj.* 意外的，想不到的
unexpectedly *adv.* 出乎意料地	unfold *v.* 展现	unfolding *adj.* 逐步展开的	unforeseeable *adj.* 不可预见的，无法预料的
unforeseen *adj.* 不可预见的，无法预料的	unheard *adj.* 听不到的；不寻常的	unheard of 前所未闻的	unicellular *adj.* 单细胞的
uniform *adj.* 始终如一的	unify *v.* 使统一	unimpeded *adj.* 畅通无阻的	uninhabited *adj.* 无人居住的
unintentional *adj.* 非故意的；无意识的	uninterrupted *adj.* 一览无余的	union *n.* 工会	union representative 工会代表
unique *adj.* 独特的	uniquely *adv.* 独特地	United Nations Conference on Environment and Development 联合国环境与发展大会	unity *n.* 团结，一致
universally *adv.* 普遍地	University of Chicago 芝加哥大学	University of Essex 埃塞克斯大学	University of Queensland 昆士兰大学
University of Reading 雷丁大学	University of Sheffield 谢菲尔德大学	unjustified *adj.* 不正当的	unleash *v.* 释放
unlikely *adj.* 不太可能的	unload *v.* 卸货，卸载	unmanageable *adj.* 难处理的；难管理的，难控制的	unmasking *v.* 脱去假面具；暴露
unnoticed *adj.* 不引人注意的	unobtrusive *adj.* 不引人注意的；谦虚的	unorthodox *adj.* 非正统的	unpaid *adj.* 未付的

unpalatable	unparalleled	unpleasant	unploughed
adj. 讨人厌的，使人不悦的	*adj.* 无比的，空前的；不平行的	*adj.* 讨厌的，使人不悦的	*adj.* 未耕的
unplug	unprecedented	unpredictable	unprincipled
v. 拔掉电源	*adj.* 空前的；前所未有的	*adj.* 不可预知的	*adj.* 没有原则的
unquestionably	unravel	unrealistic	unrecognised
adv. 无可非议地	*v.* 解开，揭开，散开，阐明	*adj.* 不切实际的	*adj.* 未被承认的，未被认可的
unrelated	unrewarded	unrivaled	unsatisfactory
adj. 无关的	*adj.* 未获得报偿的	*adj.* 无敌的，无可比拟的	*adj.* 不令人满意的
unscathed	unsolicited	unsound	unspoilt village
adj. 未受伤的	*adj.* 未经请求的	*adj.* 不稳固的	未被破坏的村庄
unstable	unstoppable	unstream	unswerving
adj. 不稳定的	*adj.* 无法阻碍的，无法停止的	*v.* 不再把……按智力分班	*adj.* 坚定的
untangle	unthreatening	untrained	unusable
v. 解开……纠结，整理，解决	*adj.* 没有威胁的	*adj.* 未经训练的	*adj.* 不能用的
unveiled	unwanted	unwind	unworthy
adj. 公布于众的	*adj.* 多余的	*v.* 放松，解开	*adj.* 不值得的，无价值的
unwrapped	up until this time	upbringing	update
adj. 打开包装的	直到这个时候	*n.* 养育	*n.* 更新
upgrade	upper limit	upright	upset
v. 升级	上限	*adj.* 垂直的 *n.* 垂直，竖立	*v.* 扰乱；打乱，搅乱
upstream	uptake	upward	Uranus
adv. 向上游地，逆流地	*n.* 摄取	*adj.* 向上的；上浮	*n.* 天王星
urban	urge	urgency	urgent
adj. 城市的	*n.* 强烈愿望 *v.* 竭力主张	*n.* 紧急，催促；紧迫；急迫；急事	*adj.* 紧急的，急迫的；进击的
urn	utilitarian	utility	utilize
n. 坟墓；骨灰瓮	*adj.* 功利的；实利的	*n.* 实用，公用事业	*v.* 利用

utter	utterance		
adj. 彻底的，完全的	*n.* 发音；说话(方式)，言辞，所说的话		

V

vacancy	vacant	vaccination	vacuum
n. 空缺，空白	*adj.* 空缺的，空闲的	*n.* 接种疫苗	*n.* 真空，真空吸尘器
vague	valid	valley	valuable
adj. 模糊的，不清楚的	*adj.* 有根据的；有效的；正当的	*n.* 山谷	*adj.* 宝贵的，有价值的
value	van	vandalism	vanish
v. 评价，重视	*n.* 厢式货车	*n.* 蓄意破坏	*n./v.* 消失，绝迹
vantage point	Vanuatu	vapour	variable
优势	*n.* 瓦努阿图(西南太平洋岛国)	*n.* 蒸汽(等于vapor)；水蒸气 *v.* 使……蒸发	*adj.* 多变的 *n.* 变数，变量，可变因素
variant	variation	variety	various
n. 变化，变体	*n.* 变化，变种，变异	*n.* 多样，种类，多样性	*adj.* 不同的，各种各样的
varnish	vary	vary from	vast
n. 清漆，亮光漆	*v.* 变化	不同	*adj.* 广阔的；大的
vast emptiness	vastly	veer off	vegetation
空荡荡	*adv.* 极大地，广大地，深远地	偏离	*n.* 植被，植物
vegetative cycle	vehicle	velocity	venomous
生长周期	*n.* 媒介物；车辆，交通工具；机动车；机动车辆	*n.* 速率	*adj.* 有毒的
vent	venture	venue	veracity
n. 出口	*v.* 冒险	*n.* 筹办地点，地点	*n.* 真实
veranda	verbal	verbally	verdant
n. 游廊；走廊	*adj.* 口头的，语言的	*adv.* 口头上	*adj.* 青翠的
versatile	version	vertebrate	vertical
adj. 多功能的	*n.* 版本，解释，描述	*n.* 脊椎动物	*adj.* 垂直的，直立的

vertical line 垂直线	vertically *adv.* 垂直地	vessel *n.* 船，舰	veteran *n.* 老手；富有经验的人
veterinary assistant 兽医助手	vexingly *adv.* 令人烦恼地	via *prep.* 渠道，通过；经由	viable *adj.* 可行的
vial *n.* 玻璃小瓶	vibration *n.* 振动	vice verse 反之亦然	vicinity *n.* 邻近，附近
vicissitude *n.* 变迁，兴衰	victim *n.* 牺牲品；受害人	victimize *v.* 使受害	view *n.* 观点 *v.* 考虑
vigilance *n.* 警戒	vigor *n.* 活力，精力	vigorous *adj.* 有力的；精力充沛的	village *n.* 村庄
villager *n.* 村民	viral *adj.* 病毒的	virtual *adj.* 事实上的	virtually *adv.* 几乎；实质上；事实上
virus *n.* 病毒	visa application 签证申请	viscous *adj.* 黏性的，黏的	visibility *n.* 能见度；明显性
visible *adj.* 明显的，看得见的；可见的	visible spectrum 可见光谱	visibly *adv.* 明显地，显而易见地	vision *n.* 视力；美景；观点
visual *adj.* 视觉的	visualise *v.* 使形象化	visualizing *n.* 肉眼观察	vital *adj.* 至关重要的；生死攸关的；有活力的；重要的
vitally *adv.* 致命地，极其	vivid *adj.* 鲜艳的；生动的	vivid style 栩栩如生的风格	vocalisation *n.* 发音
vocational *adj.* 职业的	vogue *n.* 时尚，流行的	voice *v.* 表达	voice signal 话音信号
voice-over *n.* 话外音，旁白	volatile *adj.* 挥发性的；不稳定的；爆炸性的	volcanic *adj.* 火山的	volcanic ash 火山灰
volcanism *n.* 火山现象	volcano *n.* 火山	volt *n.* 伏特（电压单位）	voltage *n.* 电压
volume *n.* 量，音量	voluntarily *adv.* 自动地	voluntary *adj.* 自愿的，志愿的	volunteer *v.* （自愿）提出，贡献

voraciously	vote	voucher	voyage
adv. 贪婪地	*n./v.* 投票；选举	*n.* 代金券	*v.* 航行，航海
voyager	vulcanologist	vulnerability	vulnerable
n. 航海者	*n.* 火山学家	*n.* 弱点，脆弱性，易损性	*adj.* 易受攻击的，易受……的攻击；易受伤害的；有弱点的；脆弱的

<h1 style="text-align:center">W</h1>

wade	wag	wage	wage labour
v. 费力行走	*v.* 摇摆	*n.* 薪酬（多指周薪）	雇用劳动
waggle	wait out	Wales	walk the line
v. 摇摆	熬过	*n.* 威尔士	行走在……间
walking shoes	warfare	warm up	warm-blooded
轻便鞋	*n.* 战争；冲突	变热	*adj.* 恒温的
warranted	warship	wary	washing area
adj. 担保的	*n.* 战船，军舰	*adj.* 谨慎的；机警的；唯恐的；考虑周到的	洗漱区
wastage	watchtower	water clock	water pump
n. 损耗；衰老	*n.* 瞭望楼	滴漏，水钟	抽水机，水泵
water-borne disease 水传疾病	watercolor *n.* 水彩画	water-intensive *adj.* 水密集型的	waterproof *adj.* 防水的
water-related	water-saving	water-soluble	waterway
adj. 与水相关的	*adj.* 节水的	*adj.* 可溶于水的	*n.* 航道，水路，水道
waved	wavy	wax	wax and wane
adj. 波浪形的，波动起伏的	*adj.* 波动起伏的	*n.* 蜡	月圆月缺，盈亏；兴衰成败
weakened	weakening	weakling	wealth
adj. 削弱的	*n.* 削弱，衰减	*n.* 懦怯的人	*n.* 财富
wealthy	wean	wear and tear	wear down
adj. 富有的	*v.* 断掉	磨损，消耗	使疲劳，损耗
wear off	weather forecaster	weave	web-based
逐渐消逝	气象预报员	*v.* 纺织	*adj.* 基于网络的
wedge	weed	weevil	weigh
n. 楔子 *v.* 挤进	*n.* 杂草	*n.* 象鼻虫	*v.* 权衡，考虑 *n.* 重量

weighing *n.* 体重	weight-driven *adj.* 重量驱动的	weird *adj.* 怪异的，不可思议的	welcome *v.* 受欢迎，引进
weld *v.* 焊接	welded *adj.* 焊接的	welfare *n.* 安宁	welfare of society 社会福利
well *adj.* 身体健康的	well-being *n.* 健康，康乐	well-established 完善的	well-known *adj.* 著名的
well-nourished *adj.* 营养良好的	well-paid *adj.* 薪酬优厚的	Wessex *n.* 威塞克斯（英国历史上一个王国的名称）	Western Asia 西亚地区
westward *adv.* 向西	wetland *n.* 湿地	whale *n.* 鲸	whale calf 幼鲸，小鲸
whaling ships 捕鲸船	wharf *n.* 码头	what's more 除此之外	wheat *n.* 小麦
wheel *n.* 方向盘	wheelbarrow *n.* 独轮手推车	wheelchair *n.* 轮椅	whereas *conj.* 然而
whichever *pron.* 无论	whilst *conj.* 同时；当……的时候	whim *n.* 奇想，怪念头	whirlwind *n.* 旋风
wholly *adv.* 完全地	widen *v.* 变宽	widespread *adj.* 广泛的，普遍的	width *n.* 宽度
wild swings 猛烈震动	wildebeest *n.* 牛羚	wilderness *n.* 原野，荒地；荒废	wildlife *n.* 野生动物
wildness *n.* 野蛮；原始	willingness *n.* 心甘情愿，乐意	Wiltshire *n.* 威尔特郡	wind *v.* 缠绕
windblown *adj.* 被风吹的	windbreaks *n.* 防风林	wind-tunnel *n.* 风洞	wing *n.* 翼，翅膀
wink *v.* 眨眼	winkle *v.* 追逐	wipe out 擦净，消灭；彻底摧毁，灭绝，了结	wire *n.* 电线
wire-frame *adj.* 线框的	wisdom *n.* 智慧，才识	wiseacre *n.* 自以为聪明者	with reference to 关于，就……而论

withdraw v. 提款	withdrawal n. 取回，取得	without warning 毫无预兆地	withstand v. 抵挡，经得起，反抗；承受住，经受住
witness n. 见证，证据；目击者	wobble v. 摇动	woe n. 麻烦，问题	wonder n. 奇迹 adj. 奇妙的 v. 猜想
wood n. 木材	wood carving 木雕	woodcarver n. 木匠，雕刻匠	wooded areas 树木繁茂的地区
wooden adj. 木制的	woodflour n. 木粉，木屑	woodland n. 林地，森林	wool n. 毛织品
woollen adj. 羊毛制成的	word-for-word 逐字地	work wonder 创造奇迹	workforce n. 劳动力
Working Time Regulations 工作时间条例	workload n. 工作量	workplace n. 工作场所，车间	worksheet n. 工作表，工作单；作业
workshop n. 工作室；车间，研讨班	workshop apprentices 车间学徒	workstation n. 工作站	workweek n. 一星期工作时间
World Bank 世界银行	world-beating adj. 举世无双的	worm n. 虫，蠕虫	worry v. (使) 担心，发愁
worsen v. 使恶化	worth v. 值得	wound n. 伤口	wounded adj. 负伤的，受了伤的
woven v. 纺织	wrap v. 用……包裹，包；缠绕	wreck n. 残骸，破坏	wrecking adj. 破坏性的
wrestling n. 摔跤；扭斗	wring v. 榨取	wrinkled adj. 起皱褶的 (动词原形 wrinkle)	writhing n. 挣扎，扭动

Y

yacht n. 游艇	Yale University 耶鲁大学	year-round adj. 整年的	Yellow Emperor 黄帝

yield *n.* 产品，产量，收益； 收入	yoga *n.* 瑜伽	yolk *n.* 蛋黄	youngster *n.* 年轻人，少年
youthful *adj.* 年轻的			

Z

Zambia *n.* 赞比亚	zero correlation 零相关	zigzag *v.* 成之字形	zigzaggy *adj.* 曲折迂回的
zinc *n.* 锌	zipper *n.* 拉链	zone *n.* 区域	zoologist *n.* 动物学家
zoology *n.* 动物学	zooplankton *n.* 浮游动物	Zurich *n.* 苏黎世	

图书在版编目 (CIP) 数据

剑桥雅思阅读考点词真经：机考笔试综合版 / 刘洪波编著. —4版. —北京：中国人民
大学出版社，2016.6

ISBN 978-7-300-23015-3

Ⅰ. ①剑… Ⅱ. ①刘… Ⅲ. ①IELTS-阅读教学-高等教育-自学参考资料 Ⅳ. ①H319.4

中国版本图书馆CIP数据核字 (2016) 第140186号

剑桥雅思阅读考点词真经（机考笔试综合版）

刘洪波　编著

Jianqiao Yasi Yuedu Kaodianci Zhenjing (Jikao Bishi Zonghe Ban)

出版发行	中国人民大学出版社		
社　　址	北京中关村大街31号	邮政编码	100080
电　　话	010-62511242（总编室）	010-62511770（质管部）	
	010-82501766（邮购部）	010-62514148（门市部）	
	010-62515195（发行公司）	010-62515275（盗版举报）	
网　　址	http://www.crup.com.cn		
	http://www.1kao.com.cn（中国1考网）		
经　　销	新华书店		
印　　刷	北京玺诚印务有限公司		
规　　格	148mm×210mm　32开本	版　　次	2013年1月第1版
			2016年6月第4版
印　　张	15.75	印　　次	2017年10月第11次印刷
字　　数	330 000	定　　价	43.00元（附赠光盘一张）